ORGANIZATIONAL
BEHAVIOR

ABRAHAM K. KORMAN

Bernard Baruch College
City University of New York

Prentice-Hall, Inc., Englewood Cliffs, New Jersey   07632

Library of Congress Cataloging in Publication Data

KORMAN, ABRAHAM K   (Date)
  Organizational behavior.

  First ed. published in 1971 under title: Industrial and organizational psychology.
  Bibliography: p.
  Includes index.
  1. Psychology, Industrial.   2. Organizational behavior.   I. Title.
HF5548.8.K576 1976   158.7   76–43991
ISBN   0–13–640938–5

to
Rhoda, Stacey, and Scott

© 1977 by Prentice-Hall, Inc., Englewood Cliffs, New Jersey 07632
(Revised edition of *Industrial and Organizational Psychology*)

Printed in the United States of America

10   9   8   7   6   5   4   3   2   1

PRENTICE-HALL INTERNATIONAL, INC., *London*
PRENTICE-HALL OF AUSTRALIA PTY. LIMITED, *Sydney*
PRENTICE-HALL OF CANADA, LTD., *Toronto*
PRENTICE-HALL OF INDIA PRIVATE LIMITED, *New Delhi*
PRENTICE-HALL OF JAPAN, INC., *Tokyo*
PRENTICE-HALL OF SOUTHEAST ASIA PTE. LTD., *Singapore*
WHITEHALL BOOKS LIMITED, *Wellington, New Zealand*

Contents

iii

chapter fifteen

THE MEASUREMENT OF JOB PERFORMANCE AND REACTIONS:
   MEASURES AND TECHNIQUES *364*

chapter sixteen

CONCLUDING REMARKS *395*

Preface

In 1971 I wrote in the precursor to this volume that I had tried to write a book that would reflect theoretical concerns, practical interests, and the ever changing demands made on those who administer our work organizations by the world around them. While much the same interests have guided me here, there are some changes also. Most significant of these, I believe, is the increased focus in this book on work as a social institution and as a psycho-social experience. This is a change which I believe is not only necessary because of societal demands that those interested in "work" should examine it, but which is also desirable if we are to make "work" a better experience for individuals, organizations, and society. To illustrate, we now have a societal movement where many women are clamoring to have the type of experience (i.e., work) that some men are clamoring to leave. Why? Paradoxes such as this come under examination here.

A second change is that I have tried to provide a perspective of the adult as a dynamic, changing individual with different needs and different demands at different points in time and as a result of different work experiences. This view of the adult life has been emerging with great rapidity from research in the psychology of motivation and it also has significant implications for understanding such organizationally relevant phenomena as work motivation, leadership, and training. I have tried to reflect these perspectives here.

A third change is that I have tried, even more than earlier, to indicate, where appropriate, my own puzzlement and my own indecision about some of the major issues and questions of the field. How far will "science" take us? What, actually, are the effects of affirmative-action programs? Frankly, I'm quite unsure about these matters, and I have so indicated, unlike other areas (e.g., leadership) where the weight of the evidence is, I believe, much stronger.

Fourth, I have attempted to make this book more of a teaching aid by providing more summary statements, concrete examples, and guides for further reading that include works of fiction and journalistic essays, as well as research articles and books. I've tried to choose the latter for their attitudinal and cognitive impact and for their value in illustrating some of the points made in the book.

Finally, in keeping with the changed title, the book more truly reflects the perspective of the field that has come to be known as Organizational Behavior. While still mostly psychology, it is now more than just an individual psychology of fitting and changing people to fit organizational life. It is now also a social psychology oriented to changing organizations to fit people and it is also a sociology, anthropology, and traditional management theory. These additional perspectives find representation here.

My thanks for help in preparing this book go to many people. Much of what I learned at Minnesota during my graduate school days remains with me and my dialogues with Jack Miner and Al Glickman continue to be intellectually and attitudinally meaningful. Although I do not know them, Philip Slater and Bernard Weiner have done much to broaden my thinking on longitudinal perspectives in human behavior and the life of the contemporary adult. Also, in a more immediate vein, I want to thank Bob Pritchard for an excellent, meaningful review of the first draft of this book, my colleagues and students in the Psychology and Management departments at Baruch College for allowing me to bounce these ideas off them and for providing such good feedback, Ted Jursek and Karen Thompson at Prentice-Hall for excellent assistance, and Mrs. Lana Smart for an outstanding typing job.

Last, but far from least, my wife Rhoda has done her usual outstanding editing job of taking my mumblings and turning them into readable English. I wish to thank her for her work, and then I want to thank her again and our children, S and S (Scott and Stacey or Stacey and Scott, read it which way you prefer) for providing the home life that makes everything else worthwhile.

PART I

HISTORICAL AND METHODOLOGICAL FOUNDATIONS

There are few, if any, human activities that spring full blown from Zeus' head. Look deep enough into almost anything that people do and you will find a history and a set of traditions which serve to identify and mark all activities in a unique fashion. So it is with the study of work behavior.

In these introductory chapters I will focus on what these traditions are. We will see that the direction of historical influence has been two-pronged. First, there has been a delimitation of content areas considered appropriate to the study of organizational behavior. Among these are work motivation, leadership, organization structure, the personnel selection process, and organizational change strategies. They, along with other topics, have entered the field at different times and for different reasons, and such differences have had important implications for how research and practice in each of the areas have developed. Chapter one is devoted to how interest in these areas developed. This examination will prove of value later when we consider the evolution of contemporary work characteristics.

The second historical influence on the field is the emphasis on scientific research methodology as a procedure for answering the questions of the field. There are many reasons for this emphasis and I will try to enumerate some of them. However, I also think that we must not delude ourselves that the scientific method is without fault and although the faults do not outweigh the advantages, they do need to be discussed. It is these matters which will concern us in chapter two.

1

The Study of Behavior at Work

This book is about people in the world of work organizations and the factors that influence their behavior in that world. Specifically, it is concerned with questions such as the following:

1. What are the organizational and personal factors that influence different types of work behavior?
2. What are the factors that make work ego enhancing? What makes work debilitating? What makes it satisfying?
3. What techniques and methods are available for increasing work performance? For making work more ego enhancing? How useful are these techniques? How can we make them better?

In answering these questions, we will focus on several dimensions. First, we will look at the research of the behavioral sciences such as psychology, sociology, political science, and anthropology. Primarily, our discussion will stem from the work of psychologists because they have been most active in answering these questions, but we will also include material from other fields wherever appropriate. Our main concern throughout will be with the characteristics of people as they affect work behavior and with the characteristics of organizations as they affect behavior through their influence on individuals and groups. Our emphasis will be mostly scientific as we discuss these questions because I was trained in the science of psychology and because, despite its problems (see chapter two), I believe that the scientific format is the best way to find answers to questions about work behavior. As part of this discussion we will spend a lot of time on theory and methodology since scientists devote much attention to developing and testing theories. However, because I think that science and theory without application too easily becomes sterile, I will also spend time discussing the practical implications of these theories. Finally, certain ethical and moral responsibilities must be met in this field. These, too, will command our attention.

Basic Assumptions

In writing this book I, like any other author, have operated within a set of value assumptions that have determined to a great extent the questions I have asked and the evaluations I have made about the subjects discussed. Although these values of mine will probably become clear as we go along, it might be worthwhile to make them explicit at this point.

First, while I believe that work achievement and performance are important, I also believe that many legitimate questions can be raised concerning our traditional acceptance of the "work ethic." These doubts have raised questions in my mind and in the minds of others and therefore I will attempt to take account of both the virtues and the problems of an emphasis on work achievement.

Second, it will be apparent that I have drawn material from all kinds of research studies. Laboratory research, field surveys, and field experiments will be discussed, as will studies of adult employees, job applicants, and college students. All other things being equal, adults constitute the most important group of people to study in this field. Unfortunately, the other factors rarely are equal and it is obvious that some kinds of questions cannot be answered easily within the adult work setting. For example, how many companies would let you start a conflict between two racial groups in order to determine how to best resolve this type of conflict? For situations like this we can, under some conditions, use studies of college students and these studies can be useful providing we accept their limitations.

Third, I believe that to write about behavior in work organizations without considering what is going on outside that system is to be unrealistic. Our society has gone through a century of revolutions in the last fifteen years, and almost all of these upheavals in some way affect (and are affected by) behavior in the world of work. It is crucial, therefore, to be highly sensitive to the implications of these changes and you will see that this book reflects this opinion.

Finally, because they serve different purposes I have found it important to distinguish between scientific research and values. Scientific research can tell us how to maximize job performance, but it cannot tell us whether or not to think that high job performance is desirable. The latter is a value question to which scientific research does not give an answer. (To say that job performance helps society does not overcome this objection; it only transfers the question to whether or not helping that society is worthwhile.) Values and scientific methodology are thus different, but both are important.

A Historical Perspective

Interest in work behavior and in organizations goes back thousands of years. You can find prescriptions for the design of work systems in the Bible, you can find them in the writings of ancient Egypt, and you can find them in Chinese lore. I shall, therefore, throughout this book, occasionally refer to major historical figures, particularly when we focus on the particular content areas with which these figures are identified. For example, when we talk of the design of organizational structures, I will be referring to Max Weber, and when we talk of alienation, I will refer to Karl Marx. Right now, however, I want to provide an overall historical perspective to the field, as it has developed from the perspective of an emphasis on scientific, research-based methodology.

The scientific study of behavior in the work setting has its origins, I believe, in industrial psychology, a field that stems from the decade prior to World War I, when there were two psychologists in the United States who could be called industrial psychologists. These two were Walter Dill Scott, a nativeborn American who had gone to Germany to take his Ph.D. with Dr. Wilhelm E. Wundt, who founded the first experimental psychology laboratory at Leipzig in 1879, and Hugo Muensterberg, a German who had come to teach at Harvard and who became active in promoting the idea that psychology would be valuable in helping management achieve its goals. Perhaps the most famous of Muensterberg's research studies was a test he developed to help select motormen for the local Boston streetcar company. Scott's activities in the Midwest were also of this type, consisting mostly of promulgating the value of psychological methods for solving business problems.

Despite the work of Scott and Muensterberg, and despite J. McKeen Cattell at Columbia University, who was citing the importance of individual differences in helping a work organization select and classify people, it could hardly be said that a bonfire of enthusiasm for the field was lit at this time. In fact, quite the contrary. Perhaps the lack of interest was partly because Muensterberg was a German in a nation getting ready to go to war with Germany. Perhaps organizations were not yet large enough to experience great problems. Perhaps most employees' motivation to work was greater than in ensuing decades. Whatever the reason, it took World War I to kindle the growth of industrial psychology in this country.

When World War I began, the U.S. Army was faced, as a result of the military draft, with the question of how to effectively utilize millions of men about whom they knew little and whom they would have available only for the duration of the war emergency. Furthermore, whatever policy decision the army officials made would have to be made quickly, since a war was being fought and upon such a decision its outcome could conceivably rest. Basically, the question was whom do you classify as suited to the advanced, skilled jobs; for example, whom do you send to Officer Candidate School? On the other hand, whom do you classify as not having the potential for being an officer and who, perhaps, might be better placed in another job? The way in which these questions were solved marks the first major psychological success in developing a method to help effect a positive change in overall organizational effectiveness. In this achievement, the psychologists involved assumed that the major difference between those who could perform difficult jobs and those who could not was a matter of intelligence.[1] Hence, what was needed was some way to ascertain the intelligence level of the draftees, a problem perhaps easily resolvable today but not in 1917, because at that time the only known measures of intelligence were the scales developed by Alfred Binet in France to aid in the educational classification of school children. These scales were very successful both in France and in the United States but they had a major flaw for the army's purposes. The Binet tests were individual tests; that is, they could be given only to one individual at a time, a procedure that the army clearly could not adopt in this case. As a result, the army psychologists developed Army Alpha, a test that measured about the same thing as the Binet scales but which could be administered to groups. In fact, Army Alpha was so successful in predicting success in Officer Candidate School that it both encouraged great growth in psychological applications to industry after World War I and directed this application toward the area of personnel selection. As a result, psychologists after WW I were put to work contributing tests and scales to be used to help screen applicants for employment.

These beginnings did not last and the mid-1920s saw disenchantment with the value of psychological techniques. First, many of the tests were not as effective as claimed; the type of job applicant being hired with the aid of the tests was no more effective than the one

---

[1] We will discuss later some contemporary views of this use of "intelligence."

hired without them. Second, it was apparent that the ability tests used were, at best, incomplete predictors of job performance and that measures of personality and motivation were necessary. However, the few psychological measures of personality that existed then were highly unsatisfactory. A third reason for the decline in interest was, perhaps, a little more subtle. This was that, to some extent, management had been interested in using psychology as a tool to place and train workers in a manner so satisfying that trade unionism would be less attractive to them. With the general affluence of the 1920s in the industrial sectors of the economy, however, trade union growth was decreasing anyway and, with this, some of the need for psychology.

There was one event, though, that took place toward the end of the 1920s which was not a part of these general negative trends and which was of crucial significance for the future of industrial psychology and the study of work behavior. This was a series of experiments conducted at the Hawthorne plant of the Western Electric Company outside Chicago. Begun in the middle 1920s, they were terminated due to the depression six years later, but not before they had resulted in findings that were of a truly discipline-shaking nature. The experiments, which became known as the Hawthorne studies, began as studies of the effects of lighting, rest pauses, and other work conditions on work performance, but before they were finished they had established, according to some researchers, the importance of such factors as the style of leadership, group standards, and other social factors on work performance. While some still claim that the Hawthorne results can be accounted for by more traditional factors such as money (cf. Carey, 1967), the effects of these studies have been such that we can date to their findings the "human relations" influence on U.S. management and some of the newer theories of effective leadership that we shall be talking about later.

The depression of the 1930s was not quite as bad for industrial psychology as for everybody else. Undoubtedly, with the decline of business activity, the prevalent pessimism toward the future, and the overwhelming concern for mere survival, the period was dreary. However, some significant developments during that time did occur.

One important series of studies, undertaken by the Department of Labor, involved the development of the Dictionary of Occupational Titles (D.O.T.), a series of volumes that describe different jobs. Over the years the D.O.T., and its revised editions have been an invaluable aid to job counselors, training officials, and students of occupational structure. Furthermore, its development provided an important training ground for the development of job analysis techniques and tools important for various types of manpower utilization programs such as personnel selection, training, and performance evaluations.

Further significant developments during this time came about from the activities of the Minnesota Employment Stabilization Research Institute, a government-supported program aimed at understanding why some people, even in the depths of the depression, were able to be employed and others were not. Under the leadership of Professor Donald Paterson of the University of Minnesota, the researchers were able to describe differences among people by using ability tests of various types. An offshoot of this program was the development of several well known tests later to be of great value for general industrial purposes.

Another significant development of the 1930s stemmed in part from management-labor conflicts and the growth of a more radical type of trade unionism than had been prevalent up to that time. These developments created considerable interest in the study of job satisfaction and in 1932 the first study on job satisfaction (Kornhauser and Sharp, 1932) was published. In addition, as part of this trend, psychologists were evidently being hired by management to help in union-prevention by surveying and increasing job satisfaction, although we do not know how many were actually employed for this purpose. That such a condition did exist, at least to some degree, is probably the case since the Society for the Psychological Study of Social Issues published in 1939 a book of psychological thinking about labor problems that was admittedly prolabor in order to balance what it felt was a too heavily promanagement approach from their industrial psychologist colleagues (Watson, 1939). In addition, a heavily promanagement approach was also evident in the founding statements of the American Association for Applied Psychology in 1937.

Finally, an event of the 1930s that had great significance was the rise of Adolf Hitler and the consequent emigration of German Jewish and other intellectuals to the United States and elsewhere. Among the émigres was Kurt Lewin, a dynamic, inspiring psychologist who in his relatively short stay in the United States had an influence that remains enormous even today, three decades after his death. One reason for this influence was that he argued that experiments with human beings were possible, even in such difficult areas as motivation. While we know today that the problems of real-life experimentation are more complex than Lewin thought, his basic argument retains considerable validity. A second reason for Lewin's importance was that much of his experimentation dealt with different kinds of leadership and their motivational effects under different conditions. As a German who was aware of Germany's cultural heritage, he shared the general worldwide concern with understanding the conditions under which a Hitler gains and keeps power. Lewin devoted a large part of his research to these questions, and his findings still strongly influence contemporary theories of leadership. Finally, Lewin was a dominant influence on figures who became the most dominant influences in contemporary U.S. social psychology. Thus, much of the research of Lewin's students has been devoted to showing that rational, utility-maximizing theories fail to account for much of work behavior, a point I will stress later in my discussion as being very important for understanding work motivation.

World War II was like World War I, only more so. Tests were developed to select and classify draftees for different kinds of training. Training methods were developed with the aid of findings from experiments in the psychology of learning, the dominant theoretical interest of American psychology in the 1940s. Findings on social and motivational factors in performance began to be incorporated into leadership training as the influence of Lewin and the Hawthorne studies began to make itself felt. Finally, the explosive growth in the sophistication of weapons systems led to increased concern with how the physical environment affects work performance, particularly when the physical environment encompasses such exceedingly complex signal systems as those on today's modern jet airliners.

The great success of the psychologists in World War II led to a similar but even greater growth than that after World War I. During the decade from 1945 to 1955, we see all the signs of a prosperous, growing field of activity. Graduate training in industrial psychology in the nation's universities increased greatly. The reorganized American Psychological Association set up as one of its original divisions the Division of Industrial Psychology. A new journal, *Personnel Psychology,* was founded to go along with the *Journal of Applied Psychology,* the traditional journal of the field. New consulting firms were started, to go along with the increasing number of psychologists employed by companies and government organizations as full-time investigators of manpower problems. The number of companies using psychological tests increased from 14% in 1939 to 75% in 1952 (Baritz, 1960), and thousands of special courses and services were offered on the nature and meaning of leadership.

Yet all was not well under the surface, and the decade from 1955 to 1965 saw industrial psychology come under as concentrated a series of attacks from as wide a variety of sources as has probably been made on any area of professional and/or scientific activity. Yet, in a sense, perhaps these attacks were a good thing because (1) they were generally deserved and (2) they led to a restructuring of the field in a manner both theoretically and administratively more meaningful.

One set of criticisms came from psychologists and other members of the intellectual community who were not committed to a management point of view in looking at organizations and their functioning. While this criticism took various shapes (cf. Baritz, 1960), the major theme was that the industrial psychologist had sold out as a member of the science of psychology to become a technical assistant to personnel management. According to this argument, a psychologist was supposed to develop theories designed to explain the factors that influence human behavior or some part of it. For the industrial psychologist, this meant that he should be trying to understand the answers to such questions as, how does a person choose his career? What makes him satisfied? What is the importance of various factors in the work organization in affecting his sense of personal value and self-esteem? Instead, the industrial psychologist was spending his time developing tools and techniques to help management do its job. He was justifying his existence on the basis of "practical usefulness."

A second complaint was that even the claim of "practical usefulness" was not being met and that the tools and techniques being utilized were outmoded. According to this point of view, the various selection and training methods being used were based on a world that no longer existed, a world of large factories employing masses of male employees in semiskilled, blue-collar, similar-type jobs and a world where children were encouraged to be better than their parents. However, the world was changing, and we now had more white-collar employees than blue-collar. Furthermore, these white-collar employees were often of high status, in unique positions, and sometimes black or female. On the other hand, at the other end of the spectrum there were masses of alienated and underprivileged workers, untrained for the white-collar job, automated out of the blue-collar job, with little hope and less aspiration. Would the methods designed for a bygone era work in the here-and-now? Increasingly, it was argued that they would not and we shall see why later.

A third complaint was that the psychologist was not being as careful as he should be, allowing faddish thinking to dominate his activities. An outstanding example of this, according to some (Brayfield and Crockett, 1955), was the tendency to promote increased job satisfaction as a key to productivity, or, overly simplified, the notion that "a happy worker is a productive worker." By the end of the 1950s, it was clear that the relationship between satisfaction and productivity was a complex one at best, that there were other types of reactions to jobs besides job satisfaction, and that simple slogans did not suffice.

Finally, it was also apparent that the perspectives of industrial psychology, as generally defined, were inadequate. Understanding behavior in the work setting involved more than studying the characteristics of people and then fitting them best into an existing organization. Organizations were changing and people were coming into work settings with new ideas of what "work success" meant. Cultures were changing and automatic interest in work success, at least as traditionally defined, could no longer be assumed. Thus, there was no reason to try to fit people into organizations which themselves had to be changed because they were operating on the basis of inadequate theories of leadership which assumed outmoded theories about men, women, and work motivation. This need for organizational change called for approaches and theorizing on both the group and organizational level, a mode of thought which required intellectual perspectives stemming more from social psychology and sociology than from industrial psychology as traditionally conceived. Technological systems, their behavioral and attitudinal effects, and their interaction with social processes came to be viewed as significant, and this interest called for sociological, social psychological, and even engineering competence. Also relevant here was the recognition that many traditional management concepts (e.g., the line-staff concept, the span of control, etc.) had significant behavioral impact because people often frame their thinking along these dimensions. These also have to be studied, it was noted, and understood for their influence on behavior, even though they are not psychological variables and come from a traditional management perspective. Similarly, the effects of ethnic membership and sex are important because people react to one another differentially along these dimensions (although, since they are only descriptive, these variables do not have behavioral significance in and of themselves). People expect differences along these dimensions and, often, they bring about differences because of these expectancies. As a result, social psychological and sociological theory had to be brought in to help understand these processes as they affect behavior in the work setting. Finally, an overriding recognition was that people at work sometimes act as individuals and sometimes as group members, and if we want to understand their behavior, we need to move back and forth across different levels of analysis, whether we call ourselves psychologists, social psychologists, or sociologists.

A Contemporary View

The result of all these criticisms was that the study of behavior in the work organization became and remains today more interdisciplinary in nature. It is still mostly psychology because most of the research in the field is undertaken by industrial and social psychologists, a fact this book will reflect. (Another reason for this emphasis is, undoubtedly, that I am a psychologist.) Nevertheless, the study of work behavior also includes sociology, political science, and traditional management theory, and as we discuss the behavior of people in work organizations we will see how contributions come from these and other disciplines.

What we now have, then, is a field concerned with understanding factors influencing people's behavior at work and willing to cross disciplines to attain that knowledge. Also important is that the behaviors we are studying are varied and diverse. Some of the behaviors that we will be trying to understand, such as work performance and job satisfaction, have traditionally been important as dependent variables (to use their scientific classification) and they remain important today. We will try to see how they are affected by such independent variables as organizational structure, leadership patterns, management policies and practices, technological characteristics, incentive systems, and the personal characteristics (e.g., work motivation) of the individuals themselves. Yet, this is only one aspect of the field. We will also examine the motivation to work in a theoretical sense and theories designed to explain this phenomenon. By understanding what influences work motivation, we will discover some hints as to what leadership (or influence) factors might influence work motivation (or job satisfaction). In this sense we are using the traditional dependent variable, work performance, to understand and predict what a good independent variable might be. Even more, the so-called independent variable (e.g., a certain type of leadership behavior) might become our dependent variable at another time in that we may try to understand the factors on which it, the leadership pattern, depends. We might do this when that type of leadership behavior (or technological structure) has been found to be particularly important as an influence on work behavior. This indicates that the terms *independent* and *dependent variable* are not inherently based in any particular concept. Any specific behavior or phenomenon can change its status (from independent to dependent variable or vice versa) depending on what you are trying to understand at the time. The behavior being studied is the dependent variable and the possible factors that are studied for influence on it are the independent variables.

The same point holds when the focus of interest is on some of the newer interests in the field. In the pages to come, for example, I will be discussing power motivation, aggression, risk taking, and creativity, as well as different types of job reactions such as ego enhancement, alienation, and social estrangement. These are of particular interest today as our definitions of the meaning of "success" are changing. Each of these is important as dependent variables in the study of work behavior today and that is primarily how we will look at them; but they are also important, as we will see, because they are significant as independent variables influencing other kinds of work behavior.

At the same time that these theoretical changes in the field have occurred, traditional professional interests have been reaffirmed and active concern with the development of techniques and methods to increase the effectiveness of manpower utilization in the modern organization both from the company and individual point of view has continued. Such a reaffirmation has come on several counts. First, there is increasing acceptance that the behavioral sciences have a role to play in helping mankind with its problems, that it is an honorable role, and that it must be well done. The professionally oriented need not apologize for existence. Second, there is acceptance of two facts. Large organizations are with us to stay, and people depend on them for their way of life. Hence, upon these organizations' success and health rests the success and health of all those dependent on them. Third, job and job success is often crucial to a sense of self-esteem and mental health. The career-oriented demands of the women's liberation movement and the desires of males to reexamine jobs and enrich them are witness to the accuracy of this statement. This desirability of professional concerns has, for these reasons, seen a continuing reexamination of the techniques and methods used and a willingness to try new methods when new problems develop.

Summary

In this chapter I have placed the study of organizational behavior in a historical context. A major overall trend is that of an increasing expansion of the field from an original concern with the characteristics of individuals and how to best fit them into an organization to a contemporary interest in the nature of organizations, leadership, and jobs and how to optimize these from the viewpoint of societies, organizations, and individuals. Such contemporary interests will constitute the major concerns of this book, beginning in the next chapter on research methodology. In chapters three and four we will examine motivational processes as they relate to work behavior along various dimensions such as achievement, aggression, and creativity. We will also be concerned with implications of research on these themes for the design and management of organizations. In chapter five I will continue this discussion of individual psychological processes, but here we will concern ourselves with cognitive and thinking processes and how they are related to different types of work behavior. This focus will broaden in chapters six and seven to include the behavioral influences of organizational structures, leadership style variables, and job characteristics; that is, the types of concerns we pointed out as reflecting more contemporary interests. We will then turn our attention in chapter eight to the effects of the physical environment and factors such as technology and noise. Chapter nine examines the effects of work experience on the emotions and attitudes of individual organizational members, both those of a personal nature and those reflecting attitudes toward one's job situation.

In chapter ten we turn to some of the more traditional, applied fields and how they are dealt with in today's world. First, we will focus on methods of making the conditions of entry into the organization satisfying for both the organization and the individual. We will see how the traditional personnel selection problem has been transformed into a different set of questions today. Following this we will talk about change and development programs in today's organizations. Among the topics treated in chapters eleven, twelve, and thirteen are several of the basic questions underlying all change programs and some of the more important techniques such as T-group (or sensitivity) training and job enrichment techniques here and abroad. We will conclude in chapters fourteen and fifteen by examining several methodological questions involved in measuring some of the key dependent variables of the field such as job performance and various types of job reactions such as job satisfaction and ego enhancement. Of particular interest will be how definitions of good and bad job outcomes have been changing in recent years.

SUGGESTIONS FOR FURTHER READING

CRONBACH, L. J. Five decades of public controversy over mental testing. *American Psychologist*, 1975, *30*, 1–14.
A highly significant paper by one of the major figures in mental testing today. The author explores the inevitable social impact of behavioral science research and takes his colleagues to task for refusing to recognize the implications of such impact.

PUGH, D. S. Modern organization theory: A psychological and sociological study. *Psychological Bulletin*, 1966, *66*, 235–251.
An excellent review of some of the historical influences on the study of organizational functioning and why it has developed the interdisciplinary focus it has today.

SLATER, P. *The pursuit of loneliness.* Boston: Beacon Press, 1970.
This is not a research paper but a critical essay examining the possible dysfunctional consequences of an unquestioning acceptance of the work achievement ethic. Many readers may not accept the author's arguments and they will undoubtedly provoke anger in others. Yet, they are well presented and constitute a challenge to those who accept work achievement as being the critical dependent variable of the field.

YANKELOVICH, D. Turbulence in the working world: Angry workers, happy grads. *Psychology Today*, 1974, *8*, 80–87.

The author of this paper is one of the most respected pollsters in the United States and has spent much time in recent years surveying changes in the work ethic. In this article he reports that such changes have indeed taken place and that they have important implications for management.

chapter two

Research on Behavior at Work

This chapter discusses scientific research methodology, a topic some people dislike because it is abstract and conceptual and not very glamorous. Yet, if we want to understand behavior in organizations and the factors that influence it, we have to use a method to find the answers. The point is that methods for this purpose differ and, as I said earlier, the method I, like other behavioral scientists, prefer is the scientific method.

In this chapter I shall discuss the characteristics of scientific research in order that you, the reader, will understand the reasons for this preference. My discussion will include both its advantages and problems so that you will see that even though it is the best of the methods, it is not without difficulties. Finally, I will conclude the chapter by discussing some aspects of research on behavior at work where the scientific method does not help (or might hurt) and what this means for our understanding of behavior in the work organization.

The Scientific Method in the Study of Work Behavior

The essence of scientific research is to determine the relationship between variables; an example would be determining the relationship between a type of leadership behavior and job performance. The two major ways of determining such relationships differ conceptually in several important ways. The first of these is the experimental method, a technique which supposedly allows causal inference about the types of independent variables (e.g., leadership patterns) that affect dependent variables (e.g., performance). Note, though, that I have used the word "supposedly." There has been much research in recent years that indicates that casual inferences in experiments with human subjects are by no means as clear and easy to make as once thought. While this has not meant giving up the benefits of the experimental method, it has led to increasing care in the interpretation of findings.

The second major research method, the correlational method, supposedly does not allow causal inference. However, this conclusion, too, is not clear-cut and certain kinds of correlational studies do allow some causal inference. In other words, while there are differences between the experimental and correlational approaches, these differences may, on occasion, become somewhat blurred.

Also, there are great similarities between them in that all scientific research, regardless of its nature, rests on common guiding principles. These principles are, in fact, what distinguish scientific research from other kinds of research in the human endeavor (such as literary works, humanistic observations, historical and philosophical analysis, and so on). Among these principles, the following are perhaps the most important:

Principle One   Conclusions, judgments, and inferences are to be based on empirical observations, not beliefs or hopes.

Principle Two   Scientific research is purposeful, not random; that is, there are reasons some questions are chosen for investigation rather than others. This statement does not mean that there is always some practical end in mind when a researcher chooses a problem, since a theoretical question may be just as purposeful. What it does mean is that the choice of a problem is considerably more purposeful than the "I wonder what would happen if . . ." type of choice sometimes used.

Principle Three   Scientific research is cumulative and self-correcting; it builds on what has gone before. "Those who do not know the mistakes of history are doomed to repeat them" Santayana once said, and it is to avoid this that the researcher spends a considerable portion of his time reading the literature. The result, hopefully, is a research investigation that extends what we know about a question rather than repeating either the knowledge or the mistakes of previous work.

Principle Four   Scientific research is replicable; that is, the procedures undertaken are stated with such explicitness that any other qualified researcher could repeat the research project if he should so wish. A claim that leadership theory A leads to more effective organizational performance than leadership theory B has no scientific basis to it unless the research operations on which such a claim is based are stated with enough clarity and specificity that any qualified person could verify the claim himself.

Principle Five Scientific research is communicable; the concepts and ideas utilized and studied are not of a private nature but of a kind that may, in principle, be utilized by all qualified individuals.

These are the principles that traditionally mark science. They are idealistic, even though they are sometimes violated either consciously or unconsciously. Yet, it is useful to state them clearly here because this is what science is supposed to be like. Most behavioral scientists do try to follow these principles and when they do, the information obtained is more reliable than information obtained in other ways.

Experimental Methods

The essence of experimentation is "control," for example, the control of causes of behavior (independent variables) such as social conditions, leadership behaviors, and administrative policies in order to determine their effects on such outcomes as job performance, satisfaction, risk taking, and so on. There are three major types of experiments that need concern us here—the laboratory experiment, the field experiment, and the simulation experiment—with each having values and disadvantags.

The laboratory experiment's major characteristic is that conditions are supposedly more controllable than for any other type of study. The experimental (or independent) variable is allowed to vary in specified ways between two or more groups, and to the extent that there is a consequent effect on the dependent variable, it is attributed to the effects of the independent variable. One problem with the lab experiment is the extent to which the results have "external validity," that is, the degree to which their results are generalizable to the "real" world of work. There is no one answer to this; sometimes they are generalizable and sometimes they are not. The fact is we *have* learned about some of the factors influencing task and work performance from laboratory experiments and the findings from these studies have *sometimes* been replicated in later, less well controlled, more realistic industrial studies.

The second kind of experiment is the field experiment. As the name indicates, it constitutes an attempt to apply the experimental method to ongoing, real-life situations. One difference between this and the laboratory experiment is in the degree of control possible. Suppose that you were interested in determining the effects of a new type of leadership on task performance as compared to the old method. If you were doing a lab experiment you would set up the research in the following way:

	EXPERIMENTAL GROUP	CONTROL GROUP
Room:	Room 304	Room 304
Time:	1:00 P.M.	1:00 P.M.
Tasks:	Construction tasks	Construction tasks
Characteristics of	Mean IQ = 120	Mean IQ = 120
work group members:	Personality — no deviation scores on adjustment inventory	Personality — no deviation scores on adjustment inventory
Method of selecting		
work group members:	Volunteers	Volunteers
Type of leadership:	New leadership	Old leadership

The only differences between the two groups is the style of leadership, and, hopefully, everything else is controlled (held constant). Suppose, now, that you wanted to do the same experiment in a realistic, field situation and you were able to find two supervisors who agreed to act in the differential manner desired. Let us assume, further, that the managers involved were the heads of sales sections in a department store. Here, then, is what you might find:

	EXPERIMENTAL GROUP	CONTROL GROUP
Room:	On main floor	On third floor
Time when job behavioral measurements are taken:	Weekly	Weekly
Characteristics of work group members:	Males	Males
Method of selecting work group members:	Regular applicant selection	Union referral
Type of leadership:	New leadership	Old leadership

The difference here is that in the field experiment the researcher has less control of possibly relevant variables. Sometimes he can perform certain statistical procedures that will increase this control, but sometimes he cannot. The result is greater ambiguity in interpretation and, perhaps, a wasted research project. The gain, when correct, is realism and a greater ability to generalize the results, as compared to the essential unreality of the laboratory experiment. Which experiment should be performed? The answer is both, because both have something useful to contribute. In addition, the fact that the methodological problems are different in the two types of experiments means that when we get similar results in both cases confidence in our findings is increased even more than if they both suffered from the same potential flaws.

The simulation experiment is a combination of the laboratory and field experiment, containing some of the advantages and disadvantages of both. As a research method it duplicates a real-life environment on a small scale so that changes may be introduced into the environment and measured for effects more easily than they can be in real life. On the other hand, it differs from the laboratory approach in that in the latter case the interest is in determining the effects of a single variable, such as leadership style, and there is little concern with whether the other external conditions of the experiment are similar to the organizational conditions in which the leadership style will be exhibited. Does this make a difference in the simulation experiment's effectiveness in terms of meaningfulness and generalizability? Although some people think so, there is little evidence to support such a claim—in fact none which I know. In addition, I do not know the answers to such questions as: (1) How wide-ranging a simulation should be set up? For example, suppose we wanted to simulate a research group in the sales and marketing department in order to study the changing effects of different marketing conditions. Should we simulate deliberations for one product? for all products? Should we simulate the administrative and bureaucratic characteristics of the unit? the nonorganizational environmental influences that may affect work performance (e.g., family problems, environmental constraints, and so forth)? (2) How long should the simulation be for maximum effectiveness? A day? A week? A month? There is a study, to indicate the problem, that argues that simulation can be too complex (Weitz and Adler, 1973).

Correlational Methods

The second major scientific research procedure is the correlational method, in which variables are observed and measured without intervention by the researcher. Basically, a correlational study determines the relationship between two variables without any attempt to control the occurrence of one of the variables to see if changes in its values will affect changes in the other variables (as we do in the experimental method). An example may be a study made to see if participative decision making is related to employee job satisfaction. In such a study the goal is to find out if variable A (the behavior of the leader) is related to variable B (the attitudes of the employees), *not* if variable A has caused variable B. Because we supposedly cannot make such causal inference in correlational research, but rather must admit that in the case of an obtained relationship B might cause A, as well as A causing B, or that they both might be caused by a third variable (C), this type of research does not have the status of the experimental method. Consider the example. If we are doing an experimental study, our procedure would be to vary the behavior of the supervisors by training them to act in the desired manner and then we would wait to see if there is an effect on job satisfaction. If there is, then we would (ideally) know to what to attribute it. We would, therefore, have a good idea as to one way to increase job satisfaction in the future. Such a conclusion, however, might not be justified if all we did was measure, at one point in time, the leader's behavior and the employees' attitudes. If a positive relationship were found, it might be due to the leader causing the job satisfaction, the job satisfaction causing the leader's behavior, or, perhaps, both of them being caused by a highly competent top management. We usually could not tell from a correlational study which conclusion to make.

Thus, the major difference between the two orientations is that the experimental method is interventionist, change-oriented, radical, and emphasizes control of variables, whereas the correlational procedure is conservative, non–change-oriented, and does not involve control of variables. Yet, as we have already mentioned, we should not accept these conclusions completely, as there are exceptions. Consider the case in which we correlate the job satisfaction of a group of managers in December 1967 with their absentee rate in February and March 1968 and find a positive relationship between the two. Obviously, we could not conclude that the absentee rate caused job satisfaction.

Another exception is when we use statistical controls to develop notions of causality. Suppose we relate intelligence test scores to job performance and find a positive relationship. Can we safely attribute a causal relationship to the intelligence of the individual? At first glance, one would think so and, yet, some might argue that since both intelligence and job performance are related to socioeconomic status, the positive relationship is due not to intelligence but to a 3rd variable, i.e. the learned achievement motivations of socioeconomic middle- and upper-class individuals. There are ways to resolve this problem by appropriate statistical controls: one would be to develop different samples at each socioeconomic level. Thus, if we had separate low, middle, and high socioeconomic samples and the same relationships between intelligence and performance were found for each, we could rule out the class variable as a causal factor. Hence, while there might be other possible causal factors in addition to intelligence, we would, at least, have ruled out socioeconomic class.

We might control for possible extraneous effects even more completely by subgrouping on two or more variables. Consider the following possible frameworks for examining this relationship:

1. RELATIONSHIP BETWEEN INTELLIGENCE AND JOB PERFORMANCE —
NO CONTROLS

Hypothetical Samples	*Sample Sizes*
	n = 600
High intelligence	300
Low intelligence	300

2. RELATIONSHIP BETWEEN INTELLIGENCE AND JOB PERFORMANCE —
CONTROLLING FOR SOCIOECONOMIC STATUS

Hypothetical Samples	*Sample Size*
	n = 600
High intelligence high socioeconomic status	100
High intelligence middle socioeconomic status	100
High intelligence low socioeconomic status	100
Low intelligence high socioeconomic status	100
Low intelligence middle socioeconomic status	100
Low intelligence low socioeconomic status	100

3. RELATIONSHIP BETWEEN INTELLIGENCE AND JOB PERFORMANCE —
CONTROLLING FOR SOCIOECONOMIC STATUS AND SEX

Hypothetical Samples	*Sample Size*
	n = 600
Males/high intelligence/ high socioeconomic status	50
Females/high intelligence/ high socioeconomic status	50
Males/high intelligence/ middle socioeconomic status	50
Females/high intelligence/ middle socioeconomic status	50
And so on.	

The problem with all this is that the sample size on which each relationship between intelligence and performance could be obtained shrinks very rapidly as variables are controlled. For example, in the second case, the sample for each analysis has shrunk from 600 to 100 just on the basis of two control variables. Since our confidence in any type of statistical analysis is in great part a function of the sample size, one can quickly reach a point of diminishing returns as controls are increased.

There is a second type of correlational study that is sometimes called causal but it is doubtful whether this description is accurate. In this type of study individuals are asked to describe what their feelings and emotions were at some previous point in time. Using this information, the researcher may then predict later behavior or explain other behaviors that took place after the significant emotions but before the research investigation. An example may be a situation in which a researcher is investigating the possible attitudinal determinants of work failure by interviewing people about their attitudes upon job entry. People whom he might interview in this type of study are those still on the job whose later behavior he will try to predict and those who have already left under unfavorable conditions. While this study has value, it is extremely doubtful that its findings could be called causal. The occurrence of selective memory, ego defense, and other such processes would seem to be so operative that whatever attitudinal factors are isolated (and there would be some), it would be unwise to assume that they were the sole causal factors of job failure.

Problems In Scientific Research

The Problem of Using
Human Subjects in Research Studies

In recent years the attention of a good number of psychologists has turned to a reexamination of the scientific method. Such attention has resulted from the realization that perhaps it does not work as well as we thought when one is dealing with human subjects who can think about, react to, and form opinions about the research in which they participate. Basically, the problem is this: the logic of the experiment or of the measurement process is that something (i.e., the experimental change or the measurement) is applied to somebody (the subject) by somebody else (the researcher) and it is assumed that this something is what the subject will react to. That is, he will react to the experimental intervention or submit to the measurement process in an automatic, reflex type of way, and he will bring to the research setting no behaviors except those being studied by the researcher. In other words, the subject is assumed to be a passive responder to stimuli, with these stimuli being those specified by the individual conducting the research project. But is this really the case? Consider the following example:

> Most managers reported (and employees confirmed) that they simply went up to the employee and notified him that he would be interviewed the next day at a particular time. Over 75% of the employees reported that their superiors either ordered them to go to be interviewed or said it in such a way that they implied that they did not want any "noise." Thus, most employees felt they knew very little about the research. Few reported open resentment (after all, they were always being ordered to do something). Many reported feeling anxious.

The reasons for anxiety seemed to vary enormously. "Why did they pick me? Who picked me? Are they going to ask personal questions? Are they trying to get rid of me? Whose crazy idea was this? Will I be able to understand a professor or a researcher? Will the questions be too difficult? Will they ask me to write? How open should I be? Will it get anyone (including me) in trouble? What effect will this have on my wages earned for the day? What effect will my absence have upon others who are working and depend on me?"

In some cases the anxiety was compounded by informal employee kidding and discussion about the research. "Who goes to see the headshrinker first?" "I hear they place a hot towel on your head and send electrical currents through you to make sure you don't lie." "They have a guy who can read your mind."

Few of these anxieties were openly stated and fewer were dealt with. Many employees, who came to be interviewed or to fill out questionnaires with varying degrees of anxiety, attempted to cope with their feelings by becoming resigned ("They do things to me unilaterally all the time"), or by mild hostility and cautious withdrawal or non-involvement (Argyris, 1968, pp. 190–91).

It is obvious in this example that whatever determined the responses of the employees, the questions of the researcher were only part of the influence. But what else determines the results if they are not completely a function of the research questions? How serious is the problem? If it is serious, what can we do about it?

There can be several types of unintended effects on research results. One of these is a problem that has come to be known as experimenter demand. Sometimes, this problem involves the case where the individual being studied goes along with the researcher (e.g., because he likes the researcher or respects science). This means that the subject of the research tries to fulfill the hypothesis if he can figure it out and often he can. On the other hand, it can also involve the "screw you" effect; that is, the subject figures out the hypothesis of the researcher and does just the opposite of what is being hypothesized. In both cases, the determinant of the response has not been the experimental (independent) variable but a social psychological interaction between the researcher and the person being studied; that is, whether the subject wants to help the researcher or not.

A second unintended effect can come from the experimenter himself who may unintentionally bias his data in favor of his hypothesis. Such unintentional manipulation is often quite powerful (Rosenthal, 1967). An example is when the researcher indicates that a particular response is better than another by some unintentional smile or similar type of cue. Most of us are very sensitive to such cues and we often look to people to help us decide what to do in an ambiguous situation.

A third type of bias is when the subject tries to look good. This process, known as social desirability, is different from experimenter demand in that here the interest is not in meeting or rejecting the demands of the researcher but in doing what one can in order not to be evaluated negatively, even if this involves distorting how one really feels in response to a particular stimulus.

How often do these contaminating factors occur in research studies? Unfortunately, we do not know. Most research has been devoted to demonstrating their occurrence, rather than determining their likelihood of occurrence in different situations.

Another problem with research on human subjects takes a somewhat different tack, one more concerned with problems resulting from the presumed expertise of the researcher and the controlling influence he may adopt in implementing the scientific method. A person whose name we will see often in this book, Chris Argyris, has been very much concerned with this problem and I have integrated his arguments from two of his papers in Figure 2.1.

Figure 2.1
Dysfunctional Implications of Traditional, Researcher-Controlled Experiments and Surveys

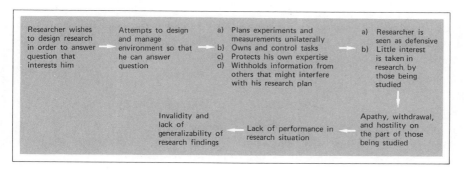

In later chapters we shall lay heavy stress on Argyris's theories on the negative behavioral effects of hierarchical, externally controlled situations such as the traditional formal organization so we shall not spend time on them here. However, Argyris has made some very telling points concerning the great similarity between the traditional experiment (in which the researcher controls the subject) and the traditional bureaucratic organization marked by pyramidal, authoritarian control mechanisms. Since the deleterious performance effects of such organizations may be considerable, as we shall see later, the difficulties outlined by Argyris in figure 2.1 are important.

What can be done about the problems of using human subjects in research, assuming the problems have at least some validity (cf. Gergen, 1973)? Although some dispute the seriousness of the problem (Schlenker, 1975), most disagree and a number of suggestions have been made to improve the situation. Perhaps the most potentially fruitful of these are the following:

1. Have the subjects in the research take an active role in designing the project; this, according to Argyris (1975), will overcome the behavioral effects of subjugation and he provides some evidence for his arguments.
2. Develop more effective ways of disguising the purpose of the research by making the relevant instruments more unobtrusive. The problem with this suggestion is that it may involve ethical problems of manipulation. It ignores the fact that people are increasingly sophisticated and may not accept manipulation (cf. Samuel, 1975).
3. Have people role play the experiment, as well as actually subjecting them to an experimental treatment such as an attitude-change attempt. If there are few differences between the results in the experiment and the role play, there would seem to be good reason to infer that there has not been much of an experimental effect (i.e., in the real experiment, the subject might have been playing a role to please the experimenter).
4. Use postexperimental inquiries to determine how much the subject was responding to the real purposes of the research as opposed to how much he was responding to demand characteristics.

The evidence for the value of each of these suggestions is still fragmentary; we have much to know about the effects of these techniques and the problems they can best overcome.

The Problems of Change Studies

Of all the different kinds of research studies, among the most important are those that have to do with the evaluation of change. How good is a new training program compared to the old? Has the attitude-change program worked? Do the supervisors really learn new attitudes in the company management-development courses? These are some of the different kinds of change studies and their obvious importance makes it even more significant that there is common agreement that there are few, if any, kinds of research studies more fraught with methodological problems. Consider the following examples of the problems to be faced in research of this nature.

the problem of control

If we introduce an attitude-change program in an organization in June and find it has an effect by a measurement in November, how do we determine the attitude changes that have occurred due to other influences on the employees during that time, e.g., societal factors? Suppose, for example, the attitudes are concerned with racial integration in the organization and race riots had occurred in the interim. The laboratory enthusiast might advise using a control group, but what control group can one use if one is a staff psychologist for company X and that is the population of interest? Company Y? This is hardly a satisfactory solution, both on the grounds that company Y might not be interested, and, even if it were, the company Y population is likely to be quite different from that of company X on other variables besides the experimental variable (i.e., the attitude-change attempt).

premeasurement effects

Take the example of trying to change attitudes toward racial integration in an organization a little further. Typically, the researcher would evaluate the current racial attitudes in order to have a base rate with which to assess the effectiveness of the change attempt. Hence, a premeasurement. But is it all this simple? As a matter of fact, probably not since any of the following might also happen:

1. At the time of the premeasurement the respondent may say to himself, "The company is getting ready to integrate and they want to know how much trouble there will be. I hate the company's guts and even though I don't particularly care about integration one way or another, I think I'll cause them a little trouble by adopting a more negative attitude than I feel."
2. At the time of the premeasurement the respondent might say, "I've never known the company was interested in (and supporting) this type of thing. I'd better adjust to this and say the proper things, even though I really feel negatively about it."
3. At the time of the premeasurement, he may also say, "Gee, I never knew the company was interested in me and my opinions. The company is really pretty nice so I must do something it obviously wants which is to be favorable toward integration, even though I really don't care one way or the other."

The problem here is an experimenter demand problem in that the premeasurement itself may set off reactions in the respondent that are not a result of the experimental design but which may, nevertheless, influence scores on the attitude measurement.

loss of sample subjects

Assume that a premeasurement of attitudes has been made in April, the change attempt has been made from May through October,

and the postmeasurement has been done in November. A simplified
table of results might be as follows:

SAMPLE SIZE

ATTITUDES	April (n = 300)	November (n = 200)
5 most favorable	100	100
4	50	25
3	50	25
2	50	25
1 least favorable	50	25
	Mean = 3.33	Mean = 3.75

What has happened between the pre- and postmeasurement? Obviously, the mean favorability score has gone up, suggesting that the
change program has worked. However, something else has also happened and that is that 75 people from the original sample left the organization and are no longer available for retesting in November. What
shall we do with their scores? There are a number of alternatives, none
wholly satisfactory. One is to throw out their scores, thereby reducing
the sample size for the study, but that would increase the instability of
any conclusions made. Also, ignoring these scores may result in an
overestimate of the effectiveness of the change programs since these
people may have left because they reacted negatively to the change attempt. On the other hand, it is also conceivable that their leaving might
have had nothing to do with the change program and that we could
keep them in the sample to give greater stability to the analysis, with
each of them being assigned the average change score of the overall
sample.

the problem of scales

Another problem with change studies is the methodological problem that in computing any effect of a change program individuals who
scored high originally can only go down (or remain the same) and
those who scored low can only go up (or remain the same). Using different scales could help solve this problem, but only partially. For example, if the scale of attitudes used ranged in possible scores from 1 to
7, as opposed to 1 to 5, then the people who scored 5 originally could
conceivably change to 7 (which they could not if it remained a 1 to 5 scale).
On the other hand, people who scored 1 still cannot go down. Overall,
the problem is messy and there is no one solution.

uncontrolled variables

Another persistent difficulty is that in many cases the characteristics evaluated in change programs are highly gross variables that have meaning administratively but which are difficult to understand and interpret psychologically. For example, the kinds of things that are important to evaluate for their change effects in an administrative sense may be different training methods (e.g., lectures versus group discussions), different leadership methods (e.g., democratic versus authoritarian), and so on. However, when research is undertaken, many variables are, of necessity, uncontrolled, and these may cause ambiguity in interpretation of results. Thus, if method A is better than method B, is this due to the fact that the methods are different or is it possibly due to the fact that instructor A used method A and that instructor B used method B and that the instructors differ in quality? One way to answer this question is to have instructor A use method B and instructor B use method A, but often this is not feasible. Even if it were, there may be another problem in that the way an instructor teaches by the second method will depend on which method he used first and this will be different for the two instructors. Another problem is that even if it were possible to isolate instructor or method differences, this would not help to identify what it is about those variables that have differential effects. For example, if we are concerned with instructor differences, what factors are responsible for the differential effects? The bearing of the instructor? His attitudes? His approach toward the students? The order of discussion topics he follows? These are the specific questions we must ask if we are really to understand the effects of change programs. However, to obtain answers to such questions might be time-consuming and costly. They are, therefore, not the kinds of things that interest the administrators or managers who pay for these programs. The solution, often, is a compromise that sometimes satisfies everybody but might, on occasion, satisfy no one.

measurement problems

A final major dilemma with change studies is that they inevitably involve some real headaches in measurement. One of these we have already mentioned in an earlier comment that an obtained relationship between original scores and change may be an artifact of the scale of measurement used. In addition, other measurement problems almost inevitable in change research are the following: (1) The ease of changing from one level to another may be different at different levels of the variable involved. For example, it may be simpler to change from antiunion to neutral toward union than it is to change from neutral toward union to prounion. How do you interpret different change scores at different levels of the scale if the difficulty of changing was different to begin with? (2) Scores on psychological measurements are rarely the same on successive measurements due to the unreliability of the instruments. It is difficult to establish conclusively that change scores are due to true change rather than the fact that people's scores generally change from measurement to measurement because of the inadequacy of the measure.

Given, then, all these problems in change studies, why undertake them? The answer is obvious. They are crucially important and *cannot* be dispensed with. Thus, we continue with change studies using the best procedure possible, at the same time being alert to new approaches to resolving the difficulties. For example, if a true experiment cannot be done in the sense of being able to isolate and control for all variables except the one independent variable under consideration, one approach is to use the quasi-experiment (Campbell, 1969), an example of this being the study of intact groups over time to see how they change as a result of both natural and staged events. In this case, each group would serve as its own control.

Another possible method for overcoming change-study problems is controlling for the possible negative effects of pretesting. This approach consists of the utilization of four groups in the research, rather than just the traditional experimental and control groups (Solomon, 1949). These four groups are as follows:

GROUP 1	GROUP 2	GROUP 3	GROUP 4
Pretest	Pretest		
Experimental treatment		Experimental treatment	
Posttest	Posttest	Posttest	Posttest

An examination of the four groups on the posttest would indicate the following:

1. If we compare groups 1 and 2, we have a traditional experimental-control comparison.
2. If we compare groups 1 and 3, we can determine whether the effects of the experimental treatment are due to the experimental treatment alone or whether they are due to the treatment and pretest in combination.
3. If we compare groups 2 and 4, we can determine how much of an effect taking a pretest alone, without any experimental intervention, might have on a posttest in terms of stimulating changes of various sorts.

The major problem with this approach, of course, is that it is difficult enough to get only two groups comparable to one another; getting four comparable groups seems almost fantasy.

Evaluating the Significance of Research Findings

Once a research study is completed, how do we interpret the findings? Suppose that the mean level of attitudes toward racial integration in an organization in November is 4.73, whereas in April it was 4.03. What does this mean?

The underlying philosophy in making inferences in research investigations is conservative because the assumption is that one should not claim positive results in an investigation unless the claim of negative results is highly improbable. In this context, positive results usually mean the establishment of a relationship, while negative results usually mean that whatever relationships we obtain between variables are of a chance, inconsequential nature and not to be relied on.

The logic involved in making these inferences can best be described by an example. Suppose we measure 10% of the women in a factory on job attitudes and 10% of the men. In each case we have taken a 10% sample from a population (e.g., the total number of women in that factory) which has a mean level of job attitudes and a variation of attitude around that mean (i.e., not everybody has the same job attitude). Hence, if we take a 10% sample from the female population, the mean of that sample will generally not be exactly the mean of the overall population since we may have sampled a little too high or a little too low from that particular group. However, it will generally not be too different and taking more samples of 10% each will make the average mean of all the means taken from the different samples the same as the overall population mean. Now, if we find that the male mean in the 10% sample is not too different, then we can claim negative results (i.e., there are no differences, and they are both samples from a population with the same mean). On the other hand, if the means of the two samples are greatly different from each other, then we can claim positive results (i.e., there are differences between males and females and the samples we have obtained are samples from populations with different means). It is the purpose of theory in statistical inference to provide various techniques to enable us to determine when the differences between two (or more) means are too great to accept the hypothesis of no difference and when real significant relationships between variables should be accepted. In this case, the technique we would use would be the *t*-test,[1] the logic of which is to compare the ratio of the difference between the obtained means to the kinds of differences we would expect if we assumed that the two means came from the same population. If the ratio is great enough, doubt is cast on the hypothesis that they are both from the same population, with a significant ratio (or *t*) generally taken to be one in which the probability that it could have occurred by chance is 5% or less. On the other hand, when the probability that they could have been taken from the same population is greater than 5%, we usually attribute the differences obtained to the random fluctuations that we said might arise from taking samples slightly above

---

[1] The relevant formulas for the *t*-test and the Pearson product-moment correlation coefficient, mentioned below, will be found in any statistics text.

or below the population mean. While this is what we shall generally mean by significant results, you should be aware that we are talking only about statistical significance here, rather than practical. Sometimes the 5% level of significance can be met when using very large samples but the actual differences obtained may be quite trivial in a practical sense.

Similar comments can be made about the other major way of determining the relationship between variables—the Pearson product-moment correlation coefficient. This is a measure of the relationship between two variables that takes as its major point of departure the extent to which two variables order people similarly. If the variables do order them similarly, the value of the relationship would approach either +1 (for a positive relationship) or −1 (for a negative relationship). A person high on one would be predicted accurately to be high on the other. On the other hand, if the correlation is low, its value would approach 0 and the level of prediction would not be high. For this measure, also, it is possible to determine whether the relationship obtained meets the 5% level of significance or whether the obtained relationship is a function of random fluctuations. In general, the higher the correlation (i.e., the more it departs from 0 and approaches either −1 or +1) the more confidence we can have in the obtained relationship, but here, also, sample size is important. The larger the sample size is, the better although, as in the *t*-test, a correlation coefficient with very large samples can be statistically significant and yet not indicate a practically strong relationship. In both cases we have to be very careful about two things: (1) not to overemphasize statistical significance if we see that the actual results do not indicate strong relationships between the variables (when the significance comes from very large samples), and (2) to make sure that the relationships obtained are based on at least sufficiently large groups to warrant some confidence. Although what constitutes a sufficiently large group depends greatly on conditions of the research, it usually means at least 30 people in each group in experimental studies and 75 to 80 in correlational studies.

Where Science May Not Help: The Choice of Problems

Until now I have discussed the logic of scientific research methodology in the study of work behavior, some of its strengths and some of its weaknesses. Overall, with its demands for observation, replication, and its attempts to control subjectivity and obtain objectivity, the scientific method provides the best way to find out the answers to questions, *once you know what the question is,* and here is the rub. The fact is that scientific methodology may not tell one what to look for and, in fact, can sometimes operate as a blinder on creativity by implicitly encouraging one to think along scientifically established, well grooved channels. When creativity is discouraged in favor of the safe but sure study the results may be a waste of effort, both for the field and for the people involved. The point is that science can help one formulate and articulate a problem once it is developed, but it doesn't necessarily stimulate original thought.

Where does meaningful, creative problem development come from? We will talk more about this later but basically it comes from an openness to experience and an awareness of the complexity of the world. More operationally, it means being open to everyday events and the problems evidenced in these occurrences (Ghiselli, 1974). It means looking at the extreme and the absurd, not because the absurd itself is that crucial but because it may illustrate something very important (Weick, 1974). You might, as an exercise, see how many or what types of meaningful research questions you can formulate from the everyday events I have taken from the newspaper which is lying on my desk as I write this:

1. the increasing number of young and middle-aged people who have rejected organizational life to go "back to the land";
2. the effect of unemployment on the esteem of low socioeconomic males and its societal implications;
3. corporations' admitting illegal bribes of domestic and foreign governments;
4. the experience of the U.S. military in racially integrating their officer corps;
5. a recent French experiment in democratizing the work setting.

For each of these I (and, I am sure, you) could formulate a whole series of researchable questions. Similarly, if we pick up any other newspaper or just keep our eyes and ears open, other questions occur. The point is to be open to what is taking place. The scientific attitude is important in evaluating the hypotheses we develop and it can, on occasion, suggest a problem on the basis of knowledge already developed. However, it can also keep us too much in already-ground paths if we rely on it too much for problem and hypothesis generation. For this, we need an openness and a sensitivity which are not the same as the scientific attitude and the scientific method but which serve as effective complements to them.

A Prognostic Remark

Even if we follow everything suggested in this chapter, that is, even if we are creative in problem development and scientifically rigorous in hypothesis evaluation, will we learn all we need to know about organizational behavior? The question of the applicability of the scientific method to human behavior is a matter about which many have had doubts for years. Clearly, the complexity is enormous and the goal of a unified theoretical framework is even harder to achieve than we used to think (Cronbach, 1975). Yet progress is being made, as this book will show, and I do not see a better alternative at this point. Science may not tell us everything, and it certainly does not give us values, which must come from other aspects of the human experience. What science does give us is one useful, meaningful way of finding out about some of the factors that influence behavior in organizations and what we can do about changing these factors. This is the emphasis we will take in this book.

Summary

This chapter has been devoted to methodology, revolving mostly around an examination of the scientific method, its characteristics, its advantages, and its faults. Two major frameworks were examined: the experimental method, which involves control of variables; and the correlational survey, which consists of studying the relationships between variables without any attempt to control their occurrence or value. Although different from one another, the two frameworks are similar in that they both rely on objectivity, replicability, and communicability. Furthermore, it was argued that the ability to control variables in experiments was not always very high and that certain types of statistical controls were possible in correlational surveys.

Along with the advantages of scientific methodology, there are also problems. Considerable discussion was devoted to the problems of experimenter demand, of change studies, and of measurement and scaling problems. Finally, the chapter emphasized the fact that science helps one to solve problems adequately but that it may not be particularly helpful in generating meaningful, exciting questions. What one needs for this is an open, inquiring interest in the world and its problems. Without it, science becomes a rigorous methodological procedure for solving problems that may not matter.

SUGGESTIONS FOR FURTHER READING

ARGYRIS, C. Dangers in applying results from experimental social psychology. *American Psychologist*, 1975, *30*, 468–485.
The author of this article has long been a critic of hierarchical

control as a mechanism of social influence, a characteristic which he sees as being descriptive of the researcher in traditional scientific methodology. Argyris discusses the negative implications of this influence, some evidence, and some possible change mechanisms.

CAMPBELL, D. T., and STANLEY, J. C. *Experimental and quasi-experimental designs for research.* Chicago: Rand-McNally, 1966.
A major effort to articulate some of the problems in conducting experiments in real-life settings and how approximations can be utilized with certain levels of confidence. A difficult book, but well worth the effort.

CRONBACH, L. J. Beyond the two disciplines of scientific methodology. *American Psychologist,* 1975, *30,* 116–127.
In this article the author critically examines some of the major theoretical assumptions of the behavioral sciences, the extent to which they have been satisfied in the past, and the prognosis for the future. The author believes that the demands of science are even more difficult than has been thought and that we might consider different approaches.

EVANS, M. G. Opportunistic organizational research: The role of patch-up designs. *Academy of Management Journal,* 1975, *18,* 98–108.
An interesting application of Campbell and Stanley's argument that approximations to experimental designs are useful in behavioral science research.

PART II

THEORETICAL PROCESSES IN ORGANIZATIONAL BEHAVIOR

"There is nothing so practical as a good theory," the great psychologist Kurt Lewin once said, and nowhere is this as true as in the study of behavior in work organizations. Theory has always been a matter of great interest to researchers in this field because theoretical investigation (1) does much to highlight the significant factors that influence attitudes and behaviors of interest (e.g., work performance, aggression, job satisfaction, etc.), (2) enables systematic investigation, and (3) provides guidelines for administrative intervention. In Part II, as we review the various types of theoretical investigations and frameworks that have marked this field, we will see how these advantages of theoretical research have contributed to the growth of our conceptual understanding of work behavior and to the development of more effective practice.

Chapters three and four discuss theories of motivation as these influence such organizationally important behaviors as work performance, aggression, creativity, risk-taking, and power. We will see that there are a number of theories in the field that are similar in some ways and different in others. Taken in context, they suggest significant directions for future theoretical development and management intervention.

In chapter five we will focus on intellectual and cognitive-processing abilities and some of the newer theoretical developments in these fields of research. We will see that there are some interesting implications in these newer developments for organizational functioning.

Chapters six, seven, and eight deal with organizational variables such as leadership structure and policies, and how differences in these influence such outcomes as work performance, aggression, and feelings about the self and others.

Finally, chapter nine focuses on theory and research relating to reactions to job experience such as effects on self-esteem, estrangement from the self and others, stress, and job satisfaction.

chapter three

The Motivation to Work

Like many other behavioral scientists, I am often called by executives in organizations to give them a one-day seminar in motivation. Most often they want to find out how they can increase work motivation to the levels at which they think they themselves are working. The techniques they have been using do not seem to work, and they want to learn others. Often, when I arrive at the organization, I am immediately told by a number of the executives that they "know darn well what to do — but the company won't let them do it." Usually, I translate this to mean that they believe that there is no need for new psychological techniques for motivating employees and that if they were allowed to use the old, traditional tools of rewarding good behavior and punishing the bad, this so-called problem of employee motivation would be resolved.

What of this? Is this all there is to the problem of employee motivation; that is, do we know what influences behavior and all we need is the opportunity to apply the appropriate rewards and punishments? Or is there something more complex involved if management actually is to influence employee behavior? Are the motivational factors influencing behavior more complex than traditionally thought? There is, in fact, good reason to think that this is so and I will try to show why in this chapter.

The Traditional Approaches:
Anxiety and Rational Economic Man

The term *traditional* has many meanings but in the context which concerns us here the meanings are clear. The traditional means of motivating workers are, to some managers, the judicious (or, perhaps, unjudicious) use of anxiety, to others the use of the rational economic man model, and, for some, the use of both. To these people, these methods are all that is needed and what they want is the freedom to use them. Our interest here is first to examine exactly what is meant by these theories of motivation (for this is what they are) and then to determine how adequate they are as theories and guides for management action.

Anxiety

It is a source of interest to me that the effects of anxiety as an influence on adult work performance in the everyday setting are just beginning to be investigated. Considering what we have just said, this is surprising. Yet, anxiety simply has not been of great interest to students of organizational behavior until very recently.

The picture is changing now, however, and we are starting to gain valuable insights, both from the laboratories of the experimental psychologist and from the field study of complex human events.

Turning first to the former body of research, anxiety has long been a favorite among the rigorous, experimentally minded psychologists because they can establish the necessary condition of anxiety quite easily in the controlled environment of a laboratory and because this interest links them to the world of complex human affairs. As a result, there is a body of anxiety-related research that has some significance for the world of work if we do not generalize it too far. (After all, anxiety that is developed in a study of learning nonsense syllables is not exactly the same as the anxiety of real-life living. The two *are* different in terms of their significance and importance.) The major results of the anxiety studies can be summarized as follows:

1. Anxiety facilitates performance on easy tasks.
2. Anxiety debilitates performance on hard tasks.
3. For any specific task there is a characteristic curve that shows that increasing anxiety facilitates performance up to a point; beyond that point, it debilitates it. The level of this point differs according to task difficulty. For easy tasks the anxiety point can be increased to a fairly high level before it becomes debilitating; for the hard task anxiety can be increased only slightly, if at all, and almost all anxiety becomes debilitating.

How does one interpret these findings? Clearly, it depends on your perspective and particular situation. For the manager who is supervising a group of employees performing relatively simple jobs there is justification for using anxiety as a motivator, whereas for those whose subordinates are performing hard jobs, the reverse is true. In this sense there is some support here for the opinions of the traditionalists concerning the value of anxiety as a motivator. Yet, they should not be too quick to claim support since a number of qualifications clearly are in order. First, the results show no support for the use of anxiety when the task is difficult. In fact, just the opposite is true. Just as important, and a qualification that illustrates the difference between the laboratory and real life, the easy–hard task distinction is very significant in the world of work because continuing to perform easy jobs may, in and of itself, have dysfunctional consequences of various kinds. As we will see, there is currently a movement against simple, repetitive jobs in favor of more challenging jobs and the simple jobs may eventually assume little importance. If this happens, it would, logically, decrease the importance of anxiety as a motivator.

Perhaps the most major qualification concerns the extent to which the anxiety of the psychological laboratory is generalizable to the anxiety in real life. I would submit that there is a real question here, particularly since it has become apparent that there are a number of different kinds of human anxiety, with each having different antecedents and consequences. In other words, since there are data supporting an overall anxiety factor and since there is also evidence for specific types of anxiety, particularly in human behavior, perhaps the best thing to do is to take account of these experimental findings, accept them as having some (but limited) generalizability to human affairs, and then turn to more specific anxiety variables such as fear of failure and fear of success, factors of considerable importance for work behavior.

fear of failure

The first of these two concepts to be studied was fear of failure, identified by John Atkinson of the University of Michigan in the 1950s (cf. Atkinson, 1958; Atkinson and Feather, 1966). Basically, fear of failure describes the anxiety that is felt about the feeling of failure, *not* objective failure itself, and it is Atkinson's hypothesis that there are individual differences in this characteristic with some people having more of this anxiety than others. Fear of failure combines, he proposes, with other characteristics of the individual and the particular task situation in influencing achievement-oriented behavior as follows:

1. Individuals who are high in fear of failure want to avoid achievement-demanding situations in general.
2. If they are forced to stay in such situations by some other motivational force such as the desire to go along with a group interested in achievement, high-fear-of-failure people will work best in situations where they

are either very likely to fail or very likely to succeed, as opposed to situations of medium risk for success. There are two reasons for this:

a. If they work at a very difficult task, nobody will blame them for failing (it is not objective failure they try to avoid, but the *feeling* of failure).

b. If they work at a very easy task, they will not be likely to fail.

One of the interesting aspects of Atkinson's framework is that he predicts some of those paradoxical behaviors that have always fascinated both psychologists and laymen (including me). For example, he predicts that a person with a high fear of failure is more likely to choose a situation in which he is likely to do poorly than one in which he has a medium probability of success, given only two choices. Atkinson's reasons for this prediction are his theoretical assumption of the desire to avoid feelings of failure rather than objective failure and the fact that a person is less likely to be blamed for failure if the task is very hard, rather than of medium difficulty. In this way Atkinson derives self-defeating behavior from an assumption that man is basically trying to achieve the best for himself. Clearly, this is a neat theoretical mechanism.

Atkinson's theory has considerable research support in its behavioral predictions and we have by now a considerable body of information and accompanying hypotheses about how people with a high fear of failure behave. Birney, Burdick, and Teevan (1969) have summarized such a person as likely to do the following:

1. avoid situations where he will be evaluated precisely;
2. prefer comparing himself against groups greatly deviant from himself;
3. prefer privacy;
4. prefer vague and imprecise measures of performance;
5. reject responsibility;
6. blame others when he fails to meet a performance standard.

When we consider these findings, in addition to Atkinson's work, there is not much doubt that fear of failure is, both actually and potentially, a very useful way of viewing the motivational processes of some people. Consider, for example, how fear of failure people would attempt to block performance appraisal programs. However, there are methodological problems with this approach which tell us we need to go slow. One is the tendency to use different measures of fear of failure in different studies, even though there is considerable evidence to indicate that the studies do not always measure the same thing (Weinstein, 1969). Another problem concerns the groups often studied. In many cases, the procedure has been to give subjects two tests—a fear-of-failure measure and a need-for-achievement measure[1]—and then rank them separately according to their scores on each. The researcher than picks those individuals who are high on one and low on the other and studies the extreme groups. Unfortunately, in this way he is ignoring those who are high on both and those who are low on both. This means that any findings are based on the behavior of only 50% of the original sample who are not randomly chosen but *preselected.* How generalizable are the findings then? Also, if we preselect on fear of failure, what else are we preselecting on? The significance of this point is seen if we realize that a study that preselects a sample on the basis of socioeconomic level also preselects on a host of other variables related to socioeconomic level such as race, religion, residence, and the like. To what population would we generalize the results of such a study? The same question can be raised in regard to Atkinson's work in this area.

I like the fear-of-failure research because it may explain such diverse behaviors as self-defeating choices, extreme risk-taking (or none at all), antagonism toward accurate performance evaluation and the reasons why "male machismo" is so dysfunctional at times. However, there are methodological problems that need to be clarified.

fear of success

Research on fear of success, our other anxiety variable, reflects many of the same concerns with paradoxical forms of human behavior that have marked the fear-of-failure research. What distinguishes it even more is that interest in it began at the same time as, and became tied in with, the women's liberation movement. Indirectly, it was inevitable that a new concept would be developed in order to explain the achievement behavior, or the lack of it, in women. The work of McClelland on need for achievement (see below) and the work of Atkinson on fear of failure has always had difficulty in predicting the achievement behavior of women. Yet, you and I know that many women achieve, and if such behavior is not predictable by the theories and ideas we use for men, what does predict it? The managers and executives of organizations who are being flooded daily by the demands of newly work-motivated women have a legitimate interest in the question, a question that began to be answered some years ago by Matina Horner in her doctoral dissertation research. It was in this work that we were first confronted with the proposal that intelligent women in our society have been socialized along mutually contradictory dimen-

---

[1] We will discuss the need-for-achievement concept later in this chapter. Basically, individuals high on this variable act in an opposite manner to those high on the fear of failure. However, it is possible to have high (or low) amounts of both.

sions. On the one hand, they have been taught to value achievement and success, as most people have been traditionally in our society, and on the other, they have been taught to fear success as college students and in the adult working world because success was considered non-feminine. Success in the world of work, they have learned, is for men, while the world of the home and the family is the appropriate sphere of activity for women. Attempts to leave the home in order to succeed in the world of work would stamp a woman as a failure, as a woman, even though she was originally encouraged to succeed in school at the lower levels. Horner maintained that this is what fear of success means and it is why she proposed that there is such a low level of vocational achievement by high-ability women.

Horner's hypothesis (1968) has been revised considerably since her original formulation. In one direction, there has been considerable support for her ideas by Broverman, et. al., (1972) who have reported interesting findings that revolve around the following perceptions, which were held by all of the samples they studied, male *and* female, and across different occupational groups:

1. The image of the ideal personality is seen to be similar to that of the successful man.
2. The image of the successful woman is opposite to that of the successful man.
3. The image of the neurotic personality is opposite to that of the ideal personality.

If you have put 2 and 2 together and have come to the conclusion that the unsuccessful woman equals the ideal personality *and* the successful man, your arithmetic is pretty good.

However, it also seems to be true that fear of success is *not* true of all women (Alper, 1974) and that it is a psychological variable which occurs in some cases but not all. The key factor for women seems to be the degree to which the family background of the woman is traditionalist in nature. If it is, she develops fear of success. If it is not (i.e., if the mother has a career and the father is supportive), then apparently she does not develop such a fear. This finding and the fact that fear of success is now also being found among large numbers of men (Hoffman, 1974; Alper, 1974; Feather and Raphelson, 1974) suggest a problem with the definition of fear of success, for clearly males have not received the contradictory socialization discussed by Horner.

One possible explanation for the occurrence of fear of success in men (Hoffman, 1974) is that achievement, traditionally a source of negative social evaluation for women, has now also become negatively evaluated by many men. There is considerable evidence for this argument. Yankelovich, in a study of nationwide samples of college youth (*Business and Society Review*, 1974), found that the belief that hard work pays off had dropped during the years from 1970 to 1973 from 79% to 56%. This change has been accompanied by an increased negative attitude toward business and its stress on monetary rewards to the exclusion of other possible job values. These results have led Yankelovich (1974) to propose several new cultural trends relevant to the work setting, among which are the changing meaning of success and doubts about the desirability of efficiency. Both of these obviously have significance for the degree of achievement motivation.

Another explanation for male disinterest in achievement relates to the fear-of-failure concept I spoke of earlier. Perhaps success has come to mean something that is negative and dehumanizing because it implies that a person must perform well to evaluate himself highly and that failure is to be avoided at all costs. It may be that some males have developed a negative attitude toward this role. Although this point has been raised recently by the men's liberation movement and by writers such as Vilar (1972), clinical psychologists have for years been familiar with the phenomenon of males rejecting responsibility in mid-life for the first time and now we are reading of such cases in journalistic accounts of "male menopause" and the like. Later I am going to discuss studies of managers by Tarnowieski (1973) and Bartoleme (1972), among others, which suggest that this rejection of success argument may have considerable viability for older men and that the attitude may have spread to their children.

Overall, the major conclusion to be made is that there is a negative attitude toward success today among some men and women, whether one calls it fear of success, a rejection of fear of failure, or a violation of new (or old) societal norms about the value and meaning of success.

implications for management

What does all this mean for management? One major implication is that it would be fruitful to reduce at least some types of anxiety in the work setting, particularly those that generate a negative reaction to success. Some of the problems are a function of other institutions besides work organizations and there is a limit to how much we can expect any organization to accomplish. However, we can expect them to accomplish something since there is reason to think that much of the anxiety may be coming from a perceived overemphasis on demands by the work system at a cost of other types of personal, familial, and societal needs. Later, when we will be examining alienation, estrangement, and similar concepts, most of which also relate to a withdrawal of interest from the work setting and a lack of concern with achievement, mechanisms and approaches to dealing with these problems will be discussed.

My own belief is that fear-of-failure anxiety needs to be moderated considerably but perhaps not eliminated completely. I think that the fear-of-failure research outlined earlier dictates such a recommendation. The problem, however, is that many of our traditional norms and beliefs say that fear of failure should be maximized as a motivating device. Why has it remained so significant in managerial thinking? I will suggest two reasons. First, there is obviously great theological and cultural support for proposing fear of failure as a significant factor in human affairs. This is hardly the place to go into these matters extensively, but it is naive to downgrade the significance of fear of failure, even in these days of human liberation. Millions of people's lives continue to be shaped by these theological and cultural traditions, either positively or negatively. Second, fear of failure may be used as a motivator because it provides a symbol of the status and power of the user. After all, is not generating fear in one's subordinates one of the most unambiguous ways of showing status? There is a considerable body of research in support of this and we will discuss the implications of hierarchical status for this behavior later.

Whatever the reasons, fear of failure will continue to be used by many managers, despite its mainly negative influence on work behavior and despite the increasing number of people who may not care about working. Its cultural support, its value for the user, and the very real threat of such management decisions as discharge, demotion, and layoffs as an influence on some people assures its continued operation, even though it would be far more optimal for those who run our organizations to encourage the growth of the need for achievement, a motivational influence discussed below which is far better for both the individual and the organization.

The Rational Economic Man Model

The other side of the traditionalist approach to work motivation can be summarized in a number of ways, but probably the easiest way is to say that it is the rational notion that performance is a function of the values one expects to get by performing, and that the more one can get, the more one will perform. In its simplest framework it states that if (1) a man or woman thinks that some kind of outcome is desirable, and (2) he or she can get the outcome by performing at a given level, then (3) he or she will be motivated to perform at that given level. You will recognize this statement as similar to the concepts of utility and subjective utility as they have been called by economists for hundreds of years, and indeed it is. Their notion, too, has been that individuals have certain preferences in that they like some things over others and, all other things being equal, they will behave in a manner designed to achieve as many of these preferred outcomes as possible, provided they believe that these desired objects are attainable on the basis of their efforts. Obviously, one does not have to be an economist to appreciate the essential logic and rationality of this type of approach to understanding work motivation. It is engraved deeply in our culture and will strike a responsive chord of familiarity in most of us as being, perhaps, just common sense.

In fact, the acceptance of this approach, along with anxiety, is so embedded within us that, together, they provide the theoretical basis on which most of the practices commonly found in our formal organizations have traditionally rested. In these organizations, the controlling influence—usually management—decides that there are certain gratifications that most people want from their jobs, gratifications which it is in the power of management to control (e.g., salary, promotion, security, and good working conditions). Management controls and increases worker performance (including their own) by making the attainment of these rewards contingent on effective work performance. These outcomes serve as incentives to the worker for better performance provided, according to the theory, that the workers believe the rewards actually are attainable through their efforts. If they believe that such rewards are not contingent on their performance, they will not react to them as incentives.

An example of this approach is given in a study by Lawler and Porter (1967). Their research was concerned with testing the hypothesis that the amount of effort a person expends on his job, as judged by his superior and peers, is related to the extent to which he perceives that he could achieve desired outcomes by engaging in such effort. In addition, they predicted that his overall performance also would be related to such perceptions of rewards. However, this relation would be at a lower level since overall performance would also be affected by such things as ability and the accuracy of role perceptions, whereas effort would not. The sample used in testing these hypotheses consisted of 154 managers in five organizations, ranging from a large manufacturing firm to a local Y.M.C.A. Table 3.1 summarizes some of the results of this study, indicating significant support for their hypotheses.

One crucial point to Lawler and Porter's work and the work of others using this framework concerns how they account for the lack of responsiveness to incentives on the part of some individuals:

> However, even if he feels that receiving a transfer does depend on performance, he may not feel that performance is related to effort. The reason for this would be a belief that, although the organization will definitely give a transfer for a certain level of performance, he himself is not capable of achieving that performance, even with a high level of effort. In other words, he might be thinking something like: "I know if I sold x amount of our products the company would transfer me, but it would be

Table 3.1

Correlations between Extent to Which a Person Perceives Valued Rewards Are Dependent on Work Performance and Various Measures of Work Performance

WORK PERFORMANCE MEASURES	CORRELATIONS
Superiors' rankings on:	
Job performance	.18
Effort	.27[a]
Peers' rankings on:	
Job performance	.21
Effort	.30[b]
Self-ratings on:	
Job performance	.38[c]
Effort	.44[c]

Source: Lawler and Porter, 1967, pp. 122–142.

[a] $p < .10$.
[b] $p < .05$.
[c] $p < .01$.

practically impossible for me to sell that much, no matter how hard I tried" (Porter and Lawler, 1968, p. 19).

Conceptually, Porter and Lawler account for unresponsiveness to incentives by suggesting that it is due to lack of confidence and belief in one's own abilities and skills. The incentive theory framework for work behavior in this contemporary version is, therefore, similar to an approach to work motivation known as a balance or a consistency model, which I am going to outline later. However, there are differences, also, as we will see.

A number of other rational economic man theories exist in the work motivation literature besides the one used by Porter and Lawler (cf. Vroom, 1964; House, 1971; Campbell, Dunnette, Lawler, and Weick, 1970). I will not list them all because basically the idea underlying all of them is similar. In all of them the idea is that behavior is a function of the value one expects to obtain from a set of behaviors (value being a function of the reward to be obtained and one's liking for the reward) and one's rational expectancy of being able to engage in the behaviors required to obtain the reward.

It is a matter of considerable interest, therefore, that the research literature testing these theories is nowhere nearly as supportive as these cultural traditions and their contemporary popularity would suggest. Table 3.2 summarizes many studies that have utilized this framework and it is clear that while support is often found, this support is not invariable. In addition, even when support is found, the relationships are often quite low, as House, Shapiro, and Wahba (1974) and Locke (1975) have pointed out.

Why? The question has interested many people (cf. Miner and Dachler, 1973; Kopelman, 1974) and a number of explanations have been offered that are worthwhile for us to consider here for their theoretical interest. We will also see that knowledge of these limitations is of considerable importance for management's ability to utilize the approach in real-life, applied situations.

One very serious problem is that the concept of value is psychologically complex. Traditionally, the economic man theory and its contemporary analogues—expectancy-value and instrumentality theory—have used as values money, advancement, pensions, security, and the like. It has become clear that this is an unnecessarily narrow view of values and that people are interested in the opportunity to achieve other types of values such as interesting, challenging, or socially responsible work. An example of the behavioral effects of trying to achieve this value is McClelland's work on need for achievement, a research program we will talk about later. There are many people whose desires are more in these newer areas rather than in the traditional ones. Hence, one reason for the relative lack of support for the approach may be that in many of these applications the most significant motivational incentives were simply not investigated.

A second explanation for the findings listed in Table 3.2 is that some of the assumptions that seem to be implicit in the application of the economic man (or expectancy-value) theory may not be valid. One of the most important of these assumptions is that more is better; that is, the greater the incentive, the greater the influence on behavior. There are at least two research programs that provide some negative evidence for this assumption. One of these is the work of Deci (1972), who engaged in a number of experiments to find out what happens when one combines traditional incentives (e.g., money) and those considered more modern (e.g., challenging work) in influencing work motivation. His results indicated that there are no overall cumulative effects when you add one incentive to behavior to another, an effect that the economic man model would not predict. Instead, Deci found that already performing a task for one incentive seems to lessen the effect of an additional incentive. A finding similar to this has also resulted from a study of naval career choice (Glickman, Goodstadt, Frey, Romanczuk, and Korman, 1974). In this study it was found that adding incentives for naval enlistment and reenlistment did not lead to greater likelihood of choosing the navy as a career. In fact, sometimes it led to less.

Other research on the preceived utility of pay incentives by Giles

Table 3.2

Summary of Research Investigations of Rational Economic-Man Approaches to Work Motivation

INVESTIGATORS	SAMPLE AND STUDY DESIGN	RESULTS
Georgopolous, Mahoney, and Jones (1957)	621 manufacturing operations employees	Performance increased as a result of the individuals' value for pay, the degree to which they saw that performance would lead to pay, and the degree to which they saw themselves as free to vary their performance.
Lawler (1966)	211 lower and middle managers	Expectancy was related to performance for individuals of high ability but not for those of low ability.
Galbraith and Cummings (1967)	32 production line employees	Complex pattern of mixed results; some were supportive and some were not. Extremely small sample makes results difficult to interpret.
Hackman and Porter (1968)	82 female service representatives	Predicted relationships reflecting the effects of higher values of outcomes and higher expectancies occurred, but highest correlation was + .40. The predicted higher relationships when these were combined did not occur.
Lawler (1968)	41 first-level and 14 higher-level managers	All correlations were as predicted. The highest correlation obtained was + .54.
Graen (1969)	169 females; experimental manipulation of work settings	Support was greatest when the relationship between performance and outcomes was concrete and clearly perceived. The effect of variations in perceived value to be obtained on performance was weak.
Gavin (1970)	192 male and 175 female candidates for management positions	Separate analyses relating expectancy and value to performance separately and combining them additively were significant. However, combining them by multiplying expectancy times value as predicted did not increase the relationships.
Goodman, Rose, and Furcon (1970)	66 scientists and engineers	Predictions from expectancy-value were supported. Highest correlation was + .39.
Mitchell and Albright (1972)	42 U.S. Navy officers	Expectancies did not relate to performance when combined with values. However, general model was supported for other criteria such as desiring to remain in Navy.
Wofford (1971)	207 white- and blue-collar employees	Performance-reward contingencies related to performance as predicted. Other predictions not significant.
Pritchard and Sanders (1973)	Government employees	Mixed results; correlations with self-reported effort higher than with supervisory ratings. One of two relationships proposed by the model supported.
Pritchard and DeLeo (1973)	Laboratory simulation	Predicted relationships did not occur.
Jorgenson, Dunnette, and Pritchard (1973)	Laboratory simulation	Predicted effects on work effort did not occur.

Table 3.2 (*cont.*)

INVESTIGATORS	SAMPLE AND STUDY DESIGN	RESULTS
Arvey (1972)	Laboratory simulation	Mixed results; belief that one's effort will lead to effective performance was positively related to poerformance, but performance-reward contingency was not. Multiplying expectancy times value did not increase the value of the theory as predicted.
Schwab and Dyer (1973)	124 blue-collar workers	Mixed results; belief that one's effort will lead to effective performance was positively related to performance, but performance-reward contingency was not. Multiplying expectancy times value did not increase the value of the theory as predicted.
Arvey and Mussio (1973)	266 female clerical workers	In general the predicted relationships of the expectancy-value model either did not occur or occurred at a very low level.
Moore and Campion (1974)	177 male blue-collar workers (63 black, 63 Mexican American, and 51 white)	For none of the three subsamples was the expectancy-value model supported.
Sobel (1971)	Laboratory experiment	Little support for the expectancy-value hypothesis.

and Barrett (1971) also indicates that increasing incentives by either adding to the value of one incentive or by combining different incentives does *not* have automatic, cumulative effects on behavior. Management cannot, therefore, apply the expectancy-value approach automatically, despite its reasonableness. There are other reasons, also, for stressing this lack of applicability. Among these, two are most worth mentioning.

First, expectancy-value theories may, in general, be losing their usefulness because they are future-oriented theories and we live in a future-is-now society. I do not know how widespread the feeling is about the future-is-now ethic, but it is certainly more widespread than it was 20 years ago. Today an increasing number of people are not willing to defer gratifications very much or for very long. Second, the value of this approach generally, but not always, increases if the organation (1) encourages accurate perceptions of the pay structure of the organization, the security structure, and the other possible incentives and (2) if it responds to differences in employee behavior (cf. Kopelman, 1974). For organizations that do not meet these requirements and many do not, the approach does not work as well in predicting behavior. Overall, then, the economic man theory has some value in predicting work behavior, but it is not *the* theory and there is much that it cannot account for.

A Different Type of Expectancy-Value Theory

For the most part the conclusions we have just outlined hold pretty well when the values under consideration are what we generally call extrinsic values. Usually, extrinsic values are defined as those that are subject to the influence of another person or social influence (e.g., money, advancement, financial security, pension rights, etc.). These, in the work situation, are generally controlled or at least influenced by management. Therefore, they can be manipulated by management in order to influence performance. As I suggested above, though, extrinsic values are not the only kind of values people want. Many of us seek values that constitute our own idiosyncratic needs and motives. To use a simple example, consider the case in which two people make the same low salaries on a job but differ in their satisfactions: one is content because he desires a sense of achievement, which he gets from his job, whereas the other is dissatisfied because he seeks only the money. Similarly, we all know of cases in which people seek a position to increase their sense of power but not necessarily their income or security levels. In these instances we are talking about intrinsic values and not extrinsic values, which are controlled and mediated by an authority system.

I am not certain that the two types of values are always distinguishable, but I do think that they comprise different ends of a continuum. Certainly, it seems that the kinds of anxiety we talked about earlier (e.g., the fear-of-failure and fear-of-success variables) are different in origin and are qualitatively dissimilar to such factors as money, promotions, and pensions. In other words, while these more idiosyncratic, intrinsic differences in motivational variables have also been developed in the expectancy-value (or economic man) framework in that they have been studied as a function of the value to be obtained by performing and the rational expectancy of attaining the value by behaving, they should be distinguished from extrinsic values on at least two counts. First, they have a different origin and the implications for management are different. Management can control extrinsic values directly, but not intrinsic values. Second, the basic hypothesis that there are differences between people in intrinsic motivational characteristics means that any solution to work problems based on these motivational variables can be only partial in nature since it is based only on those having the characteristic to a significant degree (and assuming that not everybody can be trained to develop it in equal amounts).

Of the research on intrinsic motivational variables that is of relevance to us, the work of Atkinson and Horner, which we have already discussed, is of considerable importance. At least as significant, however, is the work of David McClelland on the need for achievement, a subject to which we now turn.

McClelland's approach to achievement motivation is really the relatively common idea that some people just get a kick out of achieving or like to do well or like to be the best. While not very scientifically stated, these phrases generally explain the major ideas underlying a program of research that for over two decades has concerned itself with the implications for various kinds of task performance of individual differences in the achievement motive, or the need for achievement (abbreviated as *n Ach*). Defined as the "desire to exceed some standard of behavior," interest in the characteristic started out in psychology laboratories but later expanded into the study of various types of organizational and other kinds of achievement behavior, as well as remaining a subject for various kinds of basic laboratory analysis. There has now accumulated a fair amount of information as to how differences in this need might arise, how individual differences in this characteristic might best be measured or assessed, and what such differences mean in terms of performance. As we will see, however, despite this knowledge, there is still much to be learned about the need for achievement.

McClelland originally began his work on the need for achievement because of theoretical interests in personality and projective mechanisms. These changed, however, and his major concern became the implication for society of the presence of many individuals to whom liking to do well, liking to do better than the standard, liking to surpass previous achievements, and so on, are a source of pleasure. As a result, he evolved the following hypotheses (McClelland, 1961):

1. Individuals differ in the degree to which they find achievement a satisfying experience.
2. Individuals with a high *n Ach* tend to prefer the following situations and will work harder in them than individuals of low *n Ach:*
    a. Situations of moderate risk—feelings of achievement will be minimal in cases of little risk and achievement will probably not occur in cases of great risk.
    b. Situations where knowledge of results is provided—a person with a high achievement motive will want to know whether he has achieved or not.
    c. Situations where individual responsibility is provided—a person oriented toward achievement will want to make sure that he and not somebody else gets the credit for it.
3. Since these three types of situations are found in the business entrepreneurial role, individuals of high *n Ach* will be attracted to the entrepreneurial role as a lifetime occupation.

Assuming that the economic growth of a nation depends on successful fulfillment of the entrepreneurial role, it follows that the economic success of a society depends on the number of people attracted to the entrepreneurial function. McClelland argues that this is a function of the level of concern for achievement in that society and of the number of individuals who find achievement situations pleasant. The prediction, then, for economic growth is clear: increase achievement motivation and you increase the economic performance of the society.

How good is this hypothesis? How much of the vast set of complex behaviors we call societal growth (and decline) can we attribute to the effects of a need for achievement? How can we even test it? A necessary requirement is that we be able to derive at least two kinds of measures. First, we have to be able to measure the economic growth and decline of civilizations in a relatively satisfactory manner. Second, we have to measure the relative concern with achievement in given civilizations (on the assumption that the number of people who would be achievement oriented in a civilization would be directly related to the concern of that civilization with achievement in general). After deriving these measures, we would then follow the procedure of (1) measuring a society's concern with achievement and (2) measuring its economic growth and/or decline subsequent to the measuring of achievement, perhaps for the following 25 or 50 years (this measurement would have to be made subsequent to the achievement measurement since a causative relationship is being hypothesized).

Surprisingly, McClelland was able to perform just such a set of operations, and part of the reason he was able to do so has to do with the way he and his coworkers measured *n Ach*. In most of the individual research performed, *n Ach* has been assessed by making judgments about the extent of achievement concern in the stories an individual writes. In its most common form, this measurement procedure has involved presenting the individual with somewhat ambiguous pictures and asking the person to write stories about the pictures according to a somewhat structured outline. In general, the more these stories contain achievement-related concerns, the greater the *n Ach* inferred.

The logic McClelland followed was that if one can assess *n Ach* in an individual by studying his literary output in a situation, then one could assess the level of *n Ach* in a nation by the same method; that is, by studying its literary output. This is what he did. He studied the dominant themes in childhood stories and folktales in different nations at various times (on the assumption that the dominant characteristics of a society are most likely to show up in this area of literature), derived scores for each nation on *n Ach,* and then related this score to the subsequent economic growth and/or decline of each country. Economic growth was measured in two basic ways: electrical power and national income in international units. You might have some doubts as to whether such a research scheme is advisable at all, considering how hard it is to get an adequate sample of children's readers and folktales (e.g., just think of the regional differences in the United States alone) and how hard it is to control for the contaminating influences of wars, climate, national resources, and so on. Nevertheless, McClelland's results were intriguing and promising. Relationships were found between these sets of variables, and they were, generally, in the direction hypothesized; that is, economic growth followed rises in *n Ach* (McClelland, 1961, pp. 89–103). Table 3.3 shows some of these findings and the consistency of the patterns found is impressive considering the relatively gross and crude nature of the variables involved. In addition, McClelland attempted to construct a generalized model of the derivation of *n Ach.* Figure 3.1 shows portions of this model, which is based on the proposition that individuals with high *n Ach*

Table 3.3
National Economic Development from 1925 to 1950 (Approximately) as Related to *n Ach* Levels in 1925

COUNTRY	LEVEL OF *N ACH* IN 1925[a]	GAIN IN INCOME LEVELS OVER RANDOMLY EXPECTED VALUES[b]	GAIN IN ELECTRICITY PRODUCED OVER RANDOMLY EXPECTED VALUES
Sweden	2.19	+ 2.35	+ 3.17
United States	1.90	+ 1.28	+ 1.86
New Zealand	1.48	+ .63	+ 1.73
Canada	2.67	—.04	+ 1.73
Great Britain	2.10	—1.71	+ 1.65
Australia	2.81	+ .61	+ 1.13
Finland	1.24	+ 1.10	+ .74
South Africa	1.05	+ .70	+ .69
Ireland	3.19	+ .14	+ .33
Denmark	2.00	—1.23	+ .14
Norway	1.33	+ .44	—.03
Netherlands	.29	—.78	—.10
Austria	1.57	—1.02	—.12
Hungary	1.29	—.47	—.26
Chile	1.29	—.47	—.26
Greece	.38	—1.28	—.52
France	.81	—.92	—.55
Argentina	1.86	—.50	—.61
Uruguay	1.48		—.62
Spain	.81	—1.93	—.63
Belgium	1.00	+ 1.57	—.75
Germany	1.38	—.51	—.79
Russia	.95	+ .39	—.79

Source: From *The achieving society* by David C. McClelland, Copyright © 1961, by Litton Educational Publishing, Inc., by permission of Van Nostrand Reinhold Company, pp. 90-91.

Note: Not all data are available for all countries.
[a] Achievement level is the sum of *n Ach* scores per story divided by the number of stories per country.
[b] From C. Clark, *The Conditions of Economic Progress,* 3rd ed. (London: Macmillan, 1957).

are those who have grown up in environments in which they were expected to be competent, which gave them independence at an early age, and which had low father authoritarianism and a lack of mother dominance (since mothers have, in the past, called on traditional means of ideological and external control).

We will see later that work organizations that have analogous psychological dimensions to these are also high achieving, a replication that provides considerable support for McClelland's work. However, although this is an important empirical finding, we do not necessarily have to adopt McClelland's theory to account for it. In fact, I will suggest an alternative theoretical formulation to that of McClelland's, one

Figure 3.1
Need for Achievement

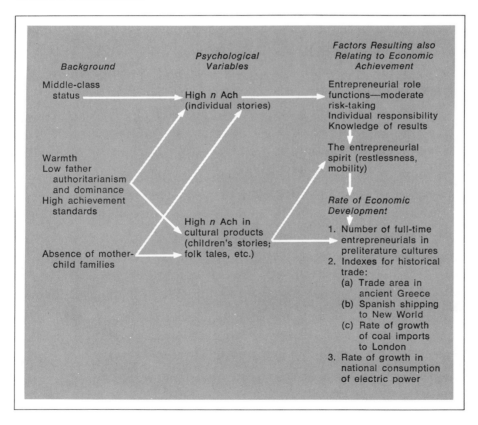

that stems from some of my own research and the work of others such as Klinger and McNelly (1969). This alternative proposes that these environment–performance relationships occur because of the desire to achieve outcomes consistent with self-perceptions, not because they encourage the growth of an achievement motive.

One reason I prefer this alternative explanation is that, exciting and interesting as McClelland's work is, there are still too many unanswered questions. One real problem is that there are many findings, summarized by Klinger and McNelly (1969), which suggest that achieved occupational level predicts later achievement behavior at a higher level than the other way around. Klinger and McNelly suggest that this finding supports a consistency formulation more than it supports the theory proposed by McClelland, and I agree with them.

A second problem is that McClelland's theory predicts in cases in which it should not. For example, if positive affect toward achievement is the key notion, then the *n Ach* measure should not predict behavior in chance situations. Yet, such relationships do occur, and the theory cannot explain why. One way of accounting for this is hypothesizing that chance situations (such as dice) take on the characteristics of skill situations in a psychological sense. But why? It is difficult to develop a rationale. In any case, changes in the meaning of a situation are not part of the theory.

Similarly, *n Ach* should not have a relationship to general administrative management success since the general management situation does not have the parameters of moderate risk taking, quick feedback, and individual responsibility. Yet, such relationships do occur (Cummin, 1967), suggesting that perhaps what is being measured is a general performance capability rather than performance varying as a function of different task and risk situations. In fact, most experiments supporting the moderate risk-taking notion, a key aspect of the theory, are highly controversial (Kogan and Wallach, 1967) because the levels of task difficulty have been defined by the experimenters who have decided what should be labeled hard tasks, moderate tasks, and easy tasks. For example, in a ring toss experiment (Atkinson and Litwin, 1960) the researchers marked off distances from the goal object and assumed that the middle distance would be the moderate risk for the subjects. However, it is obvious that what is difficult for one individual is not difficult for another. A proper test of the hypothesis requires that individual differences in perceived risk must be controlled before we can test to see whether preference for moderate risk taking is related to *n Ach,* as the risks are perceived by the decision-making subject. In the only case in which this has been done, the theory was not supported (deCharms and Dave, 1965).

The history of *n Ach* research leads overall to mixed conclusions, although there is supportive recent research. Hundal (1971) has studied entrepreneurs in India and Davies (1969) has studied the rise and fall of the Minoan civilization, both within the McClelland framework and both find support for it. Yet, the legitimate questions that have been raised and the competing theoretical frameworks that have been developed need to be taken account of in future research.

Are there any practical implications of this theoretical discussion for management, i.e, does it really make a difference whether the reason that social psychological environments of the kind McClelland proposed lead to effective work performance because they lead to high need for achievement or because people want to behave in a way consistent with the favorable self-perceptions that such environments encourage? After all, in both cases, doesn't it mean that management should develop environments of this nature? Of course it does. And yet, I think there is an important implication here and this is for the other techniques one might use in influencing achievement motivation. If we are talking about a motive, such as need for achievement, as being the crucial variable, the other techniques one would use would be different than if the crucial variable was the authority system itself. In one case you might also try to change motives; in the other you would only change the social psychological environment. Later, when we discuss explicit change programs, we will see that there are different techniques involved here, depending on which theory is accepted.

One further comment is that if the key variable is a motive like the need for achievement, the direct implications for management are different than if the key influence is something falling under the traditional expectancy-value system framework. Thus, if the key influence is an extrinsic value like money, you might change behavior just by changing the value of the incentive (e.g., offer more money). On the other hand, if the key value is more of an intrinsic nature (e.g., the need for achievement), the only way to change behavior is to change the individual's motive structure.

Consistency Motivation and a Theoretical Model

It might be useful at this point to articulate more clearly some of the threads that have been running through our discussion. First, the implicit model of man in expectancy-value (or instrumentality) theory is not totally adequate. Its view of man as value-maximizing seems only to be partially true when we look at the research studies that have sought to test it. This is not really surprising, though, is it? After all, if it was an adequate theory, why would we need a field of psychology, or any of the other behavioral sciences?

Second, just as man is not automatic in an economic man sense, so is he not in an anxiety sense. There are great differences between people in terms of the overall intensity of anxiety they experience and in terms of the factors that generate their anxiety.

The significance of these points is great, both practically and theoretically. Theoretically, it means that a model of man is needed in addition to those based on anxiety and value-maximizing. This is not an original remark with me. Indeed, attacks on value maximization go back a long time time, with one of the more significant of the recent revisions being March and Simon's (1958) argument that we are "satisfying" individuals; that is, we choose the first level of outcome that exceeds a minimum level of satisfaction, as opposed to evaluating all possible outcomes and then choosing the best.

In the following sections I suggest another alternative to expectancy-value theory, one that has come to be known as the consistency model of motivation. In doing so, I am not suggesting consistency theory as a complete replacement of value maximization. I don't think it can be for reasons that I will discuss below. Rather, it is best thought of as an alternative to value-maximization, a theory that accounts for some of the varied kinds of behavior which the expectancy-value model cannot account for, *as well as* some of the behaviors that it does explain. The consistency model is also an approach which I find useful and meaningful and which will influence much of my discussion in this book.

Consistency Theory: General Approaches

Suppose that you are given a series of tasks to do, all of them highly similar, and you find that you are relatively incompetent in all of them. This would undoubtedly lead you to a poor assessment of your abilities to perform those tasks, if you are a rational person with some degree of intelligence who is able to distinguish between failure and success. Having established this opinion of yourself, you perform another task of the same type and do it well. What would your reaction be? Would you think there was something wrong with the first task experience so that if given the opportunity, you would change your behavior to be consistent with your previous cognitions, even though such consistency was at the expense of task success? Or would you be glad for the fact of achievement and try to repeat it, given another opportunity, even though such achievement was inconsistent with your previous experience? The theory of cognitive dissonance (Festinger, 1957), which predicts the former response, is a good example of how the consistency approach to motivation is different from the expectancy-value framework in predicting the conditions under which people are motivated to achieve.

The theory of cognitive dissonance may be outlined as follows:

1. It is assumed that an individual's cognitions (ideas, attitudes, opinions, etc.) may have three types of relations to one another:
   a. Consonant: when cognition A follows from cognition B; e.g., a person has worked for company A and says company A is a good place to work. In this case, the cognition of liking is consonant with the cognition of experience.
   b. Dissonant: when cognition A does not follow from cognition B; e.g., the same person says he dislikes company A.
   c. Irrelevant: when cognition A has no relation to cognition B; e.g., the same individual with 25 years of seniority decides to take a vacation in July rather than August.
2. From these assumptions it is proposed that a dissonant set of cognitions constitutes a negative motivational state that an individual is motivated to reduce. The manner in which this negative motivational state is eliminated is by changing one's cognitions and the behavior leading to cognitions so that they will be consonant.
3. Finally, the importance of dissonance as a negative motivational state, and, therefore, as a determinant of behavior, increases with the number of cognitions that are in a dissonant relationship and with the importance of these cognitions.

Stated in this manner you may, perhaps, not see anything unusually significant about the theory of cognitive dissonance or any reason it might be of special usefulness in predicting work-oriented motivation. However, it does have such value and we shall soon see why.

A relevant study is the one that directly tested the questions with which we started this section (Aronson and Carlsmith, 1962), since it can be seen that the theory of cognitive dissonance predicts that the individual would do more poorly on a retrial in order to be consistent with the cognitions of incompetency developed on the first trial. Aronson and Carlsmith tested this prediction in a laboratory experiment in which the subjects were manipulated to think that they had either done well or poorly on a succession of four similar tasks. On the fifth task the individuals were differently treated in a way ensuring that two of the groups would perform in a manner consistent with their expectations (i.e., "high" or "low"), while the two others were given an experience different from their expectations. That is, those who were used to failing were told they passed. This was a dissonant experience and, according to the theory, dissonance can be reduced by changing one's cognitions and/or the behavior leading to the cognitions. This reasoning was based on the fact that the previous experience (involving four tasks) was stronger than the last experience (based on only one task). Given the opportunity, the subjects would try to change their behavior on the last task in order to match their expectancy based on their self-competence. Using a ruse, the authors had the subjects respond to the fifth task again, predicting that there would be a greater number of changes in the dissonant than in the consonant groups. Table 3.4 shows that this is exactly what happened, even for group C; that is, these subjects changed good responses to bad in order to be consistent. In other words, they gave up achievement in order to be consistent with themselves, a finding that an expectancy-value model would find difficult to explain.

Table 3.4
Number of Responses Changed on Repeat of Last Task

GROUP	EXPECTANCY ON LAST TASK	ACTUAL PERFORMANCE ON LAST TASK	NUMBER OF RESPONSES CHANGED
A	High	High	3.9
B	High	Low	11.1
C	Low	10.2	
D	Low	Low	6.7

Source: E. Aronson and J. M. Carlsmith, Performance expectancy as a determinant of actual performance, *Journal of Abnormal and Social Psychology,* 1962, *65,* 178-182. Copyright 1962 by the American Psychological Association, and reproduced by permission.

Is this a freak finding that could occur by chance alone? If not, we can see how important this would be for work behavior theory and management practice. In fact, there is evidence to suggest that the consistency framework is very important indeed, and I will eventually suggest an integrating principle stating that we are motivated to work at a level consistent with our cognitions of self-perceived adequacy concerning the task facing us. It is in this notion of consistency that I think we can explain many, but not all, of the findings on work motivation.

Let us now return to the theory of cognitive dissonance and see what other work-oriented studies have been done with it and what the results have been. Table 3.5 lists findings of some of these studies. Taken together, they provide impressive support for the notion of consistency as an important motivating influence in work behavior; that is, we work at a level that will achieve a just or equitable or balanced outcome, even though such consistency has to be achieved at the cost of various kinds of extrinsic rewards. Where does our definition of what would be just, equitable, or balanced come from? A number of dimensions are involved. An important one, to anticipate our later discussion, concerns self-cognitions. If individuals have negative self-cognitions, they need, according to the consistency model, negative outcomes in order to achieve a consistent result, *and this is what happens in a good many cases.*

Despite the general tenor of the findings in Table 3.5 and the fact that they are supported by other theoretical approaches detailed below, you should be aware that there are problems with dissonance theory that are as yet unresolved, although they are not so serious as to invalidate the approach completely. One difficulty comes from the fact that dissonance arousal in an individual is generally assumed to occur as a result of experimental manipulations (as in the Aronson and Carlsmith experiment described above), rather than being measured directly. Not having a direct measure of the degree to which the person has dissonant perceptions leads to both conceptual and empirical problems. One reason for such difficulty is that it is possible to reduce dissonance in more than one way. For example, one can discount the importance of one's self-cognitions prior to any behavioral choice in order to reduce the degree of dissonance about the same cognitions. While

Table 3.5

Summary of Dissonance Studies Supporting a Consistency Approach to the Understanding of Work Motivation

GENERAL FINDING	INVESTIGATORS
1. When a person is paid by piecework[a] his productivity will be greater when he perceives his piecework rate as deserved than when he feels it is not deserved.	Adams and Rosenbaum (1962)
2. Subjects who perceive they do not have the qualifications to earn a given piecework rate will produce better quality work and less quantity work than those individuals who do perceive they have the qualifications to earn a given piecework rate.	Adams and Jacobsen (1964)
3. Women of high self-esteem who want to go to college are more likely to engage in behaviors designed to achieve that goal than women who want to go to college who have low self-esteem.	Denmark and Guttentag (1967)
4. Subjects who perceive that they are getting a higher piece rate than they deserve, based on previous experience, decrease their performance, whereas individuals getting less than they perceive they deserve increase their performance.	Andrews (1967)
5. People who expect that they will have to do something unpleasant on the basis of previous experience choose to perform the unpleasant task, even when they could have chosen a more pleasant one.	Aronson, Carlsmith, and Darley (1963)
6. People who anticipate an unpleasant experience voluntarily endure more shock than people anticipating a pleasant or unspecified experience.	Walster, Aronson, and Brown (1966); Rosekraus (1967)

[a] By piecework it is meant that the person's income is a function of the *quantity* of units produced. Hence, a person who deliberately decreases his performance in terms of quantity is reducing his organizational reward (income).

the effort is made to design experiments so that dissonance may be reduced in only one way, this is not always possible to control. Hence, if an experiment does fail (and some do), we do not know whether this has been due to (1) the failure to arouse dissonance (a measure of dissonance would help here), (2) the tendency to use a different means of dissonance reduction than the one specified by the experimenter, or (3) the failure of the theory.

There are other problems with dissonance theory which I want to discuss but before I do so let me carry the supportive literature a bit further by reviewing a major theory of work motivation that has its origin in dissonance theory, the equity model of J. Stacey Adams (1965). According to Adams (1965), inequity can be defined as follows:

> Inequity exists for Person whenever he perceives that the ratio of his outcomes to inputs and the ratio of Other's outcomes to Other's inputs are unequal. This may happen either (a) when he and Other are in a direct exchange relationship or (b) when both are in an exchange relationship with a third party and Person compares himself to Other (p. 280).

Diagrammatically, Adams's model looks like this:

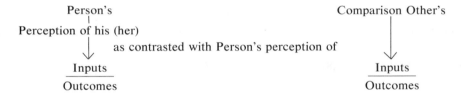

Inputs, Adams says, are anything the person might invest in a task (e.g., effort, education, time), and outcomes are anything he might receive (e.g., money, recognition, etc.). These elements, as in dissonance theory, are weighed by their importance and the motivational hypothesis is that unequal ratios lead to negative motivational states (e.g., tension, etc.), which the person tries to reduce. Adams maintains that the manner chosen to reduce tension may vary from person to person and for a particular person over time but can include any or a combination of the following: (1) distorting one's own or the other's inputs and/or outcomes, (2) withdrawing from the situation, and (3) changing the comparison person against whom he compares his input–outcome ratio. Which method will he choose? Adams suggests a minimal-cost hypothesis that predicts the person will choose whichever method is easiest. An example would be that the person would be more likely to change his perception of the comparison other's input–output ratio than his perception of his own ratio.

Because Adams's work originated while he was employed at General Electric, considerable effort was devoted to testing his notions in either the work setting directly or in laboratory and field experiments with direct work relevance. Four situations studied are particularly relevant here:

Case 1 Overpaid, hourly rate: This case involves a situation in which people are paid on an hourly or weekly basis, but the rate (outcome) is higher than they believe their qualifications (inputs) warrant.

Case 2 Underpaid, hourly rate: This is the same situation as Case 1, but the rate is lower than the people believe their inputs warrant.

Case 3 Overpaid, piecework rate: In this case, the rate of pay is based on the number of work units (pieces) achieved, as opposed to the amount of time put in, with the rate being higher than the people believe their inputs warrant.

Case 4 Underpaid, piecework rate: This is the same as Case 3 except that the piecework rate is lower than the subjects believe the perceived inputs warrant.

According to Adams, the following behaviors should take place in these four situations:

Case 1 Achievement effort (input) behaviors should increase to justify the high outcomes.

Case 2 Achievement effort (input) behaviors should decrease to justify the low outcomes.

Case 3 Achievement effort (input) behaviors should decrease in terms of quantity, since increasing input would increase the dissonance of getting too high an outcome for each unit of work produced and too high an outcome overall. Achievement effort should increase in terms of quality since each unit is worth more (i.e., the piecework rate is very high).

Case 4 Achievement effort (input) behaviors should increase since this is a way of getting equitable outcomes overall, considering one's inputs. Achievement effort should decrease in terms of quality since each unit is worth less.

How well have Adams's predictions worked out? Do people actually lower their achievement-oriented behavior in a way that will result in less financial reward, as in Case 3? Do the other predictions hold up? There have been several reviews of the many studies stimulated by Adams's theory (cf. Lawler, 1968; Pritchard, 1969; Campbell et al., 1970; Goodman and Friedman, 1971) and each review evaluates Adams's predictions somewhat differently, but they agree on several important conclusions:

1. There are different implications for achievement-oriented behavior when one is overrewarded on a piecework rate basis as opposed to being over-rewarded on an hourly rate basis.

2. Similarly, there are different implications for achievement-oriented behavior when one is underrewarded on a piecework rate basis as opposed to being underrewarded on an hourly rate basis.

3. In general, the various predictions for the separate situations have received considerable support (cf. Lawler, 1968; Pritchard, 1969; Campbell et al., 1970). However, there are cases where support for the predictions have been weaker than others. Most strongly supported is the prediction that underpaid piecework rate subjects produce more than equitably paid subjects (Goodman and Friedman, 1971). Less strongly supported are the predictions that overpaid, hourly workers produce more than those who are equitably paid; overpaid piecework rate subjects produce lower quantity and higher quality than those who are equitably paid; and underpaid hourly subjects invest less input than those who are equitably paid (Goodman and Friedman, 1971).

Since these reviews, Wood and Lawler (1971) have further supported Adams by showing that people actually do decrease their achievement-oriented behavior in piecework rate overpayment (Case 3) situations. Similarly, a comprehensive field experiment under natural employment conditions in which the people did not know they were being studied found considerable support for equity theory predictions in both the overpaid and underpaid situations (Pritchard, Dunnette, and Jorgenson, 1971).

Generally, then, it seems that the usefulness of the consistency approach to work motivation is well illustrated by these tests of Adams's models as well as by the dissonance theory research. I said earlier, however, that there were problems with this approach. These problems emphasize the fact that no theory is really a complete answer in all situations. They are just guides and aids to thinking, whether they come from cultural influences (like economic man theory) or constitute a new intruder, like the consistency model of motivation.

In addition to the problem of dissonance theory applicable here (i.e. measuring the degree of inequity in an individual), another question concerns the fact that input and outcome variables as separate, clearly distinguishable factors, such as those Adams proposes, are nowhere as distinct as they seem at first glance. Tornow (1971), for example, has pointed out that such variables as making use of abilities, making many decisions, keeping up on a variety of subjects, bearing sole responsibility, learning a new system, and working on complex tasks may be perceived by some individuals as inputs to a job. On the other hand, others may see these as outcomes or values to be derived from a good job. In fact, the job enrichment research we will talk about later is based on such perceptions.

Another problem concerns how we choose individuals for comparison. What factors determine these choices? Do these factors change over time? If so, how? Andrews and Henry (1964) and Lawler (1965) have made some preliminary steps toward resolving these questions, but much remains to be done when we consider how complex the questions are. As an example, Weick and Nesset (1968) have suggested that there are at least six different ways that the comparison process can result in an inequitable outcome. These are diagrammed below and the source of inequity is italicized in each comparison.

COMPAR- ISON	SELF- PERCEIVED INPUTS	SELF- PERCEIVED OUTCOMES		PER- CEIVED OTHER'S INPUTS	PER- CEIVED OTHER'S OUTCOMES
1	*Low*	Low	as compared to	*High*	Low
2	Low	*Low*	as compared to	Low	*High*
3	Low	*High*	as compared to	Low	*Low*
4	*High*	Low	as compared to	*Low*	Low
5	High	*High*	as compared to	High	*Low*
6	*High*	High	as compared to	*Low*	High

For each of these comparisons we might choose a different individual. In addition, the different comparisons might result both in a different type of inequity and different implications for behavior. These might also depend on whether the relationship between the person and the other was personal or impersonal (Pritchard, 1969). To add to the complexity, recent work with Adams's models seems to indicate that the basis for a feeling of inequity may not be just comparison with another person. It may also come from comparing an outcome with one's internal standard as to what is an appropriate level of outcome for the self (Pritchard, 1969; Lane and Messe, 1972). In other words, feelings of inequity may result not only from comparing yourself with another person but also from comparing yourself with what you have been used to in the past.

These added considerations make the notion of equity and what determines it more complex than Adams's original model. They also bring us closer, once we talk about the concept of the self, to some of the factors we considered in our discussion of dissonance arousal. To overcome some of these difficulties, I will introduce here a consistency theory of motivation which may overcome some of these problems.

Self-Consistency Theory: A Model of Work Behavior

I think that effective work behavior involves at least three considerations. First, it is necessary to achieve on tasks, whatever those tasks might be. Second, hostile conflict and aggression need to be kept under sufficient control so that they will not become debilitating and consume so much time and effort that goals cannot be achieved. Finally, there must be the capacity to change and be creative if the job calls for it.

Until now we have been talking mostly about the first consideration. The latter two will now also concern us since they, too, are important. My goal here is to present a theory of work motivation that involves all three factors in that it is designed to predict the conditions under which achievement, aggression, receptivity to change, and creativity occur in organizational settings.

The basic proposals can be summarized as follows:

1. Motivational processes are a function of the drive to be consistent with belief systems about the nature of the self, others, and the world.
2. Belief systems leading to differing levels of achievement, aggression, and creativity are a function of and may develop in the same types of environments.
3. Changing environments in directions specified by the theoretical model will result in changes in achievement, aggression, and creativity.

These proposals are based on two assumptions. First, a person is motivated to achieve outcomes that are consistent with his evaluative beliefs about himself and about others and the degree to which he believes that there is one set of values (whatever they may be) to guide behavior in this world. Second, a person learns about himself, others, and the world partly as a function of the actual and the symbolically stated opinions of others. Thus, holding other learning experiences about the self and others constant, the more the individual interacts with a world that encourages a certain system of beliefs about the self, others, and the world, the more these beliefs are held by the individual.

There are two rationales for these assumptions. First, the reason that a person is motivated to achieve outcomes consistent with what he has learned to believe about the nature of the self, others, and the world is that outcomes that do not conform to his beliefs are anxiety-provoking and dissatisfying. It is important to note that this motivation to achieve consistency does not mean that we seek a world of no surprises or variations. We might seek a world of constant change, for example, if this is consistent with our belief about the nature of the world. (As an illustration, look at the behavior of that exotic breed we call the jet-setters.) Fiske and Maddi (1961) have suggested a concept very similar to this in their proposal that individuals are motivated to achieve an optimal activation level (i.e., one consistent with the world as one knows it). They define activation level as a function of the variability, meaningfulness, and intensity of the internal and external stimuli to which an organism is being exposed. The level that defines optimality for the given individual is, at least in part, a function of previous experience.

The second rationale is that a person is motivated to learn about himself and others and establish a socially real world (Festinger, 1954) in the world of social behavior because there is no physical reality. The only way a person can establish a system of evaluative beliefs about the self and others and the variability of the world is to interact with others, both overtly and symbolically.

Given these assumptions, the following predictions can be made from the propositions I have listed:

1. People of high self-perceived competence should be more likely to achieve on task performance than those who have low self-perceived competence concerning the task or job at hand, since such differential task achievement would be consistent with their self-cognitions (assuming that task performance is valued).

2. People who believe that there is one set of rules to guide behavior and that there is one way of looking at the world are more likely to be opposed to creative change, change in general, and to those people or things that are different or constitute a change from themselves.

3. People who believe that people, in general, are not desirable, cannot be trusted, and must be controlled by threats and punishments are more likely to develop aggressiveness toward others and are more likely to engage in generally hostile interpersonal behavior.

Tables 3.6, 3.7, and 3.8 provide supporting evidence relevant to these predictions. Table 3.6 summarizes studies concerned with the relationship between the favorability of self-perceptions and various kinds of task performance. In each of these studies there has been some kind of direct measurement along dimensions such as self-perceived competence, self-perceived abilities, and expectancy of success—all variables that are logically subsumable under the general self-esteem variable. It might be noted, incidentally, that different measures of self-esteem correlate highly with one another (Silber and Tippett, 1965). Tables 3.7 and 3.8 report data supporting the prediction that hostility to change results from belief in a stable world and that hostility to others results from lack of esteem for others.

In Table 3.7 the measure of individual differences in belief systems cited is the F-scale (authoritarianism) (Adorno et al., 1950), and in Table 3.8 the D-scale (dogmatism) (Rokeach, 1960). Neither of these scales is as desirable for our purposes as it could be, since each is a composite measure of a number of different beliefs and values rather than a clear measure of either belief in the value of other people in general or belief in the existence of a set of rules and procedures with which to guide behavior. However, both scales have strong components of each of these two beliefs as significant contributors to their overall scores, and they are scored as negatively related to one another, in agreement with the proposals here. Nevitt Sanford, one of the original developers of the F-scale, has emphasized that the scale was designed to measure variables such as (1) belief in authority, conven-

Table 3.6

Summary of Studies Relating Self-esteem and Self-evaluation to Achievement Behaviors

BASIC FINDINGS	INVESTIGATORS
1. Women of high self-esteem who want to go to college are more likely to engage in behavior designed to achieve that goal than women who want to go to college who have low self-esteem.	Denmark and Guttentag (1967)
2. People who expect that they will have to do something unpleasant on the basis of previous experience choose to perform the unpleasant task even when they could have chosen a more pleasant one.	Aronson, Carlsmith, and Darley (1963)
3. Individuals who have high social reinforcement standards (i.e., degree to which they have been rewarded previously) are more likely to perform in a manner designed to achieve high rewards than those who have low social-reinforcement standards.	Baron (1966)
4. Self-perceived ability on a task based on previous task performance is positively related to later task performance.	Kaufman (1963); Feather (1965)
5. Individuals of high self-esteem are more likely to choose occupations in which they perceive themselves to have a great degree of ability than those of low self-esteem.	Korman (1967a); Korman (1967b)
6. Individuals who are told they are incompetent to achieve a specific goal on a task, even though they have had no previous experience with the task, will perform worse than those who are told they are competent to achieve the goal.	Korman (1968a)
7. Academic achievers have a more positive self-concept than underachievers.	Shaw (1968)
8. There is a significant positive relationship between self-concept and grade-point average.	Brookover and Thomas (1963–1964); Finkelman (1969)
9. Individuals of high self-esteem are more likely to perform a task successfully when qualifications are challenged than individuals of low self-esteem.	Finkelman (1969)

tionality, and general rules as guides to behavior, (2) opposition to reliance on imagination, subjectivity, and individually determined guides to behavior, and (3) generalized hostility toward and vilification of people (Sanford, 1956). Rokeach (1960) has viewed his D-scale as measuring very much the same types of variables, although he claims that the D-scale is more psychologically based and not as related to agreement with rightist political ideologies as the F-scale. Research has consistently shown a high positive correlation between the two scales, but not as high as each correlated with itself (Kerlinger and Rokeach, 1966). This finding tends to support Rokeach's thinking. These similarities in theory and in scoring are why I have used research with these scales as tests of these predictions. Table 3.7 presents the relationship between the F-scale and change and aggression and Table 3.8 presents the analogous relationships for the D-scale.

Turning now to the second proposition, which states that the same environments cultivate beliefs that the self and others are valuable and that change is the nature of the world, the significance of the hypothesis is that if supported, a mechanism is provided to enable management to influence behavior in the work setting. Let us assume, then, two types of environments, oversimplified a bit, but theoretically useful. Environment A is a traditional work organization; that is, it has a strong hierarchical orientation in which authority is emphasized. Individuals low in the hierarchy are required to obtain superior approval before any variation in activity from that ordered by the superiors is undertaken and it is demanded that all follow to the letter the rules

Table 3.7

Summary of Findings on the Relationship between the F-Scale and (1) Reactions to Newness, Difference, and Change and (2) Aggression and Hostility toward Others

BASIC FINDINGS	INVESTIGATORS
1. Authoritarianism is negatively correlated with favorability of attitudes toward (a) the blind and (b) the deaf.	(a) Cowen, Underberg, and Verrilo (1958); (b) Cowen et al. (1967)
2. Authoritarianism is positively correlated with the tendency to keep social distance from others in Germany, Japan, and the United States.	Triandis, Davis, and Takezawa (1965)
3. High authoritarians are more likely to be aggressive toward groups different from themselves across different situations; they are more likely to exhibit more generalized hostility toward such groups than are low authoritarians.	Epstein (1966)
4. Task groups led by leaders low in authoritarianism were more likely to adjust to changing demands of situations and to be more flexible in meeting new requirements.	Ziller (1958)
5. In an experimental game situation, authoritarianism scores were positively correlated with the tendency not to trust the other side and to act in an untrustworthy manner toward the other side.	Deutsch (1960)
6. Authoritarianism is positively related to the tendency to use physical punishment and ridicule in controlling children.	Hart (1957)
7. Authoritarianism is positively related to the use of negative (hostile) sanctions (e.g., penalties, negative evaluations) and the use of sanctions, in general, in controlling the behavior of others.	Dustin and Davis (1967)
8. Attitudes toward minority (or perceived different) groups are all highly correlated with one another, and these generalized attitudes are negatively correlated with authoritarianism.	Adorno et al. (1950)
9. Authoritarianism is highly correlated with militaristic attitudes and agreement with an aggressive foreign policy.	Eckhardt and Newcombe (1969)
10. High F-scale people are more likely to act in a hostile fashion toward others at the behest of an authority figure.	Elms and Milgram (1966)
11. High F-scale people were less likely to have demonstrated against the Vietnam war in 1969.	Izzett (1971)

and procedures specified by those high in the hierarchy. Let us assume further that not only does environment A demand that all employees pay attention to the rules, but that most of the activities are likely to be rule specified and programmed. That is, the ratio of the number of activities that are rule specified and programmed to the total number of activities is high. Finally, assume also that these externally controlled, rule-specified, programmed activities are increasingly specialized the lower one ranks in the environment. Rephrased, this would mean that the variety of activities performed increases the higher the level in the work setting.

Contrast this with organization B, which has characteristics that are at the other end of the continuum from those of the traditional work organization (environment A). There is low hierarchical orientation and great stress is placed on self-control of one's activities, once the overall objectives have been decided on. In addition, it has a low degree of programmed activity in that the ratio of the number of activities that are programmed and rule specified to the total number of activities is low and there is variety and change in everyday work behavior, even for those at low levels. As a final characteristic, the overall

Table 3.8

Summary of Findings on the Relationship between the D-Scale and (1) Reactions to Newness, Innovation, and Difference and (2) Aggression and Hostility toward Others

BASIC FINDINGS	INVESTIGATORS
1. Dogmatism is negatively correlated with the ability to learn new beliefs and to change old beliefs.	Ehrlich and Lee (1969); Torcivia and Laughlin (1968)
2. High dogmatic individuals are more likely to learn problems involving the simple following of authority, while low dogmatists are more likely to do well on problems involving the learning of new principles.	Restle, Andrews, and Rokeach (1964)
3. Resistance to compromise with the other side during collective bargaining (simulated) and the tendency to use unilateral planning (as opposed to bilateral discussion) are positively correlated with dogmatism scores.	Druckman (1967)
4. Dogmatism loads heavily on the same factor with authoritarianism and a belief in militarism and an aggressive foreign policy.[a]	Eckhardt and Newcombe (1969)
5. Dogmatism is negatively related to the likelihood of rejecting standard operating procedures and developing new procedures in a working system.	Fillenbaum and Jackman (1961)
6. Dogmatism is negatively related to a liking for new approaches in music, art, and films.	Vacchiano et. al. (1969)
7. Dogmatism is negatively related to acceptance of liturgical change among Catholics and acceptance of technological change in a factory.	Vacchiano et. al. (1969)
8. Dogmatism is positively correlated with dislike of dissimilar religions.	Berkowitz (1962)

[a] The correlation between militarism and dogmatism while positive, was not significant.

development of objectives for the organization stems from the participation of many at all levels, rather than just a few at the top.

Theoretically, I propose that work organizations of the type that I have called environment A cultivate and encourage the growth and development of low self-esteem, low esteem for others, and a belief that there is a set of rules and procedures to guide behavior as a function of the natural order of things and the nature of the world. On the other hand, environment B encourages the development of high esteem for the self and others, belief that the self and others are valuable, and belief that the world is a changing, developing, dynamic system. Table 3.9 outlines this proposal.

To state the argument more completely, in work organizations of high hierarchical orientation I would expect the growth of belief systems that would be consonant with the basic mistrust of people implicit in such control systems; that is, the growth of low self-esteem and low esteem for others. On the other hand, in more democratic organizations I would predict high self-esteem and high esteem for others. There would also be a growth of low esteem for self and others as a function of the high number of programmed activities, since programming and

Table 3.9
Summary of Model Relating Environmental Antecedents to Motivational Processes

1. Basic Theoretical Assumptions
    a. People are motivated to seek a stable world; hence, they will attempt to seek outcomes consistent with belief systems.
    b. People's belief systems are a function of environmental experience and learning.

2. Consequences of Different Environments for Behavior

Environmental Characteristics	*Consequent Belief Systems*	*Behavior*
a. High hierarchical control of behavior	a. People (both the self and others) are undesirable (since they must be controlled).	a. Low achievement
		b. High agression toward the self and others
b. High programming and routinization of activities	b. There are universal rules and principles that one should use as a guide to behavior; these principles are universal, permanent, and applicable to everyone as guides to behavior.	c. Hostility toward change and variation
c. High specialization and nonvariability of activities		
		d. Noncreative problem solving and behavior
d. Low hierarchical control of behavior		
e. Low programming and routinization of activities		
f. Low specialization and variability of activities	Opposing predictions to above	

high rule specification implies a symbolic mistrust in the ability and willingness of people to complete their tasks without direction and control of others. High self-esteem and esteem for others would also develop where there is low programming of activities because this symbolizes faith in people's ability to control themselves.

Finally, I would predict the growth of a belief system in which there are universal rules and procedures to guide behavior in hierarchical organizations for two reasons. First, the great reliance by authority figures on programming and rule specification implies that the world is stable and unchanging enough to permit the utilization of hierarchically oriented rules and programming. Second, the reliance on a relatively permanent specialization of activities, as opposed to variation, encourages a belief system that rules and routine are the order of things, whereas variations, difference, and lack of rules as guides are not.

If we look at a nonhierarchical organization I would expect a belief in a variable, changing world to develop because the lack of a hierarchical authority would be taken to mean that the world is too variable and dynamic to make hierarchically specified rules of behavior of value. In Table 3.10 I have summarized some investigations supporting these arguments.

Table 3.10

Summary of Studies Relating Environmental Variables to Belief Systems Concerning (1) the Value and Competence of the Self (2) the Value and Competence of Others and (3) Belief in the Existence of a Set of General Rules and Order as a Guide for Perceiving the World

BASIC FINDINGS	INVESTIGATORS
1. High self-esteem is positively related to low father dominance in childhood, low previous external control, and the setting of high achievement standards.	McClelland (1961)
2. High scorers on the F-scale (authoritarianism) are likely to have come from homes that stressed great reliance on formally stated external control and rigidity of behavior.	Adorno et al. (1950); Kirscht and Dillehay (1967)
3. Self-perceived competence (expectation of task success) is a positive function of extent to which parents have encouraged independence of thought and action, self versus external control, and participation in family decision making.	Rehberg, Sinclair, and Schaefer (1970)
4. Level of educational attainment that one expects to achieve is positively correlated with the degree to which the family was democratic as opposed to being hierarchically controlled.	Bowerman and Elder (1964)
5. Feelings of power and control over one's fate increase when poor people are given roles of influence and responsibility.	Gottesfeld and Dozier (1966)

Tables 3.11, 3.12, and 3.13 list investigations concerned with the influence of hierarchically structured, programmed environments on achievement, creativity, and aggression, respectively. Given the findings listed in Table 3.10 that these environments do, indeed, lead to the belief systems hypothesized, the research presented in Tables 3.11, 3.12, and 3.13 supports the basic assumptions of our theoretical model.

Before we move on I would like to point out that although this model does have considerable positive evidence attached to it, the support is not complete (cf. Leonard and Weitz, 1971). Another problem is that while a consistency model can be useful, it cannot be wholly satisfactory since we often find ourselves in inconsistent states. Other processes must be involved in developing a full understanding of motiva-

Table 3.11

Summary of Studies Relating Hierarchical Environments to Achievement Behavior

BASIC FINDINGS	INVESTIGATORS
1. Those who had their jobs redesigned to decrease specialization and enlarge responsibilities and authority increased their performance.	Davis and Valper (1968); *Business Week* (1969)
2. The more individuals feel they have control over their work activities, the higher their performance.	Bachman, Smith, and Slesinger (1966); Bucklow (1966); Tannenbaum and Kahn (1958); Smith and Brown (1964); Bowers (1964); Tannenbaum (1962)
3. Situations where individuals appraise themselves result in less defensiveness and greater performance increment.	Bassett and Meyer (1968)
4. The more that is expected of an individual in terms of goals to be achieved or the amount of time allocated for achievement, the better he will perform.	Berlew and Hall (1966); Stedry and Kay (1966); Aronson and Gerard (1966); Locke (1967); Bryan and Locke (1967); Korman (1970)
5. Participation in decision making and planning by those not used to it increases performance and productivity.	Farris (1969); Puckett (1958)
6. Choosing one's own work partners increases performance.	Van Zelst (1952)
7. The more individuals are allowed to choose their work activities, the higher they will perform on them.	Pallak, Brock, and Kiesler (1967)
8. The more an individual comes from a background of repression of independence and an overemphasis on one's own "special world" as opposed to "others," the lower his test achievement performance.	Vernon (1965)
9. The more a person has been encouraged to think independently, take part in decision making and has been expected to attain high achievement standards, the higher the achievement.	Rosen (1959); Rosen and D'Andrade (1959); McClelland (1961)

tional processes. A third problem with the model I have proposed here is that, perhaps, it is a little naive. Certainly, people can be achievers without being creative. Also, creative achievers can be aggressive (e.g., Leonardo da Vinci developed weapons of war).

Why suggest a theory, then, even if we know it does not account for everything? There are several reasons. First, no theory is immune from criticism. We choose a theory not for its truth value, for theories have none, but because they are perspectives and summary frameworks for illuminating or suggesting empirical relationships. We keep them as long as they remain useful for illuminating and suggesting these relationships, always being aware that there may be phenomena that do

Table 3.12

Summary of Studies Relating Environmental Variables to Aggression and Hostility toward Others

BASIC FINDINGS	INVESTIGATORS
1. Exposure to sensitivity-training group with its emphasis on nonhierarchy and nonprogramming increases acceptance of self and reduces prejudice toward others.	Rubin (1967)
2. Hostility between labor and management groups decreased when they were both part of a larger group where nonhierarchy, nonprogramming, and nonspecialization of activities were stressed (i.e., they met on an equal status basis, and goals were developed for all groups on an equal basis).	Blake et al. (1964); Blake, Mouton, and Sloma (1965)
3. Generalized support for finding Number 2 above in a variety of laboratory studies.	Deutsch (1969)
4. German Communists during the pre-Hitler era were more concerned with fighting those with a democratic ideology (i.e., the Social Democrats) than they were in fighting the rightist authoritarian (Nazi) group.	Draper (1969)
5. The more society legitimates differences between two groups along various hierarchical status dimensions and the more it says the two are different, the more likely it is that conflict will result between the two groups.	Triandis (1959); Lindgren (1969); McDavid and Hararri (1969)
6. The less people are committed to one specific group the more they move from group to group, the less the hostility between groups.	Deutsch (1969)
7. Work groups that are (a) homogeneous, (b) isolated from other different groups, (c) rarely interact with other different groups, and (d) view themselves as highly specialized and different from other groups are more likely to engage in strikes than groups with differing characteristics.	Kerr and Siegel (1954)
8. Children who have more positive affect toward other children and who are less likely to be aggressive and hostile are more likely to come from homes that are marked by flexibility, and a lack of parental dominance and structures.	Watson (1960)

not fit. When we discover more and more phenomena that are not explained by our theory, it begins to lose its usefulness and we seek another. So far, I think the theory I have suggested accounts for a good amount of the data, although there are clearly some cases for which it has no explanation.

Table 3.13

Summary of Studies Relating Environmental Variables to Creativity, Change, and Receptivity to Change

BASIC FINDINGS	INVESTIGATORS
1. Mothers of creative high-school males value autonomy, independence, prefer change, lack structure, and exhibit great self-assurance, the mothers of a control group scored lower on all of these variables.	Domino (1969)
2. The creation of an experimental atmosphere with decreased evaluation by others and perception of control and evaluation by others resulted in higher scores on tests of creative thinking.	Adams (1968)
3. Innovation in organizations is negatively related to hierarchical centralization of authority and positively related to lack of programming and rule orientation.	Guetzkow (1965)
4. Decreasing hierarchy, external control, and task specialization during a change program increases receptivity to the goals of that change.	Coch and French (1948); Sarason (1967)
5. Middle-class subjects are more likely to engage in alteration behavior than those from lower-class backgrounds. (Middle-class environments are generally less hierarchical than lower-class.)	Strain, Unikel, and Adams (1969)
6. Individuals in college environments where hierarchical control, programming, and specialization has been deemphasized are more likely to accept continuing changes in the university and its functioning.	Korman (1970)
7. Individuals in specialized roles and occupations are likely to be unsympathetic to people different from themselves and are less likely to communicate with such different individuals on an informal basis.	Korman (1963); Sutton and Porter (1968)
8. Individuals who have been employed in hierarchical organizations do more poorly on creative tasks than those who have not been employed by such organizations.	Maier and Hoffman (1961)
9. Creativity is positively related to the degree to which the person is in a "strong" position vis-a-vis his superior (i.e., is in a less hierarchical system of authority).	Hoffman, Harburg, and Maier (1962)
10. Groups that experience changes in membership are more creative than those that are stable.	Ziller, Behringer, and Goldstein (1962)
11. Organizations that hire unusual, different types of people are more likely to be creative organizations.	Steiner (1965)
12. Creative children come from homes marked by lack of parental dominance and structures where individual divergence is permitted and risk accepted.	Watson (1960); Getzels and Jackson (1962)

A second consideration stems from the fact that some people change considerably over time, both in positive and negative directions, while others remain consistent. Therefore, a theory of motivational processes should attempt to integrate such motivational changes and how these changes may be subject to influence. Later in this book I will discuss such changes and point out how the model I have proposed may be utilized in the study, prediction, and influence of change in organizations.

Work Performance as Self-actualization: Maslow's Hierarchy of Motives

There is a type of motivational theorizing quite popular today which is known by such names as self-actualization theory, humanistic psychology, or third-world psychology. It is an important movement among psychologists interested in such problems as personal and social growth, institutional and organizational change and development, and other similar areas. In fact, its strongest support seems to be from those who propose management and organizational development programs based on the assumption that self-actualization theories of motivation are valid. On my part, while I agree with the types of recommendations made by these practitioners, I don't think you can use self-actualization theories as justification. Other grounds are necessary, as we will now see.

Self-actualization theory stems from the work of the existential philosophers who have argued that people have a capability for a meaningful, viable, potential-filling existence, but that they have been prevented from engaging and behaving in a meaningful, self-actualizing manner by the conditions and environments in which they live. They have been forced to behave in a suboptimal manner in which they are not able to fulfill themselves because of the nature of the environmental forces surrounding them. The role of the manager (change agent) is to first understand the factors that are preventing people from reaching self-actualization and then to change these conditions.

What theory of motivational processes does the self-actualization theorist use in justifying his argument that one has the potential and desire for self-actualization, growth, and development? A number of theories have been proposed, but the most significant is the one by Maslow (1954). Maslow's theory, quite famous today, proposes that a person's behavior is organized around a hierarchy of motives, with the lowest being physiological needs, such as hunger and thirst. Once these needs are satisfied, security needs become paramount as influences on behavior (or become prepotent, in Maslow's terms), with these being followed in the hierarchy by social, self-esteem, and self-actualization needs as motivators of behavior.[2] In all cases, Maslow argues, the pre-potency of the higher need increases as a function of the satisfaction of the need immediately lower in the hierarchy.

Many writers have supported Maslow by proposing that most people today have satisfied their lower needs and are looking toward satisfying their higher-level needs in work. For this reason, we need to change our work settings to allow the opportunity to satisfy these higher-level needs if we want to have motivated, productive work be-havior. Improving work settings would be beneficial for the organiza-tion as well as for the individual since satisfying his desire for self-actualization will make him more creative, productive, less defensive, and better able to integrate with others.

It seems to me, however, that the important question here is not the popularity of Maslow's theory but its adequacy. How much support does his model receive from systematic research? Is there a hierarchy of motives organized the way he proposed? Wahba and Bridwell (in press) have reviewed studies that have directly tested the theory in three separate ways and for each they found little or no support. The first type of research design tested the hypothesis that if a large number of job motivation questions were written and spread among each of the five needs proposed by Maslow (physiological, security, social, esteem, and self-actualization), then those items measuring one need would be more highly correlated with one another than they would be with items mea-suring other needs. Of eight studies reviewed, they found moderate sup-port for this prediction in two of the studies and a lack of support in the other six. In the second type of study, the respondents were asked to rank the Maslow needs in their order of importance to them, after first being classified according to current level of satisfaction. Three studies were reviewed here involving seven samples from different occupations, with the result being a slight amount of support in one sample and an over-all lack of support in the others. Finally, a large number of studies reviewed by Wahba and Bridwell tested the hypothesis that the most important need stimulating behavior at the time is the one in which deprivation is felt to be the greatest and that the most gratified need is the least activator. Approximately thirty studies were reviewed, with an even greater number of samples, and the results were very much the same. With only an iso-lated exception, there was little support for the theory.

Perhaps the best support for Maslow's argument comes from the data we review elsewhere in this book that suggests that if we decrease hierarchical control and an overspecialization of roles, we will obtain

[2] In some publications Maslow has postulated higher needs than self-actualization. Among these are needs for understanding and cognition. It is not clear, however, how much significance Maslow attached to these cognitive needs, and most discussions of Maslow's work do not deal with them.

what Maslow calls self-actualizing behavior. Yet, this type of data is derivable from other theories also, including the one I outlined earlier in this chapter. Both expectancy-value theory and consistency theory would also predict what Maslow calls self-actualizing behavior and also under the same external conditions since decreasing hierarchical control leads to greater self-value and, hence, a greater degree of expectancy of success and value attainment. Thus, you do not need the Maslow theory to predict that decreasing hierarchical control will lead to greater seeking of values and favorable outcomes. Do we need the Maslow theory at all? Right now, I doubt it. It seems to contribute little in a theoretical sense and although there is little doubt that it is in tune with some of the great social movements of our day, I think that these social movements, along with their theory and administrative goals, would be better served by our concentrating on empirically more valid theories that make similar policy recommendations.

Theories of Work Performance: Social Influence

One more approach to the study of work achievement that I want to discuss is the influence stemming from social forces.

It has long been apparent that people frequently are influenced by other people in terms of aspiration level and behavior engaged in, with such influence often defying common sense. A famous psychology experiment by Asch (1956) found that substantial numbers of individuals, although not a majority, publicly stated that a physically shorter line was longer than one that was in fact physically longer, with such statements being made, for the most part, by individuals confronted with unanimous, though wrong, opinions of others. This conformity dropped drastically if the subject was joined by at least one other person who made a correct statement as to the physical length. Similarly, Milgram (1965) has shown that individuals can be influenced by high-status experimenters to administer physical shocks to others, even though these other individuals object violently to such punishment. The reader of such experimental research investigations cannot help but be impressed by the degree to which we are subject to other people's definitions of how to evaluate and behave in given situations, whether they be laboratory situations on a college campus or everyday work environments. In the area of work behavior, the significance of this generalization began to be realized in the late 1920s and early 1930s during the famous Hawthorne investigations mentioned in chapter one. Although quite controversial in nature because of relatively poor methodological procedures (cf. Landsberger, 1958), these studies have often been cited as examples of how <u>achievement motivation is more likely</u> <u>to be determined by social peer influences that may work for either</u> <u>better or worse performance</u> (Roethlisberger and Dickson, 1939; Vroom, 1964), <u>depending on the given situation.</u>

There are three questions that I would like to explore here, one theoretical and two with practical implications. First, why do these opinions and differing social environments influence achievement behavior? Second, what kinds of social environments are associated with differential motivation to perform? Third, under which conditions will social environments have their greatest influence on the motivation to achieve?

Looking at the first question, conforming to social demands occurs for at least two reasons. Groups and group opinions, first of all, provide definitions of reality for us as individuals, particularly when no other measures of reality are available. As I said earlier in this chapter, <u>group opinions tell us how good we are, how able we are, and what is</u> <u>just and proper in the particular case.</u> Given similar definitions and assuming, at least in some instances, the consistency model I suggested earlier, similarity in group performance is likely to occur. Second, it is also true that groups may affect the means we use to attain the various levels of performance we feel are best and the rewards we want. In this sense, we go along with the group because the group is the mechanism by which we hope to achieve the outcomes we want.

Turning to the second question, the reason high achievement norms develop is, as said earlier, a function of specific environments and the self-evaluations they cultivate (Festinger, 1954). This conclusion is also implied in the relay-room experiments in the Hawthorne studies (Roethlisberger and Dickson, 1939), in which decreasing leader authoritarianism, as one example, was associated with higher achievement norms.

As to the question of the conditions under which the influence of social environments on achievement motivation is greatest, one major hypothesis is that group influence is greatest when the individuals involved are highly attracted to one another. It would be predicted, then, that variability of performance would be less in groups of people who are highly attracted to one another; that is, they would go along with one another and would be more likely to be, as a group, either high achievers or low, with few in the middle. Conversely, in the indifferent-to-one-another groups, individuals would be less likely to conform to one another and would show a more variable distribution of task behavior. This tendency would make them more average in nature than the highly cohesive groups since it would reflect individual differences in ability and motivation and most people tend to be average. A number of findings support this prediction (cf. Shacter et al., 1951; Berkowitz, 1954; Seashore, 1954). Another point that these studies emphasize is that cohesiveness (i.e., degree of liking for one another) bears little relationship to performance. Rather, cohesiveness operates as a determinant of whether or not a person will go along with the group norm as to the level of performance, whatever the norm happens to be.

There are also some other things that we know about the conditions under which individuals will use group- and leader-defined goals as the basis for their own level of achievement motivation in a given situation. According to Walker and Heyns (1962), we should expect susceptibility to a social norm to increase with (1) the ambiguity of the situation, (2) the necessity of going along with the group for goal achievement, (3) decreased self-confidence, and (4) the appropriateness of the goals (i.e., whether the individual thinks the goals are correct for himself). Taken in essence, these findings generally fit with our expectations that we are most likely to use group definitions of reality as guides to our own behavior when (1) no other reality is available to us, (2) we do not trust these other definitions of reality, and (3) our going along with the group supports our other definitions of reality (i.e., self-defined appropriateness of the goal being offered for conforming).

Concluding Remarks

Despite the usefulness of the frameworks we have discussed here and their implication for the management of organizations, I have tried to stress that they are only tentative summarizing devices for current states of knowledge. Knowledge accumulation goes on, however, without regard to theory, eventually forcing the development of new systems. Thus, new findings serve as spurs for the development of new theories. As illustrations of two of the kinds of research findings that have significance for administration but which are not as yet understood in a theoretical sense, consider two areas.

First, what gives a social object value so that groups and people will work to achieve it? In addition to the quantity problems we spoke of earlier (cf. the discussion of Deci's work), there are other explanations in the literature and they are difficult to reconcile with one another. One is that objects gain value the more they are associated with primary reinforcing events (e.g., money attains value because you can get food with it). Conversely, there is the research stemming from dissonance theory that seems almost to suggest a self-destructive process in what we come to value. This prediction is that we come to value an object to which we are committed and which we have, with such value increasing the *less* it has served as a reinforcer in the past, up to a point. How do we reconcile these? There is little guidance as yet in the literature.

Second, some evidence suggests that different motivational processes may be involved in achieving as an individual and as a group. A strong ego is seen to be of considerable value for achievement as an individual (cf. Korman, 1971a; McClelland, 1961); on the other hand, a strong ego may be detrimental when trying to achieve as a group, where sublimation of the self may be necessary (Collins and Guetzkow, 1962). Are the two sets of findings reconcilable? Under what conditions?

The answers to these questions are unclear at this time but I believe these are the types of concerns around which much attention will be centered in the future.

Summary

The purpose of this chapter has been to review some of the major theories of work motivation and to draw from them various implications for the administration of organizations.

The theories reviewed show the influence of traditional perspectives and contemporary concerns, sometimes in the same theory. The first theory discussed was anxiety as an influence on work behavior, a framework probably as old as recorded man. Recent work with this approach has focused on such specific types of anxiety as fear of failure and fear of success. The former has considerable cultural support whereas the latter is a concept that originally was thought to be limited to women but is now seen as common also among men, but perhaps for different reasons. Both are debilitative of performance, except that fear of failure might be facilitative for very easy tasks.

A second important framework is the contemporary representation of the traditional economic man theory which has come to be known as expectancy-value or instrumentality theory. There are two versions popular today. The first is an extrinsic version in which values involved are of the type easily manipulable by management (e.g., money, promotion, etc.) and the second is an intrinsic version in which the values are particular characteristic motives that differ among individuals. The extrinsic model accounts for some work achievement, but much seems to be unexplained by the framework. The intrinsic model, as exemplified in the work by McClelland on the need for achievement, is an approach of considerable value in explaining work behavior on both an individual and societal level, even though methodological problems exist with the techniques involved.

Consistency motivation, the next of the theories reviewed, has developed as an alternative to the weaknesses of the expectancy-value model since a major characteristic of this type of approach is that it predicts paradoxical nonoptimizing behavior as a result of the desire to be consistent. The theories of this nature discussed were the theory of cognitive dissonance, the equity theory of J. Stacey Adams, and a self-consistency theory. They center around beliefs about the self, others, and the nature of the world, and significant evidence exists for each. However, each has problems and should not be regarded as totally satisfactory.

The final sections of the chapter reviewed other approaches to work motivation based on Maslow's popular self-actualization theory and on the desire to conform to social norms. Since the former has little research support, it would be more useful to focus on other explanations for self-actualizing behavior. Conformity theory, on the other hand, is quite useful as a predictor of work achievement under some conditions.

SUGGESTIONS FOR FURTHER READING

Behling, O. and Starke, F. The postulates of expectancy theory. *Academy of Management Journal,* 1973, *16,* 373–388.
An interesting examination of some of the logical and methodological problems of expectancy-value theory. It supplements well some of the questions we have raised in this chapter.

Fasteau, M. F. *The male machine.* New York: McGraw-Hill, 1974.
One of the better recent books that deal in a popular vein with some of the negative implications of the traditional male acceptance of the achievement ethic. It is of particular value in illuminating some issues underlying the growth of fear of success among males.

Korman, A. K. *The psychology of motivation.* Englewood Cliffs, N.J.: Prentice-Hall, 1974.
This book reviews some of the major theories of motivational processes and their value for predicting behavior. Some of the major theories discussed here (e.g., anxiety, expectancy-value, consistency) are examined in much greater detail.

McClelland, D. *The achieving society.* Princeton, N.J.: Van Nostrand, 1961.

An interesting account of a major research program on the need for achievement, where it comes from, and its behavioral implications. The book has particular interest in showing how similar constructs can account for behavior on both the individual and the societal level.

PORTER, L. W. and STEERS, R. *Motivation and work behavior.* New York: McGraw-Hill, 1975.

Some of the major articles in the study of work motivation are reprinted here and there is some excellent contextual material on the significance of the different studies examined.

VROOM, V. H. *Work and motivation.* New York: Wiley, 1964.

Although recent research suggests that expectancy-value theory does not account for as much behavior variation as was first hoped for, this book has significance as the first major attempt to use this framework in the study of work behavior.

chapter four

Motivational Processes: Aggression, Power, and Risk Taking

In understanding organizational behavior, task achievement is not the only motivational process of concern. As mentioned in the last chapter, matters like aggression, creativity, and receptivity to change are also of interest. We will therefore now explore (1) aggression motivation, (2) power motivation, particularly as it affects the nature and type of leadership functioning, and (3) risk-taking motivation.

Aggression Motivation

My procedure in this section will be first to discuss the frustration-aggression hypothesis, historically the most popular theory in this area, and its implications for the world of work. Then I will turn to other approaches to aggression and discuss how they also may provide an understanding of work behavior and organizational functioning.

The Frustration-Aggression Hypothesis: An Expectancy-Value Model

history of the frustration-aggression hypothesis

In 1939 the book *Frustration and Aggression* (Dollard, Doob, Miller, Mowrer, and Sears) proposed the following thesis: "Aggression is always a consequence of frustration," and "occurrence of aggressive behavior always presupposes the existence of frustration and contrariwise, the existence of frustration always leads to some form of aggression." In brief, a one-to-one relationship between frustration and aggression was postulated with frustration defined as "a condition which exists when a goal response suffers interference" (p. 11). Whenever any type of aggressive act occurs, such an act, according to the hypothesis, is always due to some frustration or interference with a goal response the organism has suffered, and conversely, whenever an organism suffers any kind of thwarting or frustration, it will aggress (Kaufman, 1970, pp. 24–25).

Despite the conceptual nicety and clarity of the original frustration-aggression proposals, the years since have provided little support for these predicted automatic linkages. The first revision came when one of the authors agreed that it would be better to assume that frustration leads only to an instigation to aggression (Miller, 1941) and that the likelihood that the aggression would *actually* take place was a function of other variables besides the frustration.

As the years went by other weaknesses of the frustration-aggression hypothesis became apparent. It was pointed out, for example, that often goal-directed responses were interfered with without aggression taking place. Similarly, great aggression often takes place as a reaction to frustrations of a relatively minor nature (e.g., the Nazi persecution of the Jews). As a result of these and other questions, Berkowitz (1962) was eventually led to propose a revised formulation, which we now consider.

According to Berkowitz the original frustration-aggression hypothesis leads to three predictions. The first is that the greater the frustration, the greater the instinct to aggression. Second, the stronger the behavioral motive being frustrated, the greater the frustration and the greater the impulse to aggression. Third, the greater the number of frustrations, the greater the aggressive response. Reviewing the research, Berkowitz concluded that the first two of these hypotheses were supported, but not the third. Rather, the data on the third suggest a curvilinear relationship in that aggression as a response to frustration increases with the number of frustrations up to a point and then it decreases, as indicated in Figure 4.1. Why does such a relationship develop? Expectancies seem to be the major answer in that as the number of frustrations increase, a person comes to expect them. Hence, when a frustration continues to occur, the reaction becomes less negative.

> In general, expected frustrations produce less intense emotional reactions than do unanticipated frustrations. Two reasons are suggested: (1) through anticipating interference with his activity, the individual may alter his actions, or even his goals, so that he actually experiences less frustration; (2) expected frustrations may be judged as less severe (Berkowitz, 1962, p. 72).

Figure 4.1
Relationship between Likelihood of Aggressive Response and
Number of Previous Frustrations

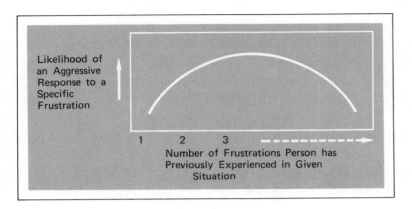

Whether or not these are the reasons that expected frustrations are not as likely to lead to aggression as those that are unexpected, aggressive behavior is not the automatic process implied in the original frustration-aggression theory. Rather, expectations, cognitions, and the previous history of the individual are also involved in influencing whether or not aggression or some other behavior will take place as a response to frustration.

It turns out that with one more step we could view the current status of frustration-aggression theory as another version of the expectancy-value framework. This step should show that the likelihood of aggressive behavior increases as a function of the expectancy that values can be achieved and negative outcomes can be avoided. As a matter of fact such evidence does exist. Thus, each of the following statements is based on research findings and when taken in context, they all lend support to the conclusion that aggression against others can be viewed as a form of behavior engaged in as a result of (1) being in a non–value-attained state at the time (i.e., being frustrated) and (2) expecting to achieve desired values as outcomes by so doing. The research evidence for such an integration is as follows:

1. Aggressive behavior as a response to frustration is inhibited when punishment for such behavior is expected.
2. Hostile behavior is inhibited the greater the degree of punishment that is expected.
3. High-status people are usually less likely to be aggressed against than low-status individuals.
4. The groups and individuals who are usually chosen as scapegoats and as targets of aggressive behavior are usually weaker individuals who do not

have the strength (economic, psychological, social) to fight back. This makes the aggression more likely to be successful.

5. The likelihood of revolution as a result of frustration is more apt to take place after a period of rising expectations (Davies, 1962). One explanation for this, which Wallace (1971) has pointed out and which is consistent with our general point, is that during periods of rising expectations rigid controls over people are progressively relaxed, protests are increasingly tolerated, and the inhibitions of downtrodden peoples to engage in violent protest are gradually lowered. In this sense, the expectancy that aggression will lead to greater value is increased, thus making it more likely that aggression will be engaged in when frustration does occur.

applicability of the frustration-aggression hypothesis to work behavior

What does all this mean for organizational behavior? Each of the following implications is suggested by these findings:

1. Aggression is more likely to be a characteristic of large organizations than small ones since (a) it is harder for large organizations to have effective surveillance to control aggression in response to frustration and (b) the complexity of large systems leads to greater possibilities for frustration.
2. Aggression is more likely in hierarchical organizations because high hierarchical individuals tend to be aggressive against individuals lower in the system in order to keep the positions constant and because individuals lower in the system are too weak to fight back.
3. We may have to live with some aggression if we want some success since success generates some aggression (see number 5 above).

Incidentally, it may be worth noting that Kelman (1973) has shown the significance of hierarchical control, routinization, and deprecation of the other in leading to major aggression against others. This is in keeping with the general findings under numbers 3, 4, and 5 above and also with the general theoretical model I proposed earlier.

Other Theories of Aggression Motivation

"modeling" and consistency models

As further support for the argument that aggression may be viewed within the same frameworks as other forms of behavior, there are other expectancy-value models in this area as well as other consistency models besides the one I proposed earlier. In the first instance, there are the "modeling" studies, which are concerned with the effects of observing the behavior of others on one's own behavior and which may, incidentally, be meaningful for understanding such behaviors as wildcat strikes.

Generally, this research has focused on the conditions under which the observation of models may be used as a basis for changing the behavior of an observer (cf. Bandura and Walters, 1963). Of relevance here is the finding that the observation of aggression that has led to some reward or the cessation of punishment is more likely to lead to the observer's repetition of the aggression than if the behavior observed is punished (Bandura, Ross, and Ross, 1963; Berkowitz and Rawlings, 1963). If we make the rather simple assumption that people learn about attainable values by observation, then this finding fits in with our conclusion that aggression is more likely to be engaged in if there is some type of value to be attained by it.

I should mention, however, that the finding that observing successful aggression in others encourages the observer's aggression has been based mostly on laboratory research and that when the same notion has been tested in the field, the reverse has occurred. A field study by Feshbach and Singer (1971) found that boys who watched aggressive behavior on television were less likely to be aggressive than those who did not watch television violence, a finding directly opposite from the modeling studies and, in fact, from the general expectancy-value framework. The best theoretical explanation for the Feshbach and Singer research is the catharsis hypothesis of Freud, which postulates that people have an inbred capacity to be hostile toward others as a result of displacing the aggression against the self. The more aggression is displaced harmlessly, as in watching television or in games, the less it will be displaced against others. Despite the adequacy of this explanation here, however, the utilization of the Freudian framework is probably not an optimal way to proceed, considering all the problems with Freud's hypotheses. What really should be done is to integrate the Feshbach and Singer findings with the other literature on modeling.

Just as the expectancy-value formulation has turned out to be viable in understanding aggressive behavior, so has the consistency theory framework. Most prominent here has been the work of Elaine and William Walster and Ellen Berscheid, all three of whom have used the consistency formulation to understand certain types of aggressive behavior. This is not so surprising since the concept of inequity as a cause of aggression is one that has a great deal of cultural support. "Unjust," "unfair," and similar terms are common in labor strikes as justification for behavior. The question, though, is what is meant by "unfair" or "inequitable"? Interestingly enough, the same definition of equity used by Adams in his work on achievement has been used by the Walsters and Berscheid for aggression.

Conceptually, they start from the point that:

$$\text{Equity} = \frac{\text{Outcomes A}}{\text{Inputs A}} = \frac{\text{Outcomes B}}{\text{Inputs B}}$$

$$\text{Inequity} = \frac{\text{Outcomes A}}{\text{Inputs A}} \neq \frac{\text{Outcomes B}}{\text{Inputs B}}$$

Considering the fact that inequity is a negative tension state that we wish to reduce, the Walsters propose and cite research support for the following propositions:

1. Under some conditions, a person will feel inequity because he receives outcomes (e.g., pay, promotions, etc.) higher than he perceives he deserves.
2. A person may reduce his feelings of inequity, under certain conditions, by (a) derogating the other person in terms of the value of the other person's inputs into the system (thus reducing the necessity for higher outputs) and (b) denying the fact of one's responsibilities for the lack of value (or outputs) that the other person receives (Walster et al., 1973).

In other words, a person who sees himself in an inequitable relationship (in which he gets too much as compared to another's input-output ratio) may try to reduce his feelings by behaving toward the other person in a manner to justify the perception that the other person *deserves less*. Since the best or at least the easiest way that this can be done is to make the other person appear to be undeserving, aggressive behavior toward that person is initiated with that goal in mind. The easiest way to do this is to deprecate him. This deprecation is most likely to take place when it is less costly, when it is less difficult, when it is more likely to be adequate in reducing inequity, when it requires little distortion of reality, and when it is most likely to increase the person's outcomes. This proposal is similar to the one made by Adams.

A lot of research jibes with this argument in addition to the experiments cited by the Walsters and Berscheid. A good illustration is the negative evaluation of the other group that takes place during a labor-management confrontation (cf. Haire and Grunes, 1955; White, 1969). Also, it has been suggested that race prejudice, certainly a form of aggression, is the development and exhibition of negative behaviors toward groups felt to be inferior in order to justify the superior status of the perpetrating group (Wrightsman, 1972; Jones, 1972). Finally, a major extension of the consistency theory approach to aggression can be found in the research by Campbell and LeVine (1968). Working primarily at the group, intergroup, and intersocietal levels, they have found support for the following predictions:

1. The more similar an outgroup is in customs, values, beliefs, and general culture, the more liked it will be.
2. Regional patterns of intergroup relations will be balanced as follows:

   an ally of an ally will be an ally;
   an enemy of an ally will be an enemy;
   an ally of an enemy will be an enemy;
   an enemy of an enemy will be an ally.

organizational size and aggression

Among the highly stable phenomena that we can count on in our rapidly changing society is that unplanned, random violence is increasing. Any casual observer of the day's events cannot help but be struck by the crime on the streets, the senseless murders and beatings of innocent people, and other similar events. The question is why. In attempting to explain this increase, Zimbardo (1969) has proposed a theory which turns out to also have implications for understanding aggressive behavior in large organizations. The reason for this is the importance that he assigns to such factors as anonymity and diffused responsibility in influencing the occurrence of aggressive behavior, factors which are a function of *both* rapid social change and large organizational size.

Zimbardo's major hypotheses are summarized as follows and in Table 4.1.

> Deindividuation is a complex, hypothesized process in which a series of antecedent social conditions lead to changes in perception of self and others and thereby to a lowered threshold of normally restrained behavior. Under appropriate conditions what results is the "release of behavior in violation of established norms of appropriateness."[1]

Such conditions permit overt expression of antisocial behavior, characterized as selfish, greedy, power-seeking, hostile, lustful, and destructive. However, they also allow a range of positive behaviors that we normally do not express overtly, such as intense feelings of happiness, sorrow, or love for others.[2] Thus, emotions and impulses usually under cognitive control are more likely to be expressed when the input conditions minimize self-observation and evaluation as well as concern over evaluation by others.

Two questions are relevant here. How much support does the theory have? Second, why does the process occur? First, the theory has some degree of empirical support but much more evidence is needed, as Zimbardo himself suggests (Zimbardo, 1969). Second, Zimbardo's motivational hypothesis as to why deindividuation results in greater aggression is that man has a desire to throw off all controls and do what his nature tells him to do.

---

[1] P. G. Zimbardo, The human choice: Individuation, reason, and order versus deindividuation, impulse, and chaos, *Nebraska Symposium on Motivation, 17,* 1969, 251. Copyright 1969 by the University of Nebraska Press. Reprinted by permission.

[2] Note that Zimbardo's model would also predict increased receptiveness to emotional training experiences (such as sensitivity training) in large organizations. We will talk about this in a later chapter.

Table 4.1
Zimbardo's Model of Deindividuation and Aggression

INPUT VARIABLES	INFERRED SUBJECTIVE CHANGES	OUTPUT BEHAVIORS
Anonymity	Minimization of self-evaluation and concern for social evaluation	Behavior emitted is emotional, impusive, irrational, and regressive, and intense behavior is not controlled by the usual external discriminative stimuli
Responsibility is shared, diffused, and given up	Weakening of controls based on guilt, shame, fear, and commitment	
Large group size, group activity		
Reliance on noncognitive interactions and feedback	Lowered threshold for expressing inhibited behaviors	Behavior is self-reinforcing and is intensified and amplified with repeated expression
		Behavior is difficult to terminate
		Perceptual distortion occurs; people become insensitive to incidental stimuli and to relating actions to other actors
		There is greater liking for group or situation associated with "released" behavior
		At extreme levels, the group dissolves as its members become autistic in their impulse gratification
		Traditional forms of social structures come under attack

Source: P. G. Zimbardo, The human choice: Individuation, reason, and order versus deindividuation, impulse, and chaos, *Nebraska symposium on motivation, 17,* 1969, 237-307. Copyright 1969 by the University of Nebraska Press. Reprinted by permission.

We must then posit a "universal need" to shatter all formal controls, albeit temporarily, as occurs in every person through dreaming. This fact is the basis of society's institutionalization of revelous behavior—harvest festivals in agrarian societies and carnivals in religious ones—where an "unproductive waste of energy" is encouraged. Functionally, such festivals serve to siphon off destructive energy, prevent unpredictable individually initiated release of impulses, and enable the deindividuated reveler to experience both the pleasure of his revels and the satisfaction of becoming reindividuated following their termination.[3]

[3] Zimbardo, *Nebraska Symposium,* 1969.

It is not essential to adopt this interpretation to make use of Zimbardo's findings in organizational settings. We might, for example, just argue that increasing organizational size leads to increasing frustration due to the difficulty of predicting the behavior of others when you interact with them less frequently. This frustration leads to increased propensity to aggression, an aggression more likely to occur because external controls inhibiting the aggression (i.e., possible punishment) are more difficult to apply because of the large size of the organization and the consequent difficulty of adequate surveillance.

authoritarianism and aggression

One final possible source of aggression in organizations was first described in a book published in 1950 that constituted an epochal event in the scientific study of intergroup relations, acceptance, and hostility. Titled *The Authoritarian Personality* (Adorno et al., 1950), it had its origin in a request by the American Jewish Committee to a group of researchers at the Berkeley campus of the University of California that they consider and study the nature of anti-Semitism. Working from both interview and questionnaire procedures, they came to conclusions about the nature of anti-Semitism that form a landmark for investigation in this area. First, it was apparent that strong anti-Semites could be and were found at all levels of the socioeconomic hierarchy and were by no means limited to those individuals who saw Jews as economic competitors to themselves. Second, individuals who were anti-Semitic also tended to be antiblack, anti-Mexican-American, and anti-Catholic, if they were not Catholic themselves. Third, highly prejudiced individuals could be described fairly well by the personality characteristics listed below:

1. *Overconventionalism:* high anxiety whenever conventional behavior standards are violated.
2. *Authoritarian submission:* high sensitivity and responsivity to authority figures and symbols.
3. *Authoritarian aggression:* high aggression toward groups that are different from oneself; this results from the great hostility the individual has toward authority figures but to which he submits because of fear of punishment.
4. *Anti-intraception:* a strong opposition to the emotional, nonpractical, dreamy, theoretical side of life. This is believed to stem from the repressed feelings of hostility which the individual has toward authority figures but which he does not want to admit to because of their anxiety-provoking nature.
5. *Power and toughness:* a tendency to identify and value strongly power, strength, and toughness in others. This is felt to be an overcompensation for having submitted to authority and a fear of valuing toughness in oneself because of its anxiety-provoking nature.

6. *High projectivity:* a strong unconscious tendency to project one's own strong emotional impulses to others because of the anxiety that would result if one were forced to recognize it in oneself.

These are the characteristics of those who would be least likely to accept blacks and other minority group members into the organization and who would be most likely to make things difficult for minorities in terms of acceptance and hostility. Therefore, it would be desirable to develop conditions in the organization that would minimize the development and encouragement of people with these characteristics.

I find it of great interest that when we look into the family backgrounds of these highly prejudiced people we discover that their maturing years were spent in family environments with the following characteristics: (1) a great reliance on formally stated rules, (2) a great reliance on means of external control and minimal reliance or internal control, (3) strong threats of punishment when rules are not followed, (4) parents and other authority figures who are highly rigid and formal. If this pattern of characteristics looks familar to you, your perception is justified. This pattern is very similar to the one proposed in the motivational model I suggested in the last chapter as being conducive to aggression. Since Kelman (1973) has also argued for a similar framework in attempting to understand massive aggression against perceived inferior groups, there seem to be implications here for organizational leadership and design, matters we will take up in a later chapter.

Power Motivation

The motivation to attain and maintain power has been one of the most controversial issues in the behavioral sciences. I believe that there are both political and conceptual reasons for this controversy. In the former case, power motivation may be one of those things one is not supposed to find interesting in our supposedly egalitarian society. If this is so, this social norm has had unfortunate consequences because (1) it has kept us from undertaking research relating to the different types of power motivation that may involve control and/or influence over others; (2) it has been hypocritical, since power motivation is clearly a great driving force for many people in our society and, in fact, is inevitable as an outcome of a competitive, individualistically oriented system that assigns great value to "getting ahead"; and (3) it has been foolish, since power-oriented behavior reflects a motivational process that is necessary to some extent for some types of task accomplishment. A much more fruitful approach is to try to understand what the nature of power motivation is, how it may vary in both a functional and dysfunctional manner, and what the optimal types of power motivation are for different organizational settings. Fortunately I think that research in the last decade is starting to move in this direction.

The Work of McClelland

David McClelland is becoming as prominent in the area of power motivation as he has been in the area of achievement and for similar reasons. In both cases, McClelland has developed careful definitions of the phenomena, constructed and tested the adequacy of measuring instruments by using the Thematic Apperception Test, and then ascertained the behavioral significance of the motivational process being examined.

For McClelland the attainment and maintenance of power is an intrinsic value in which people differ in the same sense that they differ in need for achievement. His definition of power motivation is, however, a little different in that he sees two kinds (or two "faces"). First, there is the desire for personal domination over others. McClelland views this face as somewhat negative. On the other end of the continuum is the type of power motivation which involves influencing others toward goal and task achievement. This latter type of intrinsic value develops, McClelland suggests, as a function of the controls that society normally puts on unbridled power motivation. This value, McClelland proposes, is a good one that we need to encourage, at least for some people, since people who score high on this value are marked by such work-relevant concerns as developing and formulating goals, inspiring others toward goal attainment, and being willing to influence others toward work achievement. On the other hand, people exhibiting the bad face of power motivation tend to be exploitive in interpersonal behavior and are more willing than others to use aggressive means to control others. McClelland feels that at least some people in an organization need to have the good face of power motivation or else little task-oriented effort will take place. Research evidence to support this argument comes from several sources. McClelland (1971) has cited data that people high in need for power are likely to be willing to (1) stand out by holding office in organizations, (2) engage in competition with others, and (3) influence other people in organizations. In addition, McClelland (1971) has reported experimental data that support the pattern of individuals high on this motive attempting to influence others and having a general activist viewpoint of life. There is also a supportive study by Donley and Winter (1970) of American presidents, based on an analysis of their speeches. With some exceptions, Donley and Winter's results showed a higher need for power among those presidents generally considered to be activist than those usually thought of as passive. In the former group were the Roosevelts, Truman, Kennedy, Johnson, and Wilson, whereas in the latter were Hoover, Taft, Harding, Coolidge, Eisenhower, and Nixon. (The last, it now seems, is questionable considering the Watergate affair.)

Clearly, people of this motivational pattern are important in organizational functioning, providing they are appropriately placed and do not slip into the negative form of power motivation, a continuing problem to watch for. One way to make sure this does not happen is to develop appropriate structural and organizational policy variables that lessen its likelihood. As an example, we might encourage an organization to use other mechanisms for achieving influence besides those of hierarchical control, since this type of control is likely to lead to the control of others just for the sake of maintaining one's power without concern for the functional outcome (cf. Kipnis, 1972). French and Raven (1960) have distinguished five possible mechanisms for exerting power, listed in Table 4.2. Note particularly the last three as alternative mechanisms for exerting power which an organization might encourage its managers to use.

Table 4.2
Types of Power

1. Reward power	When P has the ability to determine O's rewards, he has reward power over him.
2. Coercive power	When P has the ability to determine O's punishments, he has coercive power over him.
3. Referent power	When O wants to be like P, P has referent power over him.
4. Expert power	When O perceives that P has special knowledge in a situation, P has expert power over him.
5. Legitimate power	When O accepts a set of social norms that say he should accept influence from P, P has legitimate power over him.

Note: P = person; O = other.

The Work of Miner

Another approach to power motivation that has been quite useful in understanding leadership behavior in organizations is the hypothesis by Miner (1965) that leadership success in hierarchical organizations of at least some size is positively related to a desire for power. This motive, he maintains, is composed of positive attitudes toward the following:

1. authority figures
2. competitive situations
3. the (traditional) masculine role
4. competitive games

5. imposing wishes on others
6. standing out from the group
7. routine administrative functions

How adequate is this theory? Table 4.3 shows that it has some support, thus substantiating further the significance of power motivation. Note, though, that Miner's approach is not exactly the same as McClelland's. For example, Miner does not differentiate between types of power motivation. In addition, the theory works best in large, hierarchal organizations.

Table 4.3
Validity Studies of the Miner Sentence Completion Scale

SAMPLE	CRITERION	R	PROBABILITY
81 R & D managers	Potential for advancement ratings	.43	.01
49 R & D managers	Job grade changes	.25	.10
81 marketing managers	job grade changes	.39	.01
61 R & D and marketing managers	Rehiring recommendations	.69	.01

Source: J. B. Miner, *Studies in management education* (New York: Springer, 1965), pp. 57, 62, 65, 66.

Other Approaches

There are two other theoretical frameworks of power motivation I would like to mention briefly. Neither has been researched very much but they may well be worth examining in the future.

First is Lasswell's hypothesis that power motivation results from the desire to compensate for deprivations suffered during childhood. This is the kind of hypothesis that is intriguing to the layman, since examples such as Napoleon come quickly to mind, but this is poor evidence at best and we need more systematic research than this if we are going to understand the relationship between childhood deprivation and adult desire for power.

Second, the model we proposed in the previous chapter also has certain predictions to make about power. It states that people high in a hierarchical system are most likely to seek power for themselves and those low in the hierarchy seek to have others have power over them; in other words, they avoid power positions. There are no direct tests yet of these predictions, but there is some indirect evidence in the finding that those low in an experimental task hierarchy are less power oriented than those who are high in the system (Kipnis, 1972).

Risk-taking Motivation

Consider two cases. First, a person has two alternatives, A and B. In alternative A he has a 50% chance of winning $1,000 and a 50% chance of losing $1,000. In alternative B he has a 25% chance of winning $1,200 and a 75% chance of losing $300. Now, since it can easily be shown mathematically that a person who continually chooses alternative A would eventually wind up with nothing, whereas a person who continually chooses alternative B would eventually wind up with $75, it would appear obvious that the person should choose alternative B. The question is, does he? Second, a person has two alternatives, A and B. Alternative A is exactly like the one in the first case, whereas alternative B consists of a 50% chance of winning $10,000 and a 50% chance of losing $10,000. By the same mathematics, we would find that the eventual outcome of both, given a series of continuous choices, is nothing. Hence, both alternatives should be chosen equally. The question is, are they?

The answer to these questions, if derived from a model that says that man is rational in that he tries to maximize his outcomes, is yes. However, in real organizational life, the alternatives are often not chosen equally, raising serious doubt that rationality underlies this process. Rather, what seems to be the case is that people often prefer the extreme risk in these choices and if we are to understand these decisions, we need to understand the process that influences risk taking. Among these factors, the following seem to be the most substantiated by research data:

1. There are no clear sex differences in risk taking. Both sexes will take more risks under specified conditions.
2. People have a tendency to decrease risk taking with age (Vroom & Pohl, 1971).
3. People who have high test anxiety (i.e., sensitivity to success and failure) and high concern with maintaining an image favorable to what other people think of them will be highly consistent in risk taking, irrespective of the rational aspects of the situation. Whether they are consistently high or consistently low depends on the norms of the social group with which they identify.
4. People who have only one or neither of these characteristics are more rational in their decision making than those who have both. Hence, they will be neither consistently high nor low in risk taking but will adjust their behavior as the situation varies, usually in the direction of rationality.
5. People generally take more risks when acting in a group than when acting alone, but sometimes they may be more conservative, depending on whether the conservative or risky choices are more socially desirable and

the dominant social influences operative at the time. Basically, risk taking in groups is a function of conformity to the operative social norms.

6. Among the personal characteristics associated with risk taking are extraversion (positively), need achievement (maximal interest in moderate risks), and fear of failure (maximal interest in extreme or no risks).

Summary

The goal of this chapter has been to discuss theories relating to other motivational processes of significance to organizational functioning besides traditional work achievement and performance. Among the motivational processes reviewed are aggression, power, and risk taking.

Theories of aggression motivation are of two types. One group can be classified along the same dimensions as the motivational theories discussed in chapter three in the areas of work performance and achievement. Thus, frustration-aggression theory, a framework of great popularity originally developed in experimental laboratories, is an example of expectancy-value theory; that is, aggression is engaged in to achieve desired goals when the probability of the aggression's success is great. Consistency theory is also useful in the study of aggression, as the work of the Walsters and Berscheid shows. These researchers have utilized the same equity framework used by Adams in the study of achievement to show that one can achieve balanced outcomes by deprecating and showing aggression against others.

The second group of aggression theories are different from these in that they are more focused around aggression as such, independently of their usefulness for other phenomena. Among these are (1) Zimbardo's theory of anonymity and deindividuation as factors that lead to the loosening of societal constraints against aggression and (2) the theory of the authoritarian personality, an individual who is hostile to different others and who is a product of hierarchical, male-oriented, punitive socialization.

Power motivation has come under increasing interest in recent years as a phenomenon that needs to be studied and understood for both its positive and negative implications. McClelland has developed a meaningful research program centered around the idea of the "two faces" of power. One face is positive, that is, it involves influencing others toward achievement; whereas the other is negative in that it involves controlling others without regard for outcomes. Other theoretical work in power motivation by Miner and by French and Raven use somewhat different conceptualizations from this, but they also suggest mechanisms for clarifying power motivation.

Risk-taking motivation seems to be a function of a number of basic psychological and sociological processes such as (1) individual desires for achievement and fear of failure and (2) the characteristic social norms of the time.

SUGGESTIONS FOR FURTHER READING

BANDURA, A. *Aggression: A social learning analysis.* Englewood Cliffs, N.J.: Prentice-Hall, 1973.
The major theoretical statement on modeling as an influence on aggression by the psychologist most identified with the approach.

CARTWRIGHT, D. Determinants of scientific progress: the case of research on the risky-shift. *American Psychologist,* 1973, *28,* 222–231.
An interesting account of how a major research finding first viewed as "new" in its implications turned out to be, with continued research, another illustration of an old principle. It illustrates well the value of systematic attempts to replicate research findings in the interests of theoretical clarification.

KIPNIS, D. Does power corrupt? *Journal of Personality and Social Psychology,* 1972, *24,* 33–41.
In post–Watergate America the significance of this article is even greater than when first published. It does much to answer the questions of those who are astounded by Watergate and other examples of leadership corruption.

MCCLELLAND, D. C., and STEELE, R. S. *Human motivation: A book of readings.* Morristown, N.J.: General Learning Press, 1973, Section 6, pp. 277–316.
A number of papers on power motivation are reprinted in this book, which brings together some of the significant research stemming from McClelland's theories. An interesting application to civil rights leadership is included.

ZIMBARDO, P. G. The human choice: Individuation, reason, and order versus deindividuation, impulse, and chaos. *Nebraska Symposium on Motivation,* 1969, *17,* 231–307.
A major theoretical statement on the significance of anonymity as an influence on aggression. Several studies by the author are discussed.

chapter five

Cognitive Processes and Work Behavior

Work behavior is not simply a function of appropriate motivational variables and good leadership. We all know from observing ourselves and others that there are times when all the motivation in the world and the very best leadership do not seem to help; there is still a continued inability to perform the job. Usually we attribute this failure to the variable we call ability (or the lack of it). Yet, despite such a common attribution, it is not at all clear what abilities are and how they enter into work behavior. In fact, as research accumulates the controversies grow even greater. It is these matters which I will discuss in this chapter, as well as the importance of abilities in job performance, generally, as compared to motivational and attitudinal factors? There are actually several questions involved. First, there is the question of overall job and career success in our society. How important are abilities for getting ahead in an overall career sense? Second, how significant are abilities or skills for different jobs? Do some jobs call for more skills than others? If so, which jobs are these?

Theories of Intelligence and Human Abilities: A Historical Background

The first psychologists to be interested in human abilities were influenced strongly by the British associationist philosophers (e.g., John

Locke), among whose major tenets was that intellectual activity was a result of previous experience. Since experience is to a great extent determined by sensory and perceptual activity, these early psychologists believed that the way to measure intelligence was to measure a person's sensory discrimination characteristics. However, this type of reasoning failed (Wissler, 1901), to be supplanted by the work of the French psychologist Alfred Binet, who thought that intelligence and human ability were composites of a variety of complex symbolic processes such as verbal problem solving, memory, reasoning, spelling, and so forth. These processes, added together, provided an accurate index of an individual's ability, and it was on this basis that Binet developed the famous test of intelligence which could successfully predict school performance, whereas the sensory tests were not able to do so.

Although never developed formally by him, Binet's thinking led to the idea that intelligence could be viewed as a general characteristic of an individual, much like the hair, the eyes, and so on. This notion was given formal expression in 1904 by the British psychologist Charles Spearman as the *g* theory of intelligence. More specifically, intelligence, to Spearman, was a general factor *(g)*, supported by a myriad of specific abilities, called *s* factors. The fact that much the same people got high grades (or low ones) across a wide variety of courses was due to the general factor, whereas the lack of a perfect relationship was due to the differing specific abilities (*s* factors) called for in each course.

Spearman's theory was challenged a generation later in the United States by the psychologist Leon Thurstone, who argued that intellectual differences were not at all due to the *g* factor but rather to several relatively independent factors. His work, later called multiple-factor theory, led him to postulate a theory of intelligence composed of seven major factors (Thurstone, 1938):

1. *verbal comprehension:* to understand the meaning of words and their relationship to each other
2. *word fluency:* to be fluent in naming or making words
3. *number aptitude:* to be speedy and accurate in making simple arithmetic calculations
4. *inductive reasoning:* to be able to discover a rule or principle and apply it to the solution of a problem
5. *memory:* to have a good rote memory for paired words, lists of numbers, etc.
6. *spatial aptitude:* to perceive fixed geometric relations among figures accurately and to be able to visualize their manipulations in space
7. *perceptual speed:* to perceive visual details quickly and accurately

Thurstone's concept of intelligence proved to be more popular in the United States than the ideas of Spearman (the reverse being true in

Great Britain), with the result that considerable theoretical and methodological controversy waged for a number of years. This now has dissipated as the British psychologists have given greater importance to the *ss* in the *g* theory and as U.S. psychologists have realized that the so-called basic factors of Thurstone and the other multiple-factor theories that followed his were not really basic at all. Rather, they could be grouped in such a manner that people could be generally differentiated on a factor of general verbal ability, the characteristics of which were very similar to the *g* factor of the British psychologists. (A look at Thurstone's factors above indicates how relatively simple this can be.)

Hence, whether one started with one general factor of intelligence and then admitted less important ones, as the British psychologists did, or went at it from the other direction by grouping smaller factors into larger ones, the notion of a general factor involving the ability to manipulate concepts and ideas both of a verbal and numerical nature in a symbolic manner came to be accepted as crucial to the definition of ability, or intelligence. It is around this definition that much of the work on abilities and job performance has traditionally been organized. This tradition is now under heavy attack as we will see below.

Verbal Abilities, Cognitive Skills, and Job Performance

There is little basis for disputing the fact that a large body of research literature exists which supports the conclusion that jobs in our society can be arranged along a general (mostly symbolic) ability hierarchy and that this hierarchy generally corresponds to the importance of the job in our society. The more valuable and prestigious a job is considered, the greater the degree of verbal and numerical symbolic ability it seems to call for. Yet, all is not as it appears from Table 5.1 where I have summarized an investigation that illustrates this relationship between general abilities (i.e., verbal and numerical) and occupational membership. It seems from this study that the higher the occupation, the greater the degree of symbolic ability necessary for successful performance on the job. This conclusion also seems warranted from a review of research literature published by Ghiselli (1966) that concerned itself with integrating what was known about the relationships between various abilities (as measured by tests) and job performance when measured by training criteria (e.g., the quickness with which the job is learned) and performance criteria. Table 5.2 summarizes a portion of what Ghiselli found about the significance of intellectual (verbal and numerical) abilities for various kinds of jobs. This significance is reported in terms of the correlation coefficient; that is, the higher the

Table 5.1

Relationships between Jobs in Terms
of Verbal Abilities of Members

OCCUPATION	APPROXIMATE LEVEL OF VERBAL ABILITY
Lawyer	128
Accountant	128
Civil engineer	128
Chemist	125
Reporter	124
Draftsman	122
School teacher	122
Pharmacist	120
Photographer	118
Store manager	112
Toolmaker	111
Machinist	110
Machine operator	106
Cabinet maker	104
Plumber	103
Auto mechanic	102
Chauffeur	101
Truck driver	98
Farmhand	91
Teamster	89

Source: T. W. Harrell and M. S. Harrell, Army
general classification test scores for civilian
occupations, *Educational and Psychological
Measurement,* 1945, *5,* 229–239.

Note: Based on scores from the Army General
Classification Test, primarily a verbal test.

correlation the more important the ability is presumed to be for job
performance.

What is the problem, then, considering the consistency of the
findings in Tables 5.1 and 5.2. Why can't I be more definitive that the
general verbal symbolic factor is of great significance for career success
in our society? The reason that I believe that we should go slowly on
such a conclusion is because both studies have severe, possibly crucial,
methodological defects. One of these is that in the Ghiselli study there
has been a mixture of individuals who were tested prior to entering the
occupation and those who were tested after some occupational experience. From all that we will be discussing in this book about the effects
of work socialization, I believe it is fair to conclude that at least some
of the differences shown *reflect* different levels of occupational experience (i.e., abilities gained on the job) rather than causing them. Second,
in almost none of the research cited in both studies were the relationships corrected for differences in the participants' socioeconomic back-

Table 5.2

Summary of Relationships between Intellectual Ability and Job Performance for Different Jobs and Criteria

	INTELLECTUAL ABILITIES	
Occupation	*Training criteria*	*Performance criteria*
Executives and administration personnel		.29
Foremen		.24
General clerks	.46	.31
Recording clerks	.48	.26
Computing clerks	.52	.24
Sales clerks		—.10
Salesmen		.31
Protective service workers	.35	.23
Service personnel	.54	.03
Vehicle operators	.15	.14
Mechanical repairmen	.40	.20
Electrical workers	.50	.21
Structural workers	.29	.18
Machine tenders	—.31	.16
Bench workers	.21	.13
Packers and wrappers	.48	.17
Gross manual workers	—.03	.22

Source: E. Ghiselli, *The validity of occupational aptitude tests* (New York: Wiley, 1966), pp. 34, 37, 41, 44, 46, 48, 50, 56. © 1966. Reprinted by permission of the publisher.

ground, a variable that predicts these levels of occupational achievement as well as (or even better than) scores on the general mental ability test. As a result, when these problems are corrected, the picture turns out to be far different than the conclusions which seem to be warranted at first glance.

One of my authorities for this statement is David McClelland, a psychologist whom we have already met in different contexts. In a paper published in 1973, McClelland made some important statements about general mental ability tests of the kind we have been discussing. First, McClelland found that the research evidence for the usefulness of these tests in predicting real-life behavior is poor to minimal at best. The tests predict school grades, but little else. (School grades do not predict real-life behavior with any great degree of success, either.) Second, there is little correlation between general mental ability measures and job success when they are used to *predict* behavior at work (not reflect it). A good illustration of this statement is the Thorndike and Hagen (1959) research which reported 12,000 correlations for 10,000 respondents and found very few significant relationships. More recently, Holland and Richards (1965), Elton and Shevel (1969), and

Kent and Eisenberg (1972) have all failed to find relationships between general mental ability measures and accomplishments in such varied fields as social leadership, the arts, sciences, and police work. When relationships are found, they are uncorrected for social class status, and when these corrections are made, the correlation levels decrease greatly.

McClelland argues that the general mental ability factor, as it has traditionally been measured, is, in fact, not very important for occupational success except at the extreme points and that other kinds of skills and abilities are more important. Such skills, he maintains, are more likely to be learned by those higher in our socioeconomic strata and are, in fact, susceptible to considerable training and other types of social intervention influence. Therefore, McClelland argues, what we should be measuring and developing are such behaviors as communications skills, patience, training in goal-setting, and the like, rather than being concerned with such matters as abstract analogies and vocabulary skills. The latter are significant for success in school but not so much for success in life and work.

When we consider both the data that McClelland cites and other studies in the literature on the lack of predictive usefulness of general mental ability tests (cf. Korman, 1968) three important factors should be noted. First of all, the criticism is data-based; it is not just opinion. Second, the argument comes from people with no particular investment in a particular political ideology. Third, the argument made by these researchers leads to an interventionist, growth-oriented way of thinking about organizational behavior that is in line with current legal and social trends. In other words, they say that appropriate work experience can lead to greater cognitive abilities and more effective skill in dealing with job demands, in addition to the effects the experience may have on motivation and attitudes.

For these reasons I think that it is justifiable not to consider job-relevant abilities in the way that they have traditionally been measured for school-related purposes and then uncritically transferred to the work setting. Rather, we should think of constellations of interpersonal, cognitive, and attitudinal skills that include not only the capacity to symbolize but much more than that. As an illustration, I have listed below the kinds of concrete verbal and interaction skills that were found to be highly related to management competence in a multinational, billion-dollar corporation (Korman, Noon, and Ryan, 1975). According to them a competent manager could be expected to:

> focus in on a fast-running conversation, redirect, sum up differences, and encourage a coordinated effort.
> express ideas clearly and logically.

make a thorough analysis of alternate solutions to a problem and select the best.

pull together scattered information from various sources into a meaningful proposal.

give useful advice based on a sound grasp of current methods in his field.

state problems concisely.

take the initiative in implementing a program.

grasp essential issues, make decisions, and delegate items for action.

expedite a complicated project and see it through to completion.

be adequately prepared before discussing problems.

establish a timetable and performance goals against which to measure the success of a project.

look for ways to improve existing systems.

These behaviors are a far cry from those measured by the typical analogies on vocabulary tests. In addition, the behaviors indicated lend themselves to training and development, matters that have become very important in our society.

Recently, a number of other writers have also come to the conclusion that the school-related general mental ability concept may not be of as much use as we used to think. McKenny and Keen (1974) have suggested that cognitive skills call for information gathering (selecting and organizing data) and information evaluation (analyzing and evaluating data for problem-solving) and that different occupations call for different combinations of these behaviors. Thus, a scientist is *preceptive;* that is, he uses previously developed theories and precepts to organize incoming data whereas an accountant is *receptive;* that is, he receives a greater percentage of incoming data before he organizes and categorizes them. Similarly, a production manager is *systematic* in his evaluation and solving of problems in the sense that he may use previously developed methods, whereas an inventor may be more *intuitive* in that he is more likely to use ad hoc, trial-and-error methods for problem-solving. These proposed differences lead McKenney and Keen (1974) to suggest the framework for cognitive processes in work behavior shown in Figure 5.1, and a tentative list of occupational classifications.

I want to make it clear that this theory has not been tested yet, and it is not certain that it will be supported when it is tested. The point is that these kinds of cognitive skills (as well as those listed above) are very different from those measured by school-related tests. This does not mean that vocabulary tests are always unimportant in predicting job success. In some jobs and under some conditions they

Figure 5.1
Framework for cognitive processes in work behavior developed by
McKenney and Keen (1974)

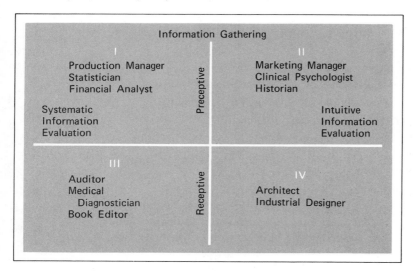

may very well be. However, much more seems to be involved in many careers and it is these skills, most of which are susceptible to intervention and training, that we should be paying more attention to in the future.

Motor Abilities

In addition to cognitive processes, other kinds of skills are important in work behavior. While the range and importance of these other skills are not as great, they have been subjected to a considerable amount of study. Among these other abilities an important group are those concerned with the physical manipulation of objects in an environment, i.e., psychomotor skills.

Since motor skills are relevant to a number of occupations (e.g., vehicle operators, secretaries, mechanics) and since they lend themselves easily to laboratory experimentation, the amount of research that has been performed on them is considerable and some fairly definitive conclusions have been reached. The most important of these is that there is little support for the idea of a general factor in manual or psychomotor abilities that would distinguish some people as generally good in them and others as generally poor. This definitely does *not* seem to be the case. Rather, various tests of motor abilities generally have low intercorrelations; an individual's score on one test of motor abilities does not generally predict very accurately his score on a different one.

A second conclusion is that not only are motor skills specific and unrelated to one another, but also the actual number of different motor skills is probably quite large. While any list that one may offer in this area would be quite tentative, the 11 separate skills suggested by Fleishman (1962), as a summary of his research over a decade, constitute what is probably the best-established grouping. These skills are as follows:

1. *control precision:* involves fine, highly controlled, but not overcontrolled muscular adjustments, primarily where larger muscle groups are involved
2. *multilimb coordination:* the ability to coordinate the movements of a number of limbs simultaneously
3. *response orientation:* unusual discriminative ability; involves the ability to make correct movements to a visual stimulus under highly speeded conditions
4. *reaction time:* the quickness of reaction to a stimulus
5. *speed of arm movement:* involves the speed of movements, not their accuracy
6. *rate control:* concerned with the making of continuous anticipatory motor adjustments relative to changes in speed and direction of a continuously moving target or object
7. *manual dexterity:* the manipulation of fairly large objects, under speed conditions, using arm-hand movements
8. *finger dexterity:* the manipulation of tiny objects using the fingers
9. *arm-hand steadiness:* the steadiness of positioning movements where strength and speed are minimized
10. *wrist-finger speed:* generally, this can be called "tapping speed"
11. *arming:* involves an accuracy of directional movements

The great specificity of psychomotor skills reflected in this list is only one reason that it is difficult to summarize the literature about the kinds of occupations for which these skills are most meaningful. Another problem is that these various skills are often combined into a single test and information of importance only for the test is available. Also, not all psychologists have used the same theoretical system for doing research. Finally, the fact that there is evidence that the necessary skills will change with practice on the task (Fleishman and Hempel, 1954) means that statements of correlational relationship that mix those measured before and after job experience need to be interpreted with caution. Table 5.3 provides such a statement and should therefore be interpreted carefully.

Table 5.3

Summary of Relationships between Various Psychomotor Abilities and Job Performance for Different Jobs and Criteria

Occupation	SPATIAL AND MECHANICAL ABILITIES		PERCEPTUAL ACCURACY		MOTOR ABILITIES	
	Training Criteria	*Performance Criteria*	*Training Criteria*	*Performance Criteria*	*Training Criteria*	*Performance Criteria*
Executives and administrators		.18		.24		
Foremen		.23		.14		
General clerks	.35	.14	.40	.26	.34	.16
Recording clerks	.30	.18	.41	.26	.15	.17
Computing clerks	.52	.26	.31	.31	.14	.09
Sales clerks			—.50			
Salesmen		.07		.21		
Protective service workers	.34	.16	.30	.17		.19
Service personnel	.42			—.10	—.05	
Vehicle operators	.30	.20	.08	.36		.30
Mechanical repairmen	.40	.20	.40	.19	.15	.15
Electrical workers	.49	.18	.33	.27	.14	.16
Structural workers	.33	.28	.25	.20	.22	.26
Machine tenders		.11		.18	.21	.15
Bench workers	.26	.19	.27	.20	.42	.21
Packers and wrappers	.46	.13		.17		.15
Gross manual workers		.35				.33

Source: E. Ghiselli, *The validity of occupational aptitude tests* (New York: Wiley, 1966), pp. 34, 37, 41, 44, 46, 48, 50, 56. © 1966. Reprinted by permission of the publisher.

Creative Abilities

By creativity we mean the ability to manipulate symbols, arrange them, and group them in ways that are *new* and that have *social utility*. Both concepts are crucial in defining creativity since the former without the latter might well be a definition of emotional disturbance. Similarly, it is quite easy to conceive of many thoughts that have social utility but which are not particularly new.

While the need for creative individuals has always been great in such fields as advertising, marketing, and certain areas of management, the demand has exploded recently with the growth of research and development departments in many corporations and with the ever-changing requirements of a dynamic society. It has become clear that a capacity to change creatively with the times must be built into any organization, or the organization will cease to exist. Therefore, great interest has developed in understanding the creative process—what stimulates it, what creative people are like—and in the development of measures of individual differences in creative abilities. As we will see, there is reason for thinking here also about a process involving a complex of skills of a cognitive and attitudinal nature that lend themselves to social influence and training. Two bodies of data illustrate much of the research in this area.

The first of these programs, reported by McKinnon (1962) and Barron (1965), involved a relatively simple procedure. After selecting various occupations that allow for creative expression, the researchers attempted to find (1) practitioners in each occupation who were considered creative by their peers and (2) practitioners who were similar to the creative group in as many aspects as possible but who differed in the degree to which they were judged creative. Since the key here was how people were ranked on creativity, the researchers spent much effort in developing procedures to make this decision as accurate as possible. The method finally used was to ask for judgments from leading experts in each occupational area, such as college professors, journal editors, medical practitioners, and so on, on the assumption that if such diverse, knowledgeable individuals as these could agree, then such a procedure would probably provide the best basis for this type of judgment. The results turned out to be better than hoped for across a variety of differing professions (e.g., mathematicians, architects, and the like) in that they showed a high degree of agreement as to who were creative and who were not. Samples of the two groups were invited to come to Berkeley for several days where they were assessed on a wide variety of psychological measures—an invitation which most, but not all accepted.

What was discovered? How do creative people differ from those who are uncreative? Table 5.4 lists how the creative people differed from the noncreative people in the fields of architecture, mathematics, and writing. While there are some specific differences, for example, the greater concern with philosophy among the creative writers than among the creative architects, the picture one gets from the various descriptions of the highly creative individuals is strikingly similar. Although we do not know whether these characteristics led to greater creativity, greater creativity led to these characteristics, or both, our discussions elsewhere in this book on the cultivation of creativity indicate that considerable confidence can be placed in the implications of these findings. (You might, for example, look at our discussions in chapter three on authoritarianism, dogmatism, and creativity).

One further aspect concerns the relation between the traditional general mental ability factor discussed earlier and the creative abilities. The work of McKinnon and Barron suggests that while the two are re-

Table 5.4

Characteristics of Creative People as Opposed to Noncreative People in Different Occupations

ARCHITECTURE *Creative people are more likely than noncreative people to:*	MATHEMATICS		WRITING *Creative people are more likely are more likely than noncreative than noncreative people to:*
	Creative people are more likely than noncreative people to be:	*Creative people are less likely than noncreative people to be:*	
Have a high degree of intellect	Individualistic	Cheerful	Have high degree of intellect
Value intellect	Original	Active	Value intellect
Value independence	Preoccupied	Appreciative	Value independence
Enjoy sensuous experience	Artistic	Considerate	Be verbally fluent
Enjoy esthetic impression	Complicated	Conventional	Enjoy esthetic impression
Have social poise	Courageous	Cooperative	Be concerned with philosophical
Have high self-aspiration	Imaginative	Helpful	problems
Have wide range of interests	Self-centered	Obliging	Have high self-aspiration
Be dependable		Organized	Have a wide range of interests
Be critical		Practical	Have unconventional thought
Be concerned with own adequacy		Realistic	processes
Be ethically consistent		Reliable	Be ethically consistent
		Sympathetic	Get things done
			Be interesting and personable
			Be straightforward in dealing
			with others

Source: Compiled from data presented in "The Psychology of Creativity" by Frank Barron, pp. 1–134, from *New Directions in Psychology II,* by Frank Barron et al. Copyright © 1965 by Holt, Rinehart and Winston, Inc.

lated, they are not the same. That is, while one needs a good degree of verbal ability in order to be creative, having more than the necessary amount does not seem to make a difference. In other words, one probably cannot be very creative unless one can handle verbal symbols well, but handling verbal symbols well does not guarantee creative behavior.

In another important research program of a somewhat different nature, Mednick (1962) has viewed creative thinking as the "forming of associative elements into new combinations which either meet specified requirements or are in some way useful. The more mutually remote the elements of the new combination, the more creative the process or solution" (p. 221). You will notice the similarity between this definition of creativity and the definition given above. Thus, if a person is presented with a group of stimuli—words, for example—and combines them in obvious ways, he is not being particularly creative. An example of this is a person who combines "bed–bug," "kill–joy," and so on. However, if he combines words into new combinations, then he is being more creative, particularly if the new combinations have social utility. Mednick suggests that a good way of measuring individual differences in creative behavior is to ask respondents to develop connections between stimuli (words) that are usually not seen as being related to one another by providing links between them that combine them into one associated group. For example, the words "rat," "blue," and "cottage" are not obviously related to one another. However, they can be connected by the word "cheese," which is easily paired with each of them. Other examples he cites are "railroad," "girl," and "class" (answer: "working"), and "wheel," "electric," and "high" (answer: "chair"). Such reasoning has led Mednick to develop the Remote Associates Test (RAT), a 30-item test that calls for individuals to find such mediating links between groups of generally unconnected words. Scores on the RAT are then compared to performance measures that are assumed to call for some degree of creative behavior.

The results have been both favorable and unfavorable. On the favorable side, it has been shown that RAT scores are very highly correlated ($r = .70$) with faculty ratings of the creativity of architecture students and also significantly related to the creative behavior of psychology graduate students (Mednick, 1962). Also in keeping with the general conceptualization of the RAT is that scores on it are related to generally liberal moral views (Kowalski, 1960) and a need for novelty (Houston and Mednick, 1963). On the negative side, the RAT did not predict the creative behavior of small samples of either physicists or engineers in a large U.S. corporation as this behavior was judged by superiors (Datta, 1964a, 1964b). Overall, while some evidence suggests that the kinds of creative abilities being measured by the RAT have occupational significance in that they predict some types of occupationally oriented training success, its degree of prediction is by no means as high as we would like it to be.

Developing Creative Skills

One of the implications of looking at creative (and other) abilities as complex, interactive processes is that this way of thinking lends itself to the development of training programs designed to increase these skills. This contrasts with the more sterile view of thinking of abilities as fixed, immutable quantities. Over the last two decades a great number of training programs for increasing creative behavior have been developed. Various types of these training programs are described below.

brainstorming

Brainstorming involves training and encouraging individuals to separate, timewise, the generation of ideas from idea evaluation. The goal is to overcome the implicit, sometimes unconscious censoring mechanisms we all have that prevent us from being as open to new ideas and approaches as we would like to be. A considerable body of research supports the value of brainstorming, particularly when it is done on an individual basis without the inhibiting influence of others and, in particular, "expert" others (cf. Bouchard, Drauden, and Barsaloux, 1974).

attribute listing

Attribute listing involves training individuals to itemize the important attributes of a particular social object and to consider how each of the attributes may be changed or improved. As an example, consider a piece of chalk. It has size, shape, color, and a certain type of material. By considering each of these qualities separately and how they might be changed, ideas for a large variety of different types of chalk may be developed.

morphological synthesis

This program is somewhat similar to attribute listing, but it is different in that the idea is to consider two dimensions of a particular social object at a time. Suppose, for example, a group of individuals wanted to develop a new type of table lamp. If they took 15 potential lamps that differed in shape, and each shape came in 20 different colors and 5 sizes, all the combinations would result in 1500 possible products ($20 \times 15 \times 5$). This is a great number of different products and many combinations rarely considered before could now be evaluated.

synectic techniques

Synectic techniques involve learning to use analogies as ways of developing creative solutions. There are four different types of analogies that can be used (Gordon, 1961):

1. *personal analogy:* imagining oneself as one of the factors under study in order to further one's understanding of the factor, e.g., a male trainer who imagines himself a woman in order to gain new insight into the problems of female managers.
2. *direct analogy:* imagining and looking for another process that would parallel the process or problem directly under consideration, e.g., the problem of underwater construction was solved by watching a worm tunnelling into a timber and observing that the worm constructed a tube for itself as it moved forward, leading to the notion of caissons.
3. *symbolic analogy:* using objective and impersonal images to describe a problem although the image or model developed may be technologically inaccurate; an example would be a computer model of managerial behavior to assist in the training function.

4. *fantasy analogy;* thinking about how to resolve a problem in a fantasy world where all other conditions are ideal for problem-solving; an example of this analogy would be to determine how to develop racial integration in organizations, ignoring for the moment all the other complexities involved.

Summary

Different abilities have traditionally been the explanation for differences in work effectiveness that do not seem to be attributable to motivation. Until recently this explanation was fairly routine, but the situation is now changing. McClelland has shown that there is little evidence that measures of intellectual ability of the type used in school settings are related to career and work success. As a result, interest is turning away from defining abilities in this manner to a view of cognitive processes as the way in which an individual collects, organizes, stores, and utilizes information. This view is in keeping with the current belief that abilities are subject in considerable degree to influence and training.

Psychomotor abilities remain important for a number of jobs but here, also, interest is starting to develop in the extent to which these skills develop as a result of different job experiences. Creative abilities have also been the subject of considerable interest. Research has been designed to identify the types of people who are creative in different occupations. The creative type seems to be relatively similar for various occupations: he is individualistic, open to esthetic experience, imaginative, and independent. Other research has involved developing tests to measure differences in creative abilities. Finally, interest in creative abilities as a process that involves using information in new, socially useful ways has led to the development of various techniques to increase creativity in work organizations.

SUGGESTIONS FOR FURTHER READING

Barron, F. *Creative person and creative process.* New York: Holt, Rinehart and Winston, 1969.

A summary of findings and implications of the major research program on creativity and occupational membership I discussed in this chapter and the author's later thinking.

Chapters on human abilities in the *Annual Review of Psychology,* Annual Reviews, Inc., Palo Alto, Calif.

These papers, while academic in nature, provide the reader with a continuing perspective on the ferment taking place in the study of human abilities.

McCLELLAND, D. C. Testing for competence rather than for "intelligence." *American Psychologist,* 1973, *28,* 1–14.

This is the paper I cited earlier on the lack of support for the relationship between traditional mental abilities and career success. A must for anybody interested in this field.

chapter six

Organizational Psychology

Every time a manager of an organization decides on a policy, adopts a practice, structures a job situation, uses a specific type of authority system, or chooses a particular type of technology, he is, in effect, implementing a particular theory of motivation. He is assuming that the particular behavior choice he is making will help achieve his desired outcomes. Most of the time these desired outcomes include organizational values as well as personally relevant values that may or may not be consistent with organizational goals.

The field known as organizational psychology is concerned with the relationships between these various choices and their behavioral and attitudinal outcomes. Given a variety of choices as to policy, authority system, and job structure, which alternatives lead to which outcomes? Do these relationships vary for different occupations, industries, and other situational factors? These are the questions explored in this chapter.

General Questions

There are, I think, three major questions in the field of organizational psychology. First, what are the processes by which organizational variables affect behavior? How do managerial policies and practices, variations in job characteristics and authority systems, and technological, physical variables influence the nature of work attitudes and work activity? This question is crucial, both for theoretical reasons and because the answer would give us some guidance as to how to increase or decrease the influence of any particular organizational variable. After all, what good would it do to know that a certain type of pay policy has a positive effect if we do not know how to increase the influence of that policy?

The second question is how to design the organizational variables, given that we know the mechanisms by which they have influence and that we know how to increase or decrease the strength of these effects. How should we design the leadership and authority system to achieve the outcomes we want? Should the leadership be hierarchical? Should tasks be variable or programmed? Although I have already touched on some of these issues in chapter three, a more intensive examination of these questions is necessary.

The third major question concerns the conditions under which the answers to the second question hold for different situations. Basically, this is the contingency question — the problem of specifying the conditions under which, for example, a given type of leadership affects behavior positively and the conditions under which it does not. Among the variables which might affect these relationships are different population groups, different job contexts, different technologies, and so forth. There is, obviously, a lot of intuitive logic to utilizing a contingency, or an "it all depends" perspective in evaluating the effectiveness of a given policy. However, this intuitive appeal is a little misleading and we will see that many problems need to be solved before the contingency approach can be used effectively for theory and practice.

Mechanisms of Influence

I can think of at least four separate mechanisms by which organizational variables such as leadership and authority systems, pay policies, job characteristics, and so on can come to influence behavior. Each one has been relatively substantiated in the behavioral science literature.

First, such variables can operate as constraint systems in both a positive and negative sense by providing knowledge of what kinds of behaviors are rewarded, punished, or ignored. An example is the rewards–punishment paradigm. Sometime back, you will recall, we said that the rewards–punishment paradigm is not the complete answer to motivation. However, this framework does provide at least a partial explanation for behavior, and the organization *can* influence behavior by attaching different rewards and punishments to varying behaviors. This assignment of different values to different behavioral outcomes would then influence the behavior of those people most interested in those specific values. In other words, setting up a financial reward for performing a certain task would influence those people for whom the money was salient in either a positive or negative sense. (Two reasons people might not be interested in a particular reward might be perceived inappropriateness for the self and peer-group disapproval of the reward.)

A second mechanism by which organizational variables might influence behavior is that they can affect the evaluation of the self and others and such evaluation will, in turn, influence behavior. Consider, for example, how a factory worker might evaluate himself in organization A as opposed to how he might evaluate himself if he were employed in organization B. The characteristics of the two organizations are as follows:

ORGANIZATION A	ORGANIZATION B
Air conditioning in both factory and office	Air conditioning only in office
Guaranteed annual salaries for both factory and office employees	Guaranteed annual salaries only for office employees; hourly pay rates for factory employees
The same lunch- and washroom facilities for both factory and office employees	Separate lunch- and washroom facilities for factory and office employees

It seems to me that I would think a lot less of myself if I were a factory worker in organization B than in A, and I suspect most of you would also.

A third mechanism through which organizational variables, as controlled by management, can influence behavior is by influencing an organization's climate. The climate of an organization may, for example, be the extent to which it is seen by either those who are inside or outside the organization as ego supportive, hierarchical, ambiguous, conflict-prone, and routinized, to cite just a few of the descriptive terms often used. Climate has, as a concept, become a matter of great controversy. Those who like the concept see the organizational climate as a set of descriptive, nonevaluative perceptions of the organization's characteristics (e.g., leadership, organizational policies, job and task characteristics, etc.). They see this composite perception as resulting from both the actual characteristics of the organization and the characteristics of the individual doing the perceiving. In this view, organizational climate is a dependent variable in that it results, at least partially, from mechanisms that management can control and it is also an independent variable in that it can influence job behaviors and attitudes.

There are psychologists who argue with this view (Guion, 1973; Johannsen, 1973). One of their arguments is that organizational climate is just another name for job attitudes. According to them, to say that an organization is high on ego supportiveness is to say something good about an organization (i.e., a person has high job satisfaction). On the other hand, to say that it is low on ego supportiveness is to say something bad about the organization (i.e., the person has low job satisfaction). I disagree with this point of view. I think that a good logical argument can be made for the concept of organizational climate if we realize that we are talking about a description of a particular set of social characteristics in a particular setting and that these do influence behavior (Pritchard and Karasick, 1973; Lawler, Hall, and Oldham, 1974). Furthermore, I believe that the argument that such descriptions are equivalent to job satisfaction is a poor one because it ignores the fact of individual differences. Not everybody likes an ego-supportive climate or an organization low on rule demands; some prefer the opposite. Also, organizational climate, when measured, is not related to the same variables as job satisfaction (Schneider and Snyder, 1975). This suggests that the two are not the same phenomenon. I would conclude, therefore, that a third way that organizational variables influence behavior is that they influence the individual to form a perception of the organization. This perception may then influence various job behaviors.

Lastly, organizational variables influence behavior because they are stimuli. As stimuli they influence an individual's arousal level, which is a motivational variable directing behavior. Briefly, arousal-level theory (also known as activation theory) proposes that there is an inverted U-shaped relationship between the activation level of the individual and performance, with activation level being viewed as the total amount of stimulation affecting the person. This stimulation may be due to stimulus complexity, the total amount of stimulation, changes in and the novelty of stimuli and the meaningfulness of stimuli. The inverted U-shaped function is proposed because low activation (e.g., low complexity and little variation) is seen as leading to a relatively low level of alertness, while a high level of activation (e.g., too much complexity and variation) involves too much stimulation, thus causing hypertension and response disorganization.

What do all of these mechanisms mean? Basically, they suggest that the managers of an organization have several alternatives open to them if they want to influence behavior. For each alternative, they must consider its advantages and disadvantages.

First, management can increase performance by increasing or decreasing the stimulus complexity, variability, and meaningfulness of the environment. The problem is in determining whether arousal should be increased or decreased in a given situation. Sometimes the choice is easy in that one can be fairly certain as to what needs or does not need to be done; for example, very few people would want to increase the noise level of a boiler factory or the New York City subway. Other times, however, it is not easy unless you take the time to measure the preferred arousal levels of the people involved. This procedure is sometimes, but not always, possible. How many arguments have you heard, for example, between people in an office who want a radio on and those who do not? A second problem in applying arousal theory is that the effects of the physical variable you are manipulating may be transformed by social and psychological influences. In fact, studies indicate that the same physical stimulus can have different effects on a subject depending on his previous experiences and the social influences around him (cf. Glass and Singer, 1972). As a result, it has been argued that the physical manipulation itself is relatively unimportant, compared to the other psychological processes involved. As I will argue later, however, I do not think you should throw out arousal theory just yet. It deserves to be considered one of the mechanisms for influencing the effects of organizational characteristics on behavior.

Another alternative that management can use in increasing the influence of an organizational variable is to make more salient the rewards and punishments involved. I have always been impressed, in a negative sense, with two aspects of organizational life: first, that there are many organizational behaviors for which either rewards and/or punishments do not exist; rather, they seem to occur without any clear idea of their appropriateness. Second, in the cases in which there are reward–punishment linkages, these linkages are either not known or not understood. It seems obvious that if this mechanism is to be used for influencing behavior, there needs to be knowledge of the linkages involved.

Finally, a third mechanism is to increase exposure to those organizational variables that cultivate favorable organizational and/or self-perception.

Design of Organizational Environments

In this section I want to develop some answers to the general question of the kind of work environment or organization we should design if our goals are to increase work motivation, increase the willingness and/or ability to engage in creative behavior, encourage a capacity for constructive conflict control, and develop optimal levels of power motivation and risk taking. How can we develop and structure a work organization? How should we design tasks? What types of leadership and authority should we use? Have the ways we have done so in the past been the best ways? These are some of the questions to which we now turn.

Design of Organizations

Some time ago two authors in the field of organizations said that it was easier to describe different organizations and their characteristics than to define what an organization actually was (March and Simon, 1958). Despite the difficulties in arriving at a good definition, most people would probably agree that an organization is a distinguishable, formally defined structure along which people's activities have been grouped in relation to one another, with all of the activities involved oriented toward a common goal.

The major questions for those interested in organizations have always been the following: How should the activities be structured? How should they be related to one another? On what basis should control systems that are designed to secure the desired outcomes be instituted? How should changes in proposed relationships be brought about? These and related questions have been the concern of organizational theorists from the time Plato formulated his plans for the ideal society and, until relatively recent years, most thinking tended to converge along similar lines. However, in the years since World War II there has been increasing ferment in this field, and a new group of organization theorists have called into question many of the traditional ways of looking at organizations. These theorists have proposed some major changes in the design of organizational structures and in the policies that are implied by such designs. While the impetus for this ferment comes from a variety of sources, some of the greatest voices for design change come from those who are trained in the behavioral sciences. In the pages to follow we will examine some of the directions those voices have taken.

traditional organization theory: the basic framework

Several writers can be cited as contributors to traditional or classic organizational theory, but among the doctrines most often cited are the works of Fayol (1949), Urwick (1943), and Koontz and O'Donnell (1964). While there are differences among them, these writers share similar assumptions about the nature of man, the nature of tasks, and the nature of the external environments within which organizations operate. The general flavor of their approach has been summarized by Etzioni:

> The classical administrative theory . . . made the division of labor its central tenet. The classical approach rests firmly on the assumption that the more a particular job can be broken down into its simplest components, the more specialized and consequently the more skilled a worker can become in carrying out his part of the job. The more skilled the worker becomes in fulfilling his particular job, the more efficient the whole production system will be. The division of labor, the classical approach pointed out, has to be balanced by a unity of control. The tasks have to be broken up into components by a central authority in line with a central plan of action; the efforts of each work unit need to be supervised; and the various job efforts leading to the final product have to be coordinated. Since each supervisor has a limited number of subordinates he can effectively control, it is necessary to appoint a number of first-line supervisors, and following that, a second-line supervisor (to supervise the supervisors) and so on up. Each 5 or 6 workers, for instance, need one first-line supervisor; each 6 first-line supervisors, and hence, every 40 workers, need 1 second-line supervisor, and so on. The number of subordinates controlled by one superior defines his "span of control." What results is a *pyramid of control* leading up to one top executive. In this way, the whole organization can be controlled from one *center of authority,* without having any supervisor control more than 5 or 10 subordinates.[1]

Is this what makes an effective organization? If we set up an organization in today's world, is this how we should do it? Would it achieve the goals which it should? Do people work better when given a simple, repetitive task to do all day under close supervision? Before examining the answers to these questions, we need to mention here the German sociologist Max Weber, who developed the most comprehensive theory of organizations based on this view of human behavior.

Weber lived in the late nineteenth century when favoritism, nepotism, and discrimination were rife in German industry. It was to the negative implications for performance of such activities that Weber was reacting when he proposed his theory of bureaucracy as the ideal type for an organization. As Gibson (1966) has pointed out, according to Weber (1947), one could avoid the negative influences of personal prejudice, irrationality, and emotionality in organizational performance if organizations were put together in the following manner:

1. All tasks necessary for the accomplishment of the goals should be broken down into the smallest possible unit; the division of labor should be carried out to the extent that specialized experts are responsible for the successful performance of specified duties.

---

[1] Amitai Etzioni, *Modern Organizations,* © 1964, pp. 22–23. Reprinted by permission of Prentice-Hall, Inc., Englewood Cliffs, New Jersey.

2. Each task should be performed according to a "consistent system of abstract rules" in order to assure uniformity and coordination of different tasks. Uncertainty in the performance of tasks due to individual differences is also theoretically eliminated.

3. Each member or officer of an organization is to be held accountable to a superior for his own decisions as well as for those of his subordinates. The authority of the superior is based on expert knowledge and is sanctioned and made legitimate by the ultimate source of authority—the chief official at the top of the hierarchical pyramid.

4. Each official in the organization is to conduct the business of his office in an impersonal, formalistic manner. He should maintain a social distance between himself and his subordinates and between himself and the clients of the organization. The purpose of this impersonal detachment is to assure that personalities do not interfere with the efficient accomplishment of the mission.

5. Employment in the bureaucratic organization should be based on technical qualifications and all employees should be protected against arbitrary dismissal. Promotions should be based on seniority and achievement.

It is in these proposals for rigid division and specialization of labor and the requirement for a dependency relationship on a superior that we see the view of man which runs through the writings of the classic organization theorists. It is the same philosophical view that became so prominent among members of industrial and other organizations and which has served as the basis for the pyramid-shaped organization that most people today think of as typical. The picture is a clear one. This is what organizations should be like if they are to compete successfully in economic activity—or so the classic theorists said.

How good are these theoretical assumptions? There is little doubt that there must have been at least some validity to these principles at one time, or our industrial enterprises that were built on such models would not have become as prosperous as they did. (It might be noted, though, that such validity might have been less than we think today. Wrage and Perroni [1974] have shown that the research of F. W. Taylor, the father of "scientific management," was far weaker than is commonly thought. Apparently, there were instances of worker rebellion, antagonism, and other negative reactions even in the days of greater worker acceptance of management authority.) However, the fact that organizations based on these assumptions were successful in the past is irrelevant; the important issue is what kinds of organizations will succeed now. Some critics argue that an organization based on traditional theory is increasingly less likely to succeed in today's world. Why? The explanation is lengthy, resulting both from logical problems of the traditional model and from research investigations on the relationship between various kinds of organizational characteristics and work behavior. The following sections deal with these matters.

traditional organization theory: the problems and some research

Problems in logic. One criticism concerns the traditional organizational principle that states that administrative and organizational efficiency will be increased by increasing task specialization. This, as it is normally stated, cannot be implemented and tested in any practical sense. The reason is that there are many ways in which a job can be specialized and there is no way of knowing, from the principle alone, which basis for specialization to follow in a given instance. For example, let us assume that a firm which markets educational materials of various sorts decides to expand from the Midwest into the New York City metropolitan area. Let us further assume that, traditionally, the firm's salesmen have been specialized on the basis of type of educational materials sold (e.g., preschool, elementary school, high school). How should they specialize in the New York area? The same way? Perhaps, in an ethnically conscious city such as New York, it would be better to specialize in terms of the needs of New York's various groups (i.e., blacks, Puerto Ricans, Jews, and others). A third possibility might be to specialize along subject areas such as English, mathematics, and so forth. Other bases are, of course, possible, but the point is that the decision cannot be made on the basis of a theoretical principle which says that specialization of tasks is desirable but does not specify the dimensions along which specialization should occur.

A second principle of the traditional organization structure states that efficiency is increased by arranging the members of the organization in a hierarchy of authority. This, the critics argue, contradicts the logic of specialization since it does not allow a person to go anywhere in the organization for guidance except to his superior, even though his superior may have less technical expertise in the area than the subordinate. For instance, an accountant who works for a sales unit in a field office may be forced to accede to his superior in matters of accounting, even though he is far more competent in his specialty than his supervisor. The contradictory aspects of this principle are obvious in the modern-day organization that employs highly trained, specialized researchers whose competence in their areas far exceeds that of their administrative superiors. The difficulties involved here have posed serious problems leading, as we shall see later, to various organizational mechanisms that, in essence, repudiate the principle stated here.

Research on the relationship between organizational characteristics and work behavior. One of the characteristics of the traditional organizational model that has been of considerable interest is that individuals are encouraged to concern themselves with and identify with matters relating only to their own jobs. This, it has been predicted, leads to cognitive processes centering on one's own subgroups, high subgroup identification, and resulting differences across subgroups. At least two studies support this consequence of the traditional organizational model. Dearborn and Simon (1958) found that middle-level executives tended to perceive that the most significant problems facing their company were those relating to their own occupations, a set of findings generally replicated by one of my own studies (1963). In addition, I found that this effect was also true of lower-line supervisors and tended to show up as early as two years after they entered the organization. (It should be noted that one problem in interpreting these results is that perhaps the occupational identifications occurred before the people entered the organization, and they may have chosen the occupations because of such identifications. However, it is relatively easy to show that, for many people, identification with a different occupational group is not related to occupational choice. Thus, if this is an explanation, it is only a partial one [Korman, 1966a, 1967b].)

How negative are the implications for performance of this fragmentation toward the "parts"? What difference does it make? Considerable data point to the conclusion that the growth of homogeneous, permanently committed and classified subgroups of the type encouraged by the traditional organizational model, with the resulting within-group similarity and between-group differences, is debilitating both for organizational creativity and for the control of conflict.

In terms of creativity, there is evidence that such relatively homogeneous, similar-thinking groups are less capable of creative change and creative expression, as summarized in Table 6.1. It would seem that the basic factors of similarity of thinking and approach that appear to be antithetical to creativity do occur in precisely the kinds of subgroups encouraged by the traditional organizations. Why is this? The rather simple answer is that creativity involves a newness and a differ-

Table 6.1
Summary of Studies Relating Group Homogeneity to Group Creativity

BASIC FINDINGS	INVESTIGATORS
1. Groups that experience changes in membership are more creative than those that are stable.	Ziller, Behringer, and Goodchilds (1962)
2. Encouraging the expression of conflicting points of group members leads to higher-quality solutions.	Hoffman, Harburg, and Maier (1962)
3. Creative problem solving is enhanced when several solutions acquire possibilities and desirability.	Hoffman (1961)
4. Organizations that hire unusual types of people are more likely to be creative.	Steiner (1965)

ence of approach, things that are quite opposite from the conformity implicit in homogeneous groups.

As for conflict, it is obvious that the growth of such different groups within an organization would lead to conflict. That is, it would encourage a lack of reliance on overall company identification, a growth of a "we–they" orientation as opposed to an "us" system of thinking, and a lack of voluntary movement across departmental and subgroup lines due not only to a belief in differences between the groups but also to a trained-in inability to so move as well as to the growth of social norms, values, and perceptions legitimizing these differences. As Table 6.2 indicates, it is precisely these types of processes that encourage intergroup conflict (Schein, 1965). Furthermore, implicit in the development of specialized groups in the traditional organization is the assumption of permanency surrounding the creation of these specialized groups because of the job-specialization principle (Simon, 1957). To the extent that this is so, we are less likely to find appreciation, knowledge, and familiarity with the positions of others within the organization. The potential for intergroup conflict therefore increases.

Table 6.2
Summary of Studies Relating Group Characteristics to
Intergroup Conflict

BASIC FINDINGS	INVESTIGATORS
1. Discrimination is based partially on perceived differences from discriminated-against group.	Sanford (1956)
2. The more society legitimizes differences between two groups along various status dimensions and the more it says the two are different, the more likely that conflict will result between the two groups.	Lindgren (1969) McDavid and Hararri (1969) Triandis (1959)

Our conclusions, then, on the basis of this kind of evidence seems clear. Such an orientation toward the parts would lead to negative outcomes such as lower creativity and a greater likelihood of intergroup conflict.

Hierarchical vs. Self-Control

Perhaps one of the most crucial criticisms made of traditional organization theory is that even when individuals are oriented toward the success of the organization as a whole, the emphasis on dependency (i.e., the approval of superiors) which is so much part of the theory will result in significant motivational deficits in a variety of ways. First, dependency is inimical to creative expression. This is true because by definition, creativity is the development of new, socially useful ideas, and as such, it can be thought of of as an attack on the assumption of the traditional organizational model that the superior has greater technical competence. It is a challenge that is less likely to occur when the object of the challenge is someone on whom the potential challenger is dependent.

Hierarchical organizations may also inhit ,creativity because of their reliance on rules and following orders. Such behavior may come to be perceived as normal and expected by the organization members themselves, leading them to reject innovation and change as being inconsistent with the world as they know it.

Argyris (1964) has suggested some behavioral implications for creativity when one is in a dependent situation (see Figure 6.1). In developing this framework, Argyris makes the following points:

1. The traditional organization, with its emphasis on rules, hierarchical authority, specialization of interests, and requirements for external control by those high in the structure over those low in it will depress each of the following behaviors:
   a. risk taking and experimenting
   b. gathering new information
   c. trusting and having concern for others
   d. owning up to and taking responsibility for one's behaviors
2. This cluster of behaviors may be called "interpersonal competence," and its occurrence in an organization can be considered to be negatively related to the extent to which the organization subscribes to the traditional organization structure.

Much of Argyris's argument is consistent with the model I proposed in chapter three. In addition, there is another group of studies, which I have listed in Table 6.3, that support both theoretical suggestions. Relevant here also is the practice of most companies that are large and prosperous enough to have research departments of placing these departments outside the hierarchical authority system. Since people engaged in research are, by definition, creative, I would guess that such companies have learned that the traditional organization structure does not allow very well for creative expression. Supporting this line of reasoning also is that most organizations that have creativity as an explicit goal (e.g., universities and research institutes) are less hierarchical in nature than other kinds of organizations. It would seem justifiable to conclude, then, that there is an inhospitability in the traditional organization structure toward creativity, a weakness which is highly important in our dynamic, "future shock" society.

Table 6.3

Summary of Studies Relating Hierarchical Organization
Systems and Dependency Relationships to Creativity

BASIC FINDINGS	INVESTIGATORS
1. Groups that are less flexible are those with a predominant number of individuals who prefer hierarchical authority social systems.	Ziller (1958)
2. Individuals highly reliant on authority figures in their cognitive processes are less able to reject standard beliefs and develop new belief systems.	Fillenbaum and Jackman (1961)
3. Innovation in organizations is negatively related to the centralization of authority and the demand for hierarchical control.	Guetzkow (1965)
4. People dependent on authority sources for cognitive processing are more resistant to change.	Ehrlich and Lee (1969)
5. The longer people have worked in formal, hierarchical organizational systems, the lower their creativity.	Maier and Hoffman (1961)

A second problem with overall organizational demands for dependency and hierarchical authority is that these tend to discourage the growth of independent, mature, high self-esteem personalities and instead encourage passivity, dependency, and less self-perceived competence. Let me suggest that you look back at the discussion of McClelland's need-for-achievement research; you will see considerable similarity between the dependence on external control that McClelland views as leading to low need for achievement and the criticism I am making here of the traditional organizational model. Argyris, the author of the model outlined in Figure 6.1, has also developed a framework of relevance here in that (1) it points out the weaknesses inherent in hierarchical structures, (2) it specifies the mechanisms by which these difficulties occur, and (3) it predicts certain behavioral and attitudinal outcomes. Although this theory is two decades old, it has remained one of the most significant and innovative in the field. For this reason, it will be outlined here in some detail.

Proposition One There is a lack of congruency between the needs of healthy individuals and the demands of the traditional formal organization.

According to Argyris, if we want to design an organization, and we use the traditional formal principles of organization (traditional chain of command, task specialization, and so forth) to create it, and if, furthermore, we hire people who were relatively mature (were pre-

Figure 6.1
Model of how the values and implicit assumptions of the traditional
organization structure depress creative expression.

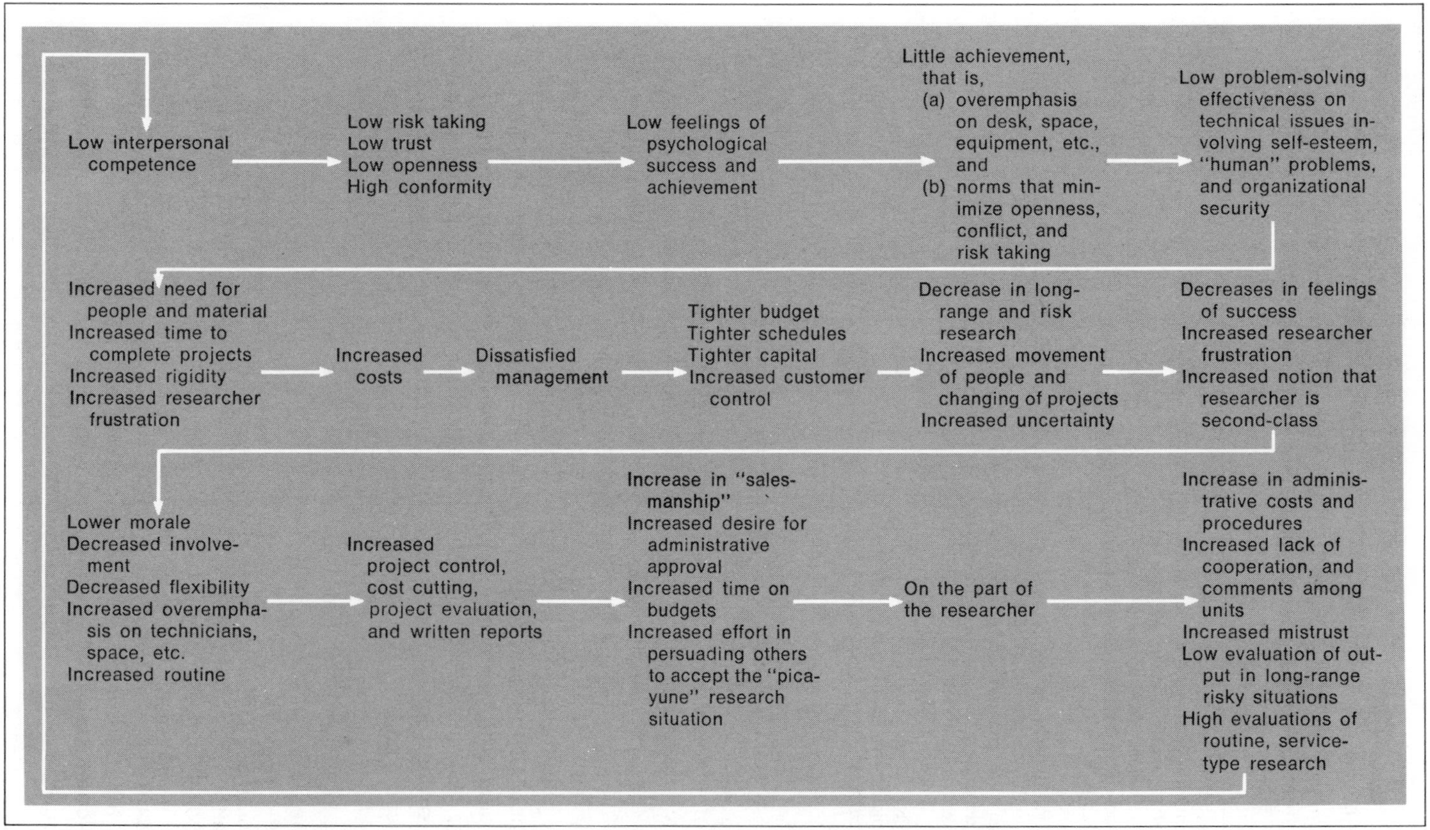

Source: Adapted from C. Argyris: *Organization and innovation.* Homewood, Ill.: Richard
D. Irwin, Inc., 1965, pp. 236–37.

disposed toward relative independence, were active, used their important abilities, liked to control their immediate work world, and the like), the result would be disturbance and dissatisfaction. The needs of mature individuals are not congruent with the requirements of the traditional formal organization, which requires that organizational members be dependent, passive, use few and unimportant abilities, and so on.

Proposition Two   The results of this disturbance are frustration, failure, short-time perspective, and conflict.

Basically, according to Argyris, the healthy organizational participant will experience frustration because his self-expression will be blocked; he will experience failure because he will not be permitted to define his own goals or the paths to these goals; he will experience short-time perspective because he will have no control over the stability and clarity of his future; and he will experience conflict because, as a a healthy agent, he will dislike frustration, failure, and short-time perspective.

Proposition Three   Under certain conditions, the degree of frustration, failure, short-time perspective, and conflict will tend to increase.

Those conditions that will increase the negative outcomes, Argyris argues, occur when the individuals involved have a higher level of maturity and when the environmental requirements for dependence, subordination, and passivity are greater. The latter is more likely to be the case as one goes down the chain of command, as directive leadership increases, and as management controls are increased.

Proposition Four   The nature of the formal principles of an organization causes the subordinates, at any given level, to experience competition, rivalry, and intersubordinate hostility, and to develop a focus toward the parts rather than the whole.

This occurs for several reasons, one being the degree of dependency that the subordinates have on the leader and another being that the number of positions above any given level in a pyramidal organization decreases as one moves up in the hierarchy. Thus, the subordinates aspiring to perform effectively and to advance will tend to find themselves in competition with, and being hostile toward, each other. A third reason stems from the organization's formal principles. Since the subordinates are directed toward and rewarded for performing their own task well, they tend to develop an orientation toward their own particular part of the organization rather than toward the whole. This increases their need for the leader, which, in turn, increases the subordinates' degree of dependence. A circular process is thus established whose impact is to maintain and/or increase the degree of dependency and the rivalry and competition for the leader's favor.

Proposition Five   Employees react to the formal organization by creating informal activities.

Among the reactions that can occur as a result of this situation, the following are among the most likely: (1) An employee may leave the organization, provided he thinks other organizations are different, or he may climb the organizational ladder, where the situation is not as bad. The viability of the latter alternative, however, depends on whether or not he has the necessary qualifications to climb. (2) He may manifest defense reactions, such as daydreaming, aggression, ambivalence, regression, and projection, and, in general, become apathetic and disinterested toward the organization, its makeup, and its goals. (3) If reaction 2 occurs, he may then create informal groups to sanction these negative reactions and give social support to them as the proper responses. He would then be more likely to formalize the informal groups and develop norms to perpetuate these behaviors, both among peers and among youth. This lack of interest and concern would then be passed on to youth as a significant cultural norm.

Proposition Six   The employees' adaptive behavior, constructive or not, maintains individual self-integration and simultaneously facilitates integration with the formal organization.

Proposition Seven   The adaptive behavior of the employees has a cumulative effect, feeds back into the formal organization, and reinforces itself.

According to Argyris:

All these adaptive reactions reinforce each other so that they not only have their individual impact on the system, but they also have a cumulative impact. Their total impact is to increase the degree of dependence, submissiveness, etc., and increase the resulting turnover, apathy, disinterest, etc. Thus, a feedback process exists where the adaptive mechanisms become self-maintaining.

The continual existence of these adaptive mechanisms tends to strengthen these norms which, in turn, act to maintain the adaptive behavior and to make it the proper behavior for the system. Therefore, employees who may desire to behave differently from the norms (e.g., rate busters) will tend to feel deviant, different, and not part of the work community.

The individual and cumulative impact of the defense mechanisms is to influence the output–input ratio in such a way that a greater input (energy, money, machines) will be required to maintain a constant output.

Proposition Eight Certain management reactions tend to increase the antagonisms underlying the adaptive behavior.

Most managements will tend to dislike the employees' adaptive behavior. However, those managements that base their judgments on the logic of the traditional hierarchical organization will tend to take corrective actions that will only reinforce the employees' maladaptive behavior even more, since such actions are the reasons that the employees adopted this behavior in the first place. Among these corrective actions are increasing the degree of directive leadership and increasing the degree of management controls.

One cannot fail to be impressed with the systematic logic, coherence, and parsimony of Argyris's critical framework. The major question is whether it is justified. I think so. Table 6.4 summarizes evidence from research studies that have tested various assumptions and pre-

Table 6.4

Summary of Studies Relating Hierarchical Organizational Systems, Dependency Relationships, and Their Derivations to Work Motivation

BASIC FINDINGS	INVESTIGATORS
1. Groups that increase their decision-making autonomy increase performance, but not as much as those in which hierarchical control experimentally increased.	Morse and Reimer (1956)
2. Those who have their jobs redesigned to decrease specialization and enlarge their responsibilities and authority increase their performance.	David and Valper (1968); *Business Week* (1969)
3. The more individuals feel they have control over their work activities, the higher their performance.	Bachman, Smith, and Slesinger (1966); Bucklow (1966); Tannenbaum and Kahn (1958); Smith and Brown (1964); Bowers (1964); Tannenbaum (1962)
4. Situations in which individuals appraise themselves result in less defensiveness and greater performance improvement than situations in which individuals are appraised solely by their superiors.	Bassett and Meyer (1968)
5. The more that is expected of individuals, in terms of goals expected or time allowed, the higher they will perform.	Berlew and Hall (1966); Stedry and Kay (1966); Aronson and Gerard (1966); Locke (1967); Korman (1970)
6. Participation in decision making and planning by those not used to it increases performance and productivity.	Farris (1969); Puckett (1958)

Table 6.4 (*cont.*)

BASIC FINDINGS	INVESTIGATORS
7. Choosing one's own work partners increases performance.	Van Zelst (1952)
8. The more individuals are allowed to choose their work activities, the higher they will perform on them.	Pallak, Brock, and Keisler (1967)
9. In a laboratory experiment, it was found that the higher the total amount of control of group members over decision making and the more equitable the control, the higher the groups' problem-solving performance and the higher the members' satisfaction.	Levine (1973)
10. Police cadet training emphasizing supervisory supportiveness and an opportunity to question and discuss orders with superiors results in more successful performance and attitude outcomes than a more traditional, hierarchical form of training.	Earle (1972)
11. The productivity of salesmen is positively correlated with their discretionary power over credit, delivery, price, and product functions. Satisfaction is related to the above and to high acceptance of salesmen's suggestions by the employer.	Pruden (1971)
12. Coercive leadership is negatively associated with the rehabilitation of prisoners.	Bigelow and Driscoll (1973)
13. Governments of a polyarchial form (i.e., democratic in nature) are more likely to be associated with a higher gross national product and a peaceful adjustment of disputes than those marked by closed hegemony types of governments (i.e., those authoritarian and denying representation to some).	Dahl (1970)
14. Managers who enter into interaction with others with an explicit intention to trust them (i.e., similar to allowing them to control their own fate) have more effective problem-solving groups than those who enter into interaction without explicit intent to trust others.	Zand (1973)
15. Organizations marked by decentralization of decision making and a relative lack of formal rules are more likely to be innovative than organizations not marked by these characteristics.	Aiken and Hage (1971)

dictions that are implied in the framework. These studies show that hierarchical control and dependency relationships are not consistent with high work motivation. In addition, other derivatives of the hierarchical control system, also included in Argyris's framework, are not facilitative of performance. The first of these other aspects is high job specialization, an explicit goal of the traditional model; and the second is low expectancy of competency. The latter seems to be justifiably classified as an assumption of the traditional model because of the demands for external control, rules, and specifications that seem to be so much a part of the model. It seems reasonable to assume that a system with this flavor is assuming a lack of trust in others and a belief in their incompetency. Hence, direct tests of the relationship between expectancy and performance do constitute relevant tests of the model, and the findings shown in Table 6.4 are, therefore, important. If you see my emphasis on these points as suggesting that Table 6.4 also supports the model I suggested in chapter three, you are right. Both my theory and the one proposed by Argyris are supported by these data.

Design of Work Groups

In addition to working within a general organization structure and policy system, most people usually spend at least part of their workday in a work group. While much of what we have said about organizational environments and how they should be structured is also applicable to the work group, there are certain unique aspects of the group that make it worthy of independent consideration. Size sometimes does make a difference. This is not because size has psychological properties in and of itself; rather, it is because it may lead to increased complexity and formalization, more rules, and greater feelings of being lost in a crowd (cf. Zimbardo's work). For these reasons and because groups are more amenable to manipulation and experimentation along such variables as size, communication patterns, and so forth, there is a wealth of data available from psychological laboratories and work environments on how groups might be structured in order to stimulate desired behavioral and attitudinal outcomes.

group size

There is a fairly consistent pattern of evidence accumulated over a period of years which suggests that although there are some exceptions, group size tends to be negatively related to performance (Porter and Lawler, 1965). However, decreasing the size of a unit can only be done up to a point since sufficient abilities and resources must be available to do the job. Perhaps the most appropriate conclusion is that there is an optimum number of individuals needed to perform a given job or task and increasing that number will lead to decreased performance.

Why is this so? Is it because of the deindividuation process that Zimbardo describes when he refers to the greater emotionality with increasing group size which leads to greater aggression and sexual behavior? Is it because the presence of too many others leads to greater anxiety and an increased fear of negative evaluation (cf. Zajonc, 1965)? Or is it a more cognitive explanation, such as the difficulties in coordinating a large number of individuals? The answers to these questions are important since if we knew them perhaps we could overcome some of these negative effects of size. Large groups are increasingly common in our society and while I think we can reduce them sometimes, we seem unable to do so universally. Thus, since we will have to learn how to live with large groups, I would like to learn how to make them better.

group homogeneity versus heterogeneity

Should groups be formed on the basis of similarity or heterogeneity of workers? The answer, as I indicated earlier depends on the difficulty and kinds of tasks involved. In creative tasks a heterogeneous group is better than a homogeneous one (Weist, Porter, and Ghiselli, 1961), whereas the reverse is probably true for repetitive tasks.

group communication structures

One area that has always greatly concerned psychologists interested in groups has been the implication for performance of different kinds of communication structures. A communication structure describes how information is distributed in a group. A single individual may be the "center of the stage" in that he receives and distributes most of the information relevant to the group purposes. This structure contrasts with that found in decentralized groups in which each individual receives information relative to the group purposes and distributes such information to the other members (see Figure 6.2). Since these communication structures are analogous to the organization structures we have described, in terms of their distribution of power and control, it supports some of our previous discussion to learn that many of the conclusions drawn from group communication structure research are similar to those we reached, as the following summary by Costello and Zalkind (1963) indicates:

> Highly centralized communications networks tend to (a) facilitate efficient performance of routine problem solving involving principally the assembling of information, (b) strengthen the leadership position of the member most central in the network (i.e., the one having the larger number of channels and the most information) and (c) result in a quickly stabilized set of interactions among members.
> Communications networks low on centralization (a) produce higher levels of satisfaction, (b) facilitate the handling of ambiguous and unpredictable situations, and (c) are more likely to be more responsive to creative and innovative solutions (p. 457).

Figure 6.2
Communication Patterns Used in Small-Group Experiments. (a) The circle: A decentralized network in which all members are equally "central." (b) The wheel: A centralized network in which position C is central and all others are peripheral. (c) The chain: A moderately centralized network in which positon C is central, positions B and D are intermediate, and positions A and E are peripheral.

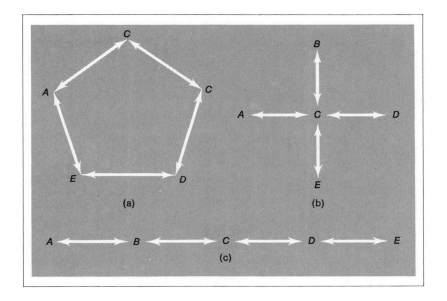

Source: From *Social psychology: A brief introduction,* by Joseph E. McGrath. Copyright ©1964 by Holt, Rinehart and Winston, Inc. Adapted and reprinted by permission of Holt, Rinehart and Winston, Inc.

The difference is that the small-group literature suggests efficient performance of routine tasks for centralized structures, whereas we have suggested a low overall performance for these authority systems. Perhaps one reason for this difference is that most small-group studies are not longitudinal in nature, a factor that is important because routine tasks may eventually encourage a person to develop low self-esteem (regardless of success). The process may be described by a statement such as, "I must be incompetent—look at what a lousy job I have." Later in this book there is a discussion on socialization processes in organizations which I think supports this explanation.

group characteristics and performance

In addition to these factors, there are a number of other findings relevant to group behavior that have important implications for understanding the conditions of their effectiveness and the kinds of effects they may have on their members. Some of these are summarized below:

1. Low-power group members spend time exhibiting deferential behavior to high-power individuals; such deferential behavior can serve to inhibit them from expressing points of disagreement where they may, in fact, be more competent.
2. Conformity to group norms, at the expense of individuality, seems to occur more in mixed-sex groups than in single-sex groups.
3. The physical characteristics of group settings seem to affect what takes place in them, e.g., persons interact more with those facing them than those sitting alongside them; concepts of personal space develop and are defended strongly; and personal status develops as a function of spatial position in the group.
4. In comparing group-versus-individual performance, most evidence is consistent with the following:
   a. Group judgments are better than individual judgments, on the average, on the kinds of tasks where particularly poor individual performances can be cancelled out by an average judgment.
   b. Groups usually produce more and better solutions to problems than individuals working alone, but groups take longer to reach their conclusions.
5. Groups may develop illusions of invulnerability that encourage excessive optimism and risk taking (Janis, 1973).
6. Group members may develop both individual and group behaviors aimed at censoring deviations from the perceived group consensus, even at the cost of minimizing their own doubts about the consensus (Janis, 1973).
7. The tendency of groups on both an individual and collective level to censor deviations from the norm generates the illusion of unanimity which, in turn, leads to even further conformity pressures (Janis, 1973).

Design of Jobs and Influences on Employee Behavior

After all is said and done, the one feature that all employees have in common is that each has a set of tasks to perform. For a long time interest in job characteristics as possible sources of influence on job behavior was not great, perhaps because of the pervasive social norm that what mattered on a job was not what one did, but what one got out of it. The more rewards (whatever these were), the better, and it did not really matter what you did to achieve them. This assumption was also encouraged by religious philosophies supporting the value of work in itself, by the general thrust of the labor union movement, and by a fairly strong value system that supported the idea of accepting one's duties in order to fit in with a greater overall social good (e.g., societal and/or organizational success). If this acceptance involved engaging in tasks that were not meaningful or exciting, then the problems that this led to could easily be made less significant by an appeal to common unity and goals and/or the payment of additional extrinsic values (e.g., money), or so it was believed.

I don't know if this historical tradition was ever as strong as I suggest here (e.g., even Adam Smith in *The Wealth of Nations* was concerned with the negative implications of repetitive, monotonous jobs), but even if it was, that's all over now. We live in an era in which headlines scream about dehumanized jobs—jobs that deaden the mind and the spirit, because they supposedly do not call for the best of human capabilities but the worst.

What are they talking about? Is the situation all that bad? What do we mean by a job that is dehumanized? Are the bad effects true for everybody or just for some? Who are the people for whom the effects are bad? Or good? Or for whom there are no effects at all? We will deal with these questions first by reviewing in some detail the various ways in which jobs can vary along the humanized–dehumanized dimension. Once we specify these dimensions, we will see a little more clearly what is generally meant by a humanized job in terms of specific behaviors.

differences between humanized and dehumanized jobs

There have been a number of suggestions as how best to conceptualize the differences between jobs. One set of dimensions that many investigators find particularly useful is listed below (Turner and Lawrence, 1965; Hackman and Lawler, 1971; Hackman and Oldham, 1974):

1. *Variety* The extent to which the employee performs a wide range of operations on the job
2. *Autonomy* The degree to which the person has an influence on the scheduling, planning, and performance of his work activities
3. *Task identity* The degree to which the job involves completing an entire piece of work which can clearly be identified as being the product of the job-holder
4. *Feedback* The extent to which the employees can learn how well they are doing as they are working
5. *Significance* The extent to which the job involves meaningful tasks
6. *Dealing with Others* The extent to which the job requires interaction with others (e.g., other employees, customers, etc.)
7. *Friendship Opportunities* The extent to which the job permits interaction with others and the establishment of informal relationships leading to friendships

To illustrate the significance of these dimensions as differentiators, consider how different jobs would score on them. A company president would probably score high on significance, variety, autonomy, and dealing with others, and somewhat lower on the other dimensions. A college professor who wrote a considerable amount might score high on all of these, with the possible exception of feedback as to his teaching. A waitress would score high on feedback and significantly lower on the other dimensions. An assembly-line worker would probably score low on all of these.

I am sure that you can think of many other examples that we could easily classify. The dimensions seem to be well defined and relatively clear in terms of the behaviors involved. The key question, though, is so what? Does it make a difference? The answer, with some exceptions that I want to talk about below, is generally yes. Jobs that are high on these dimensions (with the possible exception of numbers 6 and 7) generally lead to better outcomes in terms of both work behavior and worker satisfaction than do jobs that are low (cf. Hackman and Oldham, 1974; Ford, 1969; Hackman and Lawler, 1971; Blauner, 1964). Performance is higher (particularly work quality), work involvement is greater, absenteeism is lower, and job satisfaction is higher.

Now, however, comes another question: is this true for all jobs? Must the entire logic of job specialization and simplification be revised in the direction of job enlargement and enrichment by increasing the number and variety of tasks (horizontal job enrichment) and/or the degree of control over one's job (vertical job enrichment)? Or are there certain jobs, situations or employees for whom the traditional approach to job design should be maintained?

Two major types of contingency models have been formulated in response to this question. The first of these is a sociological argument which proposes that the significance of job characteristics is greater for those who are integrated into the work ethic than those who are not. An example of this is that if we assume that the breakdown of traditional societal values (such as the work ethic) has been greater in America's urban areas than in rural sections, it would be predicted that jobs involving greater variety, autonomy, and so forth would have greater positive effects for rural workers than for urban. The second hypothesis, which is probably not completely independent of the first, proposes more of a personality moderator to the effects of job enrichment. Actually, it is a contemporary version of the theoretical framework that deserves considerable historical credit for stimulating the breakthrough leading to the current concern with job design. Before we discuss this approach then, let us take a slight historical detour.

Herzberg's motivator-hygiene theory

You will recall that in the chapters on work motivation we devoted some attention to Maslow (1954) and his hierarchy-of-needs model. According to this framework, man is a need-oriented organism, with the needs arranged in a hierarchy from lowest to highest. The dynamic process is that a person looks to satisfy his lower needs first. Once these are satisfied, he looks for ways of fulfilling the higher needs, and so on up the ladder of needs. According to Maslow, the most basic of all needs are the physiological ones—food and drink. Then comes safety, which is the desire for protection from danger, threat, and deprivation. When a person feels psychologically comfortable and safe, the social needs become prepotent, to use Maslow's term. The social needs are belonging, association, acceptance by others, giving and receiving friendship, and love. Following the fulfillment of these needs, a person is oriented toward the ego needs for self-esteem, self-confidence, independence, achievement, competence, knowledge, status, recognition, and appreciation. Finally, a person seeks self-actualization, the desire for realizing one's potentials.

Some years ago, a psychologist named Frederick Herzberg proposed a theoretical model following from this line of thinking which led eventually to much of our concern with jobs today. According to Herzberg, these lower-level concerns are pretty much guaranteed and provided for in our society. As a result, he believed the following: (1) Having the lower needs satisfied will not lead to satisfaction since these are guaranteed by our society. The best feeling that such need fulfillment can lead to is job attitude neutrality. Not having such fulfillment will lead to dissatisfaction. (2) Therefore, being satisfied on a job is basically a function of having the higher-order needs (such as ego and self-actualization) satisfied since these are hard to get. For the same reason, not fulfilling these needs will not lead to job dissatisfaction, but rather to job attitude neutrality (Herzberg, Mausner, and Snyderman, 1959).

These considerations led Herzberg to propose what he called the two-factor theory of job satisfaction. This stated, in essence, that job satisfaction is a function of challenging, stimulating work activities or work content; these are called motivator factors. Job dissatisfaction is a function of environment, supervision, coworkers, and general job context; these are called hygiene factors. Furthermore, these are *not* opposite ends of a continuum, according to Herzberg, but can be visualized as in Figure 6.3. Because the theory implied that a) you should make jobs harder and more challenging, rather than easier, in order to be more satisfying, and because it also said that b) people, in order to be more satisfied, would work harder on harder jobs, there was a vast amount of research relating to its propositions, with some supporting but most rejecting them. To understand why there was such a refutation, one needs to go back to the original research on which the theory was based. In this study, the design was to ask samples of engineers and accountants to write stories of their

Figure 6.3
Outline of Herzberg's Job Satisfaction Model

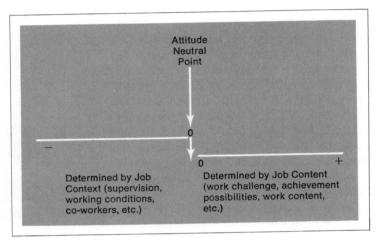

occupational histories under the following directions (Herzberg, Mausner, and Snyderman, 1959): First, they were asked to describe situations and occurrences in their work history that resulted in very high job satisfaction; second, they were asked to describe situations and occurrences in their work history that resulted in very low job satisfaction. When the incidents were coded and organized, the researchers found that in job satisfaction incidents the number of content factors was much higher than context factors, but the opposite was true for job dissatisfaction incidents. Sixty-five percent of the satisfaction incidents were content factors and twenty-five percent were from job context whereas the comparable figures for the dissatisfaction incidents were thirty-five percent for content factors and sixty-eight percent for context.

From these findings Herzberg was led to propose his two-factor theory, and it is from this same study that the controversy stems. Basically, the major difficulty has revolved around two criticisms of Herzberg's methodology: first, he used only a restricted sample of occupations; and second, his method of open-ended subjective reporting did not control for possible ego defense mechanisms. Thus, if you ask people, they might attribute good things to themselves (i.e., something they did in terms of job content and job activity that was challenging and interesting) and bad things to something else (i.e., job context factors such as superiors, coworkers, etc.).

As a result of these criticisms a wide variety of different studies were undertaken that attempted to see whether similar results could be obtained when these methodological weaknesses were not allowed to enter into the research design. The results of these studies are given in the following quotations from Dunnette, Campbell, and Hakel (1967):

> The evidence is clearcut. When employees are asked to recount some previous job event which for them was unusually satisfying or dissatisfying, they tend to mention job-content features in relation to the satisfying events and job-context features in relation to the dissatisfying events (p. 147). [When the same authors review those studies that do not have these methodological weaknesses, their conclusions are:] Results show that the Herzberg two-factor theory is a grossly oversimplified portrayal of the mechanism by which job satisfaction or dissatisfaction comes about. Satisfaction or dissatisfaction can reside in the job content, the job context, or both jointly. Moreover, certain job dimensions—notably Achievement, Responsibility, and Recognition—are more important for both satisfaction and dissatisfaction than certain other job dimensions—notably Working Conditions, Company Policies and Practices, and Security (p. 143).

These conclusions, based on the authors' own work as well as that of Ewen et al. (1966), among others, effectively laid the Herzberg theory to rest in terms of the degree to which it would be supported by well-designed studies.

recent research and theory on job characteristics

The point remained, however, that there was evidence from these studies that the motivators (in Herzberg's terms) were most important overall and the hygienes least important (cf. Dunnette, Campbell, and Hakel, 1967; Ewen et al., 1966).

One way to account for these findings has to do with the Protestant work ethic. There is reason to think that the subjects used in the Dunnette and Ewen studies, for example, were of the kind who were most likely to subscribe to white, middle-class, traditional work ethic norms. On the other hand, when other samples are used, different results are obtained (cf. Bloom and Barry, 1967).

Another explanation is that Herzberg erred by assuming that most, if not all, individuals are at the higher-order need levels. Thus, a more contemporary version of Herzberg's argument is that the complex, challenging, variable, autonomous job has the effects found by the Dunnette and Ewen studies, but only for those individuals who are operating at higher-order need levels. For those whose needs are at the lower-levels, the predicted positive effects of job enrichment would not occur. The appropriate research design, then, is to first measure people on their need levels. Once such measurement has taken place, the prediction as to the positive effects of the enriched jobs would be only for those whose currently potent needs are at the higher-order level.

Despite the apparent reasonableness of both the Protestant ethic and higher order – lower order need hypotheses, the evidence for each is mixed at best. In the first case, the argument has been used as an explanation by Turner and Lawrence (1965), Katzell, Barrett, and Parker (1961), and Blood and Hulin (1967) for the differing responses they obtained to different job characteristics. The problem, however, is that in all of these cases the explanations are post hoc in nature and none of them actually provide any data in their research to support their assumption that a difference exists between urban and rural individuals in acceptance of the Protestant ethic work norm. I, frankly, doubt the argument on several levels. Maybe there was such a difference in 1950 or even 1960 but in these days of jet planes, the influence of the "boob tube" and high levels of mobility, these differences, I believe, have just about been wiped out. (Those of you who have driven cross-country and who have tried to disentangle the unique characteristics of different communities from the commonality of the hamburger chains and the TV programs will know what I mean.) In addition, I also have doubts about this explanation on the basis of research. For example, one study that measured *directly* the effects of the degree of urban characteristics in one's life on achievement behavior among college professors and college students found few effects (Korman and Finkelman, 1974). In addition, there is another study by Wanous (1973) that also elicits doubt about the generality of *both* the urban–rural *and* higher–lower-order need models. In this study of 80 newly hired female telephone operators direct measures were obtained of urban-rural background, acceptance of the Protestant work ethic, and the potency of the different order needs. The results were as follows: (1) When job satisfaction was the criterion, the higher–lower-order need variable showed the predicted contingency effects, the Protestant work ethic showed the effect to a mild extent, and the urban–rural continuum showed few effects. (2) When job performance was the criterion, little effect of these variables could be demonstrated.

If we look at the results of the Wanous and Korman and Finkelman studies and add to it the weakness of the Maslow framework and the observation that even when results can be demonstrated in the predicted direction, they tend to be either inconclusive or only moderate (Hackman and Lawler, 1971), I would guess that the jury is still out as to where and how to put limitations on the desirability of job enrichment. Considering also the societal and organizationwide studies on this topic I am going to discuss later, these limitations may also be becoming increasingly narrow in scope.

Yet, I suspect that the limitations do exist, even if they have been hard to show consistently so far. Although I do not share his preference for using the Maslow hierarchical need system, I am in agreement with Hackman et al. (1974), whose approach I have outlined in Figure

6.4, that for any given individual at any point in life, a job can be too hard. Too-complex jobs can lead to "role overload," a variable that has come to be thought of as a source of stress in the organizational world.

Figure 6.4
Model of Effects of Job Enrichment

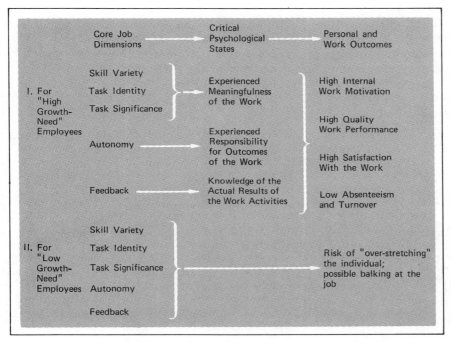

Source: Hackman et al., 1974

Management Policies and Practices as Influences on Work Behavior

Among the questions that have been intriguing an increasing number of people in the field of organizational behavior is the interest that has been developing in the behavioral implications of traditional management practices and policies. By traditional I mean basically those policies and practices that have developed on the basis of tradition and cultural norms and which now seem to be taken for granted as part of the folklore of management. Now people are beginning to question some of these practices and while there isn't very much data as yet, there is a lot of ferment and thought, as we will see.

the policy of promoting from within

The practice of promoting from within has traditionally been, in our society, almost a "mother," "God," and "apple pie" value. Most companies follow this both publicly and privately.

But should they? Are the effects of such a policy only positive? And if there are negative effects, how important are they when compared to the positive ones?

We have little research on these questions, but we do have some intriguing hypotheses by Campbell, Dunnette, Lawler, and Weick (1970). These researchers suggest that the negative outcomes may be more serious than we commonly imagine. A look at their hypotheses, as outlined in Figure 6.5, suggests that perhaps we have been assuming too much as to the value of this policy. It is also possible that the negative effects proposed by Campbell et al. would not occur and that the effects would be positive. These questions need to be researched.

Figure 6.5
Implications of Policy of Promotioning from Within

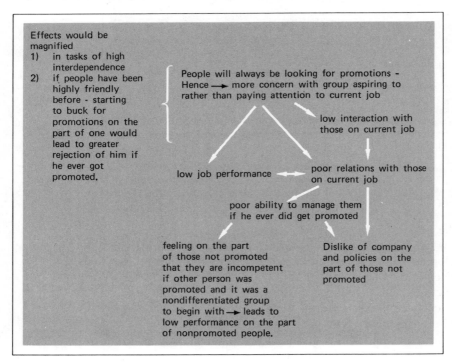

equating effectiveness with getting results

Almost equal to the promotion-from-within policy in terms of cultural support is the belief that we equate management (or any other kind of) effectiveness with getting results. But what does getting results mean? Very often, it is the bottom-line concept—how much production? How many units produced? How many units repaired?

Is this a useful approach? I shall have much to say about it later in this book when we talk about the concept of effectiveness and how we determine it. Right now, I want to refer to the implications of adopting this type of approach for classifying effective and ineffective performance. Again, little data can be cited. However, Campbell et al. (1970) have developed some interesting hypotheses here also, and I offer them in Figure 6.6 as, perhaps, a stimulant to those of you who are interested in doing research on organizational problems.

Figure 6.6
Implications of Equating Effectiveness with Getting Results

A "getting results" policy
may lead to:

a) Ignoring of means by which results are obtained -
   would lead to deterioration of social system
   which generates negative implications for long-
   term performance.

b) Over-emphasis on writing of progress reports -
   disrupts work flow and planning of work productivity
   in order to appear good →
   leads to inaccurate assessments of current state
   of system → poor future planning.

c) Emphasis on standards → tends to be set too
   low in order to decrease likelihood of failure.
   However, some people will still know they have
   failed → tends to lead to low self-esteem

                attribution of reasons for failure
                to external sources → leads to
                troubles with others

d) If unambiguous standards are not available,
   then personal standards develop for knowing
   whether "results" have been obtained → this
   leads to disagreements as to state of adequacy
   of system and problems in coordination.

days and hours of work and "flexitime"

Among the various changes in the world of work that have made the newspapers regularly in recent years, one that keeps popping up is the interest in working hours and days. Whether it is because of commutation problems, a greater desire than formerly for personal freedom of choice, technical demands, or some other reason, terms like the four-day week and "flexitime" have become common and a number of researchers and administrators have begun to concern themselves with whether management should move away from the five-day, fixed-hour patterns that have been prevalent for many years.

At first glance, there is really nothing wrong with a change of this nature. After all, we used to work six days and now we work five. Why can't we shorten the work week one day more? But the issue is a little more complicated than this. Let us assume that a company moves to a four-day week. How many hours a week should the employees work? If they still work eight hours a day, then they are only working thirty-two hours a week. Do they then get a decrease in weekly pay or do they get the same pay? If they do, will the total week's productivity be the same? If not, this is unfair to management and also inflationary. Suppose the employees work ten hours a day, four days a week, the more common pattern. Do they get overtime pay for the two hours a day above the regular eight hours? This is an additional cost that would eventually be passed on to the consumer. What about fatigue effects?

Carrying it a bit further, what does the employee do with the extra day off? Does he use it for leisure or for moonlighting? If the latter, what implications does this have for his performance on his main job? If he uses the day for leisure, do we have the type of social system that would allow increased leisure time? Or would the crowded highways and the crowded and expensive parks and recreational outlets turn it into a day of frustration?

Frankly, we do not know much about any of these implications. There are considerable data to support such positive effects of the four-day week as greater independence, feelings of self-worth, and a better marital life (Ivancevich, 1974; Glickman and Brown, 1973). However, we also know that this is not true for all people (Nord and Costigan, 1973; Goodale and Aagaard, 1974) and that negative effects on the home life and on business contacts with other companies have been reported. Interestingly enough, to cloud the issue further, there is good evidence to indicate that the disasters that were predicted for Great Britain when it had to go to a three-day week because of the energy crisis of early 1974 did not occur. For example, instead of the predicted 40% drop in productivity, the drop was actually between 10% and 20%. The reason seems to have been far greater labor productivity per hour than expected. Would higher productivity occur if the same time schedules were set up on a definitive basis by a British organization? There are little data to provide an answer.

Summary

Organizations are the mechanisms by which work activities are organized and structured in order to achieve mutually agreed upon goals. A concern of society since the beginning of collective activities has been how best to design these mechanisms in order to achieve desired outcomes. How should authority be structured? How should policies and practices be designed? How should work groups be organized? How should jobs be organized? These are the questions that have been of interest in this chapter.

Until recently the answers to all these questions were generally based on the principles that the best type of leadership is hierarchical authority and that job activities should be made simple, and more repetitive the lower the hierarchical level. Research in the last two decades has shown, however, that hierarchical leadership systems seem to generate lack of creativity, intergroup conflict, and lower performance and that highly simplified, repetitive jobs generate lower performance and lower job satisfaction. Perhaps the major exceptions to these statements are that there is some evidence from small-group studies that a hierarchical leadership system may work satisfactorily for simple, repetitive tasks in static environments and that there may be some people who prefer simple tasks to more difficult and challenging ones. The characteristics of these people have, however, been difficult to establish clearly. Finally, there is also some research data which indicate that while working in groups may have the advantage of bringing together greater input and diversity, it may also generate a dysfunctional conformity.

SUGGESTIONS FOR FURTHER READING

ARGYRIS, C. *Integrating the individual and the organization.* New York: Wiley, 1964.
Although over a decade old, this is still a highly relevant major theoretical statement by one of the most important critics of the

traditional organizational model. Argyris carries forward in a more comprehensive manner some of the arguments I have discussed in this chapter.

FILLEY, A. C. and HOUSE, R. J. *Managerial process and organizational behavior.* Glenview, Ill.: Scott, Foresman, 1969.
An excellent review of the degree of research support for the basic principles underlying the traditional organization leadership model discussed in this chapter.

FORD, R. N. *Motivation through the work itself.* New York: American Management Association, 1969.
An interesting case study of one of the most important of the job enrichment research and development programs undertaken at A.T. & T.

JANIS, I. *Victims of groupthink: A psychological study of foreign-policy decisions and fiascos.* Boston: Houghton-Mifflin, 1973.
A fascinating study of the processes of group decision making at the highest level of national affairs. The examination of the dysfunctional aspects of groupthink during the Kennedy administration's Bay of Pigs decision is of particular interest.

chapter seven

Leadership

Much of what I have had to say up to now has obvious implications for the nature and design of leadership activity in work organizations. Any time one conducts an experiment in work motivation or implements a change in policy, it is relevant to leadership effectiveness. In this chapter I will draw out some of these implications more clearly by examining the leadership process itself. In addition, other matters relevant to this area but not discussed yet will come under examination. More explicitly, our framework for discussion will stem from three perspectives.

    First, since leadership behavior in work organizations is, in part, a function of the behaviors specified for the formally defined leadership positions in that organization (by leadership positions is meant those roles in which the occupant is expected to direct the activities of another), we shall discuss the kinds of leadership behaviors that are implied by different structures and the implications of such role-behavior demands for effectiveness. Second, since leadership behavior is not just a function of the demands for behavior that some social system may make but is also a function of the type of individual involved (i.e., some people are more able to fulfill a leadership role and influence others toward some direction than others), a subject for discussion will be the kinds of personal characteristics and values that have been found to be associated with effective leadership behavior. Third, since leadership is an influence process, we will examine some of the conditions under which people accept influence from others.

Organizational Influences on Leader Behavior

An important aspect of the traditional model of organizations is the nature of the explicit role prescriptions it draws for the managers and leaders within the organization and the kinds of interpersonal relationships that it seems to demand. These expected behaviors of the traditional model were set forth by McGregor (1960) in a manner that caught the fancy and attention of managers all over the world. Labeled by him as Theory X, McGregor argued that these role prescriptions were as follows:

1. Management is responsible for organizing the elements of productive enterprise — money, materials, equipment, people — in the interest of economic ends.
2. With respect to people this is a process of directing their efforts, motivating them, controlling their actions, and modifying their behaviors to fit the needs of the organization.
3. Without this active intervention by management, people would be passive, even resistant, to organizational needs; they must, therefore, be persuaded, rewarded, punished, controlled; their activities must be directed.

These prescriptions for management, McGregor proposed, have as their basis the following assumptions about the nature of man:

1. The average person is by nature indolent; he works as little as possible.
2. He lacks ambition, dislikes responsibility, and prefers to be led.
3. He is inherently self-centered and indifferent to organizational needs.
4. He is resistant to change.
5. He is gullible, not very bright, the ready dupe of the charlatan and the demagogue.

These assumptions, McGregor argued, were not supported by research evidence. Rather, the support was for Theory Y, the assumptions of which are the following:

1. Management is responsible for organizing the elements of productive enterprise — money, materials, equipment, people — in the interest of economic ends.
2. People are not by nature passive or resistant to organizational needs but have become so as a result of experience in organizations.
3. The motivation, the potential for development, and the capacity for as-

suming responsibility toward organizational goals are all present in people. Management does not put them there.

4. The essential task of management is to arrange organizational conditions and methods of operation so that people can achieve their own goals best by directing their efforts toward organizational objectives.

It is obvious that McGregor's argument is similar to what we have been saying all along. The contrast is between the traditional, authoritarian strongman, the "I'll do the thinking around here" type of leadership with the democratic, participative, decision-making, self-controlling type of leadership *from the viewpoint of what makes for increased performance (rather than satisfaction)*. His argument is strongly for the democratic mode as being more in keeping with the research evidence. Since the traditional organizational structure implies the former kind of leadership, McGregor's arguments are very important if one is interested in developing a work environment that will maximize human performance. We need to examine, therefore, the kinds of evidence that exist in the psychological literature relevant to McGregor's arguments. We shall see that the evidence is indeed formidable and that it supports both McGregor's notions and the position we took in our discussion of organizational theory and the hierarchical structure.

One extensive series of research studies which are germane are those undertaken at the University of Michigan. Since we have already mentioned some of them in our discussion of the effects of hierarchy, we shall not review them all here but shall, instead, select only a sample for consideration. It should be noted, however, that the general trend of the Michigan studies shows that to the extent that a leader acts in a Theory Y manner (i.e., evaluates his subordinates highly and shows it by task assignments, and the like), the subordinate will internalize this evaluation into his self-concept and thus perform accordingly.

One series of studies performed by the Michigan group took place in the first decade after World War II and involved studying supervisory and managerial behavior at various large companies such as the Caterpillar Tractor Company, Detroit Edison, the Chesapeake and Ohio Railroad, and the Prudential Insurance Company. The method in all of these studies was similar. It involved determining from company records those work groups that were dissimilar in terms of performance and similar in other characteristics and then seeing how the supervisors differed from one another in their behavior toward their subordinates, as this was described by the subordinates. While these studies differed somewhat in detail, the results did not. All of them pointed to similar conclusions. These have been summarized by Miner (1963) as follows:

1. Supervisors who spend most of their time doing nonsupervisory tasks are likely to be less effective.
2. Delegating tasks to subordinates so that they may carry them out in their own way is facilitative of performance.
3. Having concern for the subordinate as a human being increases performance.
4. The effectiveness of the previous three characteristics as a determinant of performance will increase the more the supervisor has influence with his own superiors.
5. The supervisor must assume an active leadership role rather than a passive one.

Results 2 and 3 are most relevant here and can be considered to strongly support both of McGregor's notions and our earlier discussions. In fact, as a result of the consistency of these findings, one of the theoretical models that developed from the Michigan studies reads very much like Theory Y and is consistent with the research findings in work motivation and organization theory in general. This is the principle stated by Likert:

> The leadership and other processes of the organization must be such as to ensure a maximum probability that in all interactions and in all relationships within the organization, each member, in light of his background, values, desires, and expectations, will view the experience as supportive and one which builds and maintains his sense of personal worth and importance (Likert, 1961, p. 103).

Consistent with this principle and our earlier discussion on hierarchical control stemming from the Michigan research is the following theoretical principle stated by Tannenbaum, (1966) that increasing the amount of control in an organization by giving subordinates an opportunity to exert personal control over their job content and behaviors (as opposed to being subjected to external control by leaders and authority figures) will increase work motivation and organizational identification and will also lead to better communication and understanding. A number of studies support this contention quite well and therefore further support the general argument made here (cf. Bowers, 1964; Smith and Brown, 1964; Levine, 1973; Tannenbaum, 1962; Tannenbaum and Kahn, 1958). An example of the results of one of these studies is given in Table 7.1.

Just as in our discussion on overall organizational hierarchical control, support for these principles is not limited to studies at the University of Michigan or even to the United States by any means. A group from the Tavistock Institute has found in both Great Britain and India that work groups who are given control over their work processes and behavior are more likely to be effective performers, according to a variety of criteria, than those who are under traditional forms of organizational control (Bucklow, 1966; Trist et al., 1963). All in all, there seems to be considerable support for the implications for leadership behavior suggested by McGregor's ideas.

Table 7.1
Administrative Characteristics Correlated with Office Mean Criteria Scores (N = 36 Offices)

OFFICE MEAN RATINGS	CORRELATION WITH OFFICE PERFORMANCE
Control over office	
Exercised by office manager	.22
Exercised by salesmen	.39[a]
Total control	.39[a]
Interpersonal control	
Office manager's influence over salesmen	.35[a]
Salesmen's influence over office manager	.39[a]
Total interpersonal control	.41[a]

Source: J. Bachman, C. Smith, and J. Slesinger, Control, performance and satisfaction: An analysis of structural and individual effects; *Journal of Personality and Social Psychology,* 1966, *4,* 127–136. Copyright 1966 by the American Psychological Association, and reproduced by permission.
[a]Significant at the .05 level.

A problem remains, however, and it is a methodological one. Some, but not all, of the research we have cited here and earlier has been in the form of correlational studies. It is possible, therefore, that the tendency for Theory Y leadership to result in better performance may be due to the fact that the good performance affects the quality of the leadership rather than the other way around, or that both may be caused by a common third variable. What evidence do we have that the causal relationship is that Theory Y leadership leads to better performance rather than the other way around? Or are both true? The answer is probably the latter. While there is evidence that subordinate performance affects leader behavior (cf. Green, 1975), there are also experiments that support the interpretation I have given here that leadership variations may generate differences in performance if we interpret leadership in terms of the kinds of evaluations it makes of subordinates, the level of capability it expects of them, and so on. Among the experiments that support this conclusion are those by Dawson, Messe, and Phillips (1972), Levine (1973), Day and Hamblin (1964), Korman (1968a), and Solem (1958). As an illustration, in the Korman experiment subjects were presented with a series of tasks to be accomplished according to two different "sets." In the first case individuals were presented with a set of difficult goals and were told that these goals had been achieved by a group of individuals more select than they were. In the second case, the subjects were told that this other group was less select. The goals were the same in both instances, with the prediction being that individuals would perform as a function of the expectancies the experimenter had of them, even though the individuals had had no previous experience with the tests. Table 7.2 shows that this prediction was supported: those who were expected to be better than the groups that had previously achieved the goals achieved a higher score than those who were expected to be worse.

These results are in keeping with other research by Rosenthal and Jacobsen (1966) on implicit expectancies. It is fair, therefore, to conclude that leadership behavior of a nonhierarchical, Theory Y type does result in better kinds of performance outcomes. These data also provide support for the theoretical model I have proposed in that the findings show how organizational constraints on leadership behavior might be structured in order to increase performance. Thus, if the leader believes the employee to be competent and worthy of self-control, the result is an increased level of work motivation and work outcomes that reflect an increased self-evaluation.

Table 7.2

Performance as a Function of Explicit Interpersonal Expectation of the Experimenter

HIGH INTERPERSONAL EVALUATIONS		LOW INTERPERSONAL EVALUATIONS	
Number of Tasks	*Number of Individuals Who Achieved Goals for Given Number of Tasks*	*Number of Tasks*	*Number of Individuals Who Achieved Goals for Given Number of Tasks*
3	2	3	
2	6	2	3
1	16	1	8
0	21	0	20

Source: A. Korman, Self-esteem, social influence and task performance: Some tests of a theory. Paper presented at the American Psychological Association, San Francisco, 1968(a).

Characteristics of the Effective Leader

As indicated in the introduction to this chapter, an important dimension to research on leadership has been the study of the cognitive, motivational, and personality characteristics of effective performers in managerial roles in business and other work organizations. This interest reflects the traditional orientation of psychologists and many managers toward using the selection mechanism as the basic method for organizational improvement. Knowing the characteristics of effective leaders has obvious implications for the selection process and for training and development programs. For these reasons, the research we will discuss here has both theoretical and practical justification.

Two approaches will be considered. One has centered on the characteristics of the effective leader independent of different situational demands, whereas the second follows a contingency approach. The latter has involved the study of how the characteristics of the effective leader may vary according to specifiable environmental dimensions. In both cases the implicit assumption has not been that social expectations of leadership behavior are unimportant in understanding effective leadership, but that such an approach is incomplete at best. Even though one might arrange the environmental situation to be optimal for effective leadership, some people will not take advantage of the situation. Similarly, there are effective leaders even in conditions that are not conducive to good leadership. It is because of cases like these, and the fact that the necessary effective characteristics may vary according to other environmental dimensions, that some researchers have been concentrating on identifying and understanding the characteristics of the effective leader in industry.

One final point concerns the nature of the personal characteristics we will be examining. Basically, they are of two types. One of these consists of personal characteristics that are analogous to different types of social expectations. Leaders differ, for example, in authoritarian attitudes in the same way that organizational units differ from one another in the degree of their demand for authoritarian-type leadership. The reasons for different levels of effectiveness would then be due to processes similar to those we discussed earlier.

The second type of personal characteristics we will discuss are of a personal-trait nature. Those might be such characterisitcs as self-assurance, initiative, and intelligence. Why should these be related differentially to effectiveness as a leader? I would hypothesize that such traits may have their effects through such mechanisms as the following:

1. People with certain traits are more likely to engage in certain desirable leadership behaviors than those without these characterisitcs (these may or may not be analogous to social environmental demands).
2. People with certain traits are more likely to be accepted as leaders, even though their behavior does not differ from those who do not have these traits. Such acceptance is positively correlated with effectiveness.
3. A combination of both of the above.

As we go along we will, where appropriate, provide some explanation for research findings by referring to one of these mechanisms. Please be aware, however, that our suggestions will generally be post hoc and that we have little direct evidence that these mechanisms operate the way we say they do. It may be that future research will suggest other mechanisms besides the ones discussed. However, if the mechanisms do operate the way we say they do, this would be important both theoretically and practically since it would provide us with a mechanism for understanding why leaders are effective. This, in turn, would provide us with a useful tool for increasing the levels of leadership competence in situations in which such competence is lacking.

Ghiselli's Managerial Traits

If I were to pick the individual whose work has epitomized the appropriate way of developing a trait theory of managerial effectiveness, my first choice would be E. E. Ghiselli. His traits are carefully chosen, his methods of measurement are appropriately validated, and his inferences are linked closely to his data. As a result, his findings have been marked by continuing, significant results.

Ghiselli's work starts from the following assumptions: first, a number of trait characteristics are related to leadership effectiveness in formal task-oriented organizations; and second, the demands of an organization for leadership talent are common to all leadership positions but increase in importance the higher one goes in the organization. In his most recent work Ghiselli has studied eight personality and five motivational traits for their possible significance for management success. His traits and definitions are as follows:

PERSONALITY TRAITS

Intelligence: of a generally verbal and symbolic nature
Initiative: the willingness to strike off in new directions
Supervisory ability: the ability to direct others
Self-assurance: the favorability of self-evaluation
Affinity for the working class
Decisiveness
Masculinity–feminity
Maturity: conformance to age norms

MOTIVATIONAL TRAITS

Need for occupational achievement
Need for self-actualization
Need for power over others
Need for high financial reward
Need for job security

Ghiselli argues that a true managerial trait is one that relates more to management success than to supervisory and worker success; that is, there should be more of a relationship between scores on a managerial trait and success on a managerial job than on a nonmanagerial job. Within this framework, he has ascertained the usefulness of each of these traits (c.f. Ghiselli, 1963, 1971) for managerial success. Table 7.3 summarizes these findings.

Table 7.3
The Relative Importance of Thirteen Personal Traits to Managerial Talent

Very important in managerial talent	100	Supervisory ability
	76	Occupational achievement
	64	Intelligence Self-actualization
	61	Self-assurance Decisiveness
	54	Lack of need for security
	47	Working class affinity
	34	Initiative
	20	Lack of need for high financial reward
	10	Need for power over others
Plays no part in managerial talent	5	Maturity
	0	Masculinity–femininity

Source: E. E. Ghiselli, *Explorations in management talent* (Pacific Palisades, Cal.: Goodyear, 1971).

An examination of this table suggests some interesting conclusions, although these must be tempered by the fact that the traits are not independent of one another. First, cognitive characteristics are important for management success in addition to motivation (cf. the high scores for cognitively oriented supervisory ability and intelligence, which he measures in a complex behavioral sense rather than in the traditional academic way). Second, there is little support here for the hierarchical, "power over others" oriented leader as being more successful. Theory Y seems to be upheld. Also strongly supported is the importance of self-confidence in management success. Finally, the security-oriented person, content to rest on the directives of others, is not the individual who becomes a successful manager.

How supportive are other researchers of Ghiselli's work? Considerable evidence suggests that Ghiselli is on the right track. Dunnette (1967) has reviewed test research that pictures the successful executive as dominant, self-confident, and assertive, with high aspiration and a general life pattern of successful endeavor. Similarly, Nash (1965) has found that effective managers have highly verbal persuasive skills. Finally, in a study of several thousand middle- and higher-level executives, Korman, Noon, and Ryan (1975) found cognitive skills and respect for subordinates to be most highly predictive of success.

There are, in addition, two indirect lines of support. First, Ghiselli's self-assurance variable has been found to be correlated with performance by different investigators (cf. Korman, 1968c). Second, both self-assurance and self-perceived occupational level have been found to be positively related at a moderate level (average $r = .32$) with another personality measure, the Miner Sentence Completion Scale (Korman, 1965), found to be positively related to leadership behavior in some work organizations. The latter scale stems from the power-motive hypothesis we discussed earlier and which Miner has proposed as predicting leadership success in hierarchically organized, relatively authoritarian organizations of at least some size.

A Contingency Approach: The Fiedler Model

Until now we have been talking about general theories or orientations to leadership. Is this approach better than that one? Is this type of person a better leader than that one? For some of you, this discussion has, I would guess, been a problem because there may have been a nagging question that bothered you during this process. Doesn't the answer to these questions depend on the situation? At one level of analysis the answer to this has to be yes. No person would seriously propose any theoretical model to be applicable at all times to all people. Limits to the generality of one's proposals always need to be set. In the area of leadership theory there is no question that at some point in the spectrum a general proposal that has been found valuable for a number of situations will begin to break down. For example, I think that most of the data clearly favor a democratic, participative mode of leadership in today's work settings, regardless of the criterion being used. Yet, it would strike me as clearly dysfunctional for any sergeant to take a vote among his men as to how best to handle a squad of enemy soldiers advancing from 100 yards away with guns firing. Clearly, in some situations requiring quick decision making, the democratic, participative leadership mode might be dysfunctional.

This illustration, however, points up a question that has become a matter of considerable controversy. This problem concerns the point at which we begin to look at the "it all depends" limitation. Do we begin by building in the exceptions to the generalization first, right from the beginning? Or do we first see how far a generalization will take us and bring in the constraints and limitations only when they become necessary? There is the argument that since you have to do it eventually, you should build in the limitation at the start, and in this way you can understand and control the phenomena better from the beginning. At first glance, this makes a great deal of sense and there are a number of leadership theorists who have adopted this position. However, since the contingency approach has many unseen pitfalls of a methodological, philosophical, and measurement nature which I will discuss later, I must confess that my bias is in the opposite direction. I lean toward taking a particular style or approach to leadership as far as it will go and then bringing in the situational constraint, or contingency, only when it becomes necessary.

Since until now we have been talking mostly about those researchers who have used the general approach, it has not really been necessary to discuss these matters. However, as we continue our discussion into other theorists' work and other research on leadership, we will find these questions relevant.

Historically, the term *contingency* in leadership theory really became associated first with Fiedler's (1967) research. Over a period of two decades his work has consisted of empirical research of both an experimental and a correlational nature and has also involved continued testing and restructuring of his theoretical framework, the results of which are shown in Figure 7.1. Basically, Fiedler argues that environments can be ordered according to their degree of favorability for the leader and necessary leadership characteristics vary according to this degree of favorability. The favorability of an environment for a leader, according to Fiedler, is a function of three characteristics: (1) leader–member relations, (2) the task structure, and (3) the degree to which the leader has formally defined organizationally supported power. The higher each of these is (i.e., the more pleasant the relations, the more structured the task, and the greater the power), the more favorable the environment, or so Fiedler assumes. Once environments are classified along these dimensions, desirable leader characteristics vary, with this behavior being conceptualized for Fiedler along a dimension ranging from permissiveness at one end to strong control at the other. Thus, for those environments in which the degree of favorability is very high or very low, the best leader behaviors are "high control of others and activity" whereas for those environments in which the degree of favorability is moderate, the best leader behavior is "permissiveness."

These statements by Fiedler are empirically based ones resulting from a large number of studies, some of which are summarized in Figure 7.1, a figure which supports these claims since the claims are based on them. The procedure for Fiedler's studies, in essence, has been first to classify leaders according to their degree of permissiveness, then to evaluate the environments, and then to correlate the relationships between the leaders' scores on permissiveness and group task success. The measure of permissiveness used is called the LPC score, or the least preferred coworker score, and it consists of the degree to which the leader uses favorable adjectives in describing the least preferred coworkers. The greater the number of favorable adjectives used, the greater the degree of permissiveness, or so Fiedler assumes.

The real mark of a good theory, though, is not how well it accounts for the studies on which it was originally developed. Obviously,

Figure 7.1
Correlations between Leader's Least Preferred Coworker (LPC) Scores and Group Effectiveness According to Different Environments

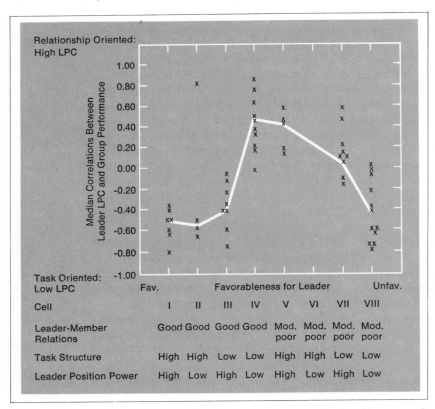

Source: Adapted from F. E. Fiedler, The effect of leadership and cultural heterogeneity on group performance: A test of the contingency model, *Journal of Experimental Social Psychology*, 1966, *2*, 237–264.

this support is strong or the theory would have never been developed. The key question is in how much or how well the theory can generate accurate predictions about behavior in new studies. Unfortunately, Fiedler's arguments have not held up too well when this criterion has been applied. A few years ago, Graen and his coworkers reviewed the research published subsequently to the development of Fiedler's model and found that these later studies did not support his theory at all. Table 7.4 summarizes the findings of their work and one can certainly see a difference between the results of the antecedent studies, the research on which the theory was developed, and the evidential studies, those studies which the theory stimulated.

Table 7.4
Summary of Graen's Review of Consequential Evidence for the Fiedler Model

	CELL							
	I	*II*	*III*	*IV*	*V*	*VI*	*VII*	*VIII*
Means								
Antecedent	$-.54$	$-.60$	$-.17$	.50	.41	—	.15	$-.47$
Evidential	$-.16$	.08	$-.12$	.04	.09	$-.21$	.15	.08
$t =$	$-1.83*$	$-2.44*$	$-.19$	$2.02*$	$2.56*$		.00	$-2.81**$
Number of studies								
Antecedent	8	3	12	10	6	0	12	12
Evidential	12	13	9	8	11	13	9	8

*The difference between these correlations is significant at the .10 level.

**The difference between these correlations is significant at the .05 level.

Since the publication of Graen's work the controversy has raged. Some writers publish papers showing lack of support for Fiedler's framework and others find that the predictions are useful. I don't think we need to review each of these studies here. There are a large number of them, some clearly relevant and some that may be more tangential, and the only pattern which has emerged is these mixed findings. Despite this ambiguity, I do think some general comments about the current state of Fiedler's theory can be made. First, the fact that the predictions are verified, sometimes, suggests that some meaningful phenomenon exists. However, this does not necessarily justify calling it a theory. A theory suggests explanations for why certain phenomena occur, and it proposes certain processes as causal. Fiedler, I do not think, has dealt with this question very well. Why should the same leadership behavior work equally well in favorable and unfavorable situations? I do not believe that this question has been sufficiently answered. Fiedler may have an empirical generalization, but not a theory.

Second, even if an empirical generalization is all Fiedler has, it could be useful, at least administratively. Yet, there are several problems here. First, there is the mixed evidence as to its predictions. Whatever the other problems, this is the most serious since if a theory (or empirical generalization) cannot predict behavior, there is little else that we care about it. Second, there are some real questions concerning the relevancy of Fiedler's task environments to organizational concerns. In fact, these task settings may contain some mutually contradictory aspects. For example, in Figure 7.1, how can a leader describe other employees in a negative fashion (i.e., low LPC) and still have a good relationship with them? Is it meaningful to think of an organizational environment in any permanent sense when relationships are poor, tasks are unstructured, and there is no formal legitimate power (Cell VIII)? Could a low LPC be effective in such an environment? Could the environment even survive?

Finally, there are a number of logic problems with a contingency approach that need to be kept in mind. One of these problems is that the approach normally is a static one that involves the fitting together of two parts. It does not take into account that part A (the environment) may affect part B (the person) over time and that such effects may vary depending on the characteristics of the particular part B. Such dynamic characteristics are not part of the approach, although they are part of organizational behavior. A second problem with a contingency approach is that you have to know beforehand what the values of the contingency variable are at which you change the type of leadership behavior that is most appropriate. Otherwise, you may change from permissive to controlling at the wrong point. But how do you know the point? When does more favorable change to medium favorable? When does high position power change to low position power? Unless you know this before you attempt to apply the theory either theoretically or administratively, serious misapplication is likely. But how do you know this? You need accurate measures of each contingency variable with high construct validity (see chapter ten) and you need to know how the meaningfulness of the measure changes in different contexts (e.g., a score signifying high position power in one context may not in another). Clearly, the complexity here is great, but complexity is what is involved in all contingency theories, not just Fiedler's (Korman, 1973a). This is one of the reasons why I would rather see an approach to leadership in which a style or an orientation is taken as far as it can go before we begin to bring in contingency factors.

Before continuing, I want to note that Fiedler and his coworkers are beginning to deal with a few of these problems. They have suggested, for example, that the measure of leadership characteristics they have been using may be a measure of cognitive complexity rather than degree of permissiveness toward subordinates (Mitchell, Biglan, Oncken, and Fiedler,

1970), although the evidence for this contention is mixed. They have also pointed out the necessity for better, more rigorous measures of the contingency variables (i.e., leader–member relations, task structure, and position power). In addition, they have pointed to the need for investigating whether the significance of peer relations on positive affect is as great as leader–member relations, and whether the theory should incorporate such a measure. However, if this addition should be made, how would each set of relations be weighted and how should the other contingency variables be assessed? They suggest that these are also relevant questions in measuring overall situational favorability.

I think that important as these considerations are, some of the more basic methodological questions I mentioned earlier will still remain, even if these attempts at revision prove successful.

An Alternative Contingency Approach: Consideration and Initiating Structure

An approach to the study of leadership which began by first conceptualizing dimensions of leadership behavior, ascertaining their significance, and then bringing in contingency factors only when needed stems from a research program that started at Ohio State University during the decade following World War II. It has had two major goals. One is identify the smallest number of dimensions that would adequately describe leader behavior, as viewed by the subordinates' perceptions of the leader's characteristic behavior and as the leader describes his own attitudes toward his job. The second aim is to see how leader variation on these dimensions is related to effectiveness and whether these relationships vary according to the situation, or contingency.

The first goal has been achieved by using extensive statistical analyses of questionnaire data. Two leadership dimensions have been isolated in various separate subordinate and leader self-description studies, and these turned out to be identical across the two cases and, also, across different European cultures (cf. Tscheulin, 1973). The names given them, and their definitions, are as follows:

Initiating structure (IS)   Reflects the extent to which an individual is likely to define and structure his role and those of his subordinates toward goal attainment. A high score on this dimension characterizes individuals who play an active role in directing group activities through planning, communicating information, scheduling, trying out new ideas, etc.

Consideration (C)   Reflects the extent to which the individual is likely to have job relationships characterized by mutual trust, respect for subordinates' ideas, and consideration of their feelings. A high score is indicative of a climate of good rapport and two-way communication.

A low score indicates that the supervisor is likely to be impersonal in his relations with group members.

Achieving the second goal has been somewhat more difficult. A decade ago, according to a review made of the literature in this area (Korman, 1966b), consistently low correlations were found in most cases for both IS and C with performance and high correlations for C with job satisfaction.

How does the situation look now? It is the same to some extent, but there are a few differences worth noting. What has not changed is the significance of considerate leadership for job satisfaction. In a recent study of 489 male employees of a large manufacturing company, Badin (1974) found a consistently high positive correlation between these two variables for situations differing in size, tenure, position power, and task structure. However, the relationship of consideration to performance and the relationship of the IS variable to both performance and satisfaction were all moderated by contingency factors. Fleishman (1973) has also pointed out the continued general significance of consideration for generating positive feelings in job situations.

Outside of this general consideration–satisfaction relationship, consistent positive findings continue to be hard to come by and contingency relationships are beginning to be explored. Although many of these explorations are still highly tentative in nature, some of this more recent work may be worth reviewing in order to indicate the nature of the more recent findings in this area. Thus, some, but not very much, evidence exists for each of the following:

1. There is some indication that those who are high on *both* C and IS are high on criterion variables (Fleishman, 1973). If a choice is to be made, it is better for a leader to have high C than high IS, since IS is positively correlated with criteria under the contingency of high C but the reverse is not true (Fleishman and Harris 1962).
2. IS may be either more beneficial or less detrimental when the needs of the employee for structure are great than when they are not great. Badin (1974) found that IS was less detrimental for groups of large size than for groups of small size.
3. Under high pressure for production, IS tends to be positively correlated with productivity and C tends to be negatively correlated with this criterion. When the pressure is low, the correlations lose their significance.

In addition to these conclusions, Kerr, Schresheim, Murphy, and Stogdill (1974) have suggested some other propositions for which there is some evidence, although much more is needed. Among these are the following:

1. The greater the congruence between subordinate expectations of leader C and IS and their observations of these behaviors, the greater will be the satisfaction and performance of subordinates.

2. The greater the upward influence of the supervisor, the more positive the relationship between C and subordinate satisfaction. This relationship will be greater for subordinates who are more dependent on their supervisor for satisfaction, freedom, and psysical and financial resources.

3. The more support shown by higher management for the C leadership style, the greater the positive relationship between C and subordinate satisfaction.

4. The greater the stress (and job ambiguity), the greater the subordinate acceptance of leader IS and the greater the positive relationship between IS and satisfaction and performance criteria.

5. The greater the intrinsic satisfaction provided by the job, the less positive the relationships between C and satisfaction and performance.

6. The greater the intrinsic satisfaction provided by the job, the less negative the relationships between IS and satisfaction and the less positive the relationship between IS and performance.

I think if one looks at these propositions, the prospects are intriguing for eventually clarifying some of the conditions under which C and IS as leadership dimensions are significant influences on organizational outcomes. Yet, I have considerable doubt that contingency approaches like these, useful as they may be, are the only mechanisms to use in studying leadership at the current state of our knowledge, both for the reasons I mentioned earlier and because of one other problem I want to deal with now.

Basically, the dilemma starts from the point that if IS is of value for individuals who work in large groups and of negative value for those who work in small groups, what leadership behavior do we encourage for those in middle-size groups or those who work in no groups at all? The problem is that as soon as you limit the value of a specific type of leadership behavior to a specific type of situation, you automatically exclude other situations from your concern. Your theory has nothing to say about them, either theoretically or administratively. What, then, do you tell the manager looking for help (Korman and Tanofsky, 1975)? The problem is not easy to solve unless you try to develop general statements of desired leadership behavior, as well as those limited to contingencies.

Recent Research in Leadership and Integrating Proposals

This section concerns a number of questions generated by my positive conclusions on the optimal effects of democratic leadership. First, it is legitimate to inquire about possible contingency variables affecting my statements. I suggested one possible contingency in the Army combat case, but some of you might feel that there are others of a more general nature. As a matter of fact, if you feel that way, you are not alone. A number of researchers in this field agree with you. Since these contingency models do exist, I want to give an illustration of one, its degree of empirical and logical support, and some of the questions that can legitimately be raised about it.

A second question that will be dealt with here concerns the relative independence of the democratic–authoritarian grouping and the consideration–initiating structure pair. Do they warrant the separate treatment given them here? Or are they two different ways of conceptualizing the same thing? Obviously, I think they are different and I will try to show this later. In addition, I will also review a recent promising approach to integrating both pairs into one leadership scheme that was developed by Yukl (1971).

Third, I want to describe other dimensions of leadership behavior besides those we have discussed so far and finally, I want to examine the conditions under which we will accept leadership from others.

contingency models of authoritarian–democratic leadership

It is not hard to find writers who have made careful, systematic attempts to delineate in a specific manner the different parameters of authoritarian and democratic leadership. Table 7.5 lists a number of these. We can see that although the writers have used different phrases and terms and somewhat different emphases, the correspondence among them is sizeable.

The description of different types of leadership does not, however, make a contingency theory; one needs to propose a set of conditions under which one of these types of leadership would work better than the other and another set of conditions under which a different type of leadership would be optimal. (My illustration of the condition of Army combat is a very narrow example of a contingency theory.) One of the most significant recent examples of such a theory is by Vroom and Yetton (1973). Their approach consists of a set of eight questions for the leader (manager) to ask himself in deciding what type of leadership style to adopt and it is on the basis of the pattern of responses to these questions that the decision is made. Table 7.6 and Figure 7.2 need to be read together in understanding this model. Table 7.6 lists the different kinds of behaviors (or decision-making procedures) a leader may follow, whereas Figure 7.2 indicates the types of diagnostic questions for him to utilize. On the basis of the pattern of responses to these questions, certain types of decision-making behaviors are recommended, that is, those on the right-hand side of Figure 7.2. These, of course, correspond to the behaviors described in Table 7.6. Operationally, Figure 7.2 may be utilized as follows:

Table 7.5

Correspondence between Different Approaches to Authoritarian and Democratic Leadership

LEWIN, LIPPITT, AND WHITE (1939)	MAIER (1953)	TANNENBAUM AND SCHMIDT (1958)	HELLER AND YUKL (1969)	LIKERT (1967)
Autocratic leadership	Autocratic management	Manager makes decisions and announces it / Manager sells decision / Manager presents ideas and invites questions	Own decision with detailed explanation / Own decision without detailed explanation	Exploitive authoritative (System 1) / Benevolent authoritative (System 2)
	Consultative management	Manager presents tentative decision, subject to change / Manager presents problem, gets suggestions, makes decision	Prior consultation with subordinates	Consultative (System 3)
Democratic leadership	Group discussion	Manager defines limits, asks group to make decision / Manager permits group to make decisions within prescribed limits	Joint decision making with subordinates	Participative Group (System 4)
Laissez-faire leadership			Delegation of decision to subordinates	

Reprinted from *Leadership and Decision Making* by Vroom & Yetton by permission of University of Pittsburgh Press. © 1973 by the University of Pittsburgh Press.

Figure 7.2
Decision Process Flow Chart for Both Individual
and Group Problems

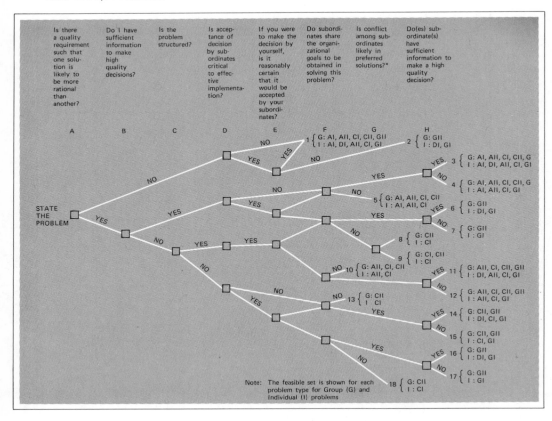

Note: The feasible set is shown for each problem type for group (G) and individual (I) problems.

Reprinted from *Leadership and Decision Making* by Vroom & Yetton by permission of the University of Pittsburgh Press. © 1973 by the University of Pittsburgh Press.

1. There are 18 types of leadership decision-making contexts identified (see the right-hand side of the flow chart).

2. Each of these contexts is defined by a different pattern of responses to the eight diagnostic questions; however, these patterns are not unique, that is, each context may be defined by more than one pattern. For example, decision-making context 1 may be defined by no's to questions A and D *or* by a no to question A and a yes to questions D and E; decision-making context 8 may be defined by yes's to questions A, B, D, and E and a no to F *or* by a yes to A, a no to B, a yes to C, D, and E, and a no to F. Differing patterns can be traced back for each problem situation.

3. For each of these contexts it is predicted that there is a set of feasible leadership approaches, which, if used, would result in more satisfactory outcomes than other leadership approaches; these are indicated by appropriate designations in Figure 7.2, with each designation corresponding to the set of behaviors listed in Table 7.6.

Table 7.6
Decision Methods for Group and Individual Problems*

GROUP PROBLEMS	INDIVIDUAL PROBLEMS
AI: You solve the problem or make the decision yourself using information available to you at the time.	AI: You solve the problem or make the decision yourself, using information available to you at the time.
AII: You obtain the necessary information from the subordinates, then decide on the solution to the problem yourself. You may or may not tell the subordinates what the problem is in getting the information from them. The role played by your subordinates in making the decision is clearly one of providing the necessary information to you rather than generating or evaluating alternative solutions.	AII: You obtain the necessary information from the subordinate, then decide on the solution to the problem yourself. You may or may not tell the subordinate what the problem is in getting the information from him. The role played by the subordinate in making the decision is clearly one of providing the necessary information to you rather than generating or evaluating alternative solutions.
CI: You share the problem with the relevant subordinates individually, getting their ideas and suggestions without bringing them together as a group. Then you make the decision, which may or may not reflect your subordinates' influence.	CI: You share the problem with the subordinate, getting his ideas and suggestions. Then you make the decision, which may or may not reflect your subordinates' influence.
CII: You share the problem with your subordinates as a group, collectively obtaining their ideas and suggestions. Then, you make the decision, which may or may not reflect your subordinates' influence.	GI: You share the problem with your subordinate and together you analyze the problem and arrive at a mutually agreeable solution.
GII: You share the problem with your subordinates as a group. Together you generate and evaluate alternatives and attempt to reach agreement on a solution.	DI: You delegate the problem to your subordinate, providing him with any relevant information that you possess, and giving him responsibility for solving the problem by himself. You may or may not request him to tell you what solution he has reached.

*Please note that Table 7.6 and Figure 7.2 are to be read together and that each of the methods described here refers to a decision-making approach which is proposed as appropriate for a specific type of answer pattern to the questions which a leader should ask in a specific situation and which are listed along the top of Figure 7.2. To illustrate, Decision Methods A I, A II, C I, C II, and G II are appropriate leadership behavior, if the leader can answer "No" to question A, "Yes" to D and E, and it is a group problem. On the other hand, if the answer to E is "No," only Decision Method G II is appropriate.

Basically, this is a proposed authoritarian–democratic dichotomy. The premise is that the less the situation calls for the skills and cooperation of the subordinates, the more authoritarian leadership is appropriate and, conversely, the more the situation calls for such skills and cooperation, the more democratic leadership is warranted.

Logically, this makes sense. Yet, I have doubts. For example, Vroom and Yetton report insignificant findings in the empirical test they made of these proposals. The original development of this model is based on their reading of the research literature, as they interpret it, but this is antecedent evidence, not consequent, and, as we saw in Fiedler's research, antecedent evidence can be misleading. The fact that Vroom and Yetton were unable to find support in the consequent test they made is, I think, important. Another problem is that we have to be mindful of the longitudinal implications of different leadership styles. It is quite likely that a contingency model of the kind proposed here might be supported in the short-run but not in a longitudinal study in which the long-range effects of an authoritarian mode of leadership may be negative implications for the individual's self-esteem, aspiration levels, and the like. It is because this occurs, and I will discuss the research evidence for this in a later chapter, that I think you get both the strong evidence for the democratic power-sharing mode of leadership, which I discussed earlier, along with the possible short-range usefulness of the authoritarian mode, the combined findings of which lead to the development of a contingency model of this type. In fact, Vroom and Yetton themselves discuss this limitation on the usefulness of a contingency model. They also note the difficulty of classifying situational contingencies adequately, a problem we cited earlier.

Most important, I think this whole issue is becoming a dead letter and we might just as well recognize it. People in this era and time, regardless of background, occupation, and so forth, are refusing to accept authoritarian controls, regardless of the contextual cues that might warrant them (cf. Yankelovich, 1974), with the possible exception of some extreme situations such as the Army case. Even in the military, though, there are strong limits to the authoritarian mode. For example, in a major study of Naval career motivation (Glickman et al., 1974) the pattern of findings showed clearly that the desire to control one's fate and to eliminate authoritarian controls is a dominant motive, regardless of occupation, age, educational level, and other such contingencies. I may be wrong, and it is possible that a contingency model for the authoritarian–democratic dimension will prove more useful than I think, but my doubts are strong that this will be the case. However, the only answer to this question will be appropriate research data and not my opinions.

*consideration, initiating structure, and the authoritarian–democratic
dimension: are they different?*

Some believe that the distinction made here between these different dimensions of leadership behavior is illusory and that consideration
is really another word for democratic leadership and initiating structure
for authoritarian. I am not of this opinion. I think that a useful distinction can be made between them. Yukl (1971) has dealt with this
question quite effectively by showing through a review of research with
a variety of samples from different studies that initiating structure is independent of the authoritarian–democratic continuum, whereas the correlation between consideration and democratic leadership is generally
positive at a low to moderate level. These findings make sense, Yukl
suggests, if we realize the following: (1) initiating structure really
means the assumption of an initiating role; however, one can initiate in
a directive (authoritarian) manner or in a democratic manner; and (2)
consideration measures how you treat people; you can treat them with
consideration even if you are an authoritarian leader (e.g., the benevolent
autocrat) and you can treat them somewhat harshly even if you are a democratic leader.

Having established these distinctions, Yukl proposes a multiple-
linkage model in which all four factors are involved in determining
leadership effectiveness. First, Yukl maintains that consideration by the
leader influences performance by motivating subordinates to work. The
reason for such influence is either or both of the following: subordinates are motivated to perform well because of the promise of consideration by the leader and/or previous consideration by the leader has
led the subordinate to identify with him and therefore adopt his norms
for performance. From the latter, Yukl predicts that the effect of consideration on performance increases the higher the leader's initiating
structure (concern for performance). This leads Yukl to the conclusion
that the most optimal situation for the leader is to have high scores on
both dimensions, an argument for which we have already noted some
support.

Second, Yukl states that democratic leadership increases subordinate motivation because individuals become ego-involved in implementing a decision they have helped to make. The positive effect on performance is maximized if it involves group support for the group decision
to work, if the individuals identify with the goals of management and if
they have the requisite skills.

Third, initiating structure influences performance because leaders
high on this dimension are likely to correct the task-skill deficiencies of
their subordinates. In addition, they are likely to take active roles in

structuring the task-role organization, an activity also likely to increase performance.

And fourth, democratic leadership will also influence task-role organization, but only under the contingency that the workers involved are skilled and motivated. Yukl's model is summarized in Figure 7.3. Although some support for it exists, much more research is needed, particularly for the contingency predictions. For our purposes here, what is important is that the leadership dimensions of consideration, initiating structure, and authoritarianism–democratic ideology seem to be relatively independent of one another and all are useful in understanding the conditions under which organizational leadership is effective.

other dimensions of leader behavior

But are these dimensions all there are? One would think so, from the amount of research they have generated. However, there are other dimensions besides these, and interest is now beginning to focus on them. One project worth citing illustrates the importance of a variety of cognitive and other motivational factors in leadership behavior, in addition to dimensions of the kind we have been discussing. In this study, the frequency of different behaviors among several thousand managers in a number of divisions of one of America's largest corporations was assessed. These assessments were then grouped by the factor-analysis

Figure 7.3
Yukl's Multiple-Linkage Model of Leader Effectiveness

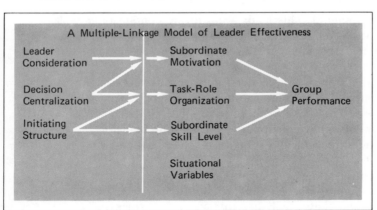

Source: G. Yukl, Toward a behavioral theory of leadership, *Organizational Behavior and Human Performance,* 1971, *6,* 414–440.

technique into five leadership behavior dimensions: (1) intellectual, planning, and analytic skills, (2) respect for subordinate competence, (3) concern and responsibility, (4) dysfunctional self-presentation, and (5) planning and adequacy of perspective (Korman, Noon, and Ryan, 1975). These results give much more justice to the complexity of leadership behavior in organizations than does trying to reduce leadership to the authoritarian–democratic dichotomy or to consideration and initiating structure. Also, almost all these factors were significantly related to evaluative ratings, thus indicating their organizational significance as well as behavioral occurrence.

Another study that gives justice to this complexity is Mintzberg's (1973) review of the literature in this area. As a result of his analysis, Mintzberg proposed that there are 10 dimensions along which managerial behavior could be categorized. These different behavioral roles are figurehead, leader, liason, monitor, disseminator, spokesman, entrepreneur, disturbance-handler, resource-allocator, and negotiator.

These are not the only studies of leadership characteristics and leadership behavior that deal with dimensions other than consideration, initiating structure, and the authoritarian–democratic continuum. There are others. The problem is that the research has been mostly scatter-shot, with little continued testing and follow-up. This, hopefully, will change in the research to come.

choice and acceptance of leaders

The attempt to understand the conditions under which people agree to be influenced by or elect other people as their leaders is of great significance to our democratic society. It has been shown (Korman, 1968b) that by far the most consistently effective predictor of leadership success is peer rating (a process by which individuals at a given level judge one another as to how effective they would be if they were placed in leadership positions). As the results summarized in Table 7.7 indicate, the extent to which one is accepted and perceived as a leader by others is an important determinant of how effective he will be (Kraut, 1975). A leader who is not accepted as a leader is not really a leader at all. He may still command behavior by external means but often these means of power are inadequate. Similarly, a leader who is accepted needs fewer external means to influence others than a leader who is not accepted. A question for us here is what kinds of people are perceived as leaders or tend to be accepted as leaders.

Three trends of research have attempted to answer this question. One of these trends has originated in the common observation that chosen leaders are often those who are perceived to follow and accept the group norm most completely, a conclusion that contradicts another observation that a leader must be an innovator so that his group will

Table 7.7
Peer Ratings as Predictive of Leadership Success

INVESTIGATORS	DESCRIPTION SAMPLE AND STUDY	N	CRITERION	RESULTS
Ricciuti (1955)	Navy officers	308–324	Overall rating	.32[a]
				.22[a]
				.33[a]
Williams and Leavitt (1947)	Marine officers	100	Combat ratings	.47[a]
				.43[a]
Hollander (1965)	Navy officers, OSC ratings	639	Overall rating	.24[a]
				.40[a]
				.39[a]
La Gaipa (1960)	Navy officers	10	Overall rating	.26[a]
	Shore duty	10	Overall rating	.24[b]
	Fleet duty		Critical incidents (effective)	.29[a]
			Critical incidents (ineffective)	−.16
Wollack and Guttman (1960)	Navy officers	108	Overall rating	.36[a]
	Fleet officers		Critical incidents (effective)	.15
			Critical incidents (ineffective)	.23[b]
			Critical incidents (average)	.23[b]
	Shore officers	81	Overall rating	.09
Haggerty (1953)	Military academy ratings	222	Overall rating	.28–.33[a]
Haggerty (1963)	Military academy ratings	78	Combat criteria ratings	.53[a]
	Military academy	420	Overall rating	.33[a]
Weitz (1958)	Insurance managers	100	Ratings	.40[a]
Roadman (1964)	Middle managers	56	Promotion rate	Generally predictive

Source: A. Korman, The prediction of managerial performance: A review, *Personnel Psychology,* 1968, *21,* 295–322.

[a] Significant at the .01 level.

[b] Significant at the .05 level.

flourish in a changing environment. The basic dilemma is how can a leader be both a conformer and an innovator at the same time? E. P. Hollander, a social psychologist, developed a theoretical hypothesis (1958) that has a great deal of empirical support and that helps considerably in illuminating this paradox. According to Hollander, individuals build up what he terms "idiosyncrasy credits" by subscribing to the norms of the group and helping the group achieve its goals. The more the individual helps the group achieve its goals by conforming to its goals and by being competent in goal achievement, the more he will build up an allowance to deviate from the group. Basically, the group is saying, "If you wish to lead us into new paths by innovation, you must first show that you are one of us by conforming to our goals and helping to achieve our goals. Providing you do this, we will agree to go along with you."

Hollander has shown that this explanation leads to certain verified predictions such as (1) a person must first conform before innovating (rather than innovating before conforming) and (2) people do choose one another for leadership on the basis of competence, a finding supported by Izard (1959) among others.

The second trend of research stems from the general hypothesis that a person evaluates another more highly the more the other is like the person, or, in brief, the greater the similarity, the greater the attraction and the willingness to be influenced by the other. There has been a great deal of research on this in recent years, but the results have not been conclusive. Although some studies indicate that attraction toward and willingness to be influenced by others is a function of perceived similarity (cf. Brock, 1965; Byrne and Nelson, 1965), others have either failed to find support or have found that relationships are much more complex than this (cf. Byrne and McGraw, 1964; Hoffman, Harburg, and Maier, 1962). The model I proposed earlier suggests a way out of this morass by proposing that the tendency to be attracted toward others and to be influenced by them may be a function of a self-esteem balance model. Thus, if one makes the assumption that for a high self-esteem person a balance situation is one in which his own needs and characteristics are being reinforced and told they are good, then such a person would be more likely to engage in this type of behavior toward a person whom he perceived to be similar to himself than one who is not similar. On the other hand, this type of relationship would not hold for the low self-esteem individual. Several of the studies I reviewed earlier support this notion (cf. R. Leonard, 1973).

Finally, a third line of research related to this question, somewhat more indirectly, is the consistent finding that whatever other characteristics a leader must have, he must act like a leader if he is to be effective. As the Michigan studies and others have persistently pointed out, an effective leader must project the image of leadership, engage in leadership-type activities (i.e., planning and decision making), and appear strong and powerful rather than weak and submissive. Similarly, Gibb (1969) has found that such characteristics as appearance, height, weight, dominance, and personality integration are associated with the leadership role. All of this seems to make sense in a balance framework since going along with others and accepting their direction and innovation is more in balance when the others have power and strength than when they are weak and powerless. Incidentally, this is probably also one of the reasons Ghiselli has obtained the results he has concerning the relative effectiveness of personality dominance in leadership. In addition, such people are also probably more effective because they are more likely to work for what they want.

Summary

Research on leadership in work organizations suggests support for a democratic–participative approach to the influence processes. Such an approach is typified by McGregor's Theory Y and by several theoretical suggestions made by researchers at the University of Michigan. In other research, the consideration and initiating structure factors have some significance as dimensions of leadership behavior, with the former being particularly important as an influence on the satisfaction of subordinates. The significance of initiating structure in general and of consideration for performance seems to be a function of various contingencies that are not yet fully understood. However, we are learning something about these contingencies. Fiedler's model, another contingency approach, has led to more conflicting results. One reason is that the contingency approach to leadership (in the sense of postulating leadership and contingency factors at the beginning) has both theoretical and administrative pitfalls. There is some value, therefore, to adopting the strategy of looking for general factors in leadership and then bringing in contingency factors only insofar as empirical research shows them to be necessary. Such an approach has been followed by the consideration and initiating structure researchers.

More recent research is focused on developing contingency models for the authoritarian–democratic leadership dichotomy and on integrating this body of literature with consideration and initiating structure research. Vroom and Yetton have proposed a contingency model in the former area that has much antecedent support but has not as yet been supported predictively. Yukl's proposals for integrating the two bodies of leadership literature is in a similar stage.

Work is now beginning on other types of leadership behavior, but few well replicated conclusions can be made. In the area of acceptance of leadership influence, research on peer ratings indicates that this is a key determinant of effectiveness. There is some support for the conclusions that individuals tend to be more effective if they conform before they innovate and if they give the appearance of being strong, dominant individuals.

SUGGESTIONS FOR FURTHER READING

FLEISHMAN, E. A., and HUNT, J. G. (Eds.) *Current developments in the study of leadership.* Carbondale, Ill.: Southern Illinois University Press, 1973.

HUNT, J. G., and LARSON, L. L. *Contingency approaches to leadership.* Carbondale, Ill.: Southern Illinois University Press, 1974.
These are the first two reports of a continuing series of symposia on leadership theory and research held at Southern Illinois University. They are of great value for those who are interested in keeping up with the changing nature of the field.

GHISELLI, E. E. *Explorations in managerial talent.* Pacific Palisades, Cal.: Goodyear, 1971.
A progress report on the development, validation, and usefulness of Ghiselli's measurement procedures for assessing managerial talent. It is an excellent case study of how constructs of theoretical and administrative usefulness are developed, measured, and examined for their fruitfulness. Not all research needs to be done exactly this way, but it is an excellent way to do it.

MINTZBERG, H. *The nature of managerial work.* New York: Harper and Row, 1973.
Both an interesting review of research studies that have attempted to determine what it is that managers do and an attempt to set up behavioral categories to guide future work. It is the type of basic research that has great practical value for planning selection, training, counseling, and assessment programs.

STOGDILL, R. M. *Handbook of leadership: A survey of theory and research.* Riverside, N.J.: Free Press, 1974.
Basically a review of much of the experimental and questionnaire research on leadership for the past several decades. It is a major scholarly effort by a noted researcher in the field. While not everybody would come to the same conclusions he does or interpret the data in the same way, the inferences made need to be examined carefully by anyone purporting to be a serious student of leadership.

chapter eight

The Physical Environment and Work Behavior

So far we have been focusing on so-called soft variables; that is, those that are not concrete. Leadership styles, motivational structures, cognitive skills, and organizational policies are all soft variables; they are conceptual constructs that are proposed to account for certain behaviors, but they cannot be known except through their manifestations and effects. In this chapter the traditional hard variables of technology and the physical work environment will be examined. However, although these variables are, at first glance, physically concrete and manipulable, the mechanisms by which their effects occur suggest that the distinction between hard and soft variables is not always as clear-cut as this first examination implies.

Physical Environments: Mechanisms of Influence

At the beginning of chapter six I discussed a number of mechanisms by which environments influence work behavior. I suggested that environments can (1) operate as constraint systems by specifying rewards and punishments for different behaviors, (2) influence opinions about the self and others, with these changed evaluations then, in turn, influencing later behavior, and (3) influence the likelihood of behavior of any kind by serving as a source of arousal–activation. Each of these mechanisms is as applicable to the study of physical variables as it is to the study of such phenomena as leadership. Here, however, I want to point out that physical environments may be important for other, more unique reasons. For example, an appropriately designed work setting can provide an individual with a great sense of security by allowing him to control the people and machinery with whom and which he interacts. A good illustration of this is the great fear that some people have of flying. These same people usually have little fear of riding in an automobile, even though the likelihood of death and injury is far greater in the latter than in the former. A number of therapists working in this area have pointed out that a major explanation for this is that in a jet airliner the passenger must give up control over what happens to him and put his life in the hands of the pilot. On the other hand, riding in a car allows for greater personal control. I would hypothesize that similar psychological processes to these operate in the work setting.

A second unique influence of the physical environment is that the setting *itself* may serve as a pleasure or an irritant, depending on factors ranging from innate physiological preferences to learned tastes for certain colors and forms. In the former case, the Gestalt psychologists have since 1913 provided continuing, convincing demonstration that certain forms and figures are almost invariably preferred over others and have proposed physiological explanations for these choices. To give validity to the fact of learned preferences, one needs only to cite the bewildering variety of color and form preferences people make when given a choice. To illustrate how this can operate in the work setting in some unusual ways, I will relate a personal experience. I was recently invited to visit a machine factory in the Midwest and when I walked in I was assaulted with a kaleidoscope of orange, blue, pink, yellow, red and multi-colored machines. My host laughed at the expression on my face and then went on to tell me that the management of the company had told the workers they could paint the machines any color they wanted and that the company would furnish the paint if they furnished the manpower. The result was a very unusual looking factory to me, although it was a pleasing work environment to those who worked there every day.

Technology

Of all the physical environmental variables in the job setting, among the most important is the technology of the work system. Technologies can differ drastically from one another and can affect individuals either directly or through the mechanism of influencing group structures and interactions which then, in turn, influence the people involved. In addition, technology can, theoretically, have a direct effect or can work as a contingency variable in that it can influence in a positive or negative way the effects of other forms of social influence such as leadership behavior and organizational design.

Before these theoretical possibilities and the relevant research are explored, the various ways in which technology may differ must be specified. Two of the most significant frameworks to describe various technologies in terms of their degree of influence were proposed by James Thompson (1967) and Joan Woodward (1965).

Thompson's framework is concerned with organizations involved in different kinds of processes, products, and services. These differences, he proposes, can be conceptualized by three technologies, as follows:

Long-Linked Technology This technology is based on a serial interdependence of tasks, i.e., completing task A depends on completing task B, whose completion, in turn, depends on completing task C, etc. Examples of organizations that use a long-linked technology are those which are involved in heavy industrial production such as automobiles or appliances.

Mediating Technology This term describes the technology used by organizations that provide a linking service between customers and clients. Such companies are marked by high levels of paper work and need to use various types of information-processing techniques. Examples of companies that have a mediating technology are advertising agencies and banks.

Intensive Technology This technology is used by organizations involved in bringing together a wide range of technological skills and services in order to service a single client. An example of an organization with an intensive client is a hospital.

Woodward's classification is different from that of Thompson in that her framework focuses only on manufacturing technologies (while Thompson includes other types of firms). Her proposals are as follows:

Process Production (or Continuous Manufacturing) This involves continuous production of goods in anticipation of consumer demand rather than in response to customer order. Examples of industries using this technology are the petroleum and chemical industries. Since this type of manufacturing lends itself to a standardization of production techniques and to automation and mechanization whenever possible, labor costs can be kept to a comparatively low level.

Unit (or Small-Batch) Production This is essentially the procedure of manufacturing a product to a specific customer order (the opposite of process production). The products are heterogeneous in nature, and labor costs are, as a result, high.

Large-Batch Production (or Intermittent Manufacturing) This is a mixture of both of the above technologies and is the most common one in American manufacturing since it includes nearly all of the mass-production firms (e.g., the automobile industry). Its characteristics are that components are made for inventory but they are combined differently for different customers, and the finished product is heterogeneous but within a range of standardized options assembled by the manufacturer. Because production is partly for inventory and partly for consumer demand, there are problems to be met in scheduling, forecasting, coordination, and inventory control.

Viewing these as some of the different types of technologies, of what significance are they?

Some aspects of this question, I might note, have been looked at elsewhere in this book. Earlier, for example, I referred to the effects of dull, repetitive jobs (cf. Chapter Six) and later I will discuss the influence of both assembly-line work and bureaucracy on self-estrangement and estrangement from others.

Let us first look at Thompson's classification system. Of what significance is it to work in one type of organization as opposed to another? An interesting analysis has been suggested by Gottman (1975) who has studied organizations in which the predominant form of labor is not physical endeavor but, rather, handling transactions between people. In Thompson's terms, this would be the difference between the long-linked technology and the mediating technology. According to Gottman, to the extent that work requires the processing, distributing, and interpreting of information, the following would be implied:

1. There is a greater premium based on specialized expertise in order to properly process, distribute, and interpret the information.
2. There is less of a premium for physical space since much information transmission is symbolic.
3. On the other hand, it is conceivable that there is an increased demand for physical space based on nonfunctional, superficial needs.
4. Work is mixed with recreation time since information transmission activities can take place at any time and anywhere.
5. Since work is mixed with recreation, demands for accountability by significant others at work and after hours (e.g., supervisors in the work setting and family members in recreation) become diffused. The alternatives are either favoring one or the other (with consequent implications for either work success or family life, depending on which is chosen) or accepting a somewhat ambiguous life style and not keying on either set of stimuli in a maximal fashion.

Some of these implications, the last in particular, may strike you as the type of outcomes which we often see discussed in papers and magazines. The conflict between job and family and how this generates family break-ups and other dysfunctional consequences is a popular magazine theme today. There are a lot of reasons for these dilemmas and later we will be talking about some of them (such as bureaucratic routine and executive-responsibility pressures). Right here, though, I simply want to note that the growth of mediating technology (which is taking place very rapidly in some segments of our society) may also serve to explain some of these conflicts.

The use of technology as an explanatory framework for understanding behavioral differences can also be found in other areas besides those suggested by Gottman. One very important concern has been with automation, a process involving the substitution of mechanical processes for human physical endeavors in the performance of specialized, routinized physical activities. What is it like to work in an automated setting? What has automation meant? It is necessary to distinguish here between societal effects and individual effects. Clearly, many people have lost their jobs because of automation, although it is also undoubtedly the case that a good number of these individuals (if not most) have been reabsorbed into the labor market within a reasonable period of time. If we turn our attention to the individual level, the effects here do not seem to have been as negative as had been feared for *those who have continued to work in the automated setting.* The reason for this is that the nature of the jobs appear to have changed in the direction of calling for skills of a more cognitive and flexible nature. Shepard (1971), in his examination of the effects of automation on blue and white-collar workers, found that the most negative feelings arose when an individual was in a mechanized work setting calling for highly specialized, routinized work activity. In settings that involved no mechanization or in automated settings where there was a low degree of specialization of activities, more positive job feelings were reported.

In addition to the continuing concern with automation, another long-standing interest has been in the implications of technological growth for overall societal processes in general. One traditional hypothesis states that an increased level of technology and sophistication of production methods generates because of the job requirements of such a system a more open society in which (1) individuals are evaluated by competence rather than status or race, (2) there is high mobility, and (3) a social consensus develops around such middle-class values as competence and work orientation. Has this happened? Research evidence has given these predictions only moderate support.

The United States is the most technologically advanced nation and yet, within the last couple of years, there has been a spate of books indicating that working-class individuals have remained isolated from the traditional middle-class values. Two of these books, those by

Levison (1974) and LeMasters (1975), are essentially subjective, almost reportorial analyses that reflect a high degree of personal involvement on the part of the writers. Despite this subjectivity, they both reach the same conclusions: a consensus toward a traditionally middle-class life style and set of values has *not* occurred with increasing technology. The working-class individual, they argue, thinks differently and acts differently from these norms and also perceives himself as acting in a different manner. Also suggesting that the predicted convergence of attitudes and values with technology will not occur is a theoretical analysis by Bell (1973). His proposal is that as technology increases and becomes more complex and as the blue-collar worker is replaced by the machine, there will be an increased dominance of the professional and technical occupational groups who provide the source of knowledge for using the technology. This dominance will lead these occupational groups into conflict with those individuals and groups who are consumers of the expertise and who will resent giving up control of themselves and their resources to those having the requisite knowledge.

From the viewpoint of research data, some of the most negative evidence for the hypothesis that increased technology will generate a more open society as described above comes from the work of Goldthorpe (1964). I have summarized his predictions and findings in Table 8.1.

I think it is fair to conclude from the work of people like Goldthorpe and from the research on automation that increasing technology is neither the road to horror nor the road to utopia. Apparently, specific kinds of behaviors do not necessarily follow invariably from certain technologies. This conclusion holds also when we look at the research literature on whether certain types of leadership behaviors are more appropriate for certain technologies than others. This hypothesis had its origin in the work of Woodward (1965) who proposed that centralized, authoritarian leadership was called for or would be more effective in large-batch mass-production organizations, whereas decentralized, more democratic leadership was called for or would be more effective in the unit or small-batch organizations and in those that call for continuous process manufacturing. This hypothesis has, however, *not* been replicated in independent studies (cf. Mohr, 1971; Hickson, Pugh, and Pheysey, 1969) and there is now some research that suggests that technological characteristics may have little importance in general in firms of 500 or more employees (Hickson et al., 1969).

Why, then, has technology become an anathema? Primarily, I think it is because technology has been developed as a tool in the service of rationality and efficiency, and this latter value has come under great attack because of its supposed implications for control and subordination of human individuality. Elsewhere in this book I have discussed the writings of Argyris and Slater, both of whom have much to say about

Table 8.1
Summary of Goldthorpe's (1964) Predictions and Findings

PREDICTIONS	RESEARCH FINDINGS

1. Increasing technology generates (a)
  a. Demand for increasing technological competence
  b. Increasing state intervention to decrease dislocation caused by technology
  c. Increasing size of middle class (from a)
  d. Increasing relative income of poor (from b)
  e. Increasing technological competence
  f. Increasing demand for role in decision making
  g. Growth of pentagon- or diamond-shaped organizations rather than pyramidal
	1. There is some indication that the dispersion of incomes is getting smaller. However, there is also evidence that there is considerable cheating in reporting income at upper levels as well as an increase in the use of legal tax shelters. Thus, there is considerable doubt as to how much leveling has actually occurred.

2. Increasing technology generates Equilibration of all status systems into one based on occupational class	2. A convergence of different status systems is not occurring. While blue-collar workers have increased income, their status has not increased and distinctly different life styles remain. The argument that convergence will occur does not take into account the fact that there are differences between those who manage and those who do not and the fact that high pay may not be offered as compensation for poor jobs.
3. Increasing technology generates Increasing number of jobs based on basis of achievement Growth of open, meritocratic society Increasing vertical mobility based on talent	3. With greater intergenerational mobility there is less intragenerational mobility because the high educational requirements make it difficult for the uneducated to get ahead. In addition, it is difficult to successfully develop small businesses in a technologically advanced setting.

this matter. Also of major relevance here is the work of Jacques Ellul (1965), a French sociologist who has been concerned with the effects of technology and *la technique,* the social psychological process he proposes technology generates.

According to Ellul, the least danger of technology is its actual physical characteristics. The real problem of technology is its capacity to destroy the human spirit since technology's success leads to the growth of the values embodied in the concept of *la technique* — the belief that good techniques and good mechanisms will automatically produce good results and that rationality will conquer all human problems. Ellul believes that man is in danger of becoming dominated by this process, a danger he sees as being manifested in the application of *la technique* to all spheres of human existence (i.e., social, cultural, recreational, and political) as well as those spheres for which it was originally explicitly designed. Man is losing his being to the process of rationality as *la technique* comes to dominate more and more of his existence.

Much of Ellul's evidence for his argument is anecdotal in nature, so it is not easy to come to any definitive judgment about its validity. Yet the argument is an important one. Some of my later discussions will suggest that man does come to value his behavior in the way that Ellul suggests. What we need to know is how far this valuation will go, when or if it becomes dysfunctional, and what to do about it when it does.

Noise

As factors in understanding how noise acts as a determinant of work performance, the type of noise and the difficulty of the task at hand must be considered. If the noise is steady, the individual adapts to it and adjusts his behavior accordingly by increased physical effort and there is little decrement in performance. However, if the noise is intermittent, it is difficult to adapt to and there may be a decrement in performance (Finkelman and Glass, 1970). The likelihood of a decrement becomes even greater as the difficulty of the task increases relative to the ability of the individual.

A significant question about noise is its possible effects on physiological health. Clearly, very high levels are quite damaging. But how high is high? Currently, companies, unions, and governmental agencies are in conflict about whether the maximum decibel levels on a job should be 85 or 90. Unfortunately, research has not helped very much here. Some studies, for example, report a negative effect of noise level on cardiac activity whereas others do not (Finkelman, Zeitlin, Romoff, and Brown, 1975).

Music

Piped-in music as a stimulant to work behavior had considerable vogue some time ago but has not come under much study recently. One reason, I suspect, is that some people came to see it as an unethical manipulation of employees. I am not certain that this is so and am of the opinion that other variables may have become of greater interest. Whatever the reason, some research findings relating to music are summarized below. They are from an article by Uhrbrook (1961):

1. Unqualified claims that increased production results from the introduction of music into the work situation are not proven.
2. Feelings of euphoria during periods of music stimulation have a physiological basis which is evidenced by changes in blood pressure that occur

in some subjects while listening to music (perhaps as a function of pre-ferred arousal level?).

3. Most but not all factory employees prefer working where music is played rather than where it is not played.

4. Quality of work can be adversely affected by music in the work situation.

5. Instrumental rather than vocal music is preferred during working hours by the majority of workers.

6. There is a negative correlation between age and preference for work music.

7. At least three investigators have reported that young, inexperienced employees engaged in doing simple, monotonous tasks increased their output when stimulated by music.

8. Evidence has been presented which demonstrates that experienced factory operators, whose work patterns were stabilized and who were performing complex tasks, did not increase their production when music was played while they worked.

9. At times music has had an adverse effect on the output of some employees, even though they reported that the music was "quite pleasant."

Illumination

General statements about necessary illumination requirements for work are difficult to make because they depend on the task and the context in which the task is performed. Optimal illumination varies according to the size of the details to be discriminated, the time available for seeing, and the brightness contrast of the details against the background. Much of the work in this area has, therefore, involved developing tables giving desirable levels of illumination for different kinds of industrial tasks using as their measure of illumination the footcandle. Although not of theoretical significance, such tables are of great practical value in specific instances.

Other investigations have focused on such areas as the effects of different colors and the consistency of illumination. Illustrative of the former type of research is a study by Berry (1961) who tested the common belief that people feel cooler in a green and blue room than in a red and orange room. The study showed few behavioral effects, despite the subjects' continuing belief in the relative coolness of the different colors. Illustrating the latter type of research is a study by Slake and Brozek (1965) which demonstrated that the common belief that intermittent, flickering illumination is a decrement to performance may not be true in all instances.

Atmospheric Conditions

There is some research on the question of desirable temperatures for different kinds of work, with most of the evidence pointing to the following results (Tiffin and McCormick, 1965):

ACTIVITY	DESIRABLE DRY-BULB TEMPERATURE
Light sedentary work — winter	68–73
Light sedentary work — summer	75–80
Moderately hard work	65
Strenuous work	60
Mean preferred temperatures: summer — 71, winter — 68	

We should note, though, that these preferred temperatures may be a function of the geographic climate in which the person is living. It seems hard to believe, for example, that the perception of a cold day is the same in Minnesota as it is in California. The writer remembers well his graduate student days in the former state when he waited for the temperature to inch up to the freezing level so that he could take off his "real" winter clothes.

Accidents

From any point of view, be it economic, social, psychological, or physical, accidents constitute one of the greatest problems known to mankind. As an indication of the extent of this problem, consider the human and economic costs in the following statistics (1963 data; Tiffin and McCormick, 1965), considering that they were compiled more than a decade ago and would be even greater today:

Total number of accidents resulting in fatalities	100,500
Motor vehicle accidents resulting in fatalities	43,400
Public accidents resulting in fatalities	17,000
Home accidents resulting in fatalities	29,000
Work accidents resulting in fatalities	14,200
Wage loss, medical expenses, overhead, insurance costs	$2,650,000,000
Indirect costs (interference with schedules, property damage)	$2,650,000,000
Total costs	$5,300,000,000

How can accidents be prevented? The first of the answers developed was the accident-proneness theory, described below.

accident proneness

Basically, the theory of accident proneness is the hypothesis that the tendency to have accidents or engage in behavior likely to lead to accidents is a consistent characteristic of an individual and thus predictable from that person's other characteristics.

Accident proneness, with its practical implication that high-accident people can be weeded out at the time of selection, was at one time considered to be highly valid. Most of the supporting evidence came from studies that showed such typical results as 10% of the population having 30% of the accidents, or 25% of the population having 75% of the accidents (Blum and Naylor, 1968). These findings were criticized, however, in a paper by Mintz and Blum (1949) who reasoned that since accidents can be considered to be "rare events," the proper statistical model to be used in interpreting the occurrence of accidents and whether these happen with greater-than-chance frequency in a given situation is the statistical model known as the Poisson distribution. According to the Poisson distribution, 9% of a given population should have 39% of the accidents, and 39.5% should have 100% of the accidents. Hence, if accident proneness is to be considered a reasonable explanation for any given distribution of accidents, then the distribution should be more extreme than these: for example, significantly fewer than 9% should have 39% of the accidents or 9% of the population should have significantly more than 39% of the accidents, and so forth.

As a result of Mintz and Blum's work the concept of accident proneness fell into considerable disrepute, with the major argument now being that the hypothesis could be supported only under three conditions (in addition to the departures from the Poisson distribution discussed above): (1) the number of accidents that people have in two time periods should be highly correlated; (2) the people who have major accidents should be more likely to have minor accidents in a later time period, and vice versa; and (3) the people who have accidents in one time period are more likely to engage in near-accident behavior in a later time period than those who do not have accidents. Although most evidence suggests that these kinds of relationships are not very high (cf. Whitlock, Clouse, and Spencer, 1963), some recent findings have provoked a great deal of interest. They suggest that the death of accident proneness as an explanatory concept might have been a bit premature. Among these recent findings, the following are typical:

1. Keehn (1959) found that Arab university students who admit to having accidents in one situation also indicate that they have been involved in accidents in other situations.
2. McFarland and Mosely (1954) found that accident repeaters commit many more violations than accident-free drivers.
3. Greenshields and Platt (1967) found that inexperienced and poor drivers have a tendency to be indecisive and thus overcorrect the controls in given situations.
4. Barbarik (1968) found that taxi-cab drivers who had an abnormal number of accidents in which they were struck from behind had a slow initiation time and fast movement time. The latter characteristic led them to have fewer accidents overall.
5. Haner (1963) found that driving attitudes are related to driver accidents.

6. Kunce (1967) reported a series of studies showing that adventure-someness relative to cautiousness is related to accidents in a wide variety of situations.

7. Block (1975), using a technique he calls the Attention Diagnostic Method (ADM), found that he could distinguish between individuals having accidents in work settings in two separate studies. The technique involves asking people to sort into correct order a set of numbers presented to them randomly on a simulated plate. Those scoring very rapidly on this task are more likely to be those with high accident frequency.

What can one conclude about the importance of personal factors as a cause of accidents? Goldstein's summary (1962) provides a useful guide:

1. Accidents seem to be predictable at a relatively low level of accuracy from measures of human characteristics such as visual accuracy, reaction time, and attitudinal measures.

2. Accident repeaters account for some, but not a great many, of the total traffic accidents on record.

3. The below 25- and above 75-year groups contribute disproportionately to the accident total.

4. Alcohol has a bad effect on driving performance at much lower levels of concentration than is generally recognized and is a contributing factor in 25% to 50% of fatal traffic accidents.

5. Accident records themselves are relatively poor measures of human behavior. They are complex phenomena, unstable over time, and greatly subject to errors in recording of both a random and biased nature. For example, it is considered manly in our society to brush off feelings of pain and the possible harmful results of accidents. Other biases in recording may come from insurance considerations, fear of punishment, etc. These characteristics about accident records probably account in part for why they are so hard to predict on the basis of psychological variables since it is always harder to predict unstable variables than stable ones.

alertness and stress as determinants of accidents

As a result of the moderate level of support for the accident-proneness hypothesis, other theoretical notions have become quite important in the study of accidents. One of these is the goal-freedom-alertness theory (Kerr, 1957) and this looks like the kind of theoretical approach I suggested earlier in this book. Indeed, one of the clearest statements of this theory reads as follows:

> We hold that great freedom to set reasonably attainable goals is accompanied typically by high-quality work performance. This theory regards an accident merely as a low-quality work behavior—a "Scrappage" that happens to a person instead of to a thing. Raising the level of quality in-

volves raising the level of alertness. Such high alertness cannot be sustained except with a rewarding psychological climate (Kerr, 1957, p. 5).

There is a considerable amount of evidence, most of it collected by Kerr and his coworkers, that increasing a worker's feeling of influence and control over his environment or increasing his feelings of competence and self-esteem will reduce the likelihood of accidents. One study found that accident rate is negatively related to such variables as job prestige, promotion probability, the degree of comfort in the work environment, and the degree of individual rather than group responsibility over work (Keenan, Kerr, and Shermon, 1951). These findings were supported in a study that showed accident rates to be negatively related to the extent to which people could transfer and feel mobile within an organization, the extent to which they used suggestion systems, and the prestige of the job (Kerr, 1950). All of these relationships are consistent with the general theoretical framework I proposed earlier that productive behavior is a function of the self-esteem and self-perceived competence of the individual with this, in turn, a function of the social psychological environment in which the individual finds himself.

Another factor leading to accidents may be too much stress, as the adjustment stress theory suggests:

> ... unusual, negative, distracting stress upon the organism increases its liability to accident or other low quality behavior (Kerr, 1957, p. 9).

What is meant by stress? The answer is given by some of the findings as to the correlates of accident frequency. These have been found to be mean-rated comfort of the shop, work place, temperature, illumination, degree of operational congestion, manual effort involved in the job, tendency for the firm to have seasonal layoffs, and the degree to which the personnel live in blighted neighborhoods (Keenan, Kerr, and Shermon, 1951; Kerr, 1957). For the variable of accident severity the results are somewhat different, but not antithetical. The key variables seem to be the punitiveness of the management for tardiness, the egalitarianism of the plant, and the presence of national unions (with this probably reflecting previous conflict) (Kerr, 1950).

From a behavioral perspective, are these latter theories more important than accident proneness? Kerr (1957) claims they are, arguing that accident rates are roughly determined by the following in terms of degree of importance:

	% OF TOTAL # OF ACCIDENTS
Accident proneness	1–15%
Alertness	30–40%
Adjustment stress	45–60%

It cannot be said, however, that the evidence is as conclusive as Kerr thinks. Perhaps the most judicious conclusion is that all these theories probably have some relevance and all should be kept until the evidence becomes clearer than it is now.

Physical Environments: General Theoretical Issues

In recent years, attention has been directed toward activation-arousal theory as a possible overall framework for understanding the effects of different physical environments and as an aid to the design of changes. I have already discussed some aspects of this framework in the chapter on organizational psychology, but here I will discuss it in a more complete manner. Following this, I will discuss some of the problems of this theory and why I think that while this approach is interesting and useful, it is far from being the whole answer to the development of a major overall theory in this area.

The essential logic of the activation-arousal framework can be summarized by the following:

1. Physical stimulation affecting a person contributes to the physiological and psychological arousal level of that person at the time.
2. The impact of a stimulus is a positive function of such variables as its intensity, its meaningfulness, its complexity, the recency of its previous occurrence, the frequency of such occurrences, and the extent to which it provides variation from previous stimulation (Fiske and Maddi, 1961; Walker, 1964).
3. For any person at a given time of day (i.e., during the sleep–wakefulness cycle), there is a level of arousal that is normal and appropriate, and behavior is motivated toward achieving that normal arousal state for that given time of day. Having attained that state, the individual is then motivated toward maintaining it by engaging in behavior to increase arousal level when it is too low or decrease it when it is too high.
4. When in a state of normal arousal, the person becomes more sensitive to other aspects of the environment and is more able to deal with them efficiently. If his behavior does not have to be directed toward the achievement of optimal arousal, it can then be directed toward whatever external demands happen to be operating in the environment at the given time. Such increased attention to external environmental demands when the person is at an optimal activation or arousal level leads, all other things being equal, to a U-shaped relationship between arousal level and task performance since it is when he is in his optimal arousal state that he can pay most attention to task demands.

You will notice that this is a balance, or consistency, formulation since it postulates that, at least in part, behavior is due to the desire to achieve an outcome that is in balance both with previous experience (either exact or relative) and with what the individual desires for that time of day, and that it rejects both too much physical stimulation and too little. The nature of the behavior that will be engaged in depends on the stimulation state at the time. If it is too high, the person is motivated to reduce the stimulation; if it is too low, he is motivated to increase it. The advantages of this approach seem obvious at first glance. It provides a rationale for deciding when to increase lighting or music, for example, and when to decrease it. Conceptually, arousal levels, and all sources of physical stimulation should be kept at an optimal level; therefore, the performance level will be optimal, as Figure 8.1 indicates. Unfortunately, however, it is not quite this simple and there are problems involved in applying this framework. These problems mean that activation-arousal theory has some usefulness at this time, but not as much as you might think.

The Physical Stimulus: How Does It Come to Have an Effect?

Let us assume that you are working in a dress factory in Manhattan surrounded by the noise of sewing machines and honking automobiles outside. Clearly, there is a great deal of physical stimulation here, whether it is measured by intensity, variability, or meaningfulness. Assume that a week later you are working on a farm in Maine, where the only noise is the rustle of leaves. The level of physical stimulation here obviously seems to be less. Taking both in context, then, the two environments should affect you differently. The question that concerns us here is the process by which these environments have their effect. You will recall the relevance of this in our discussion of Ellul's argument. Is it just a matter of the stimulus affecting the neurons of your body in a different manner? If so, then all we would need to do to affect levels of arousal would be to adjust the physical stimuli. Suppose, however, that it is more complex than this and that the effects of physical stimuli on arousal are a function also of the social psychological characteristics of the situation and of the personality of the individuals being studied. Attempts, then, to develop a viable, optimal physical environment would be considerably more difficult, since now we would have to consider the social and psychological variables involved as well as the level of physical stimulation. Perhaps arousal is not involved at all and physical stimuli, with the exception of extreme cases, have either little or no effect. Perhaps they operate only in conjunction with social psychological variables. In addition to being of theoretical interest, the answer has direct practical implications for how we change environments.

As it turns out, there are several different but not necessarily anti-

Figure 8.1
The Relationship between Arousal Level and Performance

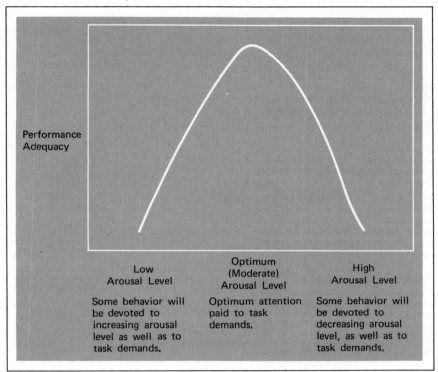

Performance
Adequacy

Low Arousal Level	Optimum (Moderate) Arousal Level	High Arousal Level
Some behavior will be devoted to increasing arousal level as well as to task demands.	Optimum attention paid to task demands.	Some behavior will be devoted to decreasing arousal level, as well as to task demands.

thetical hypotheses concerning the effects of physical stimulation on psychological processes. Table 8.2 lists several of the most important of these hypotheses and some of the research evidence attached to them.

With the possible exception of the second hypothesis in Table 8.2, and, perhaps, part of the sixth, it would be stretching it beyond a reasonable point to argue that these hypotheses are just rewordings of the activation-arousal framework. They are more than that and, therefore, they raise doubts as to the necessity and importance of the arousal hypothesis. They suggest we have little reason to assume automatically that if we manipulate a physical environment, we will affect behavior through the arousal mechanism. Research needs to be done as to when and where the arousal hypothesis holds and when and where these other hypotheses hold. Perhaps then we will be able to understand why we get such conflicting research findings as the fact that

Table 8.2

Hypotheses Concerning Processes by Which Physical Stimuli
Influence Psychological States and Behaviors

HYPOTHESES	INVESTIGATORS
1. Crowding (i.e., increased number of people per unit of space) may affect the ability to control interaction with others (or increase the costs of doing so in a physiological and/or psychological sense).	Zlutnick and Altman (1972)
2. The psychological variable of unpredictability, and the anxiety felt because of the lack of control, is more important than the physical parameter known as noise intensity in predicting adaptation to noise in task situations. The effect is the same for (a) different procedures for manipulating unpredictability, (b) different levels of physical noise, (c) both male and female subjects, and (d) different laboratories.	Glass and Singer (1972)
3. The concept of relative deprivation may explain some of the effects of physical stimulation on behavior, in that people who are being exposed to stressful physical stimuli will find these even more intolerable if they are made conscious of the fact that others comparable to themselves are being exposed to stimuli less stressful.	Glass and Singer (1972)
4. The effect of noise on performance may be understood in terms of its influence on the information-processing capacities of the individual and its tendency to utilize those processes in a manner that increases the capacity of the individual to respond adequately to other stress stimuli.	Finkelman and Glass (1970)
5. For people who are required to work under noisy conditions, high intensity has a negative influence; for people who choose to work under the poor conditions, the effects of high intensity are considerably lessened. Hence, the element of choice is crucial in affecting susceptibility to noise.	Glass and Singer (1972)
6. One's perception of being in a state of a specific type of (or as feeling a particular emotional) arousal is a function of (a) the actual physiological arousal one is in (i.e., the stimulus to which one is subject) and (b) the cognitive and sound cues that are available in order to assist one in labeling the state of arousal (or emotion) one feels.	Goldstein, Fink, and Mettee (1972); Schacter and Singer (1962); Schacter and Wheeler (1962)
7. The effect of any specific type of physical stimulation on an individual is a function of his experience with stimuli of that nature, his expectancy for that situation, and the amount of time he has been in that situation.	Helson (1964); Zlutnick and Altman (1972)

sometimes high temperature leads to dislike (Griffitt and Veitch, 1971), and other times the same high temperature is negatively related to aggression (Baron, 1972). Similarly, we might also understand why there is a lack of correlation between crowding and performance over a range of different tasks (Freedman, Klevansky, and Ehrlich, 1971; Korman and Finkelman, 1974).

Arousal: One Kind or Many?

In activation-arousal theory, one basic assumption seems clear: there is only one kind of arousal and it affects behavior in the same way, no matter its source and how it is measured. This is an important assumption since if there is more than one kind of arousal, then more than one kind of theoretical framework may be necessary. Similarly, if there is more than one type of arousal, then a research study in which arousal theory is not supported may be due to the fact that different types of arousal, unknown as to nature and intensity, are involved.

The evidence relating to this matter is ambiguous. Typically, the different measures used for assessing degree of physiological arousal (e.g., measures such as the degree of activity in the reticular formation, electrocortical activity, circulatory activity, vasomotor responses, respiratory activity, the electrical properties of the skin, and skeletal tension) are positively correlated with one another, but not always at a very high level. As a result, some psychologists have cited the lack of very high correlations as indicating the presence of more than one type of arousal (cf. Lacey, 1950), whereas others see the positive relationships as supporting a general arousal factor (cf. Berlyne, 1967). Which one is right? It depends on how one wants to look at it. In the meantime until clearer data become available, some disagreement in interpretation will remain.

Testing a Curvilinear Hypothesis

A third problem in activation-arousal theory concerns the same issue we brought up in our discussion of leadership processes: the fact that the prediction of behavior at any specific time is a function of two variables. The first of these is the degree of arousal that the person is used to; the second is the degree of arousal that the person is subjected to at the time. Only by knowing these two antecedent variables can we predict behavior, since the following could easily occur:

PERSON'S TYPICAL AROUSAL LEVEL	AROUSAL LEVEL OF CONTEMPORARY ENVIRONMENT	BEHAVIOR PREDICTED
10	7	Arousal-increasing behavior
5	7	Arousal-decreasing behavior
5	3	Arousal-increasing behavior
1	3	Arousal-decreasing behavior

In these examples, for any given level of each variable (arousal levels of person or environment), opposing behaviors would be predicted, depending on the level of the other.

Another problem is that U-shaped relationships are far more complex than linear relationships. In the latter case, a test of a hypothesis that variable A is related to variable B is relatively simple, since only two levels of the independent variable (i.e., variable A) have to be tested to determine the relationship. The higher on one variable (A) the higher on the other (B), or so such a hypothesis would have it. However, for a U-curve hypothesis (a) a minimum of three levels of the independent variable is needed; (b) the three levels used must be placed widely enough apart so that an adequate test of the U-shaped hypothesis may be made; and (c) the middle level used must be at the level of optimum performance. Thus, if we utilize three levels of variable A and find a direct linear relationship with variable B, either positive or negative, is this because we have unknowingly chosen arousal levels too close together at the low (or high) point of the arousal continuum? Table 8.3 shows clearly that the testing of a U-shaped hypothesis can be very difficult. In case A, three levels have been used for variable A, but they are all on the lower end of the continuum. As a result, a positive linear relationship between arousal level and performance has been found. Just the reverse has occurred in case B. In both cases, negative evidence for a U-shaped hypothesis has been found and would be reported, even though in actuality there has not been a true test of the theory. This has only occurred in case C, where three levels of arousal have been used, the middle one of which is the desired optimal level. From the hypothetical data given, a U-shaped relationship would then be reported quite properly. The point is that it is only in Case C that a true test of the hypothesis was possible, since it is only there that the desired level of arousal was actually included in the experimental situ-

Table 8.3
Three Examples in Testing a U-Shaped Hypothesis

CASE	INDIVIDUAL'S DESIRED AROUSAL LEVEL	AROUSAL LEVELS TESTED	PERFORMANCE LEVELS	CONCLUSIONS
A	10	2	100	Positive linear
		4	200	relationship
		6	300	between arousal
				and performance
B	10	12	300	Negative linear
		14	200	relationship between
		16	100	arousal level and
				performance
C	10	8	300	U-shaped
		10	400	relationship
		12	300	

ation. Thus, should the results be positive, as in this case, the evidence would quite properly have to be interpreted as positive for the U-shaped hypothesis in an appropriate test of the approach. If they were negative, they would also have to be properly interpreted as such, unlike Cases A and B.

Given these problems, then, how do we use activation-arousal theory to design a physical work environment? It is difficult to do so unless we know at what level of the environment's arousal potential the optimum performance will take place. Because it is so difficult to determine this, it is, perhaps, no wonder that so far as I am aware no research program meets the requirements for a full test of the theory. What the research does show is support for the approach only if we make certain assumptions in each case. For example, Scott (1966) has pointed out that the introduction of variety into dull, repetitive environments has led to increased task performance, a finding that lends support to the lower part of the U-shaped hypothesis. Table 8.4 lists some of the experiments that Scott cites in support of this derivation and others that have appeared since his paper. The problem is that these studies have not measured the subjects' preferred arousal levels prior to the experimental induction. The assumption is that these dull environments were too low in arousal-inducing properties for all respondents, an assumption that leads to ambiguous results.

A second line of evidence concerns research relating to the desire to engage in creative behavior. If we define creativity as we did earlier

Table 8.4

Summary of Studies of the Effects of Introducing Some Variation into Environments That Can Be Classified as Dull by Social Consensus

BASIC FINDINGS	INVESTIGATORS
1. A telephone message in the latter part of a clock-monitoring task leads to similar performance to that engaged in by fresh students.	Mackworth (1950)
2. Experimenter presence reduces the decrement in visual tasks of a prolonged nature.	Fraser (1953)
3. There are fewer performance decrements when there are more signals to respond to.	Deese and Ormond (1953); Holland (1958); Jenkins (1958)
4. Performance decrements tend to occur more in simple vigilance tasks than in complex tasks with many stimuli to respond to.	Frankman and Adams (1962)
5. People engage in and complete their shopping tasks more quickly, with no loss in satisfaction, when noise is introduced in a supermarket.	Smith and Curnow (1966)
6. Performance in monotonous tasks is increased by introducing noise and variety into the environment.	McBain (1961); McBain (1970)

(i.e., as new and useful behavior), there is considerable evidence, as I outlined in chapter four, to suggest that the motivation to be creative is, in part, a function of the extent to which one has engaged in varied forms of behavior in the past and the extent to which one has not been in a social psychological environment that has encouraged routinization, specialization, and sameness of behavior. Since one's normal activation level is, in part, a function of one's experience, such evidence can be considered in keeping with the prediction that an individual seeks outcomes in balance with his normal arousal level. However, in order to adequately test activation-arousal theory, we would need to measure the environments and the individual on the same scales prior to the behavior to resolve any ambiguity of interpretation. This has not been done as yet as far as I know, nor was it done in studies that involved decreasing stimulation to virtually a zero level (i.e., below anybody's adaptation level), with this leading to the development of hallucinations and increased self-stimulation (Bexton, Heron, and Scott, 1954).

Evidence shows that individuals differ systematically and consistently in their preference for levels of stimulation, and this fits in with the framework. For example, high scores on a stimulus-seeking scale (Zuckerman et al., 1964) predict preference for visual complexity, drug and alcohol usage, varied forms of heterosexual activity for both sexes, and hallucinatory activity for females (Zuckerman, Neary, and Bustman, 1970). In addition, the finding that scores on the scale vary positively as a function of educational attainment supports the conclusion that stimulus-seeking behavior is a balance process reflecting the degree of stimulation to which one has been exposed in the past (Kish and Buisse, 1968).

Overall, I think it would be fair to conclude that activation-arousal theory is a theory of conceptual value, but that it still leaves much to be desired if we want to use it to actually design a physical work environment.

Summary

Organizational characteristics can be of both a soft and hard nature. The former consists of such factors as leadership patterns, while the latter is illustrated by technology. This chapter has been concerned with the latter.

Physical environments may operate as constraints, encourage the development of opinions about the self and others, serve as a source of stimulation and/or security, or be a source of pleasure in itself. Technology is an important variable with effects that are still not well understood. Among the conflicting theories of technology, one of the most significant predicts that increasing technological growth will generate the growth of a demand for skills, which will lead, in turn, to a reduction of status based on birth, an increase of status based on accomplishment, and to an increasing uniformity of outlook. The evidence for this hypothesis is, however, conflicting. Another frequently voiced prediction that has generally not been verified is that automation will lead to lower job satisfaction. It appears from these results that the reason for the contemporary concern with the negative effects of technology has less to do with research findings than with the belief that technology generates a rationalistic mode of thinking in areas of human behavior for which it is inappropriate. As a result, much unique human expression is being lost. This hypothesis needs to be investigated further.

Noise, music, light, and temperature are other physical variables that influence work behavior under some conditions. For optimal work behavior, noise should be steady and expected and music should be periodic. Light and temperature need to be keyed to specific demands to have positive effects.

Accidents, which seem to result from both personality and environmental considerations, constitute a very critical type of work behavior. There is some evidence that accident proneness as a personality characteristic accounts for some accident behavior but it is clearly more important in preventing accidents to develop work environments that are ego-enhancing, stimulating, and satisfying.

Activation-arousal theory, which postulates a U-shaped relationship between activation and the efficiency of work behavior, is a theory of some promise. However, many problems with this theory need to be resolved before this promise is fulfilled.

SUGGESTIONS FOR FURTHER READING

FREEDMAN, J. L., LEVY, A. S., BUCHANAN, R. W., and PRICE, J. Crowding and human aggressiveness. *Journal of Experimental Social Psychology,* 1972, *8,* 528–548.

This article reports an interesting series of experiments which came to the conclusion that common sense is not always a useful guide to behavior. The article provides a good demonstration of how basic research can, at times, be of considerable value in the study of hypotheses about complex human behavior.

SCOTT, W. E., JR. Activation theory and task design. *Organizational Behavior and Human Performance,* 1966, *1,* 3–30.

The article that was primarily responsible for introducing activation-arousal theory into the field of work behavior. The author provides an excellent review of the theory and its physiological support and goes on to point out its possible fruitfulness.

SHEPARD, J. *Automation and alienation.* Cambridge; MIT Press, 1971.

A report of a research study that tested some of the supposed negative effects of automation on job satisfaction and self-worth. While not all of the results stand above dispute, the study is a good example of how meaningful research can be conducted on significant social questions.

SOMMER, R. *Personal space: The behavioral basis of design.* Englewood Cliffs, N.J. Prentice-Hall, 1969.

One of the earliest examinations of the effects of physical environment on human behavior. While many of the points made are not as research-based as one would like, it is possible to see in this book the concerns and interests that appear in much later research.

STEELE, F. I. *Physical settings and organization development.* Reading, Mass.: Addison-Wesley, 1973.

An integration of research findings with a view toward their implications for the effectiveness of organizational functioning. The author is a well-known psychologist with extensive consulting experience who is well able to draw out some of the major implications of the field.

chapter nine

Reactions to Job Experience: Alienation, Stress, and Satisfaction

This chapter will discuss attitudinal and emotional reactions to job experience. There are three major conceptual questions involved. First, what are the different types of job reactions? I have identified three in the chapter title which I will discuss separately although they do have some similarities, as we will see. Second, what types of job experiences are crucial in influencing these different reactions? Finally, what personal and other factors influence the way people react to different job characteristics? Each of these questions will come under examination in the following sections.

Alienation

One of the most frequent terms one hears today in discussions of organizational behavior is alienation. The problem of worker sabotage at the Chevrolet Vega plant in Lordstown, Ohio, for example, has been laid to the concept of alienation. Other aspects of alienation, such as executive alienation, blue-collar blues, and the decline of the work ethic, are also prevalent concerns. But what exactly is alienation?

Karl Marx first defined alienation as a condition in which man, in his everyday life, denies part of his being in order to survive. He plays a role so to speak. In this role he is separated, or estranged, or alienated from the kind of life of which he is capable. It was Marx's contention that the industrial worker of the nineteenth century was an alienated individual because of the roles he was forced to play. Such alienation took place on several levels. First, the laborer became alienated from the product of his labor and the organizational system (or the means of production) which produced these products. The reason for such alienation, according to Marx, was that the worker had given up control over his own fate and his desire for self-expression in return for a wage. This giving up of his sense of self as a result of joining the factory system led him to become estranged, or alienated, from the products of that system. Second, since the worker had to reject his desires for self-expression and control in order to survive in the factory system, he became estranged from those parts of himself that wanted self-control and meaningful experience. He, in essence, becomes alienated from those parts of his own character or psyche which he is unable to express in his everyday life. This is the second level on which alienation occurs.

At the time Marx wrote there were no empirical researchers in the field of organizational behavior as we know them today. Even if there were, the political aspects of Marx's writings would have made it doubtful that his work could have been treated and tested as a scientific theory in the way that we test such theories today.

Despite the political implications in Marx's work, his arguments constitute a theory of human behavior concerning the proposed effects of certain independent variables (i.e., the hierarchical leadership conditions and the specialization and routinization of factory work) on certain dependent variables (i.e., alienation from the conditions of work and alienation from the self). If we look at modern concepts of alienation and the alienated worker, we see the influence of Marx's ideas, although the significant factors leading to alienation and its effects, in the modern sense, are considerably more complex than Marx imagined. In addition, as we will see, alienation occurs in contexts that would have surprised Marx considerably.

Before continuing, we need to clarify the definition of alienation, a term that we have been using rather loosely until now and which has been used often in a variety of inconsistent ways. For example, under the heading of alienation, it is possible to find studies of such different concepts as powerlessness, meaninglessness, normlessness, isolation, self-estrangement, and job dissatisfaction. This, I think, is unfortunate since these terms are different from one another. Since it is not likely that we will be able to make great progress in this area until we develop some clarifying definitions, I will devote some attention to them here.

One direction for clarification has been suggested by Faunce (1968) who has proposed that powerlessness, meaninglessness, and normlessness are predisposing conditions to alienation. Alienation itself, he maintains, is composed of a sense of social isolation and self-estrangement. In other words, Faunce suggests that we view the process as:

$$
\left.
\begin{array}{l}
\text{Powerlessness} \\
\text{Normlessness} \\
\text{Meaninglessness}
\end{array}
\right\}
\rightarrow
\begin{array}{l}
\text{Social isolation (or social estrangement)} \\
\text{Self-estrangement}
\end{array}
$$

Assuming this conceptualization, each of these terms would be defined as follows:

Powerlessness   This term describes the emotions of the individual who feels that he has lost control over the events in his life that matter to him. He sees himself as a pawn reacting to events, rather than an originator of events. Faunce argues that as a result of being in a state of powerlessness, the individual is more likely to see himself as engaging in behavior that does not reflect his real self, i.e., he is more likely to see himself as being self-estranged.

Meaninglessness   The individual experiencing a sense of meaninglessness is one who has difficulty in finding and utilizing appropriate standards for judging the importance or use of actions and beliefs. What is meaningful and important and useful? Because the individual experiencing a sense of meaninglessness is one who has difficulty answering this question, he is more likely to feel a sense of isolation from effective social interaction with others.

Normlessness   This term describes the condition of an individual who sees few effective rules or standards for guiding behavior; the social system and its behavioral regulations have, for him, broken down. Normlessness describes the emotional condition of the individual for whom there are few guides, as opposed to the inappropriate guides that mark the condition of meaninglessness. In both cases, however, the results are the same in that they generate a sense of isolation and ineffective social relationships.

Social Isolation   This term describes the psychological condition of the individual who has lost the ability to interact meaningfully with others. He feels he cannot understand the attitudes of other individuals, cannot predict their behavior, and cannot explain himself and his feelings to them.

Self-Estrangement   This term describes the state of an individual who engages in behaviors that do not truly reflect his values, needs, or desires. Rather than expressing himself, he is engaging in trivial and nonmeaningful activities. (Note the similarity between this behavior and the behavior we have attributed to the low self-esteem individual. This similarity is even greater if we also consider that each construct, i.e., low self-esteem and self-estrangement, results from a sense of powerlessness. It may be that these are really the same constructs and that research will bear this out. However, for now, we will keep them separate).

Finally, we can distinguish between job dissatisfaction and these alienation phenomena by referring to the hierarchical control variable. There is good support, as we discuss throughout this book, for the conclusion that hierarchical control affects both alienation and job dissatisfaction. This suggests a positive correlation between the two, a relationship often found. However, it is also true that individuals who are not estranged from themselves and who demand that they be allowed to engage in behaviors that reflect their values can become extremely dissatisfied because they demand too much from the world. These unrealistic expectations can be very important in causing dissatisfaction, as Wanous (1975) and others have found. Here, then, we have a case in which decreasing hierarchical influences can lead to lower alienation and higher dissatisfaction. Similarly, individuals of very low self-esteem and low expectancies for satisfaction and meaningful interaction can be quite satisfied with their jobs because they expect very little.

Assuming, then, that we can clarify alienation by viewing it as a sense of isolation and/or self-estrangement which results from feelings of normlessness, powerlessness, and meaninglessness, how do these latter conditions develop?

Marx's argument that the key factors are conditions approximating those of the nineteenth-century factory is really an oversimplification. This is not to say that these conditions do not lead to feelings of powerlessness and meaninglessness. They can and do. However, such reactions are not inevitable responses to nineteenth-century century factory conditions. Form (1973), for example, did not find these reactions in studies of factory workers in four countries. In addition, feelings of powerlessness, meaninglessness, and, in particular, normlessness can occur in response to other situations. While Kornhauser's (1965) study of the automobile worker provides support for the Marxian hypothesis, other studies exist which show that alienated-type responses are not limited to this occupational group. I mentioned earlier the study of 2,821 managers by Tarnowieski (1973), which found results for this group that were comparable to those found for the automobile assembly-line worker. Yet, managers have jobs that involve far less routinization, specialization, and hierarchical control than those on the assembly line. Consider the following pattern of results from Tarnowieski's study:

> Sixty-two percent of the managers did not look to the work they were doing for a realization of their life expectations.

> Sixty-six percent did not think that the organization they were working for was either interested in or even aware of their aspirations.

> Eighty-three percent said that their attitudes toward achievement and success were changing.

Eighty-three percent did not define success in terms of their business activity.

Forty percent did not believe that the organization they worked for would allow them to achieve their personal goals.

It strikes me that if the conclusion stemming from Kornhauser's work were generalizable, one would not get these results. Also, one would not get the findings reported by Bartoleme (1972), who found in intensive interviews of successful young executives that feelings of meaninglessness in life and a loss of personal alertness and life interest were common. Nor would you get Ramey's (1972) finding of an over-representation of professional and managerial occupations among those who had decided to actively pursue a new life style.

It is because of these studies that I believe the Marxian hypothesis to be oversimplified and that there are other factors that need to be considered. For one thing, it may be that the dimensions found on the assembly line—hierarchical control, routinization, and specialization— may occur also in other radically different jobs, perhaps in different combinations. We may find feelings of isolation and self-estrangement in other groups because perceptions of powerlessness, meaninglessness, and normlessness occur in a variety of different tasks, not just in those on the assembly line. A second possible consideration is that feelings of self-estrangement and/or isolation occur among managers, for example, because of factors unique to the managerial job. Perhaps the strain of responsibility generates a detachment from others and a consequent feeling of isolation. Third, the key factors may not be different types of work experience at all, but other forms of social experience that coexist or operate in conjunction with the work milieu (e.g., family or cultural experiences). For example, I will propose later that working for and being influenced by hierarchical control mechanisms and extrinsic incentives (e.g., money) generates feelings of self-estrangement, regardless of the degree of success attained, (since one has worked for others and been controlled by others). Hierarchical influence, can, of course, come from both within or outside the work setting.

The hypotheses of Slater (1970) are relevant here because of their focus on the implications of hierarchical organization and the types of individually oriented achievement striving it seems to generate. Figure 9.1 illustrates the framework Slater has proposed.

Hierarchical structure is, clearly, a type of social experience that can occur in both work and nonwork settings as an influence on feelings of powerlessness and meaninglessness, and, eventually, self-estrangement. It is, however, not the only kind of experience that falls into this category. Faunce (1968) has proposed that isolation and self-estrangement result from the loss of those social cues that provide a sense of location, place, and security. If Faunce's argument (summarized in Figure 9.2 in slightly revised form) has some validity, there would be no reason to expect less isolation and self-estrangement among those who are higher in the organizational system than those who are lower.

In fact, Faunce's model might even suggest that isolation and self-estrangement would be greater at higher levels of the organization than at lower levels because the perception of change is greater at higher levels. On the other hand, perhaps isolation and self-estrangement are the same at different levels but for different reasons. We do not really know which statement is true because, despite considerable theory, we have only a few research studies in the area, such as those by Tar-

Figure 9.1
The Influence of Hierarchical Organization on the Effects of Achievement Striving

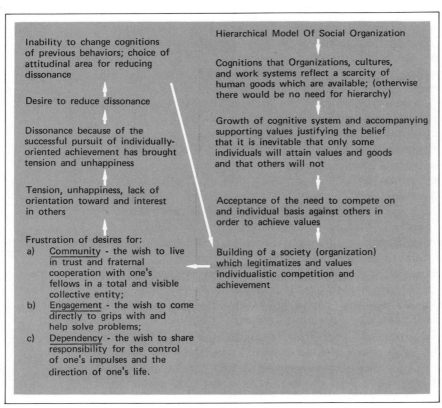

Source: Slater, 1970

nowieski. I think that the sum total of all of these is to cast doubt on the fruitfulness of a theoretical framework stemming from the Marxian hypothesis and its current forms. On the other hand, it seems clear to me that much research is necessary before we can say more definitely what these other factors might be.

There is one body of work in this area which does have a considerable data base and that is the studies conducted by researchers at the University of Michigan. Their work is also valuable because they have tried to relate indices of attitudinal reactions to work conditions to some very specific behavioral and physiological outcomes of societal interest. While it is unfortunate that they have not distinguished as well as I would have liked between reactions reflecting self-estrangement and reactions reflecting job satisfaction (or the lack of it), their work is still highly useful for several reasons. First, their work suggests that

Figure 9.2

Influence of Social and Technological Change on Self-Estrangement

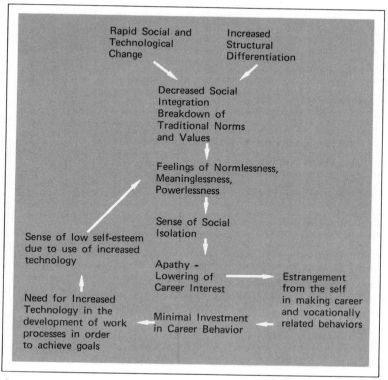

Source: Faunce, 1968

alienation can occur at different levels of the occupational hierarchy. Second, it has considerable research support. Third, it incorporates into its framework a concern with behavioral and stress-related consequences of these attitudinal reactions. Their basic concepts are outlined below (French and Caplan, 1973):

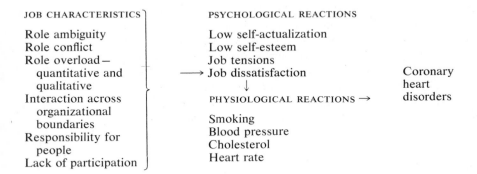

We can see that the major hypothesized independent variables (i.e., role ambiguity, role conflict, the crossing of organizational boundaries, and the others) have a very strong relationship with those suggested by Faunce. After all, concepts like role ambiguity and conflict, and the different role expectancies that may come from being at the border of two organizations (like a salesman), are all instances of *unclear social expectations,* the same kind of phenomena to which Faunce attributes such importance. For both the Michigan group and for Faunce, then, being exposed to this type of social experience is predicted to result in feelings of powerlessness, meaninglessness, normlessness and, eventually, self-estrangement. In addition, Faunce sees isolation as resulting from the same unclear social expectations, an outcome that the Michigan people have not dealt with but which which I doubt they would disagree.

A recent paper by French and Caplan (1973) has reported considerable research support for the Michigan framework. In addition, they make two other important points. First, they suggest that, to a considerable degree, these problems may be overcome by increasing the level of significant participation in organizations since effective participation by an individual will enable him to decrease the amount of role ambiguity, role conflict, overload, and so forth. This is a recommendation very much in keeping with our emphasis here. Second, French and Caplan point out that the effects of these organizational variables are not the same for all individuals. For example, these job characteristics are not quite as stressful, they think, if a person has the appropriate skills for the job, if the job meets his needs in other ways, and if the person is not Type A (i.e., if he is not highly involved in his job, if he does not dislike deadlines, if he does not feel overburdened by his work, and if he does not mind taking on responsibility).

It seems clear that if we look at the Michigan research and the other theories and research described earlier, we need to start thinking about dimensions of work experience (and other social experience) which generate feelings of isolation and self-estrangement that can occur at all levels of the occupational spectrum and in different areas of work. Suggested above are some dimensions that might overcome the narrowness of the Marxian hypothesis. Here I would like to list some others that I have taken from the work of Jacques (1970) and Terkel (1974) and which might be worthy of further research. In no particular order, these are:

1. the difficulty one has had finding a job
2. the stress of being judged and evaluated by superiors
3. the inequity common in work organizations
4. the feelings of anonymity in some organizations
5. the feeling of obsolescence with experience common in some work settings

Each of these is common to some forms of work experience and not to others. Each of these, from the face of it, looks like it might have some significant negative behavioral effects. What needs to be found out is whether these effects do occur, where they occur, and how they might be overcome.

Integrating Remarks and Further Theorizing

If we bring together our discussion, two broad speculative themes emerge. One is that hierarchical and external control, in and of themselves, generate feelings of self-estrangement and that such estrangement can occur even if one succeeds in this type of setting (cf. Kirsch and Lengermann, 1972). Second, there is the theme in the work of Faunce and the Michigan group as well as in other future-shock writers that overly rapid change and ambiguity generate self-estrangement and social isolation.

At first glance one sees a contradiction here since, traditionally, hierarchical control is supposed to overcome the problems of ambiguity and role conflict. There really is not any contradiction, though, because the point is that there is nothing wrong with setting up clear guides and norms for behavior. We need them very much. The problem comes from who sets the guides, ourselves or some external force? When the determinants are primarily external, the problems begin because the guides are not personally relevant or meaningful, they reflect too much of the norm-setter and, as a result, they generate the types of reactions we have reviewed here. The research on participation and the role of personal influence in decision making is convincing enough to lead me to think that these, as goals, would not only be valuable for society as a whole but would also be better for the organizations themselves in terms of their performance objectives. It does no good for anybody if our organizations encourage the type of worker described by Jenkins (1973):

> The detachment of worker from his work is similar to the detachment in the schizoid condition described by R. D. Laing. The individual is subjected to the stress of "a threatening experience from which there is no physical escape" develops an elaborate protective mechanism; "he becomes a mental observer, who looks on, detached and impassive at what his body is doing or what is being done to his body." For that person, "the world is a prison without bars, a concentration camp without barbed wire." Instead of experiencing reality directly, he develops a "false" self as a buffer for the real world, while the real self retires to an "inner" position of unexposed safety. All of life seems full of "futility, meaninglessness, and purposelessness," since it is not, in fact, being directly experienced. The real self is completely blocked, barred from any spontaneous expression or real freedom of action and totally sterile. In the absence of a spontaneous natural, creative relationship with the world which is free from anxiety, the "inner self" thus develops an overall sense of inner impoverishment, which is experienced in complaints of the emptiness, deadness, coldness, dryness, impotence, desolation, worthlessness, of the inner life".

Source: Excerpt from *Job Power* by David Jenkins, copyright © 1973 by David Jenkins. Reprinted by permission of Doubleday & Company, Inc. Pg. 43.

Psychological and Physiological Stress

One of the outcomes of work experience that our society is interested in is the effects of stress on physiology and health. Are certain occupations more likely to be associated with such disorders as ulcers, coronary heart disease, and even suicide? What variables are involved in leading to these outcomes? Self-estrangement? Isolation? Job dissatisfaction?

Evidence, as my comments on the Michigan group research showed, is beginning to accumulate on these questions, despite the fact that there is much that we do not know. House (1974) has reviewed the literature in this area and has come to the following conclusions:

1. Job characteristics such as low job satisfaction and high job pressures such as work overload, status inconsistency, and job mobility are consistently related to coronary heart disease.

2. A mediating variable among all of these characteristics is that they are all presumed causal determinants of stress and this stress, in turn, leads to the coronary complications.

3. However, the determination of what stress means still needs to be made. Stress has many physiological and psychological dimensions. For example, it may include what we have called isolation and job dissatisfaction, but it could also include a feeling of great exhilaration and a desire to achieve a goal.

4. In addition, we know little about the population parameters that mediate this relationship. We have, therefore, little knowledge of the extent to which this relationship holds among women and blacks.

Conceptually, if we look at House's (1974) conclusions, they would support the argument we made earlier that stress and resulting dysfunctional behavior are not necessarily simple functions of one set of job characteristics. Jobs at different levels may all have stressful effects as a result of experience in them and we should be wary of oversimplification.

Job Satisfaction

While job dissatisfaction has been studied more extensively than any other type of job reaction and is related to outcomes like stress, social isolation, and self-estrangement, they really are not the same. The totally estranged worker (in both a personal and social sense) may have highly positive feelings about his job because he expects and desires little from it. Hence, anything he gets is fine. On the other hand, there are individuals with relatively low degrees of personal and social isolation who like their jobs, perhaps because their job discourages these negative feelings. Similarly, job satisfaction can be and frequently is highest among those individuals whose jobs are quite stressful (e.g. managers and professionals). These are the reasons I have kept the discussion of job satisfaction separate from the discussions of isolation (personal and social) and stress.

In what follows I intend to:

1. discuss the various theories of job satisfaction which have been offered, some of the evidence which is relevant to them, and the degree to which they converge on a common framework;

2. summarize what has been learned about the various correlates and possible determinants of job satisfaction as these developed from empirically oriented, non-theoretical studies and judge whether these findings are generally consistent with the theoretical schema developed under #1;

3. discuss the most traditional way of looking at job satisfaction, i.e., what happens when job satisfaction is/is not achieved, or degree of job satisfaction as an effect on behavior;

4. suggest some mechanisms for controlling in a constructive fashion a common consequence of job dissatisfaction, i.e., aggression of both an individual and inter-group (e.g., management-union) nature.

Theories of Job Satisfaction

Three major theories of job satisfaction have served as either implicit or explicit reference points for much of the research in this area. While they stem from different traditions and outlooks, I believe there is some basis for integrating them into a relatively consistent framework. Before I do this, however, I want to discuss each of them separately.

need-fulfillment theory

In some respects the most rational of the theories of job satisfaction and the one which is probably the clearest analogue to the incentive theory of performance is the notion that (1) a person is satisfied if he gets what he wants and (2) the more he wants something, or the more important it is to him, the more satisfied he is when he gets it and the more dissatisfied he is when he does not get it. There are two major theories that utilize this kind of framework, one a subtractive model and the other multiplicative (Vroom, 1964). Both conceptualize job satisfaction as a direct function of the extent to which an environment corresponds to one's need structures.

The subtractive model proposes that job satisfaction is a direct negative function of the discrepancy between a person's needs and the extent to which the environment provides satisfaction of those needs. The greater the total discrepancy counting all needs, the less the satisfaction; and the less the discrepancy, the greater the satisfaction.

According to the subtractive model in Table 9.1, the individuals' rankings in terms of their satisfaction with their jobs would be predicted to be, starting from the most satisfied, C and D (tied), E, G, A, B, and F. This is the order corresponding to the order in which the individuals' needs are seen as being fulfilled on the job (i.e., their total discrepancy scores).

This subtractive procedure has certain characteristics (Vroom, 1964). One of these is that, all other things being equal, the greater a person's needs, the more job satisfaction will decrease, regardless of what happens in the environment. Similarly, the greater the amount of environment return, the more job satisfaction will increase, independent of the level of need of the individual involved. A second characteristic is that a person who has a need level of 1 and a satisfaction of 1 is considered to have the same level of satisfaction as a person whose comparable figures are 10 in desire and 10 in fulfillment. Vroom thinks

Table 9.1
Example of Differences between Subtractive and Multiplicative Methods of Job Satisfaciton

(1) INDI-VIDUAL	(2) SCORES ON			(3) FULFILLMENT OF			(4) DISCREPANCY SCORES ON			(5) TOTAL DISCREPANCY	(6) PREDICTED RANKINGS ON JOB SATISFAC-TION (SUB-TRACTIVE MODEL)	(7) TOTAL NEED FULFILLMENT (PRODUCT OF NEEDS × FULFILLMENT)	(8) PREDICTED RANKINGS ON JOB SATISFACTION (MULTIPLICATIVE MODEL)
	Need 1	Need 2	Need 3	Need 1	Need 2	Need 3	Need 1	Need 2	Need 3				
A	8	7	4	6	3	0	2	4	4	10	5	69	3
B	3	9	6	1	1	2	2	8	4	14	6	24	6
C	8	7	5	7	7	4	1	0	1	2	1	125	2
D	4	2	3	2	2	8	2	0	0	2	1	36	5
E	8	10	10	9	9	8	0	1	2	3	3	242	1
F	3	6	9	1	1	1	2	5	8	15	7	18	7
G	4	4	7	3	2	5	1	2	2	5	4	55	4

that this is a distorted conception of job satisfaction. I do not agree. The research we discussed earlier that people who are estranged from themselves and who have low expectancies of personal value satisfaction may be more satisfied than those with high expectancies is quite consistent with this. In any case, Vroom prefers a multiplicative model in which we multiply a person's needs by the degree to which the job fulfills the need and then add up the products for all needs. This total would then be the level of job satisfaction. In the example given in Table 9.1, the rankings on job satisfactions would be E, C, A, G, D, B, and F, a somewhat different ordering than under the subtractive model.

There are several studies that support these models. For the multiplicative theory, one of the best known is the one reported by Vroom himself (1959). In this investigation Vroom was concerned with the extent to which the relationship between supervisory participative practices and job satisfaction was dependent on the extent to which the individuals involved wanted to engage in decision making. The rationale here was that if they did not, it would not matter if the supervisor was participative or not. Vroom classified his sample on two scales, one of which measured the need for independence and the other of which measured authoritarianism (or liking for strong authority symbols). The results of this study are highly supportive of his hypothesis.

In addition to Vroom's study and the expectancy research discussed earlier, there are other results that indicate some usefulness for the subtractive or multiplicative models (cf. Kuhlen, 1963; Schaffer, 1953; Morse, 1953). Despite such positive findings, there is research that suggests that these models cannot be the whole answer in developing an adequate theory of job satisfaction. In the Kuhlen study (1963), for example, the subtractive model is moderately supported for men but not for women. Tosi (1970) tried to replicate Vroom's study and found no support for it. Similarly, studies by Neely (1973) and Schletzer (1966) failed to find support for the hypothesis that satisfaction is a function of the congruence between personal values and needs and job characteristics. One possible explanation for this finding comes from studies by Korman (1967d) and Berger (1968), both of which found support for the subtractive model for high self-esteem respondents but not for low.

It is fair to conclude from these studies that need-fulfillment theory, while useful, is only a partial answer in the search for an adequate theory of job satisfaction. This conclusion may puzzle you since it seems to violate rationality. Doesn't "common sense" say that job satisfaction is the discrepancy between one's values and the extent to which they are met? Yet this definition, and it's associated theoretical frameworks, is not always supported. Why not? I shall attempt to provide an answer later in this chapter.

reference-group theory

Reference-group theory is similar to need-fulfillment theory except that it takes as its point of departure not the desires, needs, and interests of the individual but, rather, the point of view and the opinions of the group to whom the individual looks for guidance. Such groups are defined as the reference group for the individual in that they define the way in which he should look at the world and evaluate various phenomena in the environment (including himself, to a great extent). It would be predicted, according to this theory, that if a job meets the interest, desires, and requirements of a person's reference group, he will like it, and if it does not, he will not like it.

A good example of this theory and how it can be empirically tested has been given by Hulin (1966a). In this study data were obtained that measured the job satisfaction of female clerical workers employed in 300 different catalogue order offices. In addition, information was also obtained about the prosperity, unemployment, living conditions, farming productivity, and general economic condition of the communities in which the catalogue order establishments were located. The major hypothesis was that such economic conditions would be negatively related to the job satisfaction of the employees; that is, with job conditions held constant, for the person living in a well-to-do neighborhood, the less likely it was that she would like the job. Hulin's results are given in Table 9.2 and, taken in total, they indicate strong support for his explanation that frames of reference for evaluation may be provided by one's social groups and general social environment.

A similar interpretation can be offered for the results of a study by Katzell, Barrett, and Parker (1961) that investigated a drug company with 72 warehousing divisions geographically spread throughout the United States. For each of these locations the following variables were computed and related to job satisfaction:

1. Size of work force—average number of warehouse employees over the course of a year
2. City size—population of the city in which the warehouse was located
3. Wage rate—total straight-time earnings expressed as a ratio to total straight-time man-hours worked
4. Unionization—whether or not warehouse employees were represented by a union
5. Percentage male—percentage of warehouse employees who were men

The relationship, in all cases, for each of these variables was negative. This is interpretable in terms of the reference-group model if we accept the assumption that the last three variables are positively related to the degree of expectation and degree of reward that is deemed to be acceptable and meeting the standards of the groups' desires. The first two variables are not quite as clear in terms of this explanation, but they probably fall into this general pattern because they are related to the last three. (In support of this interpretation, it should be noted that the relationships for the first two were smaller than for the last three.)

These are only two of a number of studies available that support this view of job satisfaction (cf. Form and Geshwender, 1962). We shall not cite the other studies now since several will be mentioned later in this chapter. Suffice it to say that there seems to be clear indication that the reference-group model can be used to interpret a considerable number of studies in job satisfaction. However, it is obvious that it must be an incomplete explanation since even the most casual observer can easily cite the fact that while some people go along with group opinions and group evaluation of organizational phenomena, many people are independent of these pressures. How we can reconcile such observations into a coherent framework with what we have said previously is a matter for later discussion.

Herzberg's motivator-hygiene theory

The third theory of job satisfaction significant during the last decade and a half is the motivator-hygiene argument of Herzberg discussed earlier in the context of job enrichment. If you reread that discussion you will see that this is a theory of both performance and satisfaction. Its basic argument is that an enriched job leads to satisfaction and that one is motivated to perform well in order to achieve satisfaction. On the other hand, a nonenriched job can only lead to lack of dissatisfaction, at best; hence, it cannot serve as a motivator to performance. As you recall, there is little research support for this theory, but there is support for the satisfying nature of enriched jobs under certain conditions.

toward a theoretical integration

It would seem, then, that considering the negative outcomes of Herzberg's theory, there is good reason to suggest a gradual convergence on two major explanations or theories of the determinants of job satisfaction. These two explanations can be summarized as follows:

1. Need-fulfillment theory: Job satisfaction is a function of, or is positively related to, the degree to which one's personal needs are fulfilled in the job situation.
2. Reference-group theory: Job satisfaction is a function of, or is positively related to, the degree to which the characteristics of the job meet with the approval and the desires of the groups to which the individual looks for guidance in evaluating the world and defining social reality.

Table 9.2
Average Correlation between Community Characteristics and Satisfaction Variables

SATISFACTION WITH	NONWHITE (%)	OWNER-OCCUPIED HOUSING (%)	MEDIAN INCOME	EARNING OVER $10,000 (%)	SOUND HOUSING (%)	PER CAPITA RETAIL SALES	MEDIAN RURAL INCOME	UNEMPLOYED WORKERS (%)
Supervision	.01	−.08	−.03	−.01	−.02	−.06	−.04	−.15
Kind of work	.14[a]	−.11	−.15[b]	−.15[a]	−.20[b]	−.14[a]	−.19[b]	0
Amount of work	.12[a]	−.11	−.16[b]	−.12[a]	−.16[b]	−.12[b]	−.20[b]	0
Coworkers	.08	−.06	−.05	−.01	−.07	−.13[a]	−.04	.04
Working conditions	.20[b]	−.08	−.24[b]	−.21[b]	−.26[b]	−.20[b]	−.26[b]	.06
Pay	.26[b]	−.15[a]	−.44[b]	−.38[b]	−.45[b]	−.24[b]	−.45[b]	.10
Career and security	.10	−.06	−.16[b]	−.12[a]	−.16[b]	−.14[a]	−.15[a]	.02
Company identification	.19[b]	−.06	.34[b]	−.30[b]	−.30[b]	−.26[b]	−.31[b]	.4

Source: C. Hulin, Effects of community characteristics on measures of job satisfaction, *Journal of Applied Psychology*, 1966, *50*, 185–192. Copyright 1966 by the American Psychological Association, and reproduced by permission.

[a] Significant at the .05 level.

[b] Significant at the .01 level.

Several questions would seem to naturally follow. First, are these two explanations compatible with one another? Second, if they are, how are they to be combined in predicting a person's job satisfaction? Do we weight them both equally or do we weight one as being more important than the other? Does the process of deciding on the weighting problem depend on specified conditions? These are questions I want to discuss here.

For the first question, the answer must obviously be yes. Human behavior is a complex, multiple-caused activity, and there is little reason to think that a phenomenon as important as job satisfaction would be a function of just one set of factors. Furthermore, there intuitively seems to be no basis for concluding that the two theories are incompatible with one another. They may both be correct.

How they relate to one another, however, is a question for which we have few answers. One hypothesis that has some promise for integrating these theories into a unified framework stems from the theory I proposed earlier. Essentially, it argues that the need-fulfillment model holds only for those high in self-esteem (defined as one's general evaluation of himself as a need-satisfying, adequate individual), since it is for them only that need fulfillment is just and in balance. This prediction is derived from the theoretical assumption that individuals will find satisfying those situations that maximize their sense of cognitive balance. Thus, for the low self-esteem individual, being in a situation in which he is adequate and in which his needs are fulfilled is not an equitable or balanced situation (as it is for the high self-esteem person). He should be no more satisfied in a case such as this than in a case where his needs are not fulfilled and where he is not adequate. The fact that there is generally not a negative relationship (although there may be, (cf. Korman, 1966a), is probably because of a social norm that says individuals should find situations more satisfying where their self-perceived needs are satisfied and where they perform well than situations in which these are not the case. According to this hypothesis, the following predictions should be true:

1. There should be a positive relationship between need fulfillment and overall job satisfaction for high self-esteem individuals but not for low.
2. There should be a positive relationship between task achievement and task liking for high self-esteem individuals but not for low.
3. There should be a greater relationship between reference-group evaluation of a job or a task and the evaluations of a low self-esteem individual than for a high self-esteem person (since the personal need-fulfillment requirement for the high self-esteem person will dilute the satisfaction that will be achieved if a job situation is in balance only in relation to group norms and desires).

There is good evidence to support differential predictions 1 and 2, but the evidence for prediction 3 is as yet inconclusive. Table 9.3 lists the results of a series of experiments that support the second prediction. It should be noted that the results shown in Table 9.3 seem to be the same whether self-esteem is measured by a personality inventory or whether it is experimentally manipulated. Siegel and Bowen (1971) and Greenhouse and Badin (1974) have also reported results that support prediction 2.

Table 9.3 also indicates that reference-group evaluations are of equal importance for both low and high self-esteem people, not just for low self-esteem people, a conclusion supported by Greenhouse (1971). This seems to invalidate our third prediction, although there is one study by Blood and Hulin (1967) which suggests that reference-group processes are more important in predicting the job satisfaction of blue-collar workers than white-collar workers, a result consistent with the prediction if we assume that blue-collar workers have lower self-esteem than white-collar workers. Yet I am not sure how adequate this assumption is today.

In addition to the mixed data, there are other reasons for caution before we accept this framework. My hesitation stems from the fact that reference-group theory looks a lot better at first glance than it does

Table 9.3
Summary of Studies of Liking for Tasks as a Function of
Task Achievement and Self-Esteem

| | MEAN LIKING SCORES | | | |
| | High Self-Esteem[b] | | Low Self-Esteem | |
EXPERIMENTAL TASKS[a]	Succeed	Fail	Succeed	Fail
1. Inferences—critical thinking	3.86	3.08	3.41	3.31
2. Recognition of assumptions—critical thinking	4.07	3.31	3.38	3.32
3. Anagrams	4.21	2.18	3.42	3.00
4. Anagrams—others like the task	7.13	4.93	5.95	6.27
5. Anagrams—others do not like the task	5.83	3.58	5.38	5.00
6. Inferences—critical thinking—others like	7.41	6.66	6.50	6.45
7. Inferences—critical thinking—others do not like	5.62	2.75	4.55	4.50

[a]For tasks 1 through 5, self-esteem was measured by a personality scale. For tasks 6 and 7, it was experimentally manipulated.

[b]All differences for the high self-esteem groups are significant at the .05 level, whereas no succeed–fail differences are significant for the low self-esteem groups.

on close examination. The problem is that it is post hoc, i.e., it helps you explain behavior after it happens. A good theory is one that enables you to predict behavior and at the current stage of its development, when it is utilized in the real world, reference-group theory does not do this. For one thing we have little idea of how people choose their reference groups. For example, who constitutes the reference group of an urban black? His parents? His friends? Or affluent whites or blacks living in expensive suburban homes? His satisfaction with a particular job depends on which group he chooses, since if he chooses his friends he is more likely to be satisfied with his job than if he chooses the affluent white or black. Yet, which does he choose? We do not know. The findings of Katzell, Ewen, and Korman (1974) show few racial differences in the evaluation of job conditions and the findings of Reilley and Roberts (1973) show fairly significant differences. This obviously leaves us with no clear-cut conclusions. Very much the same argument can be made, I think, if we look at the middle-aged woman returning to the labor market after fifteen or twenty years as a homemaker. If she looks to her generation for reference, she will be satisfied with most jobs, but if she looks to the younger generation, she might not like the possibilities open to her. The point is that we have to know to whom she looks for reference *before* we try to predict her behavior; otherwise, reference-group theory is both theoretically and administratively trivial.

I would conclude, therefore, that the integration I have suggested here has some promise, but it has a long way to go before it becomes satisfactory, particularly in regard to the reference-group aspect.

Correlates of Job Satisfaction: Environmental Effects

As I mentioned earlier, there has been considerable research aimed at determining the job characteristics that are related to job satisfaction. While much of this research was practically oriented, the information obtained has also had some theoretical value. My first goal in the following is to summarize this vast literature into some meaningful categories. Second, I will relate this literature to the tentative integrated theoretical model proposed above.

occupational level

One consistent finding is that the higher the level of the job, the greater the job satisfaction (cf. England and Stein, 1961; Herzberg et al., 1957; Vroom, 1964). Why should this be so? I think I have pretty well implied the reasons earlier in this book. They are well summarized by Tiffin and McCormick (1965):

Blauner has attempted to explain the gross differences that exist among people in different occupations and industries, and has set forth four factors that seem useful in explaining the difference. These are (1) occupational prestige, (2) control, (3) integrated work groups and (4) occupational communities. Of these, differences in occupational prestige seem to be particularly important, as reflected by the fact that the rank order of job satisfaction of various occupational groups corresponds generally with the rank order of prestige of the groups. The control factor deals with the relative amount of "control" inherent in jobs. Satisfaction generally is higher in the case of people whose jobs involve control over their own work and that of others, and is lowest for those people who are in jobs that are at the lower end of the organizational hierarchy, for whom there is little opportunity for such control . . . (p. 357).

In other words, part of the theoretical explanation for the positive relationship between occupational level and job satisfaction stems from reference-group theory in that, overall, our society values some jobs more than others. Hence, people in valued jobs will like them more than those who are in nonvalued jobs.

A second reason may stem from our other postulated determinant of job satisfaction. Jobs increase in range and spread of activities the higher one goes in the occupational world. All other things being equal, then, people who need to have their needs fulfilled in order to be satisfied are more likely to find this to be the case in the higher-level jobs rather than in the lower-level ones (cf. Porter, 1962). (One note of caution here is that one's needs may become so demanding as a result of being in a high-level position that no job could be satisfying in the sense of meeting these needs.)

job content

There is good evidence, as I mentioned earlier, to indicate that the greater the variation in job content, the greater the satisfactions of the individuals involved. Illustrative of this is a study by Walker and Guest (1952) of workers in an automobile assembly plant. They found that for those workers with jobs that involved five or more distinct operations, 69% had favorable job feelings. This contrasted with the finding that only 33% of those workers who performed a simple operation liked their jobs. Similar results have been found by Wyatt, Fraser, and Stock (1929), Baldamus (1951), Mann and Hoffman (1960), and Hackman et al. (1974) among others.

considerate leadership

There is a large number of research studies that point to the conclusion that considerate leadership results in higher job satisfaction

(Vroom, 1964; Badin, 1974) than inconsiderate leadership. Although these studies have not always used the same instruments of measurement, the same procedures, and so on, the trend of their findings is consistent. Why is this so? In addition to the explanation that people like to be treated with consideration, there are two other explanations that are consistent with these data.

First, since much of the research is of the concurrent type of design in that it involved asking individuals to describe at a given time their satisfaction with their jobs and the behavior of their superiors, one might argue that the satisfaction levels caused the supervisory behaviors. That is, it may be that the superiors adjust their behavior to the individual subordinates involved, reward noncomplainers with considerate, individual, need-oriented behavior and punish complainers with leadership behavior of the opposite type. This explanation would be consistent with many of the obtained relationships, and has been shown to occur in a variety of settings (cf. Farris, 1969;). However, as I explained in chapter seven, this explanation could not account for the positive results found when leadership is experimentally varied and the effects are as predicted.

Another explanation for these findings also stems from the weaknesses of this kind of research design in that it is conceivable that descriptions of supervisory behavior by a subordinate are not independent of his description of his own satisfaction. Thus, a subordinate who is dissatisfied with superior A may be more likely to claim that the superior engages in a specific set of negative behaviors than a different subordinate of superior A who happens to be satisfied with and like him, even though the *same* supervisory behaviors are involved. Such an occurrence would be another example of the balance notions already discussed. Again, though, there are experimental studies that show the effects of considerate leadership on satisfaction and which cannot be accounted for by this type of explanation. I would conclude, therefore, that while all the consideration and satisfaction relationships may not be a function of the causal directions suggested, a good portion of them are.

pay and promotional opportunities

All other things being equal, these two variables are positively related to job satisfaction. An explanation of this finding lies in both factors of our theoretical model. That is, both of these variables are tied up with occupational level and also have social prestige themselves. Hence, they can be considered to be supportive of reference-group theory. In addition, each of these variables also has the capacity to fulfill an increasing number of needs the more they are increased, thus meeting our proposed personal-fulfillment component of job satisfaction.

social interaction and working in a group

Does interaction itself cause satisfaction with those with whom one is interacting? While some have hypothesized this (cf. Homans, 1950), and while it may hold for voluntary groups from which one may withdraw if interaction is unsatisfying, it is likely that this does not hold for organizational contexts from which one is not always free to withdraw. There, interaction can be frustrating, and the more the interaction, the more the frustration.

Among the various hypotheses that have been offered to explain when interaction is most satisfying, the following are, perhaps, most common (Vroom, 1964):

1. Interaction is most satisfying when it results in the cognition that the other person's attitudes are similar to one's own, since this permits the ready calculability of the other's behavior and constitutes a validation of one's self.
2. Interaction is most satisfying when it results in being accepted by others.
3. Interaction is most satisfying when it facilitates the achievement of goals.

Of these three, the second has the most support, with the evidence for the third being fairly good. Research relating to the first hypothesis shows a pattern of mixed results which is perhaps understandable, considering the point we made earlier that some people (e.g., those with low self-esteem) are not interested in seeking out people like themselves.

Correlates of Job Satisfaction: Personal Variables

It is apparent that whereas various organizational variables such as occupational level, job content, and type of supervisor have been able to explain a considerable amount of variation in job satisfaction, they are not the whole story. In any situation marked by a given set of conditions, considerable individual differences in job attitudes and job satisfaction exist. This is probably because of differences in the characteristics of the individuals. For some people most jobs will be dissatisfying, irrespective of the organizational conditions involved, whereas for others most jobs will be satisfying. In this section we shall review what seem to be the most important personal characteristics related to job satisfaction. The reader should be forewarned, however, that the research is neither vast nor conclusive.

age

Most of the evidence on the relationship between age and job satisfaction, holding such factors as occupational level constant, seems to indicate that there is a generally positive relationship between the two variables up to the preretirement years (approximately the early sixties) and then there is a sharp decrease (Saleh and Otis, 1964). On the other hand, there are studies that show no relationship between age and pay satisfaction (cf. Schwab and Wallace, 1973). Given this ambiguity, it would be foolhardy to try to provide a theoretical framework for this relationship at this time.

educational level

There is a relatively consistent trend of evidence which indicates that, with occupational level held constant, there is a negative relationship between the educational level of the individual and his job satisfaction (particularly his pay satisfaction) (cf. Centers and Cantril, 1946; Cantril, 1943; Klein and Maher, 1966; Schwab and Wallace, 1973; Lawler, 1971). Most of the researchers in this area have explained their findings on the basis of theoretical frameworks similar to or identical with reference-group theory. Simply, it can be argued that the higher the educational level of the individual, the higher the level of the group he looks to for guidance as to how he should evaluate his job rewards. The higher the reference point of any group looked to, the lower the level of satisfaction with any specific job outcome.

sex

There is as yet no consistent evidence as to whether women are more satisfied with their jobs than men, holding such factors as job and occupational level constant. Even if there were, I am not sure what they would mean, considering the contemporary ferment. The discovery that jobs are as important to the life satisfaction of women as they are to men (Kavanagh, 1974) has to have a profound effect on satisfaction studies of women.

summary of factors relating to job dissatisfaction

A summary of the factors relating to job dissatisfaction, as we have discussed them here, is not difficult. The higher the job in terms of level, responsibility, autonomy, and variety, the better. However, the higher the level of the individual (in terms of his education, abilities, etc.), the higher the level of these characteristics that is necessary in order for satisfaction to be attained.

Job Dissatisfaction and its Consequences

Assume that a person becomes dissatisfied with his job. What does this mean for behavior and performance? Does it mean anything at all? This has always been an important question, since the assumption that satisfaction led to performance underlay much of the original research and recommendations for practice.

Although the early recommendations were somewhat over-simplified and led to considerable controversy during the latter part of the 1950s and early 1960s, more recent theory and research indicate that efforts to maximize job satisfaction may, in fact, result in more satisfactory job performance. However, the actual relationships will depend, among other things, on the measure of performance used and on the type of job involved.

First, there is a consistent trend of evidence which shows that job dissatisfaction is a significant predictor of a high turnover and absentee rates (Vroom, 1964). The fact that the relationships are sometimes not overly high is probably because of factors such as labor market and economic conditions in the turnover case and weather and geographic conditions for absenteeism. It is an important practical benefit when job satisfaction is maximized, since it is quite obvious that turnover and absenteeism cost money. In addition, when one minimizes absenteeism and turnover, one increases total organizational performance productivity since, for most jobs, one cannot perform when one is not present.

In turning to the question of how job satisfaction influences job performance itself, the picture is a little more clouded, with some historical perspective necessary.

In 1955 Brayfield and Crockett, after a review of the research literature on job satisfaction and job performance, concluded that there was little or no relationship between the two variables. They argued, therefore, that efforts to increase job satisfaction in order to increase performance were not based on hard facts and should be discontinued. While these conclusions were controversial at the time (Herzberg et al., 1957), for the main part they were accepted and became part of the lore of industrial psychology. For years psychologists were quick to disclaim practical benefits in increasing job satisfaction. During this period, however, other psychologists believed there was something wrong with this position. A person who is dissatisfied should behave differently than someone who experiences pleasantness in a job situation, they felt, even if for some reason, he cannot leave the job. Yet, according to Brayfield and Crockett, he does not. Why?

One answer is that the question posed above, while it is the one that has generally been asked in these studies, is not the correct one. Rather, the question that should be the subject of investigation is under which conditions does job dissatisfaction lead to decreased performance and under which conditions does it not. Since this has generally not been asked, it is premature at this point to dismiss the notion that job satisfaction has no effect on job performance (something which should never have been done anyway, considering the turnover and absenteeism data discussed above).

What are some of the conditions under which this relationship might occur? There are several factors to be considered, some relating to the model of work motivation I suggested earlier. One prediction, therefore, is that whether or not a person will engage in negative behavior as a function of job dissatisfaction will depend on the difficulty of the job relative to his self-perceived competency for the job. The more the individual considers himself competent, the more he will see work performance as a source of balance and satisfaction. Therefore, for people with high self-perceived competency for a job, a response to dissatisfaction might be high performance. On the other hand, for those with low self-perceived competency for the job, the response would more likely be negative behavior, since these individuals are more likely to consider this response as legitimate and proper, whereas they do not see high performance as legitimate, proper, and satisfying.

In investigations supporting this reasoning, Schacter et al. (1961) found that variations in the emotional state of workers do not affect performance as long as the required performance is stereotypical and does not require much attention or thought. However, during time of technological change, when work assignments become less stereotyped and require more detailed attention, job performance is affected by the emotional state of the individual. This finding has been replicated in a laboratory study by Latane and Arrowood (1963). If we equate time of job changeover with increased job difficulty (and less self-perceived competency), we have support for our hypothesis. Case (1969) has reported an experiment in which low self-esteem people decreased their performance under auditory stress but high self-esteem people did not, partially supporting this prediction. There is also a recent study by Greenhaus and Badin (1974) that supports this prediction.

Another determinant of whether poor work performance is a response to dissatisfaction may be the extent to which the individual's work behavior is under his control. Herman (1973) has shown that when people can control their work activity satisfaction predicts performance and when it does not the relationship is not found.

It is because of this research and these hypotheses that I feel that the whole question of whether or not job satisfaction determines performance, independent of its effects on turnover and absenteeism, is still an open one.

Job Dissatisfaction and Aggression

Common observation suggests that a frequent response to dissatisfaction is aggression. Since aggression as a response to dissatisfaction in the business organization is a frequent occurrence in the form of strikes and other activities of serious economic and social loss to individuals and institutions (Stagner, 1956), it is of theoretical and practical importance to be able to predict and understand the circumstances under which aggression will occur and the type of aggression that will take place. Unfortunately, empirical research and theory relating to these questions have been sparse, despite their importance, and there is not much of a substantive nature that can be cited. However, there has been some research and it is to this that we now turn.

First, joining labor organizations or developing favorable attitudes to them is a common response to job dissatisfaction (Stagner and Rosen, 1965; Sinha and Sarma, 1962). This finding is consistent with the notion that aggression is a response to dissatisfaction if we assume that labor organizations are instruments of aggression against management in that they take away from the arbitrary powers of management.

What also seems to be the case, interestingly enough, is that the type of labor organization joined and the kinds of labor activity engaged in are very much a function of the types of people involved. For example, the traditional trade union is seen primarily as being an instrument stemming from and aligned with low-status blue-collar workers, individuals who might be considered to have a low degree of self-esteem. As a result, a number of writers (cf. Blum, 1963; Kuhn, 1963) have pointed out that the growth of the U.S. trade union movement will depend primarily on either or both of two factors, given the empirical fact that our industrial structure is becoming increasingly white collar. First, the self-perceived characteristics of the white-collar worker will have to change if he is to accept the trade union as a proper instrument for him.

> Management policies, or perhaps a lack of them, may also weaken the clerks' sense of self-importance engendered by their belief that they are a part of management. To many office employees, signing a union card is proof of lack of success, a defeat—an index of decline of importance (Blum, 1963, pp. 190–191).

A second condition for the trade union movement to grow is that the traditional differences between the professional association and the labor union must disappear so that the two become indistinguishable. While occupational sociologists have long disagreed on what the term *professional* means in terms of specific characteristics, there is little doubt that there have been strong differences between the traditional trade union and the professional association. An example of these differences is given in the following quotation from an engineering union head:

> We bargain only for the broad outlines, and let the individuals fill in the details. It is like school. The professors present a curriculum, but the stu-

dents can choose what courses they want to suit their purposes. They also get the opportunity to strive for A's, B's, or C's in grades. We are trying to control only the broadest aspect of standards—like doctors. They negotiate with each patient for their fee but within the overall limits set by their professional body (Kuhn, 1963, p. 195).

Yet, I do not know how much longer the differences are going to remain, considering the strong trade union–like attitudes of the National Education Association and the concern with fee structures and the like among the American Medical Association, the American Psychological Association, and the American Bar Association. The Bar Association, in fact, has come under legal attack for regulating lawyer's fees too rigidly. I am not quite sure how much difference there is anymore between these professional associations and the traditional trade unions.

This trend also opens up the whole question of the consequences of joining a labor organization. Seeman (1966) has found support for the hypothesis that joining a voluntary labor organization gives a person a feeling of greater control over his own destiny and more sense of importance. If this is so, then we should expect that labor union members and professional association members should increasingly act alike in what we have called a high self-esteem manner, with this tendency increasing with the size, power, and prestige of the organization. However, much more research is necessary before we can understand how deriving high self-esteem from an association or a union membership is different from deriving it from management influence, if it is different at all. One interesting hypothesis here might be that the saliency of work performance would be less.

Given that aggression occurs in and between organizations and that it often has dysfunctional consequences, how can the behavioral scientist contribute to its reduction and control?

First, of course, it would be desirable to reduce levels of dissatisfaction. In addition, it is necessary to control at least three other major sources of aggression in industry. The first is the aggression that results from frustration; the second consists of intergroup differences in beliefs, attitudes, opinions, and norms; and the third involves overall social norms that legitimize and value aggression and its related behaviors. Each of these should be influenced in such a way that dysfunctional consequences do not occur, but how can this be done?

Looking first at the case of aggression as a function of frustration, I indicated previously that this is an old hypothesis in psychology. More recent research, however, has resulted in a revision of the basic formulations of the theory in a manner significant for the constructive control of aggression in organizations. In the original formulations it was hypothesized that aggression as a response to frustration increases the stronger the need or desire being frustrated, the more complete the frustration, and the more frequent the frustrations. I said earlier that recent research has supported the first two statements, but the third needs revision because aggression is not likely to occur if the frustration is anticipated. On the other hand, if it is unanticipated, aggression is more likely to take place. Obviously, the more often a person is frustrated, the more he expects it, and the less likely aggression will occur as a result of any specific frustration.

There are several interesting implications of this finding. First, it says that if we observe aggression in a person who is not used to frustration, then there is probably some type of frustrating situation which is causing the difficulty. Hence, if we can control this frustrating stimulus, we will be able to control much or all of the aggression. In principle, then, the leadership of an organization will be able to control at least some aggression if the people in the organization are not used to frustrations as their fate in life. The situation is not the same, however, if the organization is composed of people who expect frustration, since their aggressive behavior is not as stimulus controlled as it is for people who do not expect frustration. One may ask whether people who expect frustration will engage in any aggressive behavior at all. The answer to this is yes, and this brings us to the second implication of the frustration-aggression hypothesis. As the person builds up expectations of frustrations during his life experiences, he is also engaging in a large number of aggressive behaviors and eventually learns to develop aggressiveness as a habitual mode of behavior, (since he has engaged in it so often), although he is no longer as bothered by any specific frustrating situation as he was prior to developing this habit. Thus, these individuals' aggressive behaviors are less subject to influence and control by external manipulators of the environment such as organizational managers.

To control this type of aggression it is best to develop an organizational population that does not expect frustration and for whom aggression is, at least in part, a reaction to a specific frustrating stimulus. It would seem that high self-esteem people can be considered to fit into this category since we have defined a high self-esteem person as one who has learned from his life experiences that he is valuable and competent. Our previous suggestions for increasing the self-esteem of organizational populations have relevance here.

Turning now to intergroup differences in values and norms as sources of conflict, the major question for control is how to reduce the we–they orientation that such differences cause. The problem with intergroup differences, be they different departments, management–union situations, or racial group differences, is that each group develops different ways of perceiving different values and different behaviors.

They then come to value their unique characteristics and see other groups as outsiders. How do we reduce this we–they orientation? Of the most significant proposals, the solutions listed below are representative:

1. Develop goals that all groups can accept as viable and significant.
2. The effectiveness of item 1 will be greater in controlling the conflict if the goals to be achieved depend on the groups' cooperating with one another.
3. Develop procedures whereby all contact between the groups is on an equal-status basis.
4. Develop procedures whereby there is continuing interaction between the members of the two groups, with as many individuals as possible being involved in these interactions (job rotation might be one way of implementing this).
5. Develop procedures whereby each group learns as much as it can about the other groups' motives, attitudes, and values.
6. Each group should refrain from engaging in behavior designed to show one another up.
7. Each group should be as open as possible about its interactions, values, goals, and motives; secrecy tends to breed mistrust and fear.
8. A social environment should be created, overall, so that all people are perceived as competent and worthwhile.
9. Decrease the permanency of commitment to each group and increase the probability of becoming a member of different groups over time; an example of this is the project-team approach.

In addition to these, Osgood (1962) has suggested a technique called GRIT (Graduated Reciprocation in Tension Reduction). Starting from the assumption that the key need is to change the negative perceptions that groups have of each other, Stagner (1961) has summarized GRIT as follows:

1. Unilateral peace-oriented acts should be employed by one group in such a manner that they will be perceived as a low threat by the other group.
2. These acts must be accompanied by explicit invitations to the other group to reciprocate (i.e., engage in acts designed to reduce tension).
3. The unilateral actions must be executed regardless of whether the opponent makes a prior commitment to reciprocate.
4. Unilateral actions must be planned in sequence and continued over considerable periods regardless of whether the opponent overtly cooperates.
5. The acts must be announced in advance of execution and widely publicized.
6. Unilateral initiatives should, whenever possible, focus on areas of mutual interest and opportunities for cooperation.
7. Acts must be of low risk to the group making the peace offer, at least in the beginning, to avoid excessive hazards. Existing intergroup hostility has to be treated as a reality.
8. Each action must be accompanied by firmness toward the opponent.

Finally, a major source of aggression in organizations is the degree to which social norms support aggression. The more aggression is considered to be legitimate and proper, the more it will take place. While this statement has considerable support in the research literature (cf. Berkowitz, 1962), how to control it is not clear. Perhaps the most useful suggestion is that destructive aggression should never be given the stamp of legitimacy, no matter how minor it is. We very often come to value and see as proper and legitimate whatever action we perform, although it may not have been seen as such at the beginning. Once legitimization takes place, the ease of controlling it and decreasing its occurrence diminishes rapidly.

Summary

The significance of work experience and how it affects our attitudes and values about work and about ourselves is becoming increasingly recognized. Until recently the major type of job reaction studied was satisfaction with the job itself, a matter of great importance but, as it turns out, not the only type of effect important to study.

Among these other effects, a type of job outcome that has become of great interest is the phenomenon known as alienation. Unfortunately, there has been great ambiguity surrounding this term and a variety of distinctly different ideas have been indiscriminately lumped together. Faunce has provided some assistance by proposing that alienation be defined as estrangement from the self and from others. These outcomes are a function of feelings of powerlessness, meaninglessness, and normlessness. Another advance in the study of alienation has been the accumulating evidence that feelings of alienation, as defined by Faunce, are not limited to those working on blue-collar, assembly-line positions as the Marxian model would predict. Rather, it has been noted increasingly in high-level management and technical positions.

Consistent with this finding is the research data showing various types of physiological and psychological stress as a result of experience in high-level jobs. A particular finding is that the stress effects are magnified if the job occupant happens to have a high-achievement, compulsive personality.

Job satisfaction as a job reaction remains an important area of study. Theoretical research suggests that among the major factors leading to job satisfaction is the extent to which the job meets personal needs and social evaluation criteria. Recent research has posed a significant problem for those who see job satisfaction as significant for mental health because of the findings that people with low expectations of need fulfillment can be as satisfied as those with high expectation levels. Regardless of the factors influencing its level, there are strong data that job satisfaction influences significant types of work behavior.

SUGGESTIONS FOR FURTHER READING

FAUNCE, W. A. *Problems of an industrial society*. New York: McGraw-Hill, 1968.
This book constitutes an excellent attempt to integrate the morass of literature that has grown around the term *alienation*. While theoretically sophisticated, it is written at a level comprehensible to most students.

HELLER, J. *Something happened*. New York: Ballantine, 1975.
An absolutely magnificent novel about a middle-aged "successful" executive ruminating on the nature of his work and personal life and what success has meant to him. A shattering experience to many who have read it.

SEIDENBERG, R. *Corporate wives—corporate casualties?* Garden City, New York: Anchor Press, 1975.
The author is a practicing psychiatrist in New York State who is concerned with the negative effects of upward mobility of corporate executives on their family life. His case study descriptions are vivid and raise serious issues for those interested in the implications of our work environments for other aspects of the human experience.

TARNOWIESKI, D. *The changing success ethic*. New York: American Management Association, 1973.
A major research study that provides a good base of evidence for the increasingly recognized fact that a successful management career does not necessarily generate personal contentment and satisfaction. Studies such as this indicate that the effects of work experience may be far more difficult to understand than the often proposed alienated blue-collar worker syndrome.

TERKEL, S. *Working: People talk about what they do all day and how they feel about what they do*. New York: Pantheon, 1974.
A best-seller that both reflects and contributes to some of the contemporary interest in work experience. This is a series of extensive interviews with working people in which they reflect on their experience. The distinctive flavor of the work is lost unless the reading is spread out over time.

PART III

APPLICATIONS OF THE STUDY OF WORK BEHAVIOR TO ORGANIZATIONAL IMPROVEMENT

Any theoretical undertaking, no matter how exciting and thought-provoking, needs eventually to be generalized and applied to real-world problems if it is not to lose touch with significant matters and become merely a pedantic exercise. This is as true in the study of work behavior as it is in other fields.

In the chapters to follow I intend to detail how some of the basic tools of behavioral science have been applied to the improvement of organizational functioning. Two major approaches to improvement can be used. One of these is to bring better people into the organization and the second is to change them once they are in the system. Traditionally, the former mechanism has been preferred, but for a variety of reasons that will be detailed in chapter ten, this approach has become increasingly less valuable. As a result, the study of change in work settings has become a matter of great interest, with attention being focused on some of the basic processes and on the various types of change programs that are being used. In chapter eleven we will review some of the basic questions involved in the study of change while in chapter twelve we will review the complex programs that have come to be known as organizational development. Chapter thirteen is devoted to some of the more traditional change programs in attitudes and skill learning. These are of great importance in themselves and also provide a research base for some of the techniques used in organizational development.

The final chapters are devoted to one of the most basic of all questions in the study of work behavior and that is how we ascertain the "goodness" of a particular type of behavior or job reaction. There are a number of conceptual and methodological issues involved here and they need to be discussed for their importance in helping to evaluate the effects of both practical programs and theoretical research.

chapter ten

Organizational Entry: Concepts and Procedures

Most psychologists would probably agree that industrial psychology, as a profession devoted to assisting in the achievement of organizational and individual objectives in the world of work, has its greatest historical support in, and continues to be predominantly identified with, the personnel selection process. It is in the development and refinement of procedures and methodology relating to the question of the basis on which individuals enter an organization that industrial psychology first developed as a recognizable entity, and it is in this area that many practitioners continue to work today.

Despite this tradition, the conditions under which individuals enter organizations is a highly controversial matter today. Recent years have seen continuing argument on such issues as how to reconcile the bases for organizational and/or job entry with civil rights concerns, the problem of satisfying both an individual's right to privacy and the legitimate needs of the organization for job relevant information about the individual and, finally, an examination of the entire philosophy underlying, and the practicality of, the traditional personnel selection process.

This chapter is concerned first with the process, the values, and the questions relating to traditional personnel selection procedures. We shall then discuss how contemporary societal characteristics and changes are generating demands for the development and utilization of techniques to govern the conditions of organizational entry that will allow and encourage the satisfaction of the legitimate needs of the individual, the organization, and society.

Mechanisms for Organizational Entry: Traditional Personnel Selection Models

Two major questions have traditionally concerned organizations that need to select people and that view the process as essentially one during which they will make the decision from a group of applicants. One of these questions has to do with the need for measures of job applicants that can be used to predict job performance and that are available to the company prior to the time of the hiring decision. The second problem has to do with the need for appropriate methodologies for evaluating whether or not a given predictor is actually operating effectively; that is, whether it is recommending the selection of the people it should be recommending. In this book we shall be concerned with the latter question for the most part, since an adequate discussion of the former would require much more space than can be given here.

Until recently, those who were interested in developing effective personnel selection procedures within this traditional framework all tried to do much the same thing, regardless of the particular situation. These procedures, known as predictive and concurrent validity models, will be discussed here and in the next section as a series of steps. At first glance they seem to be highly appropriate. However, as we examine them further, we will see that these models contain a set of assumptions about the nature of work and human characteristics that in today's society are sometimes dubious. These doubts, in fact, have contributed to the development of the newer approaches to determining organizational entry that we will be discussing later in this chapter.

The Predictive Validity Model

step one: the job analysis

The first step in the predictive validity model is the study of the characteristics and required behaviors of the job. The procedure for finding out this information (which also has value for other organizational functions such as training, job transfer, and performance appraisal) is known as a job analysis, which consists, usually, of a description of the various behaviors, characteristics, and abilities required of the occupant of that job. The ways in which this information is obtained vary with the company, the job, the occupant, and so forth, but in essence there are two major procedures.

One way is to ask the current job occupant to describe what he does, either subjectively or along some defined dimensions. This method has some advantages. It elicits worker cooperation by bringing him in on the decision making and possibly enhancing his self-esteem at the same time. A second advantage is that the job occupant probably knows the job better than anybody else. However, there is the disadvantage that the job occupant may be motivated to distort, either consciously or unconsciously, his description in a favored direction. Furthermore, the occupant may not be psychologically, educationally, or emotionally equipped to write an accurate description of his job duties.

Advantages and disadvantages also attach themselves to the other major job analysis method, that of observation. This has the advantage of eliminating distortion to a great extent, since an observer is generally more objective than the job occupant. Furthermore, most often the observer will be qualified. However, the first advantage could be illusory in that the job occupant may fake his performance, either consciously or subconsciously, if he knows that someone is watching him. A second disadvantage is that this procedure is completely inappropriate for "thinking" jobs and for jobs that involve a long period of time before a specific activity is finished. (The comparison here is between the division manager who might be working on a decentralization plan taking five years as opposed to someone who performs a mechanical, repetitive job.) Since these long-cycle jobs are becoming increasingly common in our society, we might expect to see a decrease in the method of observation in job analysis as time goes on.

Besides the advantages and disadvantages of each of these methods, there are problems in job analysis that are common to both and, in fact, to any system involving the rating of such social objects as jobs and people. One set of these problems has been called the judgment errors and can be summarized as follows:

The halo error. The tendency to allow one characteristic of a rating object to dominate ratings along other dimensions of the object. An example is when we are more likely to attribute intellectual qualities to a person who wears glasses than to a person who does not.

The central tendency error. The tendency to rate all rating objects around the middle or mean of a continuum and not to use the extremes.

The leniency error. The tendency to rate all social objects in a relatively favorable manner and not to attribute negative aspects to them. (The obverse to this is that some people are likely to be error-prone in the opposite direction.)

Although there are other judgment errors, these are probably the most important. There is little agreement about how to overcome them.

In fact, some argue that these may not be errors at all and that one of the reasons they are considered as such is because of the stubborn refusal of psychologists to admit that (1) some kinds of human behavior may not be distributed according to the normal bell-shaped curve (e.g., in some cases all people might be good), and (2) some people may actually have all their personality characteristics dominated by a main characteristic such as their social skills (i.e., the halo error is not an error). This seems extreme, however. Suffice it to say for our purposes that these behaviors are probably errors in the traditional sense, but their importance and possible remedial actions will probably vary according to a given situation.

A second problem of what might be more serious import is how to incorporate into a job description some recognition of the fact that jobs are becoming increasingly of the type in which the job behaviors cannot be totally specified in advance but will also result from the characteristics of the person who happens to fulfill the role at that particular time. Look at the differences between a management role and the role of a sewing-machine operator in a dress factory. It is much simpler to specify in advance what the behavior of the latter should be than the former. In fact, it is probably very much the case that one requirement of the managerial role is success in the ability to handle problems that cannot be specified or programmed in advance. While this difference in potential specificity of roles has always been a problem for job analysts, its significance is increasing because many jobs in our automated society are becoming more like that of the manager and less like that of the sewing-machine operator.

It should be emphasized that I am not suggesting that we do away with the job analysis as an aid in selection and manpower utilization programs. For one thing, some job planning is necessary because the alternative is chaos. Second, job analysis is of value in other management concerns besides selection. Previously I mentioned briefly its significance for planning job transfers, for training content, and for performance appraisal programs. There are other values, also. Consider, for example, the following procedures, all of which might be undertaken with the aid of job analysis:

1. Diagnosing organizational coordination (Are people doing what is planned? Is there unnecessary repetition or overlap?)
2. Diagnosing the degree of organizational prejudice (Are blacks on the same job as whites actually doing the same work?)
3. Evaluating training programs (Are training courses teaching deadbeat material that is irrelevant to what is being done on the job?)
4. Assessing administrators' knowledge of tasks (Do the administrators actually know the tasks being done in the organization?)

Since job analysis data can be used in each of these cases, it seems to me that job analysis is still very important, and perhaps even more now than ever. What needs to be done is to determine how it can best be done in the world of nonprogrammed, long-perspective, nonroutinized jobs.

step two: hypothesis development

The second step is to derive from the job analysis hypotheses about the kinds of individuals who would be most likely to fit the behavioral demands of the job. This step can be a subjective one based on an appraisal of the job analysis information. It would thus be highly dependent on the cognitive characteristics of the person developing the hypotheses. Unfortunately, we know little about the kinds of people who would be particularly good at this type of thing. This situation is, undoubtedly, one of the reasons why the more common procedure in job analysis has been to describe jobs in terms of more objective psychological dimensions and then to verify such descriptions by either giving job occupants unambiguous tests of these dimensions or getting qualified interjudge agreement of the importance of the dimensions for the given job. Because of the difficulty of getting tests that are unambiguous measures of simple psychological dimensions, particularly in nonability areas, the latter verification procedure is more common. These descriptions are then used for developing an hypothesis about the type of person to be sought for the job.

step three: predictor development

The third step consists of deciding how one is to measure individual differences in job applicants on the relevant variables. Most important, it is necessary to choose a measure that actually measures the relevant psychological variable that is demanded by the job. The reasons for this are simple. If the chosen measure is not an actual measure of the relevant variable, two possible problems develop, depending on whether or not the measure is actually related to job performance. First, we may reject a good hypothesis as to the cause of good job performance in a given job and not know it. Hence, whatever else we eventually learn about the job in terms of selection and training, this knowledge will always be incomplete, perhaps seriously so. Suppose, however, that the mistake works; that is, suppose we have hypothesized sociability as an important variable but have measured anxiety by mistake (without knowing it) and that anxiety does actually predict job performance. It does not matter, the practical person says, that it does not measure what it is supposed to measure, since it predicts job performance and hence can be used for selection. The answer to this is that this is a wasteful, shortsighted, uneconomical attitude.[1] One reason this is so can be seen if we assume that the relevant important psychological variable is sociability (when it is really anxiety). First, all of the recommendations for managerial action in training, development, appraisal, and promotion that would follow from such a successful prediction would be based on a mistaken belief. A second reason this attitude is impractical is that jobs do change, and sometimes a variable that used to predict performance no longer does. Hence, if we find that our measure of sociability (which is really anxiety) no longer predicts job performance, we start looking for new predictors, eliminating sociability, although a good measure of sociability might now be a good predictor on the changed job.

How does one decide if a measure is actually a measure of the desired variable? The best process for this is a procedure known as construct validity. This consists of looking at all the relationships that the proposed measure of the variable has with other variables and then deciding whether or not these observed relationships are consistent with what they should be if the measure were really measuring what it says it is. As an example, let us look at Table 10.1, which lists the results of a construct validity study of a scale known as the Ghiselli Self-Assurance Scale, defined as a measure of the extent to which people see themselves as competent, need-satisfying, and able to deal with their problems. It can be seen in this table that the relationships with other variables are about as they should be, given this definition. Were they not, we would have a basis for inferring that the scale is not a measure of what it claims to be.

The process of establishing the construct validity of a scale is never-ending. We must continually be concerned with obtaining new information on the construct validity of our instrument since the more we know about it, the more we can have confidence that we are actually measuring what we claim we are measuring. In this sense, the development of the construct validity of a measure is similar to the testing of the utility of a theory.

What kinds of predictors are typically chosen? I mentioned earlier that the development of measures that will be good predictors of performance has been a primary concern of industrial psychologists. The result is that a wide variety of different measures may be used. We may summarize them into the following categories:

Cognitive tests. Measures of verbal and other cognitive skills (see chapter five).

---

[1] Actually, this was the implicit attitude of some practical industrial psychologists for many years. Even these, however, paid lip service to our step 3, although they did not follow it very often.

Objective personality tests. Measures of personality characteristics that have a relatively structured format; i.e., the individual respondent describes himself along dimensions defined by the test constructor rather than along dimensions he defines.

Projective personality tests. Measures of personality characteristics that have an unstructured format and that allow the individual to respond along any dimension he wishes.

Table 10.1

Relationships between Ghiselli Self-Assurance Scale and Other Psychological Measures

NATURE OF SAMPLE	MEASURE	N	MEAN OF "HIGHS"[a]	N	MEAN OF "LOWS"	SIGNIFI- CANCE LEVEL[b]
Engineering students	Gough Adjective Checklist— *Self-Confidence Scale*	14	52.60	20	46.60	.05
Industrial foremen	Miner *Sentence Completion Scale* (a projective test of organizational power orientation)	10	4.70	12	.60	.05
Business students	Crites *Need for Social Service* (Likert-type scale)	35	5.77	36	7.97	.05
Business students	Crites *Need for* Job freedom (Likert-type scale)	35	9.60	36	8.22	.10
Industrial foremen	Biographical data frequency with which parents supervised their jobs and tasks (lower score = greater frequency of supervision)	15	2.93	23	2.30	.05
Industrial foremen	Biographical data frequency with which they argued with their parents during teens (higher score = greater frequency of arguments)	15	2.73	23	2.34	.05
Liberal arts students	Marlow-Crowne SD Scale[c]	89	$r = .16$		No score	
Business students	Bass *Self-Orientation* (force-choice tetrads)	20	27.10	15	24.06	.10

Source: A. Korman, Task success, task popularity and self-esteem as influences on task living, *Journal of Applied Psychology,* 1968, *52,* 484–490. Copyright 1968 by the American Psychological Association, and reproduced by permission.

[a] Division between "highs" and "lows" was based on the median of national norms.

[b] All significance tests are two-tailed.

[c] I am indebted to Virginia Dunda and Charles Miller for these data.

Objective life-history items. Questions concerning relatively objective characteristics of a person's school, work, and personal background; the rationale for these is that they are measures of various attitudinal and personal characteristics that are not measured by other means.

Interviews and other judgmental assessments. Judgments by various individuals of the extent to which the applicant possesses the behavioral characteristics that are felt to be necessary for adequate job performance.

Which of these is the best? There is no single answer. It depends on the criteria used, the occupation involved, various ethical problems, theoretical measurement problems, and so forth. The rest of this chapter will explore these factors and how they might operate to influence the value of these measures.

step four: administration of predictors to applicant sample

Once the measures have been decided on, they are administered to the applicants for the job. However, the measures are *not* used as a basis for selection at this time. Rather, the applicants are selected on the basis of whatever procedures are being used at the time and the scores on the hypothesized predictor measures are filed away, to be used in connection with step 5 (see below).

The reasoning behind this procedure can be explained quite simply. If we use the hypothesized measure as a basis for hiring, we would never know what the job performance would have been of those individuals who were not hired. That is, if the company were to take in only those with high scores, it would not know the eventual performance of those with low scores, and vice versa. For all the company would know, the unselected group might have been better in job performance than the selected group.

step five: relating predictor test scores to measure of job performance

After the applicants have been hired and been on the job for a long enough time to get some meaningful measure of differences in job performance, the first critical point in this process is reached. This is the relating of scores on the predictor variable to the measure of job performance—the criterion. There are two questions involved. First, what measures of relationship should be used, and what are the advantages and disadvantages of each of these measures? Second, how shall we interpret the results found in terms of their practical significance for organizational action?

The correlation coefficient. The most popular method for describing the relationship between two variables in personnel selection research has been one of the statistical techniques discussed in chapter two, the correlation coefficient, or r. One reason for this popularity is that most industrial psychologists are familiar with it, having studied it in their graduate training. Second, it is a convenient way of summarizing a relationship into one generally descriptive term. When we say that a correlation is .60, it is agreed that this means something different from a correlation that is .10 or $-$ .35. Third, there is a considerable amount of theory about r that is concerned with how much confidence we can have in obtained results, given certain assumptions. Therefore, because the theory concerning the correlation coefficient is well developed, we are able to specify, given these assumptions, the likelihood that our results are not due to chance or unstable factors, and we can also estimate the degree to which our specifications will be in error. Related to this is that any obtained r is directly convertible into a measure of predictive accuracy, the purpose of the whole selection mechanism process.

These advantages hold whether we have either a single or multiple predictor. In the latter case, r is known as a multiple r, and it can be interpreted in the same way as the simple r.[2] A value of .00 means no relationship between the two variables, a value of $+$ 1.00 means a perfect positive relationship (i.e., the highest individual on one variable is the highest on the other, the second highest on one is the second highest on the other, etc.) and a value of $-$ 1.00 means a perfect negative relationship (i.e., the highest individual on one variable is the lowest on the other, etc.).

One problem with using r stems precisely from the fact that r measures the extent to which two variables order a group of people similarly. The greater the similarity in ordering, the higher the r, and the greater the discrepancy in ordering of the individuals, the lower the r. The problem is that any discrepancies in ranking individuals have a negative effect on r, no matter the score levels on each. Thus, two predictors of job performance can have the same relationship with job performance and yet differ in value in that one makes errors in prediction only for those who are all very good, whereas the other makes errors in predicting a bad performer to be good and a good performer to be bad. Clearly, the first would be more useful since it does not really make a difference, usually, if you mistake the best applicant for the second best (or the worst applicant for the second worst). In the first

---

[2] You may wish to consult a statistics textbook to see why this is so and to under- stand more fully the logic of the multiple r. The major difference, I might note, is that the multiple r will tend to be too high a value and that a cross-validation study is crucial to verify results. However, as I will explain later, a cross-validation is crucial for *both* single and multiple r. Thus, there are no differences between the two for our purposes.

case, both would normally be accepted, and in the latter both would normally be rejected.

Another problem with using *r* is that it assumes that the relationship between the two sets of scores is best described by a linear formula (i.e., the higher a person is on one variable, the higher (or lower) he should be on the other). Yet, it is conceivable that some predictors would not be related to job behavior linearly but curvilinearly. For example, suppose that we wish to use a test of intelligence to predict performance as a department store sales clerk. One might assume that a certain level of intelligence is required to write sales slips, take returns, and so on. Hence, one would predict a positive correlation between intelligence and performance, or would we? Would this relationship also be so once we sampled above the average in intelligence? Would it not be just as likely here that the relationship would turn negative, since high-intelligence people would become bored with the job? If this were so, then the relationship would be a U-shaped one, as in Figure 10.1. While most relationships studied in work settings have been found to be linear, the possibility that they can be curvilinear should make one wary of using *r* without studying the specific prediction situation.

Figure 10.1
A Curvilinear Relationship between Intelligence and Job Performance

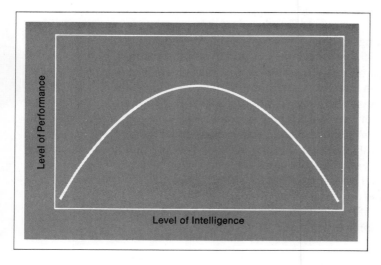

Other problems with *r* concern interpretation. One difficulty is the tendency to interpret *r* as the proportion of predictive accuracy; for example, an *r* of + .50 is twice as accurate as an *r* of + .25. This is *not* so. The most that can be said is that r^2s can be compared with one another. That is, an r of .50 is equal to an r^2 of .25 (.50 × .50), an r of .70 is equal to an r^2 of .49 (.70 × .70), and the latter explains or is about twice as useful as the former. However, for the r figure itself, about all that can be said is that an r of .50 is greater than an r of .30, and so on. Another problem is the interpretation of the actual level of r itself, a problem discussed in chapter two. What is a significant relationship between two variables? Normally, we use the various formulas that are designed to provide a guide for determining whether a given correlation is significant or not, given the size of the sample on which it is based (i.e., whether it is a result of chance fluctuation or whether it really does seem to indicate a true relationship between variables). There have been some objections to this, however, with the major one being that a significant correlation (i.e., one cited as being a real relationship between a given predictor and a measure of job behavior) may actually be one that is very small in actual size, if it is based on a large enough sample size. For example, a correlation of .10, based on a sample of 400, is significant at the .05 level (i.e., there is less than 5% chance that this relationship could have occurred by chance alone, given the size of the obtained relationship and the sample size). Since this correlation is only equal to about 1% of the predictive accuracy ($r^2 = .10 × .10$), we can see why there have been some complaints about this concept of statistically defined significance. Surely, being able to improve the accuracy in prediction 1% hardly seems significant! As a result, Dunnette and Kirchner (1965), among others, have argued that the correlations obtained in prediction studies should be evaluated in terms of practical rather than statistical significance. Although I agree with this point, I must admit that how one translates practical significance into guides for decision making is still a question.

Perhaps the only way of even approaching some kind of meaningful judgment as to whether a given correlation is of practical significance is to view it in terms of the specifics of a given situation since it is these specifics that may play an important part in determining whether or not to use selection instruments at all. For example, contrast the different base rates of success in the situations described in Table 10.2. Assume now that we do not have any selection instruments

Table 10.2
Selection Situations with Different Success Base Rates

SITUATION A	SITUATION B	SITUATION C
Job is very simple: 90% of the applicant population could perform it, e.g., assembly-line workers.	Job is of medium difficulty: 45% of the applicant population could perform it, e.g., first-line supervisors	Job is of great difficulty: 10% of the applicant population could perform it, e.g., middle-level managers

at all and we hire all the people who apply for each job; that is, we predict that *all* will succeed. The number of mistakes in prediction we make in each case is as follows:

> Situation A — 10% (the base rate of success is 90%)
> Situation B — 55% (the base rate of success is 45%)
> Situation C — 90% (the base rate of success is 10%)

These statistics indicate that if a test is to be of practical usefulness, its correlation coefficient must be higher in situation A than in situation B and much higher than in situation C, since ignoring selection instruments and just hiring people at random would result in much higher success in the former case than the latter. (It is for this reason that selection instruments that are often utilized in managerial and high-level selection would be considered to be too low to be of practical usefulness when dealing with lower-level employees.) This base rate of success level is one factor that enables us to determine when a correlation coefficient is practically useful.

A second factor is the selection ratio. Consider the situation in which we need to select only 1 of 100 applicants for a job, as opposed to a case in which we must select 50 of 100. Since in the first case we can take only the best, a selection instrument does not have to be very accurate in increasing our ability to predict job behavior over chance levels. It only has to be a little bit better than chance in order to help us in picking out the best person for the job. On the other hand, this is not the case in the latter situation, where we must pick out 50 and where the accuracy of the selection instrument must be high to be useful. The former case is called a low selection ratio situation and the latter a high selection ratio.

These two factors, then, the base rate of success (or difficulty level of the job) and the selection ratio, are the major guides in determining the practical usefulness of an obtained correlation coefficient in a specific situation. The higher each is, the higher the level that r needs to be for it to be practically useful.

Expectancy charts and cut-off systems. To overcome some of the weaknesses of the correlation coefficient, many psychologists suggest the use of simple and multiple cut-off systems. These are expectancy charts and/or tables that depict the level of job performance that is to be expected from those scoring at different levels of the predictor. Once these charts are developed, cut-offs can be developed for selection purposes that will maximize the level of performance. An example of a simple predictor expectancy chart is given in Figure 10.2.

Although the cut-off methods do not provide convenient summary figures for describing the obtained relationships, a look at this chart indicates the advantages that account for its usage. First, it is clear and easy to interpret. Second, it can be keyed to either type of relationship, linear or curvilinear. Consider the example given in Figure 10.2. Logically, a curvilinear relationship could be depicted there and the logic of interpretation and utilization would be the same, whether one predictor or a combination of predictors is used.[3]

Which is better, *r* or the cut-off technique? There is no simple answer. In many cases simple expectancy charts are quite satisfactory, particularly since they easily lend themselves to practical selection recommendations. Sometimes, however, we would like to know how useful a given job predictor is and for this *r* is very useful. Perhaps the best answer is to use both, one for understanding and the other for administrative recommendations.

step six: cross-validation

The next step in the predictive validity model depends on whether or not the results in step 5 look promising. If they do, it is necessary to *repeat the entire procedure,* using the same job, the same measure of performance, the same kinds of applicants, and so on. The reason for this stems from the essentially conservative nature of the scientific endeavor. It is always conceivable that a single obtained result, no matter how positive the obtained relationship, could occur on the basis of chance factors alone. To have greater confidence in the results, one should always replicate the study. This is the purpose of the cross-validation step.

Unfortunately, it is often the case that the results of step 5 are not promising enough to continue to the cross-validation attempt. In this case, there is nothing else to do, according to the predictive validity model, but start all over again with a new set of potential predictors.

step seven: recommendation for selection

The last step, assuming that step 6 works out, is to make recommendations for selection. The point is to specify the kinds of scores that will be acceptable for selection and then to set up guidelines for the administration of such recommendations. Often such recommended guidelines may take the form of the tables given in Figure 10.2 with the desired scores outlined in some manner. Since this whole procedure depends very much on the specifics of a given situation, we shall not bother to discuss it further here.

---

[3] Textbooks in statistics or tests and measurements provide meaningful illustrations of multiple cut-off techniques.

Figure 10.2

Examples of Simple Cut-off Systems Relating Test Scores to Job Behavior. *(Top)* Chart showing relation between pilot aptitude score and successful completion of pilot training (Psychological activities in training command AAF, *Psychological Bulletin,* 1945, *42,* 46). *(Bottom)* Chart showing relation between biographical "score" and length of service for female office employees (Development of a weighted application blank to aid in the selection of office employees. *Research Report No. 7,* Personnel Research, 3M Co., 1956).

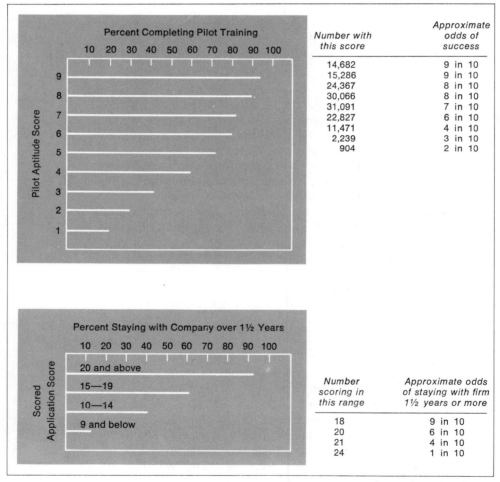

Source: M. Dunnette and W. Kirchner, *Psychology applied to business, and industry* (New York: Appleton-Century-Crofts, 1965).

assumptions and problems

This, then, is the predictive validity procedure. Its advantages are that it is statistically based, it attempt to limit human error, and it provides checks on the various steps along the way. Generally, it should work well and it does, when the implicit assumptions involved in it are met. However, these assumptions are being met less and less in today's world and new models and procedures in personnel selection are becoming necessary. In fact, severe questioning of the whole logic underlying personnel selection is taking place with recommendations for some radical change being heard. Before we turn to some of these recommendations, let us see what the assumptions of the traditional predictive validity model are.

The first major assumption is a belief in a static world relating to both jobs and people. There is a strong assumption that the kinds of people who apply for a given job will not change over time, nor will the characteristics of the job. Is this reasonable? It probably was in the days when our organized work force consisted predominantly of blue-collar individuals engaged in semi-skilled, manual factory employment, but these jobs are less the case today. We now have more white-collar than blue-collar employed people, and the discrepancy is increasing all the time. Since white-collar work is generally less routinized than factory work (although by no means is all white-collar work that innovative), the opportunities for job change by particular job occupants are much greater. In addition, an increasing number of workers have jobs in which the opportunity for job innovation and self-expression are either expressly engineered into the job or demanded by the job occupant. Clearly, the assumption of the static job is increasingly difficult to meet.

A related argument can be made for the assumption of similarity of applicant populations. We live in a dynamic society, and we are constantly subjected to changing legal, social, and ethical constraints on our behavior. An obvious example of this is the greatly increased concern with minority-group employment and utilization and the implications for selection, training, and development which we shall discuss in more detail later. Suffice it to say at this point that it should be obvious to all that a large company in a downtown metropolitan area is proceeding in a somewhat foolhardy manner if it assumes, without checking, that its applicant pool is equivalent psychologically to the type of applicants the company had 10 or even 5 years ago.

Another problem with the predictive validity model is that of sample size. We cannot apply this procedure unless there is a considerable number of people doing the same job, with this number not decreasing over time. Again, one can see the remains here of a way of thinking that was adequate for the industrial world of 30 years ago but which is increasingly less so today. The very essence of managerial, technical, and other white-collar jobs is their uniqueness in the organization. While there are many jobs in which this assumption still holds, it is obvious that there are many in which it does not.

A third problem is the amount of time involved in implementing the predictive validity procedure. To develop a set of predictor instruments utilizing the traditional personnel selection model, a longitudinal study must be undertaken with no guarantee that the attempt will be successful (see step 6). This, of course, makes it a problem to sell to management.

Finally, there is the assumption that when we find a set of successful predictors of job behavior these will be equally applicable to all individuals applying for that job. In other words, the traditional predictive validity model assumes that if a person is to succeed on a job, it is because he has the required amount of that characteristic and if he is to fail, it is because he lacks the characteristic. It does not acknowledge the possibility that a subgroup of the applicant population might succeed on the job for a different reason. Consider a case in which one hundred women apply for a position as salesperson. Sixty-seven of these women would use perseverance as a method of job behavior if they were hired; none would use tact. Thirty-three would use tact, none would use perseverance. If all of these women were thrown into the same applicant pool and analyzed as a group, the psychological variable that would be of greatest predictive importance would be perseverance. Hence, all the women who would use tact as a way of succeeding and who would succeed, if given the opportunity, would be prevented from doing so. This is unfair to these applicants since it prevents them from obtaining a job in which they would be successful. In addition, it is also unfair to the organization, since it is losing a potential group of successful employees and its selection technique will, overall, be inefficient.

Recognition of the fact that people may use different routes to job success has become necessary as a result of two factors. First, there has been an increase in the number of jobs that allow personal innovation and differing ways of suceeding. For example, to assume that one may succeed as a research personnel psychologist only by performing experiments in the area of training and development is a foolish and dangerous process. The individual interested in personnel selection might develop a procedure of far greater benefit if given the opportunity.

A second factor is the presence of culturally deprived groups such as blacks and Latin Americans in occupations where they never were previously. The question is whether these different cultural groups succeed in various achievement situations for different reasons. In some cases, there is evidence that they do (cf. Kirkpatrick, Ewen, Barrett, and Katzell, 1968). On the other hand, a number of studies do not find such differences in prediction for different racial groups (Boehm, 1972). We will talk more about this later. The point is that we need to allow for the possibility that this can occur, and it is because of this possibility that the moderator variable approach to personnel selection has achieved considerable importance. Basically, this approach involves choosing a variable (in this case, ethnic group) that moderates or determines how two other variables might be related (e.g., aptitude and work achievement). As a technique for selection that has become necessary in some instances, it generates even more doubt about the usefulness of the traditional predictive validity model.

The Concurrent Validity Model

Attempts to meet these and other problems discussed later are a great source of controversy today, as we will see. One revision which, in fact, dates back many years is the concurrent validity technique. Its goal is to eliminate the delay between the administration of the predictor measures and the collection of job behavior measures by using present, already working groups of employees as test groups on which to determine whether potential predictors are related to job performance. In other words, the procedure is very much the same as predictive validity except that the hypothesized predictors of successful job performance are administered to those for whom job performance data are immediately available. If the expected relationships occur and are replicated in a cross-validation step, the measures are recommended for administrative use in selection procedures.

There is little doubt that it is because this procedure overcomes the time problem that it became popular for developing selection instruments. Yet, there are some who feel that this benefit does not compensate for the very serious disadvantages entailed, disadvantages that include almost all of those in the traditional model plus several others.

In addition to the fact that the concurrent validity model makes the same assumptions as the predictive validity model about the static nature of the job, the constant large influx of applicants with similar characteristics, and the necessity for large numbers of individuals performing the same job, it also assumes the following: (1) the motivational determinants of responding to a possible selection instrument (such as personality tests, attitude questionnaires, etc.) are the same for those already on the job as for those applying for the job; and (2) scores on a potential predictor of job behavior are not related in any systematic manner to experience on the job.

Obviously, if these two assumptions did not hold, it would destroy the validity of this procedure. How often are they violated? It would appear hard to believe from all that we have said elsewhere in this book about socialization and change in work settings that attitudes and cognitions do not reflect organizational experience to a great extent. Similarly, when a person who is working and has union security is asked about his motivational characteristics, it is hard to believe that the psychological determinants of his answers are similar to those of a person who may have been out of work for several months.

A third problem associated with the concurrent validity procedure is a technical one. Consider the situation in which an organization has a job category involving 40 positions but which now has 5 available openings. Who are the 35 currently on the job? Technically, they are a subgroup of those who were originally hired for that position, differing from the 5 who left in that they remained on the job. Now if we assume that, in general, the person who stays on the job or who is not fired is more competent than the one who quits or is fired, then the 35 now on the job would, in general, show less variation in job performance than the original unrestricted group of 40. If this were so, it would be harder to find any correlation between a predictor and job performance, since a correlation measures the similarity in variation between two variables and one of the variables does not have much variation. This, in turn, would depress the level of the correlation to a level perhaps lower than it would be if we had used it in a predictive validity situation.

Mechanisms for Organizational Entry: Alternate Models for Personnel Selection

There are two solutions to the problems we have discussed with the traditional personnel selection models. One is to develop alternate approaches to the selection process, still within the framework in which the organization does the decision making. The second is to develop mechanisms whereby organizational entry decisions are made from a different framework. First I want to discuss the former approach, while later in this chapter I will deal with the latter.

The Moderator Variable Model

Among the newer approaches to personnel selection that have gained some adherents is one that we mentioned briefly in our discussion on cultural variation problems in personnel selection—the moderator variable model. As stated there, this model involves the identification of some population characteristics by which we first divide some applicant population into two or more subgroups. Following this step, we then compute predictor systems for each separate group, with the average predictive accuracy of each then being greater than if we used the same predictor formula over the entire sample.

Consider the following example:

1. Variable X has been found to be correlated with job success for applicant sample A at a level of $r = .40$. Variable Z is correlated at $r = .05$.
2. However, sample A can be subgrouped into sample A_1 and sample A_2 on the basis of some other variable, say variable Y.
3. Once we perform the subdivision indicated in step 2, we find the following correlations with job success:

	CORRELATION OF X WITH JOB SUCCESS	CORRELATION OF Z WITH JOB SUCCESS
Subsample A_1	.52	.03
Subsample A_2	.10	.48

Variable Y can be considered to be a successful moderator in this instance.

How do we find successful moderators that can be used at the time of job application? One might find useful moderators by studying socially significant variables of various kinds (e.g., race, sex, and significant personality characteristics such as self-esteem) or by using powerful data analysis procedures to search out variables of this nature.

But do we find and use moderators in real life? Here the evidence is mixed. One problem is that while the moderator approach does have the advantage of increasing prediction accuracy, it has the disadvantage of requiring an even larger N than the traditional model. (In fact, in terms of having equal confidence in the stability of the results obtained, we would need a sample size of $2N$ if we split into two groups, $3N$ if we split into three groups, and so on). To illustrate, in Table 10.3 there is a study reported with Naval samples (Kipnis, 1962) which supports the author's interpretation that his Hand Skills Test, which he interprets to be a test of motivation to persist beyond minimum standards, should be a more effective predictor of job performance for those who need the motivation to succeed (low-ability people) than for those who do not need it (high-ability people). In this case, intelligence or ability has moderated the relationship between motivation to persist and performance. Notice, however, the different sample sizes in the separate analyses.

Table 10.3

Correlations between a Test of Motivation and Job Performance
for Those with Differing Levels of Intelligence

APTITUDE LEVEL	PHI CORRELATION	N
High		
AM	.03	63
RM	.12	61
NP	.04	56
OC	.13	53
Low		
AM	.43[a]	57
RM	.47[a]	61
NP	.39[a]	61
OC	.26[b]	55
Totals		
AM	.23[b]	120
RM	.29[b]	122
NP	.23[b]	117
OC	.21[b]	108

Source: D. Kipnis, A noncognitive correlate of performance among lower aptitude men, *Journal of Applied Psychology,* 1962, *46,* 76–80. Copyright 1962 by the American Psychological Association, and reproduced by permission.

[a]Significant beyond the .01 level.

[b]Significant beyond the .05 level.

Another example of the moderator variable approach that may have some social significance is Banas's study (1964) of handicapped and nonhandicapped workers. Banas found that certain intellectual test factors in the General Aptitude Test Battery differed in their ability to predict job performance between handicapped and nonhandicapped and that such differences in predictability depended on the job the person was in.

On the other hand, moderators often are not found in the real world and when they are, their effects are not consistent in different situations (cf. Cronbach 1975). The question is why, assuming it is not always a sample size problem, which it is not. One reason, I believe, is that the moderator variable is formally and logically equivalent to the contingency variable used in leadership theory. In both cases the hypothesis is that the correlation between two variables is different for different levels of a third variable. All the problems that I outlined for contingency theories are true here: the difficulty of knowing and defining the crucial score on the contingency (moderator) variable on an a priori basis in a given situation, their limited value (since most people normally fall between the extreme scores on the moderator), and the unreliability of any given finding because of statistical regression effects. You might do well at this point to review that discussion on contingency models. Its implications for us here are that, yes, moderators can and do occur but they are hard to find and when they are found, their practical usefulness and consistency are questionable.

The Synthetic Validity Approach

A characteristic of all the approaches to personnel selection that we have discussed so far is that they depend on relatively large numbers of individuals performing the same job. This poses a problem for personnel selection in these days of specialized, high-level personnel in jobs that are ever-changing in demands and requirements. Hence, there has been an interest in one proposed remedy to this problem, an approach known as the synthetic validity method. Consider Table 10.4, which proposes a series of dimensions of job behavior that are applicable in various degrees to each of 12 jobs; that is, each of the values listed is a rating of the importance of that behavior dimension for the job at the left. Since these are specific behaviors, it should be possible to find specific tests or predictors that would predict differences in performance on each. That is, we should be able to find tests that are able to predict differences in performance on dimension A, differences in performance on dimension B, and so on. In order to determine if the test actually makes such discriminations, we would use current occupants on each job, comparing the level of test performance of those in jobs in which the skill is very important with those in jobs in which the skill is unimportant. Using behavior dimension A, then, the basic logic is that those who are now in job 12 will exhibit more of these behaviors than those in job 4 since it is important for performance on that job. If this is so, scores on a predictor variable measuring this dimension would be an effective predictor of performance on job 12.

Table 10.4
Ratings of Importance of Dimensions of Behavior for Each Job

Jobs	JOB BEHAVIOR Dimension A	Dimension B	Dimension C	Dimension N
1	6	7	3	2
2	9	5	8	6
3	4	3	7	9
4	1	4	1	5
.	.	.	.	.
.	.	.	.	.
.	.	.	.	.
12	10	1	2	7

To be more specific, assume that dimension A is verbal ability, dimension B is the personality trait of dominance, and dimension C is spatial ability. This would suggest the following:

	Verbal Ability	Dominance	Spatial Ability
Manager	9	8	2
Salesman	9	4	1
Mechanic	4	5	9

If we were able to find tests that correlated with verbal performance, dominant behaviors, and spatial performance, the validation groups for which would be current members on the three jobs, we might be able to use these tests for selection in the following possible ways:

1. Applicant A, who is high on the predictor for verbal ability but relatively low for dominance and spatial ability, might be selected for salesman.
2. Applicant B, who is high on both verbal ability and dominance, might be selected for manager, and so on.

The major advantage is that, instead of developing selection instruments on one specific occupational group, we use several occupations. In other words, the problem that develops when we have only ten people in each occupation is overcome if we can use six or seven occupations, each of which has ten individuals.

Synthetic validity assumes that dimensions can be found that apply across a group of occupations, an assumption that constitutes its major problem. Although there are a couple of studies which have shown some support and which indicate that this assumption might be met (cf. Guion, 1965), these have mostly been with low-level jobs. There is as yet little evidence that enough dimensions of similarity can be found across such innovative, self-directed positions as sales manager, research director, and chief engineer, for example, to make this a feasible approach, and these are the types of occupations that are of greatest concern. It would seem reasonable to conclude that while this approach has some promise, much more needs to be done before an accurate evaluation of its fruitfulness can be made.

Clinical or Judgmental Prediction

Because the question of sample size is crucial to most personnel selection models and because the most difficult and important selection problems are the high-level unique jobs (i.e., those where the sample size is smallest), attention has focused on clinical or judgmental prediction methods. This process involves taking measurements on a set of applicants for a given position (such measurements might consist of test data, interviews, ratings from peers, superiors, and psychologists, etc.) and making some overall judgment about that person for the job. The correlation between these judgments (or predictions) and some measure of success on the job constitutes a measure of how good that person's judgments are or how good a predictor he happens to be. Judges may be psychologists, employment office interviewers, managers, and so on.

There are differences between this method of combining variables for the purpose of predicting job performance and the purely statistical methods discussed earlier. First, the necessity for large samples to establish a measure of the quality of the prediction system is less necessary here, since what we are actually concerned with is the quality of the judge. How good is he? Does he make good predictions? Establishing a measure of quality can be done quickly, since by the time he makes as few as five or six predictions we can make a judgment. Consider the following: if the probability of succeeding on a given job is 50%, then the chance probability of making a correct prediction in a given case is 50% or 1/2; the chance probability of making two correct predictions is $1/2 \times 1/2$ or 1/4 or 25%; the chance probability of making three correct predictions is $1/2 \times 1/2 \times 1/2$ or 1/8 or 12 1/2%; the chance probability of making four correct predictions is $1/2 \times 1/2 \times 1/2 \times 1/2$ or 1/16 or 6 1/4%, and so on. If we were to get a judge who made five correct predictions out of five, the probability of doing this is so small that we would have good reason for thinking that we have a judge who is really good.

A second difference concerns the flexibility of the judgmental approach versus the statistical procedures. The latter are rigorous and follow the rules set. There are certain formulas to be utilized and the numbers derived dictate what is to be done. Such rigorous, cookbook-type procedures are, conceptually, not the bases for the clinical or judgmental prediction model. Here the individual judge can use predictors of job behavior in any way he wants. He can use one predictor for person 1 and another for person 2, he can reverse this later in the interviewing process, he can drop one predictor completely, and so on. All different ways of combination, simple and complex, are at least conceptually possible in the judgmental prediction model.

These differences have generated a controversy for years between advocates of the statistical approach to prediction and advocates of the clinical-judgmental procedure as to which is more accurate (cf. Meehl, 1954). There is little need to go into this here except to note that the either-or aspect of the controversy makes little sense. For one thing, you can find support for both techniques and you can find studies in which neither has been supported. Some time ago I reviewed the literature on the prediction of managerial performance and found considerable support for the clinical-judgmental model and less for the value of predictions based on the statistical model (Korman, 1968b). A couple of years earlier, Ghiselli (1966) found considerable support for the statistical model in predicting success in a variety of jobs. The pattern has remained the same since then in that evidence can be found for the usefulness of both, with the clinical-judgmental model being particularly useful for management selection. Relevant here is the work on assessment centers, a procedure for which evidence is beginning to accumulate.

Basically, the assessment center involves a set of judgments by multiple assessors (i.e., psychologists and/or management personnel) of the potential performance of a group of either applicants or current employees being assessed for other, usually higher careers in the organization. In making their judgments the assessors use a wide variety of cues such as interviews, job simulation performance, psychological test data, and group interaction observations, with such information usually gathered over several days by direct observation in a specific setting. Assessment centers have consistently been shown to have good validity for predicting later behavior, even when methodological problems have been controlled (Howard, 1974).

To me, the either-or argument between clinical and statistical prediction is silly. Clinical and statistical predictions are useful for different situations and both need to be developed further. Additionally, and I suggest this primarily to the statistical advocates, there sometimes is simply no alternative to using a clinical prediction system, for example when there are only a small number of people to be selected for rather unique jobs. There are also the problems I mentioned earlier with the traditional statistical models. Thus, we have to accept clinical prediction as a sometimes necessary tool, and we need to develop it further. For one thing, we need to know more about the process itself and the factors that influence judgments of this nature. If we knew more about these factors, we could, for example, develop training programs to overcome some of the problems and biasing effects that lead to poor decision making. This would help make both human and computer simulation decision making in this area more accurate.

The following list summarizes some of the findings about various influences on judgments in the selection situation. An examination of these will show that although much is known, a lot more remains to be determined.

1. Interviewers tend to develop a stereotype of a good candidate and then seem to match applicants with stereotypes (Webster, 1964).
2. Biases are established early in the interview (Webster, 1964; Mayfield, 1964).

3. During an interview in which the applicant is accepted, the interviewer talks more and in a more favorable tone than in an interview in which the applicant is rejected (Webster, 1964).

4. Interviewers are influenced more by unfavorable than by favorable information (Webster, 1964; Rowe, 1967; Mayfield and Carlson, 1966).

5. Seeing negative candidates before positive candidates will result in a greater number of favorable acceptances than the other way around (Rowe, 1967).

6. There are reliable and consistent individual differences between people in the total number of people they see as being acceptable (Rowe, 1963).

7. Factual written data seem to be more important than physical appearance in determining judgments (Carlson, 1967a); this increases with interviewing experience (Carlson, 1967b).

8. Situational measures of behavior designed to simulate job conditions are weighted more heavily than ability tests which are, in turn, weighted more heavily than personality tests (Bray and Grant, 1966).

9. Although the immediately previous job applicant has an influence on ratings of the current applicant, the effect seems to be relatively small (Carlson, 1970; Hakel, Ohnesorge, and Dunnette, 1970).

10. Although individual interviewers may use the same psychological structure for evaluating people, they may not agree on where particular individuals score on the traits comprising the structure (Hakel, 1971).

11. An interviewee is awarded a more extreme evaluation when proceeded by an interviewee of opposing value (Carlson, 1970).

Problems in Personnel Selection:

The Movement for Equal Employment Opportunity

A crucial problem that threatens the very foundation of the personnel selection process has developed in recent years as a result of societal concern with civil rights matters in employment opportunities. Basically, the dilemma stems from the following considerations:

Fact One It is against national policy to discriminate in employment matters on the basis of race, color, creed, or sex.

Fact Two Almost invariably, with the exception of various unique local conditions, culturally disadvantaged groups score lower on achievement tests of various kinds than do culturally nondisadvantaged groups. (The reader should keep in mind that this is a descriptive statement that does not imply any conclusions concerning the relative importance of heredity or environment in determining these results.)

As a result of these two conditions the last decade has seen an explosion of legal, psychological, and sociological interest in the nature of employment testing and the conditions under which it may be utilized as a basis for organizational entry. As a result, I am going to offer some opinions here as to what implications all of this has for traditional approaches to personnel selection as mechanisms for deciding conditions of organizational entry.

I think the dimensions of the problem stem from the legitimate concerns of all three major participants in the controversy—the company, the individual, and society in general. It is not just one party alone that needs to be considered. Given this, it is important to recognize first that these groups are not always in conflict with one another; they do show points of convergence. From both the company and the long-range societal perspective, it is necessary that we have healthy organizations. Therefore, the best person for any given job should be hired. On the other hand, from both an individual and company perspective, the person to be hired should be the most likely to succeed since most (not all) people want at least a modicum of success in their job. However, there is also the concern of others and of society in general that the cycle of poor jobs, low income, and their accompanying social pathology be broken. How does one do this without ignoring the fact that certain social and/or family backgrounds are more likely to stimulate the growth of high achievers and that this fact has implications for the type of people one is most likely to hire? The problem is that the traditional personnel selection process is essentially a conservative strategy for organizational improvement that reflects all those factors in society that stimulate different levels of competency, whether these factors have operated fairly or not.

If you look at recent court decisions and the controversies that developed as a result of these decisions, some possible resolutions to these problems are beginning to appear as these are being reflected in the work of the various agencies that are charged with enforcing our governmental commitments. I am referring here to such agencies as the Equal Employment Opportunity Commission of the U.S. Government. Below are summarized some of the latest guidelines in this area, as I understand them. We should note, however, that they are constantly changing. Following this, I will turn to some of the remaining ambiguities, particularly in such areas as affirmative action and quotas.

1. The Civil Rights Act of 1964 forbids both overt discrimination *and* practices that are fair in form but which operate in a discriminatory fashion. The key question is whether the employment practice is related to business necessity. If the practice that excludes members of the minority group is not related to job performance for *both* majority and minority groups, the practice is prohibited.

2. Nothing in the Civil Rights Act forbids the use of tests or other employment practices; what is forbidden is the use of these measures if they are not related to performance. The Act does *not* say that you must hire less qualified minority group applicants as opposed to better qualified major-

ity group applicants. What it does try to do is to insure that such considerations as race, sex, and religion are irrelevant to employment and that only ability to do the job is considered relevant.[4]

3. The burden of showing that the test or other employment measure is actually related to job performance is on the employer.

4. There are four ways of demonstrating the relationship between any test or employment practice and job performance. Three of these I have already discussed, i.e., predictive, concurrent, and construct validity methods; the fourth mechanism is the content validity method and is illustrated by the requirement for secretarial job applicants to pass a typing test. More generally, content validity can be claimed if the test adequately samples the skills and knowledge required by the job. For a secretary, content validity might very well be useful as a mechanism for evaluating possible tests and other predictors. For others such as managers or salesmen, it may not be as useful.

5. Among the types of employment practices that come under this legal structure, the following are illustrative without being inclusive:

   a. psychological tests of all kinds

   b. minimum educational requirements (e.g., high-school graduation)

   c. arrest records

   d. interview decisions

From the viewpoint of legal considerations, it is clear what needs to be done. Yet, operational implementation of these guidelines does not solve all the problems, nor do I think they can. For example, in very few cases is there a sufficient number of job applicants of a minority group background to allow sufficiently stable estimates of the validity of a test for this group. One result is that sometimes selection tests cannot be used at all for these individuals. In addition, while it is true that differences in test validity between the minority and majority groups tested are sometimes found to be nonsignificant and it is recommended that the groups be merged for personnel selection purposes (cf. Boehm, 1972), it is also true that differences in validity do occur. In the latter cases, the tests cannot be used.

A second problem concerns the adequacy of the criterion data. As I will discuss later, there are studies which suggest, that in some instances, a racial bias in criterion ratings takes place in the direction of favoring one's own race. The illegitimacy of such criteria clearly casts doubt on the validity of the whole selection process.

Overall, though, there is the continuing social problem that results when all of the EEOC guidelines have been *met,* but the result still is that there are fewer minority group employees than the company and the community feel is desirable. What to do then? Hold to the legal po-

---

[4] However, this does not mean that this potential problem does not exist. It has developed in a highly controversial fashion under the affirmative action programs discussed later in the chapter.

sition, one quite defensible? Or engage in other selection procedures that involve more long-range community concerns such as the affirmative action programs?

The term *affirmative action* refers basically to the demand by the federal government that organizations take positive actions to hire minority group members in sufficient numbers and at diverse enough levels so that their representation at different levels in the organization approaches that of their representation in the population which is drawn on as a labor force. The penalty is the loss of whatever federal funds the employing organization is eligible to receive. Since its implementation, affirmative action has been a source of heated controversy for several reasons. First, does affirmative action constitute a requirement for a quota system, as its opponents say, or is it a statement of goals, as its proponents say? If it is the former, it is in violation of the Civil Rights Act of 1964 and Executive Order 11246. If it is the latter, how do goals differ from quotas in an operational sense? Second, whatever affirmative action is, a quota system or a goal system, does it generate an acceptance of lower quality personnel as part of the intent to increasingly utilize minority group personnel?

There are no easy answers to these questions, partially, I think because of their extremely controversial, highly political nature. Many people feel that the questions are irrelevant; that is, that the long-range interests of society demand that an increased input of minority groups into organizations take place regardless of whether it is called meeting quotas or goals and regardless of whether there is a temporary decrease in the quality of organizational functioning until the people hired increase their competence. (They do not believe the decrease would be permanent.) On the other hand, others claim just as vociferously that this constitutes a reverse form of discrimination against majority groups because no government pressure is being executed in their behalf. In addition, they claim that it is morally, ethically, and financially insane to deliberately tolerate lower levels of competence in our organizations than is necessary. Finally, they argue that it produces states of normlessness and meaninglessness to explicitly inform large segments of our population that hard work and effort may not pay off in increased job rewards but that these rewards will be awarded on the basis of variables over which people have no control (i.e., sex, race, etc.). It is hard enough to build a society that can effectively control the awarding of illegitimate rewards; to deliberately encourage this behavior is self-destructive. Finally, to complicate the issue further, there are the arguments that affirmative action programs have not helped the people they were designed to help. An article in *The New York Times* (February 9, 1975) reported data that integration has proceeded more rapidly without affirmative action, that it has led to conflict, and that it has encouraged self-doubt on the part of those benefiting from it.

What is the answer? Frankly, I do not think there is any. There are good arguments to be made for both sides. There is little doubt in my mind that without special governmental help such as affirmative action programs, discrimination on the basis of religion, race, and sex would remain unabated in many organizations, even if minority group members were equally as qualified as majority group applicants. I also think it is psychologically damaging for a government to tell individuals explicitly that hard work and effort may not pay off in increased job rewards. The alienating effects on the individual and the eventual destructive effects on the society itself would be quite harmful. As a result of these good arguments on both sides, the result has been two predictable outcomes. First, there has been continuing conflict between opponents and proponents of these programs with no real resolution and probably no prospect of such in the future. Second, there has been, overall, both because of these problems and also those discussed earlier, a decreased interest in the use of traditional personnel selection mechanisms. Organizations just do not want to be continually involved with these difficulties. Yet, it is also clear that from the viewpoint of the individuals involved, the organizations, and society, some matching between persons and jobs needs to take place. The question is how? I will discuss below some of the alternative mechanisms that might be used in addition to, or instead of, the traditional personnel selection approaches, after I first review two other problems that also support the desirability of the changes I will be suggesting.

Ethical Questions

Another matter of concern in the area of personnel selection as it has traditionally been practiced in business and industry relates to privacy and a person's constitutional right not to have to bear witness against himself. The relevance here has to do with the use, especially for executive and managerial selection, of personality questionnaires of various sorts. There are two major problems with such usage. First, these questionnaires may ask a person to describe various aspects of his personal life that have, on a face basis, only a tangential relationship to job requirements. Second, such questionnaire responses often become a part of a person's file in the organization, to be used, perhaps, in ways that are improper and that were not intended by the original test administrator.

How shall one answer these criticisms? Psychologists are by no means agreed, since there are various moral, ethical, legal, and technical questions involved. On one hand, most psychologists would probably feel that a company has a right to inquire about a person's personal attitudes, since these could conceivably be related to job performance. However, it is now legally required that such relationships be empirically established, something that has been difficult to do with personality questionnaires thus far (cf. Guion and Gottier, 1965). In addition, there is an ethical position that all job applicants who are given personality questionnaires should have a right to know the results of these questionnaires and what the administering psychologist will conclude from them. In most cases, this position is adopted and carried out, a position that has been legally implemented by a 1974 federal law.

The second problem is, perhaps, not as easily resolved by the psychological community as is the first since this involves the ways in which organizations are administered. While there is little doubt that almost all psychologists would severely condemn improper usage of psychological tests, how one controls it is a different matter. Perhaps one way to control it is to destroy all records once their original purpose has been served. While this may seem drastic, and there is not much chance that it would ever be accepted by the management that pays for these tests, nor perhaps should it since these data can continue to be useful, the importance of the problem is so great that such a drastic solution might spur a search for something more acceptable.

Social Influences on Test Performance

A significant problem in personnel selection stems from the fact that test behavior is a sample of human behavior under standardized conditions (Anastasi, 1958). As such, performance on tests is subject to the same influences that affect performance in other areas, including the social influence that we have spoken of earlier. There is evidence that scores on psychological tests are subject to and influenced by the expectancies of the test giver, both implicit (Rosenthal, Friedman, and Kurland, 1966) and explicit (Korman, 1968a) and that scores on such tests are predictable from the opinions of the test giver about the abilities, skills, and characteristics of those taking the test. In addition to such social influences, another obvious contaminating variable is that performance scores on a personality test are often a reflection of the test taker's opinion of what will make him look socially desirable in the eyes of the company and/or the test giver.

The insidious problem with these social influences on test performances is that these influences may be applied unknowingly by the test giver in a differential manner to different groups of applicants and thus operate in an unfair manner. An example here is that of the middle-class test giver communicating differential expectancies to lower-class test takers. While there is unfortunately no research on how often such differential influences take place in actual selection contexts, they probably occur often enough to result in some real problems in interpreting test scores. There is need for research on this problem and how best to overcome it.

Alternative Approaches to Determining Organizational Entry

If you were to look for one major underlying theme in this chapter, it would be that selection in its rigid, automatic, in-or-out form is decreasing in importance as an organizational improvement mechanism. Starting from the observation that one cannot develop statistical formulas for selection when sample sizes are small and when the world is a dynamic one, we cited in rather rapid succession other problems such as the various weaknesses of the different selection models. Problems in ethnic discrimination, ethical questions, and testing situation influences on test performance with their possible discriminatory implications are also very much with us.

There has been a variety of responses to this situation, with one being a greater concern with methods for changing people and organizations. We will talk about these in later chapters. In addition, there is now great interest in other methods for determining organizational entry. One suggestion has been to set up minimum standards for personnel selection and then sample randomly within that pool of manpower without regard to affirmative action guidelines and similar considerations. The effect of this method would be to minimize the discrimination problems and throw greater reliance on training and development procedures.

In another direction there is increasing interest in using self-selection as a basis for organizational entry decisions. The idea here is to view this decision as one in which both the individual and the organization attempt to see whether they can be mutually beneficial to one another. Although this activity is currently taking place mostly at an executive or managerial level, it is also being used at least to some degree by organizations that have hired large numbers of employees who could not meet normal selection standards but, who, nevertheless, have become part of the organization. While the process is obviously different at the two levels, the differences are mostly differences in degree, not in kind. Hence, there is, in both situations, a concern with how well these individuals can be placed into the organizations. How can they be helped to make good job and career choices? How can they best be counseled to make their work careers meaningful and worthwhile?

There are a number of ways in which this approach can be utilized, but most common is to begin by giving the person a complete assessment of his interests, his capabilities, and an assessment of the jobs and careers available in the organization for which he meets certain minimum standards. (In addition, if available, he would be given the results of test data showing the likelihood of his success in the different careers.) Within this context, he is then encouraged to choose the job and career he wants, with this choice quite often taking place with the aid of managers or trained counselors. A number of major corporations such as IBM have recently attempted variations of this approach with individuals who were already employed and whose further career development was being encouraged. In addition, there is an experimental program being run by the Department of Personnel in the state of Arizona that has been concerned with the predictive validity for job performance of self-estimates of ability and which seems promising,[5] but definitive data are not as yet available. I hope that this changes in the near future since the idea seems highly promising in terms of overcoming some of the problems of organizational entry we talked about in this chapter and some of the problems that are inherently involved in any hierarchical management policy such as the traditional personnel selection process. This alternative assumes that, in general, the mistakes made in assuming that people know themselves as well as tests come to know them, and that they will not knowingly choose a job that will lead to failure (and there will be mistakes here), will lead to fewer dysfunctional organizational and personnel effects than the traditional personnel selection models. The validity of this assumption can come only from research data, not from philosophical or theoretical arguments.

Summary

Developing procedures for systematizing the personnel selection process and maximizing its effectiveness is the area in which psychology first made its contributions to organizational effectiveness. Since the years prior to World War I psychologists have worked on techniques for accurate assessment of applicants and on a methodology for evaluating their effectiveness. This chapter outlines in considerable detail a procedure known as the predictive validity model which served as the optimal approach to this goal for many years. Basically, it involves assessment of job requirements, hypotheses as to appropriate applicants, the testing of these hypotheses using rigorous statistical tech-

---

[5] E. Levine, personal communication.

niques, and the development of recommendations based on the results of the statistical analyses.

Cultural and legal changes have made this model somewhat less useful in the last decade. Among the problems are that, first, the predictive validity model assumes a stability of applicants and job characteristics that is increasingly less true today. Crucial here also is that the increasing utilization of minority group members and women in jobs that were previously closed to them has made it more difficult to use this procedure because of possible differences between these groups. However, it is still not certain how significant these differences are for developing predictors of job behavior. Overriding all of these considerations is the degree to which personnel selection procedures may be used at all, considering legal and cultural demands for increased minority group utilization and affirmative action. It is still not clear what the solution to some of these problems are, particularly since the other selection techniques developed to deal with some of these difficulties introduce other problems. These alternate techniques include moderator variables, the synthetic validity method, and judgmental prediction. Future procedures governing organizational entry may involve more joint decision making by the individual and the organization than is the case today.

SUGGESTIONS FOR FURTHER READING

AMERICAN PSYCHOLOGICAL ASSOCIATION, Division of Industrial-Organizational Psychology. *Principles for the validation and use of personnel selection procedures,* 1975.

This division of the APA has been actively involved in trying to reformulate the logic of personnel selection procedures in light of some of the legal and cultural considerations discussed in this chapter, with this being the latest of their recommendations. Like all such proposals, some aspects are controversial. Yet, they are important as reflections of some of the major contributors to this field.

BOEHM, V. R. Negro-white differences in validity of employment and training selection procedures: Summary of research evidence. *Journal of Applied Psychology,* 1972, *56,* 33–39.

An important review article on some of the methodological questions and the research findings on a matter of importance to the design of personnel selection programs.

HOWARD, A. An assessment of assessment centers. *Academy of Management Journal,* 1974, *17,* 115–134.

One of the best of the recent reviews of the usefulness of assessment centers in organizational settings. The author points out some of the methodological and practical issues involved, reviews and categorizes the research literature, and comes to conclusions of a positive nature.

KRAUT, A. I. A hard look at management assessment centers and their future. *Personnel Journal,* 1972, *51,* 317–326.

The author is a well-known researcher in the field of assessment centers. In this paper he reviews some of what has been learned in this field and what it means for management.

chapter eleven

Change in Work Settings: Basic Processes

Conceptually, controlling the conditions of job entry is an organizational improvement mechanism that involves control of the skills, abilities, and attitudes that people bring into the organization. This is clearly not the only way, however, to effect improvement. We can also change people once they are in the system. Change is the subject of this and the next two chapters. First, I will discuss some of the basic processes we need to understand in developing our knowledge of change in work settings. Following this, I will show how these basic ideas have been translated into explicit change programs and what the results of these interventions have been.

Socialization Processes in Organizations

Perhaps the most meaningful point at which to begin any discussion of change is to emphasize that *change will take place, regardless of whether or not explicit programs are introduced.* Thus, one of the most important findings in studies of the adult personality over the past decade has been that, under some conditions, men and women change in relatively important ways as a function of different kinds of everyday experience, even at the adult level (cf. Mischel, 1973; Weiner, 1972; Korman, 1976). This does not mean that changes are inevitable or that they occur quickly. It is clear that some individuals remain pretty much the same over time regardless of experience and that any investigation of them at a single point in time would be a fairly accurate statement of their characteristics. One does not need longitudinal research for them. However, others *do* change and some of them change in rather significant ways. In other words, we can no longer assume a fixed model of traits and characteristics for these people during their adult lives; we have to take account of the possibility of continuing changes in their personality and attitudinal characteristics as a function of everyday experience in their jobs.

Recognition of this possibility for change and an examination of the frequency and the conditions of its occurrence has important theoretical, social, and administrative significance. It is important theoretically because it enables us to develop a more adequate theory of work behavior; it is important in a social sense because it enables us to understand more fully the meaning of work as a significant social institution in our society and the roles and functions it plays in affecting people and their characteristics; and it is important administratively because an examination of different types of work experiences and their effects may provide explicit guidelines for the management of organizations as to how and what needs to be changed in order to achieve desired outcomes. For these reasons I want to spend considerable time on these matters in the following pages.

Why do Adults Change?: The Attribution Process and Internal–External Control

The best place to start in this discussion is first to defend the proposition that these changes actually occur. After all, aren't people pretty well shaped by the age of 18 or so? For a long time psychologists, educators, and a lot of other people thought so, and many still do. Yet, an increasing number now think that significant personal change at the adult level is much more common than we thought. Why this revision?

First, one can hardly deny that these changes often take place, even if one is a psychologist, sociologist, or some other type of behavioral scientist. For example, most people do not get married with the intention of getting a divorce. Yet, the divorce rate in this country is about one out of three, and in some geographic areas it is considerably greater. Some changes must be taking place among most of these individuals and they are all adults, at least chronologically. It is not likely that all of these divorces have been due to delusional thinking prior to marriage. A little bit closer to our concerns here are new societal phenomena such as "male menopause," midcareer change, and the like, all reflecting significant motivational changes in adults of a career-related nature. Although not yet systematically understood and little researched until now, the occurrence of these phenomena and their meaningfulness can hardly be doubted.

Changes happen. Why? One reason is a process called attribution.

> Attribution theory concerns the process by which an individual interprets events as being caused by a particular part of a relatively stable environment (Kelley, 1967, p. 193).

The basic logic of the attribution process stems from the theoretical assumption that man is motivated to attain a cognitive understanding of the nature of his environment and, more specifically, an understanding of what causes particular events. If he understands what has caused specific events in the past, presumably he will be able to control, by actual intervention or by the pattern of his choices, what will happen to him in the future. Because of this hope for control, people make attributions of reasons for events. This attribution process may then, in turn, cause change throughout life, as the following depicts:

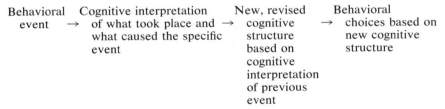

Behavioral event → Cognitive interpretation of what took place and what caused the specific event → New, revised cognitive structure based on cognitive interpretation of previous event → Behavioral choices based on new cognitive structure

The key fact to keep in mind is that change takes place because the causes of events cannot be observed directly and causality needs to be imposed on or ascribed to events by the perceivers. In the area of behavioral events, such ascription of causes will be generally made either to the individual engaging in the behavior, to the environment, or to either or both under different conditions, since these are generally considered to be the causes of behavior within a scientific perspective (Heider, 1958). The effects on later behavior will be different, depending on which attribution is made.

Let us take, for example, a newly hired saleswoman who has done well in her first month. To whom or what should she attribute her success? If we work out the derivations, we get some interesting predictions. If she attributes the success to herself, she has a greater expectancy of achieving success in the future (since she has achieved success in the past because of her own efforts), and she will work harder because of this increased expectancy in order to achieve in the future. (I might note that this prediction holds regardless of one's theoretical preference. Thus, her increased expectancy might lead her to work harder for the values she wants, if you adopt the expectancy-value model, or because increased performance is in balance with the higher self-esteem that has resulted from the success she has achieved, if you adopt the consistency model.) In addition, another result of attributing success to herself is that she will now take pride in what she has done and will anticipate even greater pleasure from achievement in the future, since she sees it as due to her own efforts. This increased anticipated value from achievement will increase the likelihood of increased achievement-oriented behavior in the future even further.

Suppose, however, that the newly employed saleswoman does not attribute the success to herself but to external environmental influence, such as her supervisor, the company training program, her coworkers, the great desirability of the product itself, and so on. What happens here? One prediction is that success would not breed a greater likelihood of future success. In fact, her later behavior would be independent of her previous behavior, since she would not gain increasing confidence with success (because she would not see the success as due to her efforts), and she would not learn from failure (since she would not see failure as her fault). As a result, management will have lost an important means of influencing this employee since she has not, with success, increased her perceived likelihood of achieving the values that management offers, and thus she will be less likely to try to obtain them. Additionally, even if she attains the values being offered, they will provide her with little pleasure because she would not see their attainment as due to her efforts. One implication of this theoretical analysis is that management should encourage attribution of the causes of behavior to personal rather than external causation, since this would lead to more effective job behavior. Is such an analysis supported by empirical data? I think so.

There is a considerable body of research on different reactions to success and failure in situations in which the people believe that the outcomes are due to their own efforts (as a result of experimental manipulation) and situations in which the outcomes are attributed to external influences. Generally, these findings show that in the former case success leads to increased expectancy of success in similar task situations and failure leads to decreased expectancy (Weiner, 1972; Phares, 1973). For the external control situation, these changes in expectancy do not occur. In this case, we are more likely to see the occurrence of behavior likely to lead to failure because of failure to learn from experience.

When we turn to the research literature where belief in internal and external control has been measured by psychological scales (Rotter, 1966) rather than experimentally manipulated, the findings are consistent in that people high in belief in internal control are more likely to have successful vocational careers in general (Valecha, 1972). Also consistent with these findings is Weiner's (1972) work with achievement motivation. This starts from the same assumption that we made above; that is, cognitive processes intervene between the outcomes of a given behavioral act and later behaviors. The nature of these intervening processes is that they affect the directionality and likelihood of later behaviors by affecting the expectancy of successfully engaging in these later acts and the degree of positive affect to be attached to them.

In the area of achievement behavior, Weiner proposes that several kinds of cognitive activities can take place as a result of a behavior that has led to achievement (Weiner, 1974). Most relevant is his argument that under some conditions (e.g., when the individual has a high need for achievement and when the social norms are appropriate), the individual is more likely to attribute success to his own efforts. When this happens, the person is likely to keep achieving because of the following process:

Success →   Attribution of success → Augmented pride   →   Increased probability of achievement
   experience   to oneself   in accomplishment   behavior

How well does Weiner's approach account for the data? He has reviewed considerable research, both his and others, and the evidence, while not always consistent, is strong (Weiner, 1972, 1974). In addition, besides his own specific hypotheses, his work supports the position that significant motivational processes do change over time and that the internal–external attribution variable may influence the direction of those changes.

In fact, I have been so impressed with the major thrust of these findings and their significance for organizational behavior (where the concept of internal–external control is so important) that I have tried to develop an expanded version of the theoretical model I proposed earlier, one that incorporates some of these considerations. In this expanded version I have, while keeping the basic form of that framework (because I think it has been generally supported), tried to take account of this concept of attribution as an influence on changes in motivation. Another reason I am suggesting this extension is that the original hypothesis I proposed predicts that high self-esteem people will develop increasingly high self-esteem because of the pattern of their choices, while those who have low self-esteem will develop lower self-esteem. Similarly, those who exhibit high creativity will become even more creative; those with low aggression will become even less aggressive, and so on. On reflection, I think there is something wrong with this conception. People do change over time and sometimes radically. Not all successful people become increasingly successful and not all failures fail increasingly. Sometimes, people who were once achievers become less so, those who were once aggressive become less so, and we do get flashes of creativity, at times, from people from whom we least expect it. The question is why? Can we ascertain the types of conditions or factors that lead to these changes? If we can, we would be able to understand, and perhaps influence, both those factors leading to the decline of career success once success has been attained and those factors that lead a person to respond constructively to failure. Similarly, we might also influence the course of creative behavior and aggression as these behaviors might change over time, and so on.

Since I do not think that the framework I proposed earlier, useful as it is, can account for these processes, some type of revision is necessary. My proposal is that change (or the lack of it) results from the extent to which one's personality generates choices that are similar to those encouraged by environmental influences to which one is subject and which may change over time. If the environmental influences are different, I predict that changes in behavior reflecting these influences will also take place. If the environmental influences are consistent, there will be no change.

To be more concrete, let us start from the basic assumption that individuals who are high in self-esteem and/or who are in nonhierarchical organizations are more likely to be internally controlled in their attributions (both Phares 1973 and Weiner 1972 have reported considerable evidence in support of this assumption). These individuals are more likely to attribute the results of both their behavioral outcomes and the behaviors of others to the individuals involved than to external forces (e.g., leadership factors). On the other hand, for those who are low in self-esteem and/or who are in hierarchical organizational environments, opposite attributional tendencies would occur; that is, they would attribute the causes of events to external factors. I would suggest the following outcomes would then occur under the three possible situations in organizational settings.

condition a:

Contemporary organizational influences are not salient. An individual who is high in self-esteem, value for others, and belief in a variable world as relatively persisting personality and attitudinal character-, istics will attribute the outcomes of his behavior to himself; to the extent that situational environmental influences are not greatly salient at the time, the results of successful task-achieving behavior will then be:

1. increased self-esteem (since the success is due to himself)

2. increased value for others (since the positive feedback from others as a result of his own behavior is due to himself)
3. increased belief that the world can be changed (since change has occurred, and the individual attributes it to himself)

The results of unsuccessful behavior will be:

1. redoubled effort for success (because he has violated personal and social norms for success, and it is due to the self)
2. redoubled effort for positive affect from others (because he has violated personal and social norms for positive affect with others, and it is due to the self)
3. redoubled effort for meaningful change and development (because he has violated personal and social norms for meaningful change and development, and it is due to the self)

Individuals who are low in self-esteem, value for others, and receptivity to change are more likely to attribute their behavior to external influences. Hence, we would expect to see mirror images of the above behaviors for these individuals. The results of successful task-achieving behaviors would be:

1. no increase in self-esteem (since the success is due to others, e.g., leadership, and not the self)
2. no increase in value for others (since the positive affect from others is due to others, and not the self)
3. no increase in acceptance of the possibility that change can occur (since the change has been controlled by others)

The results of unsuccessful behavior will be as follows:

1. unsuccessful behavior will be accepted as appropriate (since external influences are responsible)
2. behavior involving negative affect with others will be accepted (since external influences are responsible)
3. behavior involving lack of growth and development will be accepted (since external influences are responsible)

To summarize, I suggest that in condition A, behavior remains relatively stable over time because of the belief systems of the individual, the attributional processes indicated, and the lack of any salient organizational influences to counteract these effects.

condition b:

Contemporary organizational influences are salient and consistent with belief system. Condition B is an amplification of condition A in that the environmental influences operate to reinforce the behavior patterns influenced by the preexisting personality dispositions. In other words, this is the situation in which a high self-esteem individual finds himself in a nonhierarchical organization and a low self-esteem person finds himself in a hierarchical system. Since these environmental variables have effects on behavior similar to the preexisting personality pattern, the outcomes are the same as under condition A, only more so (since two sources of influence are operating).

condition c:

Contemporary organizational influences are salient and inconsistent with belief system. It is under this condition that attitudes and behavior will change over time. The mechanism through which this would operate is that as a particular environmental influence increases in salience relative to the influence of the individual's preexisting personality and belief system, there are accompanying changes in both the belief system of the individual (as a function of the social influence and social reality) and also changes in the attributional processes used. Since the environmental influence here would be opposite to that of the belief system (e.g., the high self-esteem person would be in a hierarchical setting and/or the low self-esteem person in a nonhierarchical), I would predict an eventual change in the individual from his original belief system to one reflecting the environmental influence, if the latter is strong and persistent enough. Behavior would then change in order to be consistent with that influence, as that influence became internalized by the individual into his belief system.

To illustrate this process more fully, consider the following (using the relationship between self-esteem and achievement as one illustration):

case 1:

When the organization, occupation, and/or work culture encourages hierarchical and external control, and achievement success has occurred, the leaders who helped in the career success (e.g., parents, teachers, manager, etc.) become more valued as a result of the tendency of both the individual and the social influences around him (including the leadership) to attribute the causes of the successful behavior to these external influences and the rewards and punishments they control. This leads to the growth of personal attitudes and values favoring hierarchical systems of authority (after all, they have been responsible for success). Once developed, it is predicted that these attitudes lead to failure because, with increased favorability of attitude to authority, there will be increased exposure and acceptance of hierarchical systems, and hierarchical systems lead to low self-esteem. In this way a high self-esteem person who succeeds may eventually become a non-achiever (and a low self-esteem individual who achieves in some context and might have continued to achieve does not do so).

case 2:

When failure occurs, and there are prevailing social standards for achievement, and when the environment encourages both nonhierarchical thinking (i.e., positive self-evaluation) and the attribution of causes for behavior to internal causes, I would predict that this positive self-evaluation and internal attribution will lead eventually to higher self-evaluation (and, consequently, higher achievement). For the low self-esteem person who has failed and has not met social standards for achievement, the fact that he is encouraged and socialized to evaluate himself positively in this environment will lead him to explore new kinds of behavior. Eventually, this will result in greater success than that resulting for the original low self-esteem induced behavior. This success will, in turn, lead to a higher valuation of self (because of the tendency to attribute the success to the self) and the eventual performance of behaviors that would be appropriate to achieving career success. For the high self-esteem person, the failure is also perceived as due to the self (because of the tendency by the self and others to use internal attribution in interpreting their behavior). Since both the belief system and the environment also encourage high self-esteem as well as internal attribution, the reaction to the failure will be increased motivation to seek successful outcomes.

Overall, then, if we consider conditions A, B, and C together, I am hypothesizing a set of processes whereby sometimes success breeds success and sometimes it breeds failure. Similarly, failure sometimes breeds failure and, sometimes, success. In this way, we may be able to account both for the fact that people may change as a function of everyday experience and that, sometimes, successful people become unsuccessful and, sometimes, unsuccessful people become successful.

Is there research evidence for these proposals? Not much as yet. However, there is some that comes from studies conducted in other contexts by a number of different investigators and their results are consistent with these general propositions, as Table 11.1 indicates. Despite this general favorability, however, much more research is needed before we come to any firm conclusions on these hypotheses. In addition, I want to note that some data already exist that may be inconsistent with what I have proposed. Maracek and Mettee (1972) have found in a laboratory study that internal-control subjects are more likely to accept failure than those of external control. Reconciliation of these findings with the data in Table 11.1 is clearly necessary.

Table 11.1
Summary of Evidence Relating to Longitudinal Model of Work
Behavior

BASIC FINDINGS	INVESTIGATORS
1. Low self-esteem subjects who denied a social manipulation aimed at inducing low self-esteem do better at a later task than those low self-esteem subjects who did not protest the manipulation.	Pepitone, Faucheaux, Moscovici, Cesa Bianchi, Magistieth, and Iacono (1969)
2. Low self-esteem boys who were held in high esteem by their peers and teachers had greater achievement and self-improvement motivation than those low self-esteem boys who did not have high ratings from their peers and teachers.	Coopersmith (1967)
3. Individuals from backgrounds encouraging belief in control over one's life react more constructively to stress situations than do those coming from backgrounds encouraging powerlessness.	Tiffany and Tiffany (1973)
4. The more hierarchical a society (in terms of economic inequality), the more members of that society will endorse approaches to leadership that involve mistrust of individuals and the need to manipulate them in a political manner.	Bass and Franke (1972)
5. Individuals of high external control are more likely to utilize hierarchical, traditionally authoritarian forms of leadership than those of high internal control.	Goodstadt and Hjelle (1973)
6. Individuals who believe in personal control of behavior outcomes expend more effort on similar tasks subsequent to failure than do those who believe in external control of behavior outcomes.	Weiss and Sherman (1973)
7. Individuals who have performed tasks for money in the past are less likely to perform tasks in the future when money is withdrawn than those who have not performed tasks for money in the past.	Deci (1972)

I might note also that this extension of the theory to account for changes in work behavior has considerable relevance for a number of other matters that are discussed in this book. Each of the hypotheses listed below is predicted by this model and is discussed elsewhere, with the evidence for the first two more compelling at this point than for the last. Work needs to be undertaken on this last hypothesis (which is of considerable interest today).

Hypothesis One Organizational development programs designed to increase task success which *include the active participation of the individuals involved,* even if these individuals have not been successful in the past, will be better in the long run than the exclusive use of expertise without contribution from the people involved.

Hypothesis Two The introduction of management practices designed to match the preferences of individuals will lead to satisfaction in the short run but in the long run it will lead to performance that exacerbates differential motivation toward high and low achievement stemming from original personality predispositions. I would predict that to provide authoritarian leadership for those preferring it would increase their satisfactions on a short-range basis but minimize their performances in the long run. In addition, their satisfaction would also eventually decrease as they fail to meet societal standards for achievement. However, their dissatisfaction would not be as great as that of the high self-esteem individual who failed to achieve.

Hypothesis Three   The more an individual has used extrinsic rewards (e.g., money) controlled by leadership figures as a criterion for self-evaluation and has attributed his reasons for behavior to these external-control mechanisms, the more the following are likely to occur: (1) He will come to view himself as being controlled by others; he will see himself as an unworthy individual, incompetent, and without the confidence to influence his own fate (i.e., he will develop low self-esteem), with this being independent of his actual degree of success in achieving these extrinsic values. For this reason, I would predict that phenomena such as middle-age apathy (e.g., male menopause) and lack of work involvement are as likely to occur with materialistic success as with materialistic failure. (2) He will see himself as unworthy of rewards in general, intrinsic and extrinsic, and will not be motivated to attain them (i.e., he will develop low self-esteem). (3) He will become alienated from his feelings, emotions, and values and will not use them as a guide to his behavior in determining the choices he makes and the degree to which he will be satisfied with the outcomes of his choices (i.e., he will develop low self-esteem).

Why Do Adults Change?: Post-Behavioral Valuation, Familiarization, and Other Processes

Although attribution processes and the internal–external control variable are significant in helping us to understand the manner in which work behavior may change as a result of everyday work experience, you should not think that these are the only factors involved. There are several other psychological phenomena that need to be considered.

One of the most important of these other processes stems from a theory I discussed extensively earlier in this book, the theory of cognitive dissonance. If you look back, you will see that a very important part of the theory is that it predicts attitude change as a result of the interpretation of one's previous behavior. In general, the less that one's previous behavior can be justified rationally (e.g., personal preference, external justification, etc.), the more one's attitudes change toward justifying previous behavior. On the other hand, the more that it can be justified, the less attitudes change. To illustrate, individuals in an organization are less likely to develop favorable attitudes toward the job if they have been overpaid than if they have been underpaid (at least on an hourly basis). Surprising as it may seem, you will recall that there is considerable evidence for just such a prediction. Dissonance theory, then, also postulates an individual who (1) behaves at time 1 as a function of needs and cognitive structures, (2) interprets the results of his behavior as a function of certain personal and social influences, (3) incorporates his interpretations into his cognitive and attitudinal structures, and (4) behaves at time 2 as a result of this new psychological structure. I might note, however, that as in the study of motivation, there is controversy over the effects of external justification in influencing change in attitudes. Significant here is the work of Breer and Locke (1965) who predict that changes in attitude as a result of work experience are positively related to the amount of reward associated with that experience. The basic logic of their position can be summarized as follows:

> In any task situation certain patterns of behavior will have greater reward value than others. By virtue of the reinforcing quality of task outcomes these particular forms of behavior will have a better chance of being emitted than others. At the same time, individuals working on the task can be expected to respond cognitively (through apprehending the instrumental nature of the acts), cathetically (by developing a positive attachment to this behavior), and evaluatively (by defining such behavior as legitimate and normally desirable).

Source: Breer, P. and E. A. Locke. *Task experience as a source of attitudes.* (Homewood, Ill., Dorsey Press, 1965) p. 15.

Breer and Locke also hypothesize that, through a process of induction, the beliefs, preferences, and values are generalized laterally to other similar tasks, and vertically in terms of level of abstraction. *Lateral generalization* may be illustrated as follows: A group performs a task successfully. If the members of the group think that being in the group helped to achieve task success, the above theory suggests that each should develop positive attitudes toward collective behavior and working in groups in other work situations. *Vertical generalization* proceeds from the specific to the abstract. Thus, if an individual develops a positive attitude toward working in groups, he will generalize this so that collective behavior becomes desirable not only in work, but in life overall. Since there is considerable support for these arguments (cf. Goodman and Baloff, 1968; Goodman and Theodore, 1973; Tefft, 1971), I think there will eventually have to be a reconciliation between this and dissonance theory. Later in this chapter I will suggest some possibilities in this area.

Stemming from a different theoretical perspective there is the work of McClelland (1965), who has been actively engaged in developing programs designed to change adult achievement motivation (McClelland and Winter, 1969). As the theoretical underpinning for this work, he has used his familiarization hypothesis, which states that we are motivated to approach those outcomes that are moderately discrepant from previous outcomes and avoid those outcomes that are greatly discrepant. This hypothesis predicts that the motivational processes of adults may change as a function of their work experience; for example, any stimulus that becomes more familiar on the basis of experience, up to a point, becomes a source of positive motivation. Opposite predictions would be made for those stimuli that become increasinly unfamiliar.

As the final evidence we will cite for the argument that people may change simply as a function of everyday work experience, there is a separate body of literature from personality theory that has led to such conclusions as the following (Mischel, 1973):

> Response patterns even in highly similar situations often fail to be strongly related. Individuals show far less cross-situational consistency in their behavior than has been assumed by trait-state theories . . . Even seemingly trivial situational differences may reduce correlations to zero . . . Activities that are substantially associated with aspects of intelligence and with problem solving behavior — like achievement behaviors, cognitive styles, response speed — tend to be most consistent. (Mischel, 1968, pp. 177 and 253)

Mischel has suggested on the basis of these conclusions that personality might best be viewed as a function of individuals' expectancies, subjective stimulus value, and other variables that may change as a function of experience. Placing his argument within an overall context, we obtain a view of man as a flexible, changing individual reflecting continuing interactions with his environment, a picture that is, of course, highly consistent with the argument I have proposed here.

Occupational Socialization and Conformity

One more question on this subject of change as a function of everyday work experience which I think is important to bring in here concerns the nature of any general processes operating in most work settings, independent of the effects of any specific job experience. More exactly, the question that interests me here is whether the process of change as a result of organizational and work socialization operate, in general, to produce conformity to a specific norm and increasing homogeneity of thoughts, attitudes, and behaviors.

At one level, the answer is obviously no. After all, we all know doctors who differ from one another, managers who differ from one another, and so on. However, the question is not all that simple. For one thing, there clearly might be pressure toward conformity in a work setting that some can resist but most cannot. It would be important for us to know this, both from the viewpoint of pressures on individuals and from a societal perspective. In addition, it is important to know this from the organizational perspective since increasing conformity generates an eventual incapacity to deal with problems that may confront those working in a changing, dynamic society.

When does conformity result in response to general socialization processes in the work setting and when doesn't it? At the current time, we have little research in this area, although we do have some theorizing. It may be argued (and there is some evidence) that conformity to an occupational norm may be a function of anticipatory socialization; that is, modeling yourself on the perceived characteristics of the occupation prior to actually entering it. In this case the result would be high homogeneity of attitude, thought, and feelings of people in a specific occupation or work setting, but it would not be a function of work experience (cf. Rokeach, Miller, and Snyder, 1971). Yet, it is doubtful that anticipatory socialization is the whole answer. Longitudinal research in a work setting has shown some increasing conformity pressures (cf. Hinrichs, 1972).

Schein (1971) has suggested hypotheses as to when socialization in the direction of increased conformity will take place and although the evidence for his framework is not great, there are some data for it. A major advantage also is that it does provide some possible direction for further research. Schein's hypotheses are as follows:

1. Acceptance of organizational norms occurs primarily as a person moves up or down in the hierarchy or as that individual becomes part of the inside group in the organization, i.e., as he becomes an insider or part of the system. However, movement from one type of work to another involves changes in skills and abilities, rather than concern with organizational norms and values.
2. Acceptance of and conformity to norms will be greatest as a person approaches a time when he will move higher in the hierarchy or become accepted into the group at a higher level and immediately after he makes the passage.
3. In general, acceptance of organizational norms will occur more early in a career and innovation will take place later. However, both can occur at all times.
4. There will be a tendency to conform only to demands relating to factors that the individual feels are important if he feels free to leave the work setting. If he feels committed to the work situation so that he cannot leave it, he will conform to most demands, significant or not.

Strategies for Change

The fact that change in individual characteristics takes place as a result of work experience for the reasons that I have indicated has an important implication for the design of change programs in work settings. It makes it useful to distinguish between two different strategies for designing change programs. One is the approach involving the appropriate use of incentives and the other involves the control, application, and manipulation of work experience, rather than allowing it to occur without direct influence. The two frameworks are not antithetical (and actually are complementary), but it is useful to distinguish between them because they suggest different types of behavior that may be used to influence change.

Type I: Incentive Manipulation

The first type of change strategy, which we will call Type I, involves changing people by rewarding those behaviors that are desired and not rewarding those that are not wanted. Also called an incentive manipulation strategy, this change approach can operate in two ways. First, it may affect directly the behaviors involved and the likelihood of their occurrence. In addition, it can affect the later behaviors of the individuals by influencing their attitudes and motives as a result of the secondary reinforcement process. By secondary reinforcement we mean that as a specific type of behavior is rewarded, those stimuli that occur at the same time as the behavior become viewed more positively. These changes in attitude toward specific objects as a result of this association will then, in turn, affect later behavior.

Type I change strategy may be utilized by either rewarding the behaviors of the individual directly or by having him observe the behavior of others. Through such observation the individual comes also to learn what behaviors are likely to be rewarded and to develop positive attitudes toward those objects associated with the rewarded behaviors. As I said earlier in the discussion on aggression, this observational learning framework has been called social learning theory.

To summarize, the basic logic of the Type I change strategy is that we change behavior by shaping it through rewards and then we maintain it through basically similar mechanisms. In addition, the objects associated with the rewards come to be valued through secondary reinforcement, and these new valuations also serve to direct the future activities of the individual. Let us now look at some of the conditions under which this approach is most effective.

the importance of reinforcement

Integral to Type I change, as we have discussed it here, is the concept of reward or, to be more technical, positive reinforcement. One fact is eminently clear: behavior that is positively reinforced, that is, one which is followed by a satisfying state of affairs, tends to be re-

Table 11.2
The Social Learning Theory Framework

Individual views relationships between ⟶ the behavior of certain individuals (e.g., executives) and outcomes of the behaviors (i.e., the degree to which the behavior is rewarded).	These relationships are learned as a result of ⟶ those perceptions.*	After learning the relationships between these behaviors and their outcomes, he engages in behaviors which, according to these learned cognitions, will enable him to achieve his desired outcomes. (For example, if he wishes to achieve organizational success and he sees that the president of the company behaves in a certain way in order to achieve sucess, he is likely to behave in the same manner.) ↓ The eventual development of: 1. learned behaviors that lead to desired outcomes 2. increased value for the stimuli and objects associated with the rewarded behaviors as a result of secondary reinforcement processes.

*Research has by now fairly well established that contiguity is a sufficient condition for learning that two stimuli are associated; reward is not necessary (Korman, 1974).

peated. This statement, known as the empirical law of effect, is agreed upon by most laymen as only common sense. Despite such agreement, however, and the fact that it seems to lead to a clear practical implication that the way to develop effective change programs is to positively reinforce people for changing, the actual implementation of this principle has by no means been this easy in the everyday world of work. There are at least two reasons for such difficulty.

First, it is apparent that what constitutes a satisfying state of affairs for one person may not constitute a satisfying state for another; hence, what will constitute a positive reinforcement for one person may not for another. Second, the manner and structure in which reinforcement is provided during the change process affects later behavior very differently. Most significantly, there is a highly consistent research finding that if we do not reinforce every new (changed) behavior but instead reinforce only a portion of them, the new behavior will be much more likely to be continued without reinforcement (i.e., it will be much more resistant to extinction) than if the behavior had been positively reinforced more frequently during the change process. This puzzling phenomenon has proved a constant embarrassment both to those theorists who accept a simple reinforcement theory of change and to those businessmen who argue that psychology and the other behavioral sciences have never provided anything but a repetition of the obvious. The latter aspect is particularly significant for those interested in practical questions since a moment's reflection will indicate that the partial reinforcement phenomenon can have enormous implications for organizational performance. The reason for this is that a behavior developed through partial reinforcement will continue to be performed, even though it may become inappropriate, undesired, and not positively reinforced by those in a position to give reinforcements.

If this discussion of partial reinforcement is making you think that using positive reinforcement to change people (a key component of the Type I strategy) is not as easy as it seems at first glance, this is only the beginning. There are other problems, and though they are not fatal to the approach, they do indicate that we need to go slowly. Consider the following three difficulties in applying this method.

First, incentives may lose their effectiveness over time, sometimes when we least expect it. The reason for this is that we adapt to the incentive and it loses its ability to stimulate us. (You will remember here our earlier discussion of activation-arousal theory and its prediction that we adapt to stimuli so that they do not arouse us. Somewhat the same process is involved here.) The problem is that we need a way of knowing and predicting beforehand when this adaptation process will occur so that we can control for it in our planning of the change program. Unfortunately, however, such knowledge is not yet in our possession.

Second, sometimes the effectiveness of one incentive is influenced by the presence of another. As I said in an earlier chapter, the effect of increasing incentive payments for performing a particular task will often depend on whether or not the task is already perceived as leading to the possibility of promotion. If it is, the increased opportunity to make money may have little effect on behavior. In fact, it is even conceivable that the increased incentive will have a boomerang effect and the overall influence on behavior will be negative. A good example of this comes from an extensive series of studies on how increasing incentives influenced the likelihood of choosing a Naval career. Basically, it was found that more was not better. In fact, in many cases it was just the opposite in that as incentives were added, the likelihood of choosing a Naval career diminished (cf. Frey, et al., 1974). The researchers offered as possible explanations the view that the increased incentives were perceived as inequitable (in either a personal or social sense) or as an attempt at bribery, thus violating one's sense of personal freedom. Whatever the reason, and both might be valid, the point is that a straightforward utilization of the Type I change logic resulted in outcomes opposite to those that would be expected.

Third, one last complication I want to mention is that for some people the promise of reward for performance has little effect because they believe that their behavior is not under their control. The individuals to whom we are referring are the external-control individuals of whom we spoke earlier. To offer these people a reward for certain types of behavior is obviously not going to do much good over the long run if they don't see their behavior as being under their control. It is paradoxical and indicative of the fascination of this field that a clear implication here is that the more that management exerts external control over their employees in order to influence behavior, the less actual influence they will have.

Let me not belabor the point much further. Type I change strategy uses positive reinforcers to influence behavior. At one level, this approach makes a great deal of sense and, also, has a great deal of cultural and lay support. Furthermore, there is no question that it can and should be used, at least under some conditions. The point I have tried to make here is that the application of this approach involves far more questions than appear on the surface.

One provocative theoretical question is how to reconcile some of these characteristics of reinforcement with the theoretical framework I proposed earlier. There are two ways I can do this. One way concerns the more-is-not-better finding mentioned above. The framework I proposed predicts that for any given population there will be some point at which the reward becomes too much. Hence, the finding that more is not better is consistent with this proposal. In addition, I think I can also reconcile the framework with the partial reinforcement phenomenon when the change situation involves the learning of skills. Let us first assume that when a person is told he is correct, this constitutes a form of social evaluation. Eventually, continual reinforcement becomes incorporated into the self-concept as a type of positive evaluation through the mechanism of secondary reinforcement. Since it is such positive self-evaluation that I postulated as being one of the key determinants of performance motivation, it is logical to conclude that increasing reinforcement is a mechanism for increasing learning and, eventually, performance after learning. Hence, as Table 11.3 shows, introducing reinforcement as part of the training conditions will generally serve as a facilitating influence on both learning and later performance. Furthermore, the more frequent the reinforcement during the learning, the better.

the importance of feedback

A second condition that research shows to be important if a Type I change strategy is to be effective is that outcomes are facilitated by the provision of knowledge of results, or feedback. A person's performance is facilitated by the extent to which he knows the outcomes of his behavior.

Table 11.3
Influence of Reinforcement Schedules on Self-Evaluation and Performance Motivation

	LEARNING PERIOD		POSTLEARNING PERFORMANCE PERIOD	PERIOD WHEN LEARNED RESPONSES ARE NO LONGER APPROPRIATE AND WHEN THEY WILL NOT BE REINFORCED
Case A	High frequency of being told "you are correct" during the learning period	High self-perceived competence in the area	High desire to seek out situations where the individual will attain value and reinforcement since these are "appropriate" and "in balance" for him; high seeking out of organizationally appropriate behaviors since they are reinforced	Dropping out of "learned" responses when they are not reinforced
Case B	Low frequency of being told "you are correct" during the learning period	Low self-perceived competence in the area	Low desire to seek out situations where the individual will attain value and reinforcement since these are not as "appropriate" or "in balance" for him; less seeking out of organizationally appropriate behaviors, i.e., those which are reinforced	Retention of "learned" responses even though they may now be incorrect and not reinforced

Why is this? One answer is obvious. A person cannot perform the correct response unless he is told what the correct response is. Otherwise, he may go on and on and on, performing incorrectly and never knowing it. Second, knowledge of results provides a sense of reinforcement to the individual and, hence, may operate in the manner we have described above. In addition, some psychologists feel that feedback serves as an incentive to performance over other factors. However, there has never been a clear theoretical rationale why this should be and, indeed, an experiment by Chapanis (1964) has cast serious doubt on the general usefulness of this hypothesis.

massed versus distributed practice

How should training sessions using a Type I strategy be scheduled when the change program involves the learning of skills? All at once (massed), or spaced out with rest breaks in between (distributed)? This question has long been a subject of major study, both for its theoretical interest and because it lends itself easily to various practical manipulations.

For a long time it was generally thought that distributed practice was more effective than massed. However, recent research has begun to cast doubt on the generality of this finding and it now appears that the answer depends on a number of other variables such as the amount of material to be learned and its meaningfulness. The following conclusions appear to be the safest that can be made at this time:

1. The harder the material to be learned, the greater the advantage of distributed practice over massed practice.
2. The less meaningful the material to be learned, the greater the advantage of distributed practice over massed practice.
3. The less the ability of the trainee, the greater the advantage of distributed practice over massed practice.

whole versus part learning

When the change program involves learning, should all the material be presented at once, or should a step-at-a-time approach be used? As a condition possibly affecting the learning process (which is also easily susceptible to practical change), this has been the subject of considerable research. The results have been inconclusive here, too, since the answer depends on other conditions. In general, these conditions are such that it is most advantageous to use the whole rather than a part-learning procedure when (1) the trainee is highly competent, (2) the training is distributed rather than massed, and (3) the material is highly organized and difficult (Bass and Vaughan, 1967). To the extent that these conditions do not hold, it is probably best to use a part-learning procedure, at least in the beginning stages.

Type 2: Environmental Manipulation

Environmental manipulation as a change strategy is the deliberate, explicit use of the change processes discussed under the category of socialization in the work setting. Thus, if we take any kind of leadership policy of practice (e.g., technological change, budgetary practices, etc.), institute it, and keep it in force over a period of time, some people will change in some way their attitudes, cognitions, and behavior as a result of these environmental manipulations and the processes discussed in the first part of this chapter.

Theoretically and philosophically there are an infinite number of ways in which an environment may be manipulated in order to foster change. Practically, though, only a relatively small number of strategies for manipulating environments have been tried in real work settings. Below I will outline several of these and in the next chapter I will discuss them more completely. After this discussion I think you will see why it is relatively easy to defend the position that Type II as a change strategy has great potential.

One kind of Type II change strategy is the structuring of group support for new kinds of behavior. Such structuring has the effect of decreasing the anxiety attached to the new behaviors, thus making it more likely that it will occur. A good example of this type of application is T-group or sensitivity training.

A second Type II change strategy is providing increased exposure to a particular stimulus and thus increasing familiarity with it. This has several effects. First, the increased exposure to the object enables the individual to develop coping strategies relevant to that object which he might not have had prior to the exposure. Second, the increased familiarity makes the stimulus less anxiety-provoking and, therefore, more likely to serve as a source of positive attraction. An example of this is McClelland's need-achievement training, a program mentioned earlier.

A third Type II strategy is anticipating the occurrence of and accepting the inevitability of negative outcomes. The logic of this type of environmental manipulation stems from the belief that effective behavior depends on the development of a veridical cognitive structure concerning the nature of the world. Since the world in which we live is obviously imperfect and since most of us, in the interests of protecting our ego, like to blot out the negative aspects, change programs structured along this dimension try to train individuals to change their cognitive structures of the world. Much of this is often imaginal environmental manipulation, but the basis for it is real. Rational Leadership Training, developed by a well-known clinical psychologist named Albert Ellis, is an example of this type of approach.

The practical advantages of a Type II strategy are obvious, *when it works*. However, it will not work all the time, even when the environmental manipulations are relatively permanent and it clearly will not work all the time when the manipulations are relatively temporary. The crucial point is to understand when it does, a problem of major importance because of the continuing questions in using this strategy. Consider the following three factors.

First is the question of reinforcement. I mentioned earlier that there is disagreement about the importance of reinforcement in influencing change when the change involves the individual's being subjected to environmental experience (either deliberately designed or through general everyday experience). Dissonance theory says that above some level of reward there is a negative relationship between positive reinforcement and the effects of a manipulation while others (e.g., Breer and Locke, 1965) say that the more rewarding an experience has been, the greater its effect on the individual. My own feeling is that we have to differentiate between those conditions under which each of these processes is valid. Although we have nothing to go on but hypotheses at this time, one hypothesis that is worth investigating states that reward would facilitate change if the person has not participated in the environmental manipulation and reward would either be negatively or nonrelated to change by environmental manipulation if the person has freely chosen and participated in the process.

Second, consider the roles of commitment and job involvement. Do these make a difference in how someone responds to a Type II environmental manipulation? Are commitment and job involvement just other words for participation, and would the same hypotheses hold? There are differing perspectives on this matter. My own guess is that they are related but not the same. Furthermore, I would also hypothesize that commitment and job involvement would be positively related to the effectiveness of a particular manipulation. However, please remember that this is only a hypothesis and research may show entirely different results.

Third, independent of the amount of reward and the degree of commitment of the individuals toward their jobs, how should we introduce an environmental manipulation? There are two major approaches. The first is to introduce the change by the traditional, management-controlled external directive. This has a number of advantages. It is easy to use, it is familiar and accepted by management, and in some cases there may be no time for participation. On the other hand, consider the advantages of using a participative approach to environmental manipulation: (1) it uses the skills and abilities available in the subordinate work force; (2) it encourages the growth of cooperative thinking in the organization rather than competitive aggression between groups and individuals, which can be costly; (3) it encourages the individual to come to value himself more, since he is acting in an autonomous fashion; (4) if groups are used, it brings group pressure to bear in support of the decisions made; (5) it stimulates acceptance of the change on an individual level; (6) it is ethically appropriate for a democracy. All of these reasons, plus the research results cited earlier in the book, are significant support for suggesting that the participative approach would work better than a management-imposed program. However, it may be that under some conditions management directives would work effectively as a change strategy. The point is that we have to find out when.

I believe a Type II approach does work and I am going to spend a lot of time in the following pages discussing the different ways in which it has been utilized. However, if it is going to work even more effectively than it does and if we are not going to waste our time trying to apply it to areas in which it is clearly inappropriate, we have to begin to develop answers to questions of the kind discussed here.

The Characteristics of Change Programs

Regardless of the change program chosen (Type I, Type II, or some combination), there are a number of general characteristics about instituting change programs that need to be kept in mind. Slater (1974) has listed some of these as follows:

1. All change programs will involve some stress, even if the change is positive. Change involves a loss of being able to predict what will happen and this is always disquieting.
2. All change programs are implanted on social systems that are also in change. The world and the people in it are not static (a point made earlier in this chapter).
3. Change programs are not all that objective. While there are general attempts to diagnose objectives and formulate goals, the fact is that we are usually part of any change program. Our own desires, wishes, and goals inevitably get incorporated into any change program and make it subjective, either fully or partially. It is important to recognize this subjectivity so that we may account for it as best we can.
4. Regardless of the laudability of the formal goals of any change programs, results are usually multidimensional, with some bad and some good. More confusing is that it is not always clear what is good and what is bad. For example, a change program that increases skills in work behaviors may also increase expectancies of promotion. For a corporation with minimal opportunities for promoting individuals, this could be a problem. For the individual, his increased desires could be beneficial to him if the opportunities exist. On the other hand, if they do not, his desires would serve as a source of frustration.

Summary

Change programs have assumed increasing importance as mechanisms for organizational improvement due to the decline of traditional personnel selection mechanisms because of legal, social, and cultural complications.

However, the design of programs in this area needs to take into account some of the basic processes involved in work-related change. One very important point is that change in work and personal attitudes takes place as a result of everyday work experience. Research is consistent with the argument that we continually interpret our behavior, attribute causality to events, and, on the basis of these attributions, change our cognitive structure. This changed cognitive structure influences later behavior. Among the factors involved here is the extent to which we attribute the causes of behavior to internal or external causes, since it is only in the former case that we will learn from experience. Another implication of the internal–external control variable is that the former type of attribution is more likely to lead to successful behavior, even though one has failed originally, while the latter attribution eventually leads to failure, even though one has succeeded originally. Some of the implications of this were laid out in an extension proposed to the theoretical model discussed in chapter three. Finally, changes over time were also shown to be due to other factors such as dissonance reduction, our tendency to value factors related to success, and our preference for familiar objects.

A second question about change concerns the basic models that might be used. Traditionally, change has been viewed as controllable by the manipulation of incentives. This model, termed here Type I, is still useful, although there are severe weaknesses in the approach. One of the most important of these concerns the difficulty of knowing when an incentive (or reinforcement) is operating as desired. A second major change model was defined as environmental manipulation. This technique, termed Type II, constitutes a deliberate application and control of the types of environmental experience and change that occur independent of any explicit attempts at change. Finally, a number of characteristics of any change program were reviewed. Among these were their multidimensional effects, their subjectivity, and the inevitable stresses involved.

SUGGESTIONS FOR FURTHER READING

BRAY, D. W., CAMPBELL, R. J., and GRANT, D. C. *Formative years in business: A long-term A.T. & T. study of managerial lives.* New York: John Wiley, 1974.
A.T. & T. has been the corporation that has most actively supported basic research on management. It has looked into how to assess managers and the effects of their work experiences upon them. This monograph reports one of the few bodies of meaningful research on what it has meant to be an organization man in an American corporation during the third quarter of the twentieth century.

BREER, P., and LOCKE, E. A. *Task experience as a source of attitudes.* Homewood, Ill.: Dorsey, 1965.

An innovative series of research experiments on the effects of the nature of work experience (and success) on personal attitudes and values of societal significance. Not all of the experiments were successful, but the overall thrust of the findings supports the main arguments of the researchers.

NORD, W. R. Beyond the teaching machine: The neglected area of operant conditioning in the theory and practice of management. *Organizational Behavior and Human Performance,* 1969, *4,* 375–401.

This article's major importance is that it reintroduced the logic of reinforcement theory and Skinnerian behaviorism to those concerned with management processes. I believe that the usefulness of the approach is not as great as argued for the reasons I outlined in this chapter, but you may disagree after reading this article.

SCHEIN, E. H. The individual, the organization and the career: A conceptual scheme. In D. A. Kolb, I. M. Rubin and J. M. McIntyre (Eds.), *Organizational psychology.* Englewood Cliffs, N.J.: Prentice-Hall, 1971, 333–349.

Schein's original theoretical statement on the characteristics of experience in work settings, when conformity occurs, when innovation takes place, etc. The research evidence for the proposals still does not exist for the most part, but their potential usefulness remains high.

WEINER, B. *Theories of motivation: From mechanism to cognition.* Chicago: Markham, 1972.

A major historical and theoretical statement on motivational processes and why a view of man as a changing individual who reacts to experience has become necessary. The author has made his own research contributions to this field and he integrates this work with that of other researchers.

chapter twelve

Organizational Development

If we summarize the general thrust of our discussion of all the topics we discussed under the headings of organization structure, leadership, job design, alienation, job satisfaction, and organizational socialization, the implications seem clear that changes in traditional ways of thinking are called for. But what kind of changes? After all, not all tradition is bad and it is generally a good idea to know what a replacement is before you buy it. What we want, I would think, are suggestions for change in the world of work which are research-based and which also take cognizance of the necessity to keep what is good about the traditional.

This chapter reviews some of the literature that has developed around the term *organizational development*. This is a catch-all term which incorporates within it the wide variety of change programs that have been developed to maximize work motivation and creativity and reduce processes such as isolation, self-estrangement, job dissatisfaction, and aggressive conflict. As we review the various change programs that have been instituted in different organizations and nations, it will be seen that they are enormously complex in nature. Hence, in few, if any, of the cases discussed will it be possible to indentify and isolate a single specific variable and point to it as being *the* critical variable that has influenced the result. The complexity of undertaking research and change programs in real-world settings makes it unlikely that we will ever be able to satisfy the demand of the research paradigm to the degree that we would like. However, although it is important, I would not overemphasize this limitation. For one thing, if we keep getting a basically similar result in a variety of different contexts (a situation that I think is true here), then I would submit that we are justified in concluding that this result has a high enough probability of being the case to warrant our attention. Second, despite the complexity of real-world research, it is sometimes possible to use complex multivariate designs that allow greater levels of understanding. Admittedly, some ambiguity will always remain but, as a former graduate-school professor of mine once said, "If you can't tolerate a little ambiguity, real-world research is not for you."

One further note is that although I will be talking about a wide variety of change activities ranging from job enrichment to sensitivity training, you should not assume that I will be covering all of the possible techniques. As a matter of fact, the number of activities possible is limited only by the imagination of the change agent. To illustrate the possibilities, I have listed in Table 12.1 parts of one framework for categorizing the activities that have been called organizational development.

Rather than focus on all of these, I will concentrate on those techniques about which much is known and/or about which there is considerable theoretical interest.

Job Enrichment as Organizational Development Intervention

There are by now a considerable number of company experiments in job enrichment that have been publicly reported (and many more that undoubtedly have not). These reports cover both types of job enrichment discussed in chapter five. That is, horizontal job enrichment (in which individuals are given a greater variety of tasks to do with no increase in the level of decision-making responsibility) and vertical job enrichment (in which individuals are encouraged to take a greater role in decision making relative to job responsibilities).

As I concluded earlier, even if we assume some biased reporting in that the favorable outcomes are more likely to see the light of day, I think that the results of interventions based on job enrichment are highly impressive. (I am not even certain that this type of bias exists to a great degree. A lot of people are ideologically committed to maintenance of the status quo and are very much interested in seeing that negative results relating to change programs of this nature are published).

Be that as it may, I have reproduced in Table 12.2 a summary of those company applications of job enrichment that were originally pub-

Table 12.1
Possible Organizational Development Interventions

TARGET GROUP	TYPES OF INTERVENTIONS
Individuals	Life and career planning activities
	Role analysis technique
	Coaching and counseling
	T-group (sensitivity) training
	Education and training to increase skills and knowledge in the areas of technical task needs, relationship skills, process skills, and problem-solving, planning, and goal-setting skills.
Dyads/triads	Process consultation
	Third-party peacemaking
Teams and groups	Team building—task directed and process directed
	Family T-group
	Survey feedback
	Process consultation
	Role analysis technique
	"Start-up" team-building activities
	Education in decision making, problem solving, planning, and goal setting in groups
Intergroup relations	Intergroup activities—process directed and task directed
	Organizational mirroring
	Technostructural interventions
	Process consultation
	Third-party peacemaking at group level
	Survey feedback
Total organization	Technostructural interventions
	Confrontation meetings
	Strategic planning activities
	Survey feedback

Source: W.L. French and C.H. Bell, Jr., *Organizational development: Behavioral science interventions for organization improvement* (Englewood Cliffs, N.J.: Prentice-Hall, 1973), p. 108.

lished in the Labor Department report titled *Work in America* (1973). These examples very much support the logic of this type of intervention. In addition, the cases also illustrate a point we have made elsewhere: the changes that seem desirable apply to other countries besides the United States.

One note of caution, though, before we proceed. The consistently favorable findings in Table 12.2 along both human and economic dimensions should not lead you to think that a magic formula is involved. There are dangers and practical problems involved in applying these approaches which I will talk about a little later. However, the fact that these findings are so favorable suggests that these possible flaws and difficulties are not fatal and that they generally can be overcome.

Industrial Democracy on a Societal Level as Intervention

The idea that society in general has an interest in alleviating alienation and dissatisfaction that are thought to be induced primarily by conditions of employment has only recently begun to take hold in this country and it still elicits enormous resistance in many quarters. Primarily, this has been considered a matter for the organization and the individual and, as we see in Table 12.2, in many organizations in this country and others with related cultural backgrounds (e.g., England), there have been serious, far-reaching attempts to deal with these problems. In addition, other nongovernmental attempts in this direction are being reported in nations such as Norway.

In some of the other societies that are faced with similar problems of alienation and discontent, the belief is that government has a duty and an obligation to deal with these problems, by persuasion sometimes, and by legislation if necessary. As a result, there is now a body of literature based on the experiences of other nations as to what has happened when industrial democracy has been engineered into the workplace more by governmental than private initiative. Since these effects constitute a type of intervention for organizational development, I will discuss a number of these attempts.

First we will review what is meant by industrial democracy as it is generally used in those nations that have attempted to develop it on a societal level. As Jenkins (1973) points out, the central feature of industrial democracy is the possession of real decision-making power over substantial matters by employees of an enterprise. Thus, industrial democracy is not profit-sharing or incentive schemes, although it could include these features. The central idea is power sharing, not just money sharing. Similarly, it does not involve the appointment of public or consumer representatives, although these may be beneficial to the organization on other counts. These factors are independent and should perhaps be undertaken, but they are not industrial democracy, which involves power sharing by employees, not consumers. Neither is industrial democracy the same as trade unionism. Unions have traditionally not exercised nor exhibited much interest in sharing decision-making power over job activities. Their interests have almost always been in extrinsic incentives such as money, working conditions, pensions, and so forth (although this may be changing today). Furthermore industrial democracy does not imply permissiveness, where everybody does exactly as he pleases without regard to the goals of the enterprise. It is not just being nice to one another, and it is not corporate democracy

Table 12.2
Results of Organizational Intervention Programs

TYPE OF ORGANIZATIONAL INTERVENTION	ORGANIZATIONS	CHANGE	
		Attitudinal Results	*Performance Results*
Development of autonomous work groups who are responsible for performance with: a. group bonuses for performance b. pay based on number of jobs worker can do	General Foods	Positive— also increase in civic activity	Positive on various measures
	State of Ohio; Highways Department	Positive	Positive
	Micro Wax (England)	Not discussed	Performance increased; absenteeism decreased
	Phillips (Holland)	Positive	Increased quality
	Ferado (England)	Positive	Performance efficiency increased
	Novsk (Norway)	Positive	Peformance increased; absenteeism decreased
	Texas Instruments, maintenance	Not discussed	Performance increased; turnover decreased
	Corning Glass Works	Positive	Performance quality increased; absenteeism decreased
	Syntex	Positive	Performance increased
	I.C.I. (England)	Not discussed	Performance increased
	Monsanto, chemical	Positive	Performance efficiency increased
	Texas Instruments, assembly	Positive	Positive on various measures
	Hunstos (Norway)	Positive	Positive
	Nob Fabrikker A/S (Norway)	Positive	Performance increased; absenteeism decreased
Vertical enlargement (increase in responsibility	A.T. & T. (foremen)	Positive—also grievance reductions	Slight increase

Table 12.2 (*cont.*)

TYPE OF ORGANIZATIONAL INTERVENTION	ORGANIZATIONS	CHANGE	
		Attitudinal Results	*Performance Results*
and decision making for own job for foremen and/or workers)	A.T. & T (clerical employees)	Positive	Absenteeism and turnover decreased
	Kaiser Aluminum	Positive	Worker quality increased
	Bankers trust	Positive	Increase in all measures
	Monsanto, textiles	Positive	Positive
	Alcan	Positive	Performance increased absenteeism decreased
	Oldsmobile	Positive	Absenteeism decreased; quality increased
	Montanto, agriculture division	Not discussed	Productivity increased
	P.P.G	Positive	Performance increased
	Monsanto, electronics	Not discussed	Turnover decreased
Job rotation	Polaroid	Mixed	Absenteeism and turnover decreased; recruitment easier
Horizontal enlargement	P.T.T. (Netherlands)	Positive	High performance increase
Salaries are self-determined; responsibility is also assigned to each individual for increasing productivity	Donnelly Mirrors	Not discussed	Wages, costs, and profits increased as company lowered prices

Source: *Work in America,* (Cambridge, Mass.: MIT Press, 1973), pgs. 188–201.

where the shareholders assume supervision over management. (The apathy of stockholders is notorious.) Industrial democracy is not an instant system ready to apply in three easy steps. It is, basically, a way of thinking about how to run a work enterprise and the development of methods for implementing this way of thinking. It violates long-established patterns as to how work systems should be run, and it also, implicitly, is a threat to many individuals who see themselves as unworthy and insignificant and who have learned to look to strong authority figures for needed sources of strength. (This latter situation is clearly a matter of great relevance in some cultures.)

The Israeli Kibbutz

One of the most significant societal attempts at industrial democracy and one that has attracted worldwide interest is the kibbutz system of Israel. The word *kibbutz* means group in Hebrew and there are approximately 230 of these in Israel today, with a total membership of 90,000. Although they account for only 3.5% of the population, their influence and significance far transcends their figures. They exert a crucial impact on Israeli work and life situations, providing manpower and cognitive input far out of proportion to their numbers, and their ideology provided the impetus for the development of the nation. For these reasons, they are worthy of specific study.

Ideologically, the kibbutz bases its activities on the following philosophical assumptions:

1. Labor is morally valuable.
2. Work is not a punishment; it is a joy.
3. Labor and work are not a means for satisfying needs; to work itself is a need that we wish to satisfy. (You might notice the differences between this assumption and the assumptions underlying expectancy-value theories of behavior.)
4. The noblest form of work is manual, physical labor; intellectual work is parasitical and not of direct value in building a society.

As a result of these assumptions, kibbutzim have traditionally been highly democratic and have practiced rotation among jobs for its members (including supervisory jobs). In addition, there has, traditionally, been no real salary system, with all receiving equal treatment and with private property forbidden. While the years since World War II have seen slight modifications in these traditions, (for example, older workers are not rotated into the physically most demanding jobs; there is more technical and industrial work as opposed to just agriculture; and there are some workers who are hired from the outside and treated in a more hierarchical fashion), these original values have remained fairly strong. It is important to note, then, that kibbutz members are considered to be among the most nonalienated and committed workers in the world today and their productivity levels compare favorably with those working under other systems of management.

The Worker-Management Councils of Yugoslavia

Yugoslavia is a Communist nation with a one-party system and everything else that such a political process implies. Yet, the management of work enterprises in this nation is, structurally, among the most democratic to be found anywhere in the world. The key mechanism is the workers' council, one of which must exist in every organization. In those organizations in which there are fewer than 30 employees, all are members of the council; in larger enterprises, the council may have from 15 to 120 members, elected directly on a one-employee, one-vote principle. All formal management power is vested in the council; it approves all management decisions, appoints management personnel, sets salary scales, decides on hiring and firing, establishes capital investment programs, and carries out long-term planning. All members are elected to a two-year term, serve without extra compensation, and continue on their regular jobs while serving on the council. In addition, there is generally a managing board, composed of three to ten council members, who take an active, day-to-day role in running the enterprise.

Over the years the power of the workers has been strengthened considerably, particularly in regard to the allocation and control of money, and today these councils are a far cry from the powerless consultative boards originally established in Europe after World War II. The workers on these councils have shown considerable financial responsibility and this has, in turn, led to such recent developments as separate councils for departments of large organizations in order that power remains at the worker level and not become diluted in too large a system.

Does the system work? There are considerable data to support the conclusion that the councils of Yugoslavia have not hurt the society and, if anything, have helped it. For the years 1962 to 1965 Yugoslavia had an annual growth rate of 7.75%, second to Japan among the world's industrial nations for this period. In addition, there are also research findings showing that the more successful companies are those in which the councils are more active and exercise more influence (Jenkins, 1973). Along another dimension, there are also survey data showing that 85% of the Yugoslav work force would be opposed to abolishing the councils.

Despite this favorable picture some problems do exist. For one thing, there is still a tendency for the workers to concentrate on trivia instead of major problems at council meetings. This problem does not seem to be crucial, however, and its occurrence may be decreasing. A more important problem, though, is the structural problem that, outside the councils, the manager–worker relationship is hierarchical. The disparity between the two settings can cause considerable tension.

West Germany: Social Reform Through
CoDetermination

The oldest true Western system of industrial democracy is the system of *Mitbestimmung* (codetermination, or joint management), introduced in the steel and coal mining industries of West Germany in 1951. By government legislation employees were given one-half of the places in the supreme body of authority in these companies, thus placing in their hands real decision-making power. (More recently, the West German government has established workers councils in other industries. However, here there has been minority representation. Only in the iron and steel industry do the workers have true decision-making power).

Mitbestimmung is, essentially, a highly formalistic system in which workers elect representatives who serve as a check on management. Overall, the results have been mixed (Jenkins, 1973). Some studies have shown that the workers really do not care much about it, with one reason being that its representational and formalistic nature makes it too abstract. As a result, a condiderable number of employees are not too certain about how the system operates in their companies. On the other hand, the codetermination machinery seems to work well in times of crisis and recent evaluation suggests it has generally been working well. It has helped to lower tension, reduce social conflict, and aided in the general adaptation of the organizations to change. One problem of *Mitbestimmung* has been the belief that too much of its operation is under the control of unions. Workers should be represented directly, rather than through their unions, is the feeling of these critics. As an illustration, they say, *Mitbestimmung* has not really helped to overcome the tedium of work, a failure possibly traceable to the traditional lack of interest of labor unions in this area. Economically, there seems little reason to conclude that codetermination has hurt. The companies that have used it have operated quite successfully, and, overall, the attitudes of workers are positive (Jenkins, 1973). In fact, the results have been so favorable that the power of the workers under *Mitbestimmung* was expanded in 1972.

On the basis of what we now know about job enrichment and industrial democracy there is little doubt that these types of interventions are quite meaningful and, more often than not, positive in their results. In addition, there are also developments in France, the Netherlands, and Scandinavia that support these conclusions. For example, the Swedish parliament has in the past several years approved the following legislation:

1. Employee representation on corporate boards of directors is required.
2. Safety ombudsmen—ordinary workers with additional safety and health

responsibilities—have been given the right to close down jobs they feel are dangerous or unhealthy.

3. Job security laws have been strengthened. A minimum of one month and up to six months notice for layoffs is required, and no firings are permitted without good cause.
4. Workers on plant councils are permitted to call in their own outside experts to help in council tasks.
5. Union shop stewards are allowed to do union work on company time.
6. All foreign workers have the right to 240 hours of Swedish language classes on company time at normal pay rates.
7. Workers have the right to take leaves of absence for studies, and, additionally, apply for the governmental subsidies and loans available. (France also has adopted this policy.)

Do these developments mean that we have found the golden panacea? I said earlier that I didn't think so and I want to repeat this here. Rather, there are strengths and weaknesses in these interventions and they need to be incorporated with other efforts in the area of organizational development. O'Toole (1974) has summarized some of these implications as follows:

1. Job enrichment of lower-level jobs can have significant implications for overall organizational development since the range of intelligence on these jobs is tremendous. (Three times more laborers have IQs over 130 than PhDs, and often these bright individuals are sources of trouble on these jobs.)
2. Lack of worker interest should not be misinterpreted. Apathy has been the result of disbelief that changes were possible. However, awareness that change is possible is increasing, and we can expect increased demands in the future.
3. Job redesign and enrichment are only partial answers to organizational development. We also need midcareer counseling, decreased racial and sexual discrimination, and other change programs.
4. Job redesign and participation may not be possible in very low-level jobs. Here, possible answers may be more money, improved people–job matching (e.g., utilize the mentally retarded for low-level positions), and rotation of workers so that no one has this kind of job permanently. (Temporary workers such as college students might be used for these jobs since they would not feel permanently trapped.)

Sensitivity Training: Group Support as a Mechanism for Change

Probably the most popular method used by practitioners in the field of organizational development for achieving decreased anxiety, more satisfactory interpersonal competence, and less intergroup conflict is what has come to be known as sensitivity (or T-group or laboratory) training. What is also refreshing is that it has stimulated a considerable amount of research. Before turning to this research, let us first describe the process itself.

Campbell and Dunnette (1968) have described the goals of sensitivity training as follows:

Goal One To increase self-insight concerning one's behavior in a social context, to learn how others see and interpret one's own behavior, and to gain insight into why one acts the way one does in different interpersonal situations.

Goal Two To increase sensitivity to the behavior of others (reciprocal to goal 1), i.e., to increase awareness of the stimuli emitted by other persons and the development of the ability to infer accurately the emotional bases for interpersonal communications.

Goal Three To increase awareness of the processes that facilitate or inhibit group functioning. For example, why do some members participate actively while others do not? Why do subgroups form and wage war against each other? Why do different groups, who may actually share the same goals, sometimes create seemingly insoluble conflict situations?

Goal Four To increase diagnostic and action-oriented skills in social, interpersonal, and intergroup situations.

Goal Five To teach a person to learn how to learn, i.e., to teach him how to continually analyze his own interpersonal behavior in order to reach and engage in more effective interpersonal interactions with others.[1]

The assumptions of the sensitivity training procedure are that, if these goals are achieved, one will become less defensive about himself, less fearful of the intentions of others, more responsive to others and their needs, and less likely to misinterpret others' behaviors in a negative fashion. The result, it is argued, will be greater creativity (since one is less fearful of others and less defensive), less hostility toward others (due to greater understanding of others), and greater sensitivity to social psychological influences on work behavior.

How are these goals achieved? Unfortunately, or perhaps fortunately, there is no single T-group procedure since this may vary according to the purposes and composition of the groups. However, most T-groups do have a similar framework on which specific characteristics may be built. This common framework has been described by Campbell and Dunnette (1968) as follows:

---

[1] J. P. Campbell and M. D. Dunnette, Effectiveness of T-group experiences in managerial training and development, *Psychological Bulletin,* 1968, *70,* 73–104. Copyright 1968 by the American Psychological Association, and reproduced by permission.

Thus, the typical learning experience has as its focal point the small, unstructured, face-to-face group, usually consisting of 10–15 people. No activities or topics for discussion are planned. A trainer is usually present, but he does not accept, in fact he overtly rejects, any leadership role. The participants are to discuss themselves and the way they portray themselves in the group. In the language of T-grouping, the focus is on the "here and now," that is, behavior emitted *in the group* rather than behavior involving past experiences or future problems. The here and now includes the feelings and emotions experienced by the group members. Cognitive or intellectual aspects of the problems are ancillary to this affect-laden overlay. Focusing on the here and now is facilitated by the trainer's abdication of the leadership role and his lack of responsiveness to the status symbols brought to the group by the participants (e.g., company positions, education, family background, etc.). Frequently, the trainer merely specifies the length of time the group will be meeting and that the major concern is with seeking to understand one's own and others' behaviors. He then falls silent or otherwise refuses further guidance.

The vacuum is very often filled by feelings of frustration, expressions of hostility, and eventual attempts by some members to impose an organized, and usually hierarchical (leaders, committees, etc.) structure on the group. These initial attempts to assume a leadership role are usually resented by other members, and either spontaneously or because of the trainer's intervention, they begin to consider why the self-appointed leader tried to force his will on the group. Hopefully, such a focus on the here and now generalizes and other members and other behaviors become the basis for discussion so that every participant has an opportunity to learn about his own group behavior as well as a wide range of others' group behaviors.

Given the unstructured group as the vehicle and the behavior emitted in the group as the principal topic of conversation, the success of the venture depends on the crucial process of feedback. Thus, the participants must be able to inform each other how their behavior is being seen and interpreted and to describe the kinds of feelings generated. This is the primary process by which the delegates "learn." They must receive *articulate* and *meaningful* feedback about their own behavior, including their own feedback attempts (feedback on feedback) and their efforts to interpret group processes (e.g., did the other group members think individual X was correct when he observed that Y and Z were forming a clique because they both felt rejected?)

For the feedback process to contribute to the goals of the training, at least two additional elements are believed necessary. First, a certain amount of anxiety or tension must be generated, particularly in the early part of the group's life. Anxiety supposedly results when an individual discovers how deficient his previous role-bound methods are for successful functioning in this new type of group situation. . . .

. . . The second necessary element for assuming effective feedback is . . . a climate of "psychological safety." That is, no matter what an individual does in a group or what he reveals about himself, the group must feel that it is safe to expose his feelings, drop his defenses, and try out new ways of interacting.

The role of the trainer also constitutes a dominant technological element bearing on the group's effectiveness for giving feedback and promoting psychological support. The trainer serves as a model for the participants to imitate. That is, he absorbs feelings of hostility and frustration without becoming defensive, provides feedback for others, expresses his own feelings openly and honestly, and is strongly supportive of the expression of feelings in others. In short, he exhibits for consideration the very processes deemed necessary for maximum learning to occur.[2]

This, then, comprises the essentials of the sensitivity training experience, but it is, perhaps, not very satisfying to read since even such a long explanation as this does not adequately describe what T-groups are like. To see this, let us look at a case experience cited by Tannenbaum, Wechsler, and Massarik (1961):

At the fifth meeting the group's feeling about its own progress became the initial focus of discussion. The "talkers" participated as usual, conversation shifting rapidly from one point to another. Dissatisfaction was mounting, expressed through loud, snide remarks by some and through apathy by others.

George Franklin appeared particularly disturbed. Finally pounding the table, he exclaimed, "I don't know what is going on here! I should be paid for listening to this drivel! I'm getting just a bit sick of wasting my time here. If the profs don't put out—I quit!" George was pleased; he was angry, and he said so. As he sat back in his chair, he felt he had the group behind him. He felt he had the guts to say what most of the others were thinking! Some members of the group applauded loudly, but others showed obvious disapproval. They wondered why George was excited over so insignificant an issue, why he hadn't done something constructive rather than just sounding off as usual. Why, they wondered, did he say their comments were "drivel"?

George Franklin became the focus of discussion. "What do you mean, George, by saying this is nonsense?" "What do you expect, a neat set of rules to meet all your problems?"

George was getting uncomfortable. These were questions difficult for him to answer. Gradually he began to realize that a large part of the group disagreed with him; then he began to wonder why. He was learning something about people he hadn't known before. ". . . How does it feel, George, to have people disagree with you when you thought you had them behind you? . . ."

Bob White was first annoyed with George and now with the discussion. He was getting tense, a bit shaky perhaps. Bob didn't like anybody to get a raw deal, and he felt that George was getting it. At first Bob tried to minimize George's outburst, and then he suggested that the group get on

[2] J. P. Campbell and M. D. Dunnette, Effectiveness of T-group experiences in managerial training and development, *Psychological Bulletin*, 1968, *70*, 75–76. Copyright 1968 by the American Psychological Association, and reproduced by permission.

to the real issues; but the group continued to focus on George. Finally, Bob said, "Why don't you leave George alone and stop picking on him? We're not getting anywhere this way."

With the help of the leaders, the group focused on Bob. "What do you mean, 'picking' on him?" "Why, Bob, have you tried to change the discussion?" "Why are you so protective of George?" Bob began to realize that the group wanted to focus on George; he also saw that George didn't think he was being picked on, but felt he was learning something about himself and how others reacted to him. "Why do I always get upset," Bob began to wonder, "when people get angry at each other?" . . . Now Bob was learning something about how people saw him while gaining some insight into his own behavior.[3]

This, then, is the T-group experience, and it seems to be the same whether the type of T-group we are referring to is a "stranger" group (composed of people from different occupations and different organizations), a "cousin" group (composed of people from the same organization but having different occupations), a "diagonal slice" group (composed of people from the same organization but different departments and having different ranks), or a "family" group (composed of intact work groups, i.e., a superior and his subordinates).

A number of questions are warranted at this point. First, where did such a training method come from? What are the influences on its development, and how much research support do those influences have? These questions are important because the more these influences are based on solid, substantive research findings, the more indirect support is provided for T-group training. This support is important because it is hard to undertake direct evaluative research on a complex process such as T-group training. Therefore, it is necessary to review these influences and their research support. In addition, it behooves us to review some of the direct evaluations of the method since such research does exist, despite the complexities. Finally, it is valuable to conjecture, given all this information, where T-group training might go in the future.

The question of where T-group training comes from is complex. I can cite at least seven major sources, although there are probably more. First, there was the influence of Kurt Lewin and his principle of contemporaneity, which states that behavior choice and direction is a function of both the characteristics of the person and the concurrent environmental demands and pressures. Change either one of these, i.e., the person or the environment, and the behavior would be changed. This is a historical approach to the change process and leads directly

---

[3] From *Leadership and organization: A behavioral science approach* by R. Tannenbaum, I. Wechsler, and F. Massarik, p. 123. Copyright 1961 by McGraw-Hill Book Company. Used with permission of McGraw-Hill Book Company.

to the formulation of the Type II strategy I discussed earlier and of which T-group training serves as an illustration, albeit partially. Lewin's basic principle has by now been so firmly established in psychology that its position as an influence on T-group training provides considerable indirect support to the utilization of that method.

Ego psychology provides a second major influence on T-group training, with the names of Carl Rogers and Abraham Maslow of particular relevance. As you would imagine from our earlier discussion of the latter, ego psychology, in a general sense, is based on an emphasis and belief in man's ability to grow and his ability to cope. Maslow's hierarchy of motives and his concept of self-actualization fit in neatly, as does Rogers' theory of nondirective counseling. Such an approach to the therapy process assumes that individuals have the capacity to change their own lives, if the environment is appropriate. T-group training is, as we have seen, designed to provide such an environment.

How much evidence is there for ego psychology and its assumptions? The evidence for Maslow's theory is, we have seen, minimal. However, the assumption that individuals can behave in a self-actualizing, creative way, given appropriate environmental conditions, is valid and can be accounted for by other theoretical systems, as I previously stated. For this reason, this influence on T-group training does provide some indirect support for the T-group approach.

The other influences on T-group training are summarized in Table 12.3, with each one having some research support. All of them provide indirect support for utilizing the T-group approach for training and change.

How about direct evidence for the value of T-group training? One of the most extensive reviews of the research literature on the effectiveness of sensitivity training was undertaken by Campbell and Dunnette (1968), with their overall conclusions summarized as follows:

> Laboratory education has not been shown to bring about marked change in one's standing on objective measures of attitudes, values, outlooks, interpersonal perceptions, self-awareness, or interpersonal sensitivity. In spite of these essentially negative results on objective measures, individuals who have been trained by laboratory education methods are more likely to be seen as changing their job behavior than are individuals in similar job settings who have not been trained. These reported changes are in the direction of more openness, better self- and interpersonal understanding, and improved communications and leadership skills. Unfortunately, these behavior reports suffer from many possible sources of bias and must, therefore, be taken with a grain of salt. Moreover, we have practically no evidence about possible effects of laboratory education on individual's skills in analyzing problem situations, synthesizing information, facing up to and resolving interpersonal conflict, and deriving and implementing solutions to organizational problems. Most research has been restricted to "demonstrating" the so-called human relations ef-

fects of T-groups and has given little attention to other equally important areas in the total process of recognizing, diagnosing, and solving problems in an organizational setting.

(*Source:* Dunnette & Campbell, 1968, p. 25)

Table 12.3
Influences on T-Groups

INFLUENCE	NATURE OF INFLUENCE
J.R. Moreno's utilization of psychodrama as an approach to change	Established a theater that used spontaneity and role playing in order to afford the person insight into how he feels toward others and how others feel toward him by assuming their roles.[1] In general, the greater the number of different roles assumed and played, the more open the person would be about himself and others.
Existentialist philosophy	Existentialist philosophy proposes that life is essentially the choices and decisions that are made and the responsibilities that are assumed. There are no inherent values or truths except the choices and decisions one makes. The T-group is a microcosm of life; nothing will happen to the leaderless, structureless, unorganized T-group unless the members do it themselves. Related to this is the existentialist proposal that one comes to know others only by sharing experiences with them, i.e., others are people, not conceptual categories such as those defined by socioeconomic class membership. T-group training provides these shared experiences and thus helps one to come to know others.
The growth of technology and bureaucracy	As a result of the growth of technology and bureaucracy, there has grown a pervasive belief that people have overemphasized the rational, cognitive, and logical aspects of human behavior. Hence, there is an increasing desire for greater emotional experience.
The growth of an affluent society	As a result of the growth of affluence, there has been a desire to break loose from traditional restraints and inhibitions and an increasing alienation from traditional institutions. This has led to an interest in exploring new ways of relating to others and the development of desires for individualization and greater freedom from constraint.
The growth of specialization in organizations	The growth of specialization and accompanying intergroup conflict has led to an increasing realization of the need for developing more effective ways for helping groups to work with one another.

[1] The influence of the sociologist George Herbert Mead should also be noted here.

Unfortunately, since the Campbell and Dunnette review, the situation has not changed much. We have contrary evidence in the fact that T-groups can influence interpersonal and personal attitudes, at least under some conditions, but their success in influencing some of the other outcomes mentioned by Campbell and Dunnette is still under considerable doubt.

One possible solution is to design research studies that do not assume that T-group training has an effect under all conditions but only under some. The question, of course, is what conditions and can we specify them in advance. Unless we can do this, as we said earlier, we cannot use this contingency approach. Below, I have distilled some of the recommendations of Bennis, Schein, Dunnette, and others as to what some of these conditions might be; some indirect evidence exists for each of these, but direct evidence is hard to come by.

1. Key people in the organization must support the legitimacy of the planned change.
2. Employment security of the change agent must be guaranteed.
3. Legitimacy of interpersonal influence must be accepted in the organization.
4. Opportunity must be provided for practicing the skills learned in T-groups.
5. Groups should focus on a particular goal, e.g., skill training or interpersonal competence. There should not be a mixture of goals in a particular program; the goals and, hence, the program should be specific.

Further guidelines have also been suggested by Howard (1972) in her review of the criticisms that have been made of encounter groups. Although generally favorable toward T-groups, she feels these criticisms need to be corrected in future applications. Among these criticisms those of most relevance to T-groups in the organizational field, and Howard's comments about them, are shown in Table 12.4.

Summary

If we look at the criticisms listed in Table 12.4 and the other comments we have made about T-group training, some conclusions seem warranted. Sensitivity training can increase interpersonal understanding, tolerance of others, and understanding of the self. The effects are not invariant, however, and goals are often not attained. Yet, despite these qualifications and the need to develop further understanding of when T-group training is most functional, we should not overlook the effects it does have. T-group deserves and will, I think, get the further research and attention it warrants.

Rational Training: Acceptance of Environmental Nonperfection as a Mechanism for Change

One of the most important disadvantages of having a specific technique become a fad is that it distracts researchers from investigating other ways of achieving the same goals. This statement seems particularly apt vis-a-vis sensitivity training as a method for decreasing anxiety, increasing creativity, and making interpersonal relationships more effective. The faddish aspects of sensitivity training have sometimes seemed to drown out systematic investigation of alternative means of achieving these goals, a situation that the responsible adherents of sensitivity training clearly have not supported.

Recently, however, an alternative method of achieving these goals

Table 12.4
Criticisms of T-Groups

CRITICISM	COMMENTS
T-groups can be run by charlatans who are corrupt, mediocre, or both.	There is little doubt this can happen; on the other hand, it should not serve as an excuse deprecating the entire approach. What needs to be done is to recognize and get rid of the charlatan.
T-groups invade privacy.	This is true, but it is not certain whether it is a criticism. Openness is one of the goals of the sensitivity-training program.
T-groups can do psychological damage to participants.	This is a difficult issue about which very little accurate data exist due to its sensitivity. However, it probably has occurred and to forestall it, an increasingly common procedure among ethical sensitivity trainers is to preselect individuals for group experience.
T-groups can be guilty of the same failings they are designed to overcome: they may generate superficial, nonmeaningful interactions, cheapen real emotion, cultivate an "in" jargon, and encourage participants to think of themselves as an elitist cult.	There is little doubt that this occurs; however, this problem is tied up with the charlatan question and will not be resolved until this latter question is resolved.
The emphasis on the group is wrong; it is the individual who is important.	This is a pseudo-criticism made only by those adopting a dogmatic, nonfunctional approach. Both groups and individuals are important; we can study and understand both.
T-groups may have the effects predicted, but the effects are not valid because they do not last.	While it may be true that effects do not last, this may not be because of invalidity but because the world and the organization discourage the perpetuation of the values and behaviors learned in sensitivity-training groups.

Source: Howard (1972).

in organizational contexts has stimulated considerable interest and although the evidence for it is primarily indirect, its promise is sufficiently great for us to devote some time to it here. The method we are referring to is known as rational leadership training. Suggested by a clinical psychologist, Albert Ellis, and an industrial psychologist, Milton Blum, its logic is to encourage the individual to alter his environmental perceptions so as to allow the possibility and inevitability, at times, of failure, and, more importantly, a lack of self-perfection. The possibility of failure thus becomes less traumatic and anxiety-provoking, leaving the individual better able to engage in creative, risk-taking behavior.

Conceptually, the argument revolves around what Ellis calls the irrational trinity, which he defines as a system of beliefs that demands perfection from the self, from others, and from the world. It is these beliefs and demands that cause difficulties, fears, and anxieties, according to Ellis (1973). Actual objective events are not that crucial:

> Most people tend to believe several unrealistic ideas. They hold to these ideas with dreadful results in terms of their emotions and behaviors. As far as I have been able to determine, all of these beliefs are forms of absolutism. They consist of unqualified demands and needs, instead of preferences or desires. Consequently, they have nothing to do with reality.
>
> *The Irrational Trinity*. There are perhaps 10 to 15 supreme "necessities" that people commonly impose on themselves and others. These can be reduced to three dictates that cause immense emotional difficulties.
>
> The first dictate is: "Because it would be highly preferable if I were outstandingly competent, I absolutely should and must be; it is awful when I am not; and I am therefore a worthless individual."
>
> The second irrational (and unprovable) idea is: "Because it is highly desirable that others treat me considerately and fairly, they absolutely should and must and they are rotten people who deserve to be utterly damned when they do not."
>
> The third impossible dictate is: "Because it is preferable that I experience pleasure rather than pain, the world absolutely should arrange this and life is horrible and I can't bear it when the world doesn't.
>
> These three fundamental irrational beliefs, and their many corollaries and sub-ideas are the main factors in what we often call neurosis, character disorder, or psychosis. They are not the sole causes of these disorders, since they, in their own turn, have their own origins or "causes." However, the original causes of an individual's main irrational Beliefs are not that important . . . what is important, and what philosophers rather than psychologists have tended to see for many centuries, is a concerted uprooting of the disturbed person's irrational Belief system and a replacing of it by a considerably sounder, reality-oriented philosophy.[4]

[4] Ellis, Albert. The no cop-out therapy. *Psychology Today,* 1973, *7,* 56–62. Copyright © 1973 by Ziff-Davis Publishing Company and Reprinted by permission of *Psychology Today* Magazine.

If we diagram Ellis's argument for our purposes here, it looks somewhat like the following:

A	B	C
Activating ⟶ experience	Irrational ⟶ belief	Inappropriate reactions to A

Examples:

Supervisor ⟶ suggests an improvement in proposal	Suggestion indicates ⟶ I am not perfect	Massive depression concerning future on job
Coworkers do ⟶ not go along with suggestions for work improvement	Others are not ⟶ perfect	Anger and hostility toward others
Superior ⟶ arranges to have	World is not ⟶ perfect	Depression
relative of doubt-ful qualifications given job		

Assuming man's ability to control his own fate, the most meaningful procedure is to encourage him to give up the "irrational trinity" and develop a more appropriate set of cognitions about the nature of the self, others, the world, and their imperfections. The following dialogue indicates how this might take place:

LESTER: Exactly! Isn't that kind of perfectionism good, then?

LEADER: Yes, *that kind*. But that's not exactly the kind that John has; he seems to have quite another kind of perfectionism.

LESTER: Meaning?

LEADER: Well, think about it for a moment. John obviously, like most of us, would like to do a well-nigh perfect job—to get his firm, for example, to make the right products and to promote them adequately. But he's also demanding that something *else* be perfect, too. Now what is that?

HARRIET: *Himself*—that's what!

LEADER: Right—that's what!

JOHN: Yes, I guess that's right. I'm not only trying to see that the product and the advertising are right. I am trying to see that I'm right.

LESTER: So? What's wrong with that? Why shouldn't he try to see that he's right?

LEADER: Well, first of all, he's not merely trying—he's *demanding*. That's where his *should* comes in. He's not merely saying, "I want to be right about my view of the products, about talking up about my view, about convincing the others, and about everything finally turning out well." He's really saying "I *should* be, I *ought* to be, I've *got* to be right!"

LESTER: And that leads to?

LEADER: Inevitable anxiety, hypertension, terrible conviction of failure. For if he *wants* to be right, tries hard to be, and still fails, he can logically conclude, "Too bad! I did my best and, this time, it was not good enough. Now let's see if I can do a little better next time." But if he *needs* to be, he has *got* to be right, and he actually fails, what can he possibly conclude but "how awful! What a terrible person *I* am for failing. How can a great failure like me ever possibly succeed in the future?"

DONALD: Not to mention, if he's *got* to be right, he's also *got* to be anxious.

JOHN: Yes, that's the way that I'm beginning to see it, and that's most important to me. I don't know if I would conclude, if I failed to pick the right product or convince others it was the right one to advertise widely, that I could never succeed in anything again. I'm not sure that I'm *that* much of a perfectionist. But I do see that if I'm telling myself that I've *got* to be right, that there is always a good chance that I won't be. And if I've got to be—why, that means that I just keep worrying all the time that what I've got to be might *not* be.

HARRIET: And how terrible *that* would be!

LEADER: Meaning, if you look at it a little more closely, "How terrible *I* would be." Isn't that the *real* core of almost all acute anxiety: That *I* would be pretty awful if the thing I am anxious about—or am demanding I will succeed at—did not turn out correctly?

LESTER: I think I'm beginning to get it. If John is a perfectionist in the sense that he *wants* to succeed very much at making the right decision about these products and convincing the others he is right, he gets himself into little trouble. But if he *has* to succeed—or *thinks* he has to—he then puts such a high stake on succeeding . . .

LEADER: Or on himself as a succeeder . . .

LESTER: Yes, I see; or on himself as a succeeder, that he thinks too much about the horror of his possibly not succeeding and too little of what he might do in case he temporarily fails. He thereby makes himself very anxious and—Oh, yes! I see this too—he even interferes with his own success.

LEADER: Right! By focusing so much on *himself,* and wrongly contending that *he* will be pretty worthless if his *performance* or his *task* doesn't turn out too well, John makes himself so anxious that he often hardly even looks, any more, at the ways to succeed at this task, but worrisomely keeps ruminating about his *own* imperfections, and thereby probably does worse and worse, performance-wise.

JOHN: That's exactly it! I get so tied up, when I have to make these important decisions, in how terrible it would be, and what a worm I would be, if I did the wrong thing, or even did the right thing and didn't manage to make it come out well that I soon find myself, as I said, right at the beginning, making decisions that I never ordinarily would tend to make, and almost always making just the wrong ones at that.

RANDOLPH: So, in the situation you're in now, you'll probably tend to make yourself so anxious about not standing up for what you really believe, or about standing up in the wrong way, that you may well stand up too firmly, or stand up for something you don't even believe in, and thereby really put your foot in it!

JOHN: Right again! In instances like this, in the past, I have been so afraid that I wouldn't stand up for what I really believe that I forcefully said the darndest things when the chips were finally down; and more often than not, I antagonized almost everyone and got absolutely nowhere. That's what I'm afraid will happen this time. That's why I brought this problem up—so you can help me *not* to do this again.

LEADER: All right: in the light of what we've brought out so far, what do you think you can do about the current decision you have to make?

JOHN: First of all, I think it's pretty clear that I should speak up and tell the board of directors what my views are about the product the advertising agency wants to push.

LEADER: Because?

JOHN: Because they *are* my views and I don't see any good reason why I should not stick by them. Even if I don't speak up about them, I'll still have them. And I'll never know whether the others would have agreed with me.[5]

How much evidence is there for Ellis's general argument? Directly, in the organizational setting, very little. Ellis is not a researcher, nor are most of the people with whom he works. However, there is considerable support for his ideas in a body of literature in organizational behavior that is becoming quite large and that is quite consistent in its findings. This is known as the expectancy-disconfirmation literature, with its characteristic finding being that the more individuals enter a job setting with a realistic picture of what they will find, including the job's good and bad points, the more favorable the eventual job outcomes in both a performance and satisfaction sense. Porter and Steers (1973) have recently reviewed much of this literature and there seems to be little doubt that honest, realistic recruiting that describes both a job's virtues and faults rather than encouraging unreal job demands results in less turnover and dissatisfaction (cf. Wanous, 1973). The support for Ellis in these and other papers, even though indirect, suggests the usefulness of this approach. One point I want to mention before we leave Ellis is that you should not think that Ellis is proposing either a lowering of achievement motivation or a lowering of concern for success. Far from it. Ellis values achievement striving quite strongly and feels that it is important that we try. What he wants us to do is to understand the actual nature of the world in which we live and not react dysfunctionally when the inevitable failures and disappointments occur.

---

[5] Reprinted with permission of author and publisher: Ellis, Albert, and Milton L. Blum, Rational training: A new method of facilitating management and labor relations. *Psychological Reports*, 1967, *20*, 1267–1284, (Monograph Supplement. V20)

Need-for-Achievement Training: Stimulus
Familiarization as Environmental Manipulation

One of the most carefully worked out and systematic of the different approaches that have been developed for influencing work motivation in the contemporary organization has been McClelland's development of a theoretical system to guide him in increasing the need for achievement, a variable whose importance we discussed earlier. His approach has been to develop a set of propositions that can be used in developing specific training programs designed to increase this motivation and then to test these propositions by having himself or his coworkers conduct such programs. To the extent that achievement motivation is increased by the programs, the propositions and course structure based on them receive support as a method by which to change people's motives in socially significant ways.

McClelland's propositions are listed below:

1. The more reasons an individual has in advance to believe that he can, will, or should develop a motive, the more educational attempts designed to develop that motive are likely to succeed.

2. The more an individual perceives that developing a motive is consistent with the demands of reality and reason, the more educational attempts designed to develop that motive are likely to succeed.

3. The more thoroughly an individual develops and clearly conceptualizes the associative network defining the motive, the more likely he is to develop the motive.

4. The more an individual can link the newly developed network to related actions, the more the change in both thought and action is likely to occur and endure.

5. The more an individual can link the newly conceptualized association-action complex (or motive) to events in his everyday life, the more likely the motive complex is to influence his thoughts and actions in situations outside the training experience.

6. The more an individual can perceive and experience the newly conceptualized motive as an improvement in the self-image, the more the motive is likely to influence his future thoughts and actions.

7. The more an individual can perceive and experience the newly conceptualized motive as an improvement on prevailing cultural values, the more likely the motive is to influence his future thoughts and actions.

8. The more an individual commits himself to achieving concrete goals in life related to the newly formed motive, the more the motive is likely to influence his future thoughts and actions.

9. The more an individual keeps a record of his progress toward achieving goals to which he is committed, the more the newly formed motive is likely to influence his future thoughts and actions.

10. Changes in motives are more likely to occur in an interpersonal atmosphere in which the individual feels warmly but honestly supported and

respected by others as a person capable of guiding and directing his own future behavior.

11. Changes in motives are more likely to occur the more the setting dramatizes the importance of self-study and lifts it out of the routine of everyday life.

12. Changes in motives are more likely to occur and persist if the new motive is a sign of membership in a new reference group.[6]

Conceptually, the logic of McClelland's approach to change stems from the original theoretical framework he proposed concerning the nature of motivational processes. This framework I have outlined earlier as follows:

1. People are motivated to approach certain stimuli and to avoid others. Hence, human motivation can be viewed as showing both approach and avoidance characteristics.

2. People are motivated to approach those stimuli that are mildly discrepant from previous experience and stimulation.

3. People are motivated to avoid those stimuli that are greatly discrepant from previous experience and stimulation.

4. People are indifferent to those stimuli that are the same as previous stimulation.

If we combine these basic statements of the theory and McClelland's propositions for change, we find the proposed change mechanism is to give the individuals being trained both cognitive and attitudinal input that certain stimuli — achievement, for example — are only mildly discrepant from their previous experience. Once the trainees are convinced that the stimuli are only mildly discrepant and thus relatively appropriate and desirable for them, the stimuli become sources of positive motivation. In effect, what has happened is that the individuals' motivational processes have been changed. (Theoretically, of course, you would use a reverse process if you wanted to develop new sources of avoidance motivation.)

McClelland has also used other general psychological findings and theory in developing his approach to change. The importance of meaningfulness of the motive (propositions 3, 4, and 5), the emphasis on self-determination as an influence on behavior (propositions 8 and 11), the role of feedback (proposition 9), and the role of the chance to improve self and others (propositions 6 and 7) are all concepts we have run across before.

In terms of reported research on the usefulness of this approach

---

[6] D. C. McClelland, Toward a theory of motive acquisition, *American Psychologist*, 1965, *20*, 321–333. Copyright 1965 by the American Psychological Association, and reproduced by permission.

for increasing need for achievement, the data available tend to be favorable. Kolb (1965) has reported a successful attempt to increase the need for achievement among middle-class male adolescents but not among lower-class boys. This finding makes sense if we remember that there is much more in the psychosocial environment of the middle-class boy to support increasing his need for achievement than there is in the environment of the lower-class male. In addition, McClelland (1965) has reported studies of businessmen in India whose entrepreneurial activity (a function of need for achievement) increased significantly after taking the change course as opposed to their level of motivation before taking the course and as opposed to changes in control groups.

Most recently, there is a study of considerable interest in showing the benefits of McClelland's approach for small and potential entrepreneurs from the Washington, D.C. black ghetto and depressed rural areas in Oklahoma (Timmons, 1971). Table 12.5 summarizes some of the results of these programs. Although there are some inconsistencies the overall thrust is quite favorable to the approach.

Other Suggestions for Organizational Development

We have been discussing some of the more popular and commonly used types of interventions in organizations and societies. Now I would like to turn to some other possibilities for organizational development that either have (or have promise of) value. For some of these, research data exist, whereas for others, the suggestions are mostly in the idea stage. Brought together, however, they present some interesting possibilities for further research and application.

1. The organization should hire idea people whose function is to suggest newer, more creative ways of developing answers to problems. This procedure would overcome the effects of the need for conformity with the ideas of the authority figures which seems to be inherent in any traditional authority system.

2. The organization should hire individuals who are explicitly different from those who have been hired in the past. This might include those who would typically be considered unusual and even marginal in employability. The rationale is that such individuals are more likely to have ideas that differ systematically from the high authority figures and thus would add to the creativity of the organization.

3. As I suggested earlier, individuals should be hired and tested on the basis of where they can be placed in the organization and the

Table 12.5
Comparative Summary of Findings Six Months After Achievement Training

OKLAHOMA GROUP	WASHINGTON, D.C. GROUP

Business-related activity

Course participants were significantly more active than their untrained counterparts in five of eight key areas: initiating steps toward forming new businesses, establishing expansion plans for existing businesses, improving procedures, increasing involvement in their businesses, and being promoted.

Compared with 24% of the untrained group, 61% of the trained group showed six or more signs of increased business activity.

Overall personal activity

Course participants were significantly more active than the untrained group as measured by a comprehensive, weighted and unweighted, 62-variable personal activity index.

New business activity

Course participants launched six new businesses, two of which were started by men not in ownership positions. The untrained group started five new businesses, all of which were begun by men already in an ownership position. Only the difference in new business profits was statistically significant between the two groups, in favor of the untrained.

Minimum overall business activity

Course participants added a mean of $3,192 in new capital, while the untrained group added a mean of $8,452. Sales increases of the trained group averaged $9,548, while increases of the untrained group averaged $2,190. Profits of the trained group increased a mean of $676 for the untrained group.

Maximum overall business activity

Course participants added a mean of $7,291 in new capital, while the untrained group averaged $9,246.

Sales increases of course participants were significantly higher than those of the untrained group, with a mean of $16,828 versus $1,847.

A significantly greater percentage of course participants attained larger profit increases than the untrained group, with a mean of $3,485 versus $544.

Course participants were significantly more active than nonparticipants in seven of eight key areas (including all identified in Oklahoma), and also increased their involvement in community leadership activities and improved their education.

Compared with 28% of the untrained group, 73% of the trained group showed six or more signs of increased business activity.

Course participants were significantly more active than the untrained group in terms of the same weighted and unweighted personal activity index.

Course participants launched eight new businesses, three of which were initiated by men not in ownership positions. No new businesses were started by the untrained group. Significantly, more of the trained group than the untrained group showed new business capital expenditures and new jobs created in new businesses.

Course participants added significantly more new capital than the untrained group, with a mean addition of $4,259 versus $1,420. Sales increases by course participants averaged $2,104, compared with $4,242 for the untrained group. Profit increases of participants averaged $24, compared with $511 for the untrained group.

Course participants invested significantly more new capital, and the mean expenditure of $45,548 was significantly greater than that of the untrained group's mean investment of $1,420.

Course participants experienced average sales decreases of $3,776, compared with a mean increase of $4,242 for the untrained group.

Profits of the trained group declined an average of $33, while the untrained group had a mean increase of $511. (The difference was not statistically significant.)

Table 12.5 *(cont.)*

OKLAHOMA GROUP	WASHINGTON, D.C. GROUP
Job creations	
Course participants created a minimum of 20, and a maximum of 211, new jobs, compared with 23 and 81, respectively, for the untrained group. The maximum mean jobs created for the trained group was 3.53, compared with 1.13 for the untrained group. It was predicted that the participants would create 27 to 90 new jobs during the six months following training.	Course participants created a minimum of 56, and a maximum of 70 new jobs, compared with 38 for the untrained group. The maximum mean jobs created by the trained group was 1.25, compared with .60 for the untrained group. It was predicted that the course participants would create 32 to 84 new jobs during the six months following training.

Note: The mean figures are calculated on the basis of data obtained in the six-month period following training compared with the last data available prior to the training. Pretraining data were gathered from participants and nonparticipants in both areas in June 1967.

Source: Timmons, 1971.

job that would be best for them, rather than whether they will be allowed into the organization at all. This would overcome the feelings of dependency and low self-esteem which result from being subject to the whim of others (which seems to reside inherently in any system of personnel allocation where only one person does the talking).

4. Managerial innovations such as the Scanlon Plan and multiple management, both of which involve asking members to undertake decision-making roles of a managerial nature outside officially prescribed duties, should be encouraged. The former plan in particular is promising. Its key elements involve (a) the utilization of nonsupervisory employees in the planning of work activities and (b) the distribution of the resulting additional profits on a relatively equitable basis. While the Scanlon Plan has not worked everywhere it has been introduced, its success rate is such that it generally warrants examination as a possible intervention technique.

5. The organization should institute and maintain procedures whereby new ideas may be put forth without fear of ridicule or negative evaluation. Such procedures may range from something as simple as a suggestion box to something as complex as an idea seminar for executives at a mountain retreat, but the key idea is that strong organizational support should be maintained for these innovative attempts at overcoming the traditional tendency to conform to the wishes of higher authority.

6. Professionalism among employees should be encouraged because having another social group with which the individual identifies

should make him less dependent on the organization and its prescribed norms and codes for his definitions of reality and for the level of his desired outcomes. This might lead to greater creativity.

7. Evaluation should be less of a guide to organizational life. Some slackness should be encouraged in order that newness may be introduced without the fear of negative outcomes that an evaluation-oriented organization implies.

8. So far as possible, new ideas in an organization should be evaluated on an autonomous basis. Every attempt should be made to eliminate the probability that new ideas will be evaluated on the basis of who says them.

9. The project team or matrix form of organization should be used wherever possible. In essence, this involves the organizing of different work forces around specific problems (Argyris, 1967a):

> A project team is created to solve a particular problem. It is composed of people representing all the relevant managerial functions (e.g., marketing, manufacturing, engineering, and finance). Each member is given equal responsibility and power to solve the problem. The members are expected to work as a cohesive unit. Once the problem is solved, the team is given a new assignment or disbanded. If the problem is a recurring one, the team remains active. . . . This results in an organization that looks like a matrix; hence the title of matrix organization (p. 33).

Figure 12.1 provides an example of how a matrix organization might look. Although there is not yet enough research to come to any conclusions, it appears that an approach such as this might do much to overcome the problem of lack of creativity due to the permanent subgroup identification which we spoke of previously. One problem with this method is that the temporary, fluctuating nature of the relationships formed will put a great stress on the need for coordination and on

Figure 12.1
A Matrix Organization

Representation of	Project 1	Project 2	Project 3
Manufacturing	X	X	
Engineering	X	X	X
Marketing	X		X
Finance		X	X
	Team 1	Team 2	Team 3

the development of individuals who will be able to speak the differing languages of these project teams in order to coordinate their activities. It is also conceivable that the temporary aspect of the relationships might be stressful since roles might be less defined, thus leading to role-conflict problems. However, these problems also occur in the traditional model, and they can be overcome.

10. A possible structural change for encouraging the voicing of one's opinions concerning matters related to one's own work unit is the overlapping group approach suggested by Likert (1961). Figure 12.2 illustrates the different linkages between people that would result under this approach. Basically, organizational functioning would take place primarily through the operation of the face-to-face groups (the enclosed circles), with each group having some member who is also a member of another group. Hence, this person serves as a link in that he is the medium of communication through which the activities, opinions, and decisions of each group are coordinated with one another. Although there are as yet few complete tests of the Likert model, whatever evidence there is tends to be favorable (Bass, 1963).

11. There should be a system of consumer representation in the planning of organizational behavior. By consumer representation I mean participation by those individuals whom the organization or organizational subunit provides with its goods or services. Hence, the con-

Figure 12.2
The Likert Model and the Traditional Form of Organization

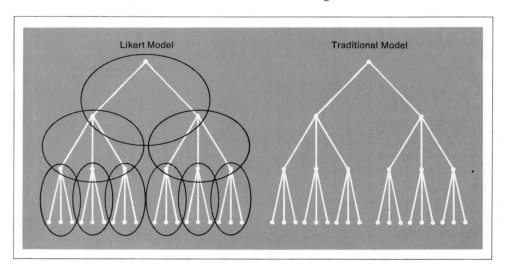

sumer might be an organizational subunit, or more traditionally, someone outside the organization. There are several values in this type of change. First, it recognizes the fact that unless the consumer is satisfied the organization will cease to exist. This is a way of finding out what the consumer wants. Second, it serves as a source of new ideas.

12. Performance appraisals should include self and peer appraisals. This would have the advantage of providing an environment in which individuals learn that their opinions are valued and sought after, and also add information about the nature of performance (Korman, 1968a). Related to this point is the concept of management by objectives, a currently popular technique. The purpose of management by objectives is to foster the implementation of planning decisions through personal commitment. It tries to do this by encouraging personal statements of commitment to self or mutually established (with one's supervisor) goal objectives. There is considerable variation from company to company about the degree of reliance placed on the subordinate in establishing the goals, but in all cases the key factor is that there must be acceptance of the goals by the superior and the subordinate. Such acceptance, it is predicted, will be likely to lead to performance designed to achieve the goal.

Research generally supports the management by objectives approach and, usually, the use of subordinate participation in setting the goals, particularly for those with high self-assurance (Carroll and Tosi, 1973). On the other hand, like other organizational interventions, using this approach without continuing follow-up will generate a loss in effectiveness. Basically, organizational change needs to be systemwide and continuing. Scatter-shot, one-time approaches rarely are meaningful.

13. Planning departments are generally of considerable value in reducing the hierarchical authority system because they bring into the organization a rational basis for ignoring the demands of hierarchy if they are found to be incompetent and/or illegitimate.

14. The organization should upgrade the skill and education of their employees in general because this leads to a greater valuation of the self and, hence, greater levels of achievement motivation.

15. Approaches such as the Planned Program Budgeting System should be implemented. This involves the lump sum budgeting of a program and its evaluation according to all immediate and delayed, direct and indirect social costs. This approach to budgeting reduces the ability of authoritarian leaders to implement their pet projects without regard to costs.

Of course, one highly controversial way of cutting down the arbitrary authority of management is the formation of labor unions. Clearly, labor unions are very strong instruments in this direction. However, whether or not unions increase personal control over one's life or are really just a substitution of one authority figure for another is a matter of dispute. In any case, unionization is not a technique likely to be used by management to increase the autonomy of employee dicision making.

Problems in Using Democratic Leadership as a Leadership Technique

I think it is obvious by now what I believe the general thrust of the research findings indicates for the direction of organizational development. Despite these conclusions on my part, though, I do not believe that the implementation of the types of changes we have discussed will take place without problems. To the contrary. I think there clearly are problems involved and we need to be aware of difficulties if the implementation of these changes is going to be effective.

Campbell et al. (1970) have listed some of the problems of using group participation as a leadership technique as follows:

1. Organizations value reaching a consensus quickly. As mentioned earlier in my discussion of some work by Janis, group members may withhold valuable information if they feel that a consensus is forming, a consensus which they feel is necessary and which they do not want to spoil. This process may, of course, result in poor decision making.

2. It is sometimes difficult to maintain one's sense of individuality under conditions of group participation. A loss of a sense of individuality can lead to self-estrangement, a sense of isolation, and a consequent lack of functional, work-oriented behavior, as you will recall from our earlier discussion of these topics.

3. The problems of management may not be very important to some workers, and asking them to participate in problem solving may lead to irresponsibility and behavior reflecting random choices.

4. People belong to different groups and asking them to meet can make for possible conflicts of a very serious nature. Not all people get along together, and very often it is difficult for them to agree on even a general statement, much less specific work-related decisions.

How serious are these problems? For some of them (e.g., problem 2), evidence already exists. For others, evidence is beginning to appear as, for example, the study by Janis (1973) of decision making during the Kennedy presidency, which seems to support the seriousness of problem 1. Clearly, group participation is not an immediate panacea, and if it is going to be used, the manager who uses it has to be aware of the problems suggested here.

Still another problem is that some people find it difficult to meet these new demands; they prefer having authoritarian leaders. I think it is foolish to deny that there are some individuals of this nature. The question is what to do. Should the authoritarian system be used because it is preferred, or should the participative method be used over objections? My preference is for the latter since I think it would result in the long run in more value for the individual and the organization. Also, I think there is research to support this, as I suggested in my discussion of longitudinal processes. However, there is little question that in many cases such introduction would be extremely difficult and may not, in fact, be feasible. In such cases, perhaps, there is no alternative except to hope for and develop competent authoritarian leaders.

Yet another difficulty is that some leaders cannot, or find it difficult to, act in a participative manner. The comments I made in the previous paragraph are, I think, equally applicable here.

Summary

Organizational development has become a quite well known term in the last decade. While there is some variation in defining it, most of the definitions used focus on the idea that it generally consists of change programs that utilize a variety of techniques in restructuring organizational functioning in order to make them more capable of surviving in a dynamic society and of providing more satisfying, ego-enhancing experiences to employees.

In this chapter various techniques commonly used in organizational development programs have been reviewed. Job enrichment and increased participation in decision making on both an individual and group level have been extensively used in both this country and elsewhere with generally favorable results. Societal restructuring as a result of government legislation has taken place in a number of nations including Israel, Yugoslavia, West Germany, Sweden, and France. The results have generally been favorable, and this type of restructuring seems to be increasing.

Among the more explicit training programs used in organizational development programs are T-group training, need-achievement training, and, less frequently, rational training. The first of these techniques is an opening-up approach in which individuals are encouraged to explore their reactions to others and others' reactions to them. Among the goals of T-groups are to increase the effectiveness of group functioning and to reduce interpersonal anxieties and frustrations. Research has found that T-group training can have positive effects, but a number of conditions can negate its effectiveness. Need-achievement training uses the concept of increasing one's familiarization with achievement stimuli in order to positively motivate trainees toward achievement. This approach stems from McClelland's theory of motivation and has had some positive results. Rational training uses cognitive restructuring as a mechanism for reducing individual demands of the self and the world and, thus, one's anxiety about not meeting demands. Indirect research has supported the value of this approach. More research would be desirable for these and other techniques used in organizational development.

SUGGESTIONS FOR FURTHER READING

ARGYRIS, C. *Intervention theory and method: A behavioral science view.* Reading, Mass.: Addison-Wesley, 1970.

> The author of this monograph is one of the most radical, innovative thinkers and practitioners in this field and has contributed much to the newer thrusts I have discussed. In this book he applies some of this thought to the problem of changing organizational functioning.

ELLIS, A. *Executive leadership: A rational approach.* Secaucas, N.J.: Citadel Press, 1972.

> Not a research monograph but a statement of the applicability of a basic theory of personality functioning to organizational life. The arguments are strongly made (perhaps too much so) and do not show an appreciation of research data as support. Yet, this book is highly stimulating and provoking.

FRIEDLANDER, F., and BROWN, L. D. Organization development, *Annual Review of Psychology,* vol. 25. Palo Alto, Calif.: Annual Reviews, 1974, pp. 313–342.

> A systematic attempt to integrate the field of organizational development along slightly different lines to those I have suggested. The perspectives are well developed and provide a good overview of recent research.

JENKINS, D. *Job power.* Garden City, N.Y.: Doubleday, 1973.

A solid, readable book on the growth of industrial democracy in different countries, including our own. The author, a journalist, is knowledgeable, well read, and moderate in his statements. All in all, he has written a book worth reading by anyone interested in the changing work scene.

McCLELLAND, D. C., and WINTER, D. G. *Motivating economic achievement.* Homewood, Ill.: Free Press, 1969.

A monograph that reports attempts at real-world applications of McClelland's achievement training model. Not everything works and the inferences are occasionally tenuous but, overall, the thrust is positive.

chapter thirteen

Change Programs: Attitudes and Skills

As in many other areas of human endeavor, change programs in work settings differ in their degree of glamour and in the extent to which they have caught both professional and lay interest. Sensitivity-training and job enrichment programs rank high on this dimension, as do perhaps a few others that fall under the organizational development umbrella.

Yet, there are many other types of change undertaken in the work environment that are equally important, but because they are more of a bread-and-butter nature, they do not make the newspapers and Sunday supplements as often. In this chapter I am going to discuss some of these lesser publicized but nevertheless important change programs. Another value of these programs is that they have much research attached to them and this body of research often provides needed guidelines for choosing techniques to be utilized in the more complex organizational development programs.

Attitude Change

Conceptually, the techniques that we have talked about under the organizational development heading are similar to one another in that they attempt to change one's emotional, attitudinal, noncognitive ways of perceiving the world. Basically, they try to change what we value and what we do not value.

Under what conditions will they be effective and under what conditions will they not be? As I have indicated, there are a number of fairly complex factors involved in answering this question. One previously undiscussed factor is the extent to which the method utilized satisfies some of the other factors we know to be significant in influencing attitude change, as these have developed from the voluminous literature on attitude research that has accumulated in laboratory and pragmatic field studies. In this section I want to review first what some of the problems are, and then I will discuss some of the positive facilitating factors as well as some of the continuing questions. While not very profound, the research I will review here is clearly of significance to anyone who wishes to design an attitudinal or motivational change program, whether of the complex organizational development kind or one of a more narrowly focused nature.

Difficulties in Real-Life Attitude Change Attempts

Perhaps the place to begin is to note that in real-life situations such as the business organization or the marketplace the effectiveness of attitude change methods is far lower than the effectiveness of attempts to change attitudes in a psychological laboratory experiment. Therefore, we need to reconcile ourselves to a relatively low level of aspiration in this field. However, this does not mean that attempts to change attitudes in the real-life situation are not worth the effort. This is not the case, as I will explain below. First, let us see why there is a disparity between the two situations in terms of effectiveness. There are a number of reasons, as Hovland (1959) points out, and the reasons do make sense. Furthermore, understanding these reasons for differential effectiveness will help us to understand better how real-life attitude change attempts should be constructed in the future.

One difference between the two stems from the fact that in a laboratory situation the person to be influenced is paying attention to the message, at least at some level of awareness, whether he agrees with it or not. After all, that is what he is there for, and it is not easy for him to ignore explicitly what is being said, particularly if he does not know what is coming. On the other hand, audiences in real-life situations are self-selected in that they have made the choice to listen or not to listen. For example, a person's attitude toward the company management cannot be changed if he chooses to ignore all of the management's attempts to change him by not listening at meetings, not reading the company newspaper, and so forth. Although it is by no means certain that we understand all of the conditions under which people will agree to receive messages into their cognitions, it is likely that one of the major determinants is the extent to which they believe that the message will agree with them. For many people a potentially disagreeable message will be ignored. Hence, the message could not possibly change the attitude.

A second reason real-life attempts at attitude change are usually less effective than laboratory attempts is the significance of the attitudes involved. In the laboratory case, the attitudes often dealt with are of a more minor, inconsequential nature than in the real-life situation. For example, a frequent type of attitude often used in laboratory experiments is one related to campus events such as whether the football team should be allowed to engage in postseason bowl games, the nature of student government, and so on. When this is contrasted with such attitudes as racial discrimination in the plant, union recognition, and topics frequently examined in sensitivity-training seminars, we can see that the latter are far more significant, are more deeply rooted, involve a much higher degree of commitment, and may receive a higher degree of social support from one's reference groups. Hence, the process of selective attention described above is also likely to operate here.

A third reason the two methods show differing results is somewhat related to the second but can be conceptually distinguished from it. This is that the attempt to change attitudes on a real-life basis will reach an individual in his regular, everyday environment where all the forces supporting his previous attitude are still operating. For example, if a company were to attempt to change an employee's attitudes toward desegregation of the work place, one of the worst ways to do this would be to attempt to influence him while he is surrounded by all of the social influences (e.g., peers, family, etc.) that may have pushed him toward segregationist attitudes in the first place. The contrast here with the laboratory attempt at attitude change, where those being influenced are isolated from previous supports of any kind, is obvious. For this reason, T-groups tend to emphasize the value of getting away from it all.

A fourth reason that attempts to change attitudes in real life run into difficulty is that in the laboratory the individual attempting the influence is generally a faculty member or an advanced graduate student, both of whom may have considerable prestige and credibility with the average college sophomore, the typical subject in laboratory experiments. This variable has been found to be related to effectiveness of attitude change attempts under certain conditions. On the other hand, most of the research on real-life attitude change has involved managers, political figures, advertisers, and the like, few of whom seem to have a great degree of credibility in our society, whether deserved or not.

Finally, a fifth reason for the differential effectiveness of the two methods concerns methodological considerations. Usually, in a laboratory attempt at attitude change, the effectiveness is measured right after the attempt at change, whereas the real-life effectiveness measure most often cannot take place immediately after the attempt at change has been made. For example, the effectiveness of a new advertising commercial is most often assessed at least a day or two after the attempt, rather than immediately after the time of viewing. This, of course, provides an opportunity for the operation of all the influences that mitigate effectiveness which we mentioned previously.

Despite these factors, we should not give up attempts to change attitudes in real life. What we need to do is to overcome the difficulties by increasing the likelihood of the message being attended to, separating the individual from his everyday environment, etc. The laboratory emphasis in T-group training is, in many respects, an attempt to meet these problems, albeit an imperfect one. Other techniques can also be incorporated into T-groups and other programs, and it is to a discussion of these that we now turn.

Techniques for Structuring Attitude-Change Messages

characteristics of the communication

Consider an attitude change attempt of the following nature: company A has been located in a downtown office building in a large eastern city for 25 years but is now going to move to a suburban location. The problem of the company is how best to get the staff to look upon the move favorably.

For example, assume that a Type I strategy has been adopted and the advantages of the move will be stressed. In developing an incentive for attitude change, should the advantages of the suburban location alone be presented? Or should the advantages of both urban and suburban be presented, allowing the recipients of the message to contrast the two? This is the one-sided versus two-sided question, and the answer depends on the audience, with the two-sided communication working best with more highly educated individuals and the one-sided communication for those with not as much education. There are several possible reasons for this fact, with these not necessarily being antithetical. One explanation is that the two-sided communication is more appealing to the intellect and more likely to be seen as appropriate for the curious. Since the more highly educated are more likely to see themselves as being curious, they are more likely to enter the situation and behave in a manner consistent with this self-image. Another possible explanation is that the two-sided communication is more likely to be controversial and hence generate more discussion in those groups that are more verbal; that is, those groups composed of the highly educated individuals. Thus, group pressures toward conformity and resulting change are more likely to operate in this situation.

One advantage of the two-sided approach is that those who

change their attitudes as a result of this kind of communication are less likely to change back; in other words, they are more resistant to counterinfluence. Probably the best explanation for this fact is that they have become inoculated against the arguments of side B by learning of their arguments prior to adopting a position favoring side A.

A second variation in the structure of a communication concerns conclusion stating. Should a communicator wind up his attitude change message by drawing a conclusion for his audience or should he let them draw their own conclusions. (It should be noted that this question is relevant for both one-sided and two-sided messages.) While this may seem like a minor question to some, it turns out that the choice does make a difference. If the material happens to be unfamiliar and difficult for the individuals involved, explicit conclusions should be stated. If the material is easy, it does not seem to make much of a difference. Since difficulty can be defined in terms of the intellectual abilities of the people involved relative to the material, this conclusion fits in with our previous comment. That is, if a person thinks he is competent in a given area, he will look favorably on those who treat him in a manner consistent with this self-image; that is, if they treat him as competent to draw his own conclusions. On the other hand, those who do not see themselves as competent will evaluate more favorably those who remind them of their own incompetence; that is, those who draw conclusions for them.

Another question concerning how an attitude change communication may be structured for maximum effectiveness is the order in which the arguments are presented. There are also several related questions involved, depending on the type of argument being used. For example, in a one-sided argument, is it better to use a climax procedure (stating the strongest arguments at the end) or anticlimax procedure (making the strongest arguments at the beginning)? Again, it depends on the audience. If the audience is interested in the communication, a climax order will be effective since an anticlimax procedure fails to fulfill the expectations created by the initial portions of the communication and may produce a let-down promoting resentment and forgetting. However, if the audience is uninterested, an anticlimax order is best, since the strong arguments will serve as an attention-getting device during the beginning of the presentation. The situation in which a two-sided argument is used has some analogous elements, but also some differences. One question is whether the pro argument should come first (supporting a primacy effect hypothesis) or last (supporting a recency effect). Again, audience variables are important and in a somewhat similar fashion to the one-sided appeal. If the audience is not interested, primacy is more effective than recency. However, if the audience is interested, it does not make much difference.

There are, in addition, other elements important in structuring the order of presentation in a two-sided communication, with one of these being the degree of public commitment. If, after hearing only the first side of a controversial issue, a recipient makes a response that publicly indicates his position on the issue, the result is a primacy effect. On the other hand, if there is no public commitment or if the person merely states his opinion anonymously after hearing the first side of the issue, there is neither a primacy nor a recency effect. A primacy effect may also occur if a single communication contains contradictory information. There is good evidence, though, that this effect may be overcome by warning the individual against the fallibility of first impressions.

A third dimension by which an attitude change communication may be varied in structure concerns the emotionality or rationality of the appeal. Despite the theoretical significance of this question, its relative ease of susceptibility to empirical testing, and its enormous practical significance, it is surprising how little research is available on it. We know very little about the different strengths of these appeals, whether they differ according to content, audience, and so forth. One area in which there has been some research is in the area of fear-arousal or threat appeals.

The model for research here is a simple one and can be diagrammed in four stages, as in Figure 13.1. The model is a relatively straightforward Type I manipulation (i.e., the promise of reduced danger if change takes place). Here again, however, we see how applying this approach is not as easy as it looks. Thus, at stage 2 a defensive process may set in whereby the individual, in order to protect himself

Figure 13.1
Model for Using Fear to Elicit Attitude Change

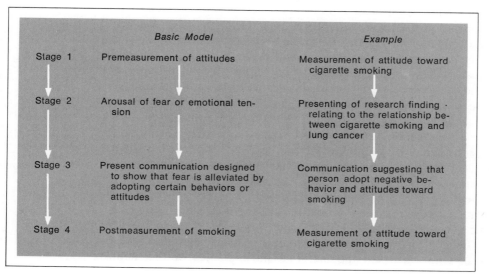

from the threat, blocks out the whole situation and does not attend to the communications in stage 3. One way to overcome this block is to have the person role-play a set of behaviors in which he or she cannot block out the fear-arousing message. Some recent studies by Mann and Janis (1968) and Steltzer and Kock (1968) have suggested that when students play lung cancer patients, significant changes in cigarette-related attitudes occur.

Of further support that fear can lead to attitude change if we force people to attend to the message is the research on two categories of people known as copers and avoiders. The first type is those who tend to meet and deal with threats head-on, whereas the second type avoids threats. As we might predict, research has shown that both high and low fear-inducing material will affect the behavior of copers, whereas only the latter type of material has an effect on the avoiders. In addition to this type of audience difference, another important variable affecting the influence of emotional appeals may be self-esteem, as we shall see later.

characteristics of the communicator

There is clear evidence that the greater the credibility of the communicator and the less manipulative his intent, the greater the effect on the attitude change when this is measured immediately after the attempt has been made. A second relatively consistent finding is that this effect of communicator credibility may wear off over time if the recipient of the message is not reminded of the communicator's credibility. When the effectiveness of the attitude change attempt is measured some time later, there is often no longer any association with communicator credibility.

Despite these empirical findings, there is as yet no clear theoretical explanation that can account for both the immediate effect and the delayed effect (in particular the latter) within a single framework. For example, one might argue that we will agree more with a credible communicator than a noncredible communicator since it is more appropriate and in balance with our social norms to reward the first type of individual as opposed to the second, and since agreeing with another person is a way of rewarding him. This type of explanation is, of course, in agreement with the theory I suggested earlier in this book. (As further support for the balance hypothesis, I have cited evidence that high self-esteem people are more likely to support other people who are similar to themselves than are low self-esteem individuals.)

A second reason for the first finding is that agreeing with a credible communicator provides more reward value. Since these explanations account only for the first effect, however, how do we deal with the second? One possible explanation has been suggested by Cohen (1964), who discussed the fact that most studies of this nature have been done with college student samples. It may be that during the time between the attitude change attempt and the delayed measurement of its effectiveness the students who have been subject to the credible communicator interact with those who have been subjected to the non-credible communicator. This interaction leads to greater conformity of opinion and, subsequently, a wiping out of any effect due to communicator differences.

A second possible explanation, equally plausible, is that perhaps the communicator was just not credible enough. If he were, the effect would not wear off, or so this argument goes. The usefulness of this explanation is questionable, however, since a reminder of differential communicator credibility reestablishes the relationship.

Personality Considerations in the Attitude Change Process

One of the questions that has always intrigued researchers in the field of attitude change both from a scientific viewpoint and from a concern with the values of a democratic society is whether there is a general personality trait of persuasibility that promotes acceptance of communications, independently of the particular topic involved, the form of communication used, and so on. Despite such interest, though, and despite a large number of research studies, there is no clear answer. Apparently, the most that can be said at this time is that some personality traits are related to persuasibility under specified conditions. Let us see what some of these traits are.

self-esteem

One of the first and most often investigated traits in this area has been one that we have heavily stressed throughout this book, the variable known as self-esteem. There are probably two major reasons this has been so important a focus of study. First, there is the definition and conceptual meaning of the variable itself. It has seemed logical to many that if we conceive of high self-esteem people as liking and having confidence in themselves and low self-esteem individuals as being the opposite, the obvious deduction would be that the greater the confidence in oneself, the less one would be swayed by the opinion of others. Hence, a long-standing hypothesis has been that self-esteem is negatively related to persuasibility. A second reason for the interest in this variable is that self-esteem seems to be highly correlated with many socioeconomic and ethnic groupings in our society. Research along this dimension has been seen by many as having significance for understanding the political, economic, and social behavior of these groups.

Unfortunately, despite the interest and research, the actual relationship between self-esteem and persuasibility is by no means clear. Although most of the early studies seemed to support the simple negative relationship, more recent work has been equivocal and several contaminating variables have begun to appear.

For one thing, it seems from a few studies (cf. McGuire, 1969) that the way in which self-esteem is related to persuasibility might depend on the kind of appeal being made. Thus, high self-esteem people are more susceptible to rational appeals, while low self-esteem people are more susceptible to irrational or emotional appeals. (Notice the conceptual similarity between these findings and the findings on one-sided versus two-sided communications.)

Furthermore, there now seems to be some evidence that self-esteem may be curvilinearly related to persuasibility, with the greatest susceptibility coming in the middle group (Cox and Bauer, 1964). The logic that has been suggested here is that the very high groups rely on their own opinions, whereas the very low are highly defensive about their inadequacies, making them less susceptible to appeals from others.

For these two reasons, what was for a while considered a relatively simple relationship with a good degree of support is no longer considered as such. The door is left open for the eventual development of a somewhat more complex framework than we currently have.

authoritarianism

Some evidence exists that those who have great respect for authority figures are more likely to be influenced by such figures than those who do not hold such opinions. One possible explanation for this finding may simply be differences in the credibility that these figures have for the different groups, but research supporting this interpretation is not as yet available.

social isolation

People who do not find others satisfying and who do not view other people in a positive manner are, on the average, less likely to be influenced by them (Hovland, Janis, and Kelley, 1953).

Speculations on Attitude Change Method as a Social Influence Process

One point, stemming from Type II change considerations, concerns some possible implications of the method of change utilized for the recipient's self-evaluation. It is clear that the type of procedure recommended for high-level individuals (e.g., two-sided messages with no conclusions drawn) poses a different type of environmental evaluation than the method suggested for the low-level individual (e.g., one-sided messages with conclusions drawn). The question arises as to whether we should use the latter means of attitude change for the low-level individual, even though it is likely to result in greater success, when it might at the same time have negative long-range personal and performance implications. Perhaps it would be better always to use the approach that assumes a high-level educated population (and, in fact, I suggested this in the theoretical extension proposed in chapter eleven). This might not be as effective a method of attitude change at the beginning for the low-level group, but eventually this group might be influenced to become a higher-level group for whom the attitude change method would then be appropriate. In addition, we would also have had the benefits of higher performance motivation during the process of growth and change.

These are some of the advantages of Type II thinking and suggestions for improvement. While there is considerable evidence to support this way of thinking in the research on leadership, I would like to see more research on this question in actual change situations.

Skill Training

For the most part, we have been talking in this chapter and the last about models and techniques of attitude and motivational change. However, most of the change programs in work settings deal with skill training. Many organizations that have little interest in organizational development still conduct training programs for job competence. Much of this work is very pragmatic, since the goal generally has been not to test a theoretical prediction (e.g., the effectiveness of massed versus distributed practice) but, rather, to help a person learn his job. Therefore, the training procedures felt to be desirable are frequently far too complex to allow one to understand the influence of a single possible variable such as the organization of practice. Even if the trainer wanted to, it would be hard to design training programs that allowed clear, unambiguous tests of theoretically important variables; the exigencies of the everyday business world make this very difficult. (Least understandable, but very important, there is some reluctance among practical people to design any project in order to investigate theoretically relevant variables. This attitude, while fast disappearing, still exists in some quarters, even though experience has shown the value of Kurt Lewin's dictum that the best way to develop effective practice is through good theory.)

The upshot is that, for the most part, industrial skill training techniques have been instituted, until recently, without much regard for the degree to which they meet the various conditions related to effective learning. One finds a wide variety of training techniques in popular use in industry, with little research surrounding them and with few firm conclusions that can be made of their effectiveness. Yet, some statements can be made about their potential usefulness. In this section, I want to review some of these major skill training techniques, their relative advantages and disadvantages, the kinds of situations in which they are useful, and why.

The Lecture Method

The lecture method of teaching and training individuals is, of course, a carry-over from the formal educational system and carries with it similar problems and disadvantages to those that it has in other educational contexts.

First, there seems to be good reason to argue that the lecture format is analogous to the authoritarian structure inherent in traditional organization theory. The lecture method therefore has implications for negative behavior similar to those of other external control techniques. While there is not a great deal of evidence testing this proposition, there does seem to be a converging trend of findings which shows that to the degree to which learning is not self-controlled, it is a negative contributor to performance, independent of any other effects it may have (Pressey, 1965). Similarly, there has been research showing negative feedback to television training, a technique that symbolizes this approach (Campbell, 1971).

Second, there seem to be certain limits as to the amount of transfer that can be obtained with the lecture method. It is obvious that whatever can be transferred from the lecture learning situation to the performance situation must almost always be limited to conceptual principles, rules, and other information. The actual skills necessary for a job, be they motor, interpersonal or verbal, *cannot* be learned through the lecture method, thus making this type of training for jobs requiring these skills incomplete. (However, it may be that learning the conceptual materials through this method may assist in, or positively transfer to, the learning of specific skills through another method.)

A third problem with the lecture method of training is that for some people, such as low-socioeconomic individuals, the stress on verbal and symbolic understanding is anxiety-provoking and thus debilitative of performance. For example, Reissman (1965) has pointed out that individuals from these lower educational, social, and economic backgrounds are more oriented in their thinking and cognitions to physical, rather than verbal, ways of viewing the world.

Finally, the lecture method of training does not seem to be capable of meeting the various conditions that facilitate learning according to the Type I model. It is very difficult to arrange reinforcements and feedback systematically with this method. In addition, the meaningfulness of the material presented to the individual may not be very high, depending on the individual trainee.

Given this rather imposing list of faults, why is the lecture method used at all? There are several reasons. One, undoubtedly, is the force of cultural norms. The lecture method is the predominant mode of teaching in our formal educational system, and since training is a form of education, etc., etc. This is not a good reason, but it is a powerful one. Behaviors sanctioned by force of tradition are very powerful in determining behavior!

A second reason, again a powerful but not a very good one, is that it provides a means of ego enhancement to the trainer or teacher. Being in the center of the stage is a valued position in our society, and since it is usually the trainer who has an important voice in deciding the technique to be used, the results are, perhaps, understandable, if not desirable.

Finally, the reason most often given for the method is its economy. Most of the other training methods are limited in size of classes whereas, theoretically, the size of the class for a lecture is limited only by the characteristics of the communication medium used. A televised lecture could be, and is, given to audiences numbering in the millions. However, one might question if it is more economical or not, if few people learn what is being taught.

The Conference Method

This method, which underlies sensitivity training and which is also known as the group discussion method, is, essentially, an attempt to have the learning and training experience take place through democratic, participative procedures whereby each learner takes an active role in the learning and knowledge development process. In this respect it is, compared to the lecture method, in the same position as democratic management is to authoritarian means of control (or Theory X is to Theory Y). Hence, we would expect it to have an advantage over the lecture method, at least in this sense.

A second advantage that the conference method may have over the lecture method is that some sort of reinforcement and feedback as to one's behavior is generally more available. In this sense, it allows the Type I change model to be more effectively utilized. For example, let us assume a lecturer for a sales training group suggests that "when meeting a potential client for XYZ product, one should generally point out that our product was developed by research scientists of Ivy League University." One of the reactions of a trainee might be: "I don't know whether such a sales message would go over in my territory, since most of the people are non–high-school graduates and they might resent it. On the other hand, maybe this kind of pitch would have even more influence with them than it would with those who have been to an Ivy League university; I just don't know." Under the lecture method, the trainee would leave the session in a quandary, whereas, under the conference method, he might be able to broach his indecision to others and receive feedback.

A third advantage is that groups can provide a more definitive environmental manipulation than can an individual. Hence, the power and force of the Type II approach can be utilized here also.

For these reasons, the conference method does have some advantages over the lecture method. However, it has disadvantages also. One of these is that the number of people involved in each training session must be kept relatively small; otherwise participation and its effects will be limited. This, of course, makes the conference method more expensive and time-consuming than the lecture method.

A second disadvantage is that there seems to be some evidence that individuals who are quiet and reserved are less likely to participate and make their feelings known than the more talkative types. It may be that they do not obtain the full benefits from this procedure. (This may be a particular problem for the low-socioeconomic individual thrown in with a training group in which the others come from more verbal, middle-class backgrounds.)

Simulation Methods

By simulation training is meant a technique whereby a deliberate attempt is made to duplicate in the training session the essential components of the to-be-entered performance situation. The essential value of this procedure is believed to be that it maximizes transfer of training possibilities since it maximizes stimulus similarity and calls for similar responses.

Based on this reasoning a wide variety of simulation-training techniques have been developed, ranging all the way from simulation of a cockpit for airplane pilot training to the business game. In the latter the players simulate being managers under certain constraint conditions, make decisions, receive feedback on these decisions (sometimes with the assistance of computers), and then make decisions based on this feedback.

There are other reasons for the enormous popularity of these simulation methods besides their obvious relevance to transfer of training.

It is comparatively simple to engineer into the technique such aids to learning as reinforcement, knowledge of results, and so on. Similarly, one might also engineer in self-control with relative ease. Clearly, simulations can be effective training tools (cf. Rubinsky and Smith, 1973).

However, there are problems, too. One obvious one is that by designing in such aspects as reinforcement and feedback, we may be decreasing the extent to which it is really a simulation of the job situation. A second problem is that these simulation methods may often take on the aspects of a game rather than a training experience. Hence, what will actually be transferred to the job situation becomes doubtful.

Finally, and perhaps most importantly, we have little information of a systematic nature as to exactly what we mean by a simulation. What constitutes an effective simulation and what does not? We have little knowledge about this question, although one series of possibilities has been suggested by Crawford (1966). He feels that among the major questions that must be raised about the effectiveness of simulation are (1) the scope or segment of the environment represented in the simulation, (2) the duration of the experience provided by it, and (3) the amount of involvement of the participants in the simulation activities; that is, the degree to which the participants have to become extensively involved in the simulation. That these questions will not be easy to answer is suggested by the research of Weitz and Adler (1973) who have found that simulations can become too elaborate. Such complexity leads to learning behaviors that are specific to the training and which should not be transferred to the job. They suggest that simple simulations that teach general job strategies might in the long run be better than complex simulations.

Programmed Learning

Of all the training and educational techniques developed during the last generation, programmed learning is one of the most important. What makes it so important? The answer is that it attempts to incorporate within it many of the conditions that characterize the Type I strategy. Hence, it is no surprise that most of the accumulated evidence shows it to be superior as a training tool to more conventional methods in the sense that individuals learn faster with no loss in proficiency or short-run retention (Campbell, 1971). Long-range retention, however, is still an open question. Table 13.1 gives an example of some typical results with this method.

Programmed learning consists, in essence, of four basic features. One is that the training material is broken down into a series of basic components or discrete steps. Second, each of these steps, known as frames, is placed in order so that there is a logical progression. Third, at the end of each frame the trainee is asked to make some kind of response (either overt or covert) that is designed to measure his comprehension of the material in that frame. Finally, the trainee is given immediate reinforcement and feedback as to whether his response is correct before going on to the next frame. Inherent in this technique, of course, is that the person controls his own pace while going through the program.

Even this brief summary indicates why the method is effective. It contains within it reinforcement, knowledge of results, self-control rather than authoritarian control, and expected activity on the part of the trainee. As we have said previously, the fact that the research evidence on it is good is not surprising. All that it does not contain is provision for transfer of training to the performance situation but, as we have seen, this method is not unique on that basis.

There is more than one kind of programmed learning and much of what has been learned about this technique is based on what is typically called a linear program. However, while there are other types of programs, they are all similar to one another in that they all include the important conditions for learning we have stated. As a result, there is probably little basis for choosing one over the other at this point in terms of their applicability for industrial training. Similarly, there is

Table 13.1

Examples of Improved Performance and Savings in Training Time Associated with the Use of Programmed Instruction

	AVERAGE PERFORMANCE SCORE		AVERAGE LENGTH OF TIME (HOURS)	
Course	*Conventional Instruction*	*Programmed Instruction*	*Conventional Instruction*	*Programmed Instruction*
7070 computer nomenclature	86.2	95.1	15	11.0
Reading engineering drawings	81.2	91.2	17	12.8
Dermatology and mycology	60.1	91.9	—	—
Basic electricity				
Facts	64.9	76.8	—	—
Concepts	47.5	—	—	—
Analogue computation	—	—	40	11.0
Package billing	—	—	40	26.0

Source: J.R. Murphy and I.A. Goldberg, Strategies for using programmed instruction, *Harvard Business Review,* 1964, *42,* 115–132.

Note: Dashes indicate that information is not available.

little basis for choosing between the use of books or machines, written or oral presentations, or a high or low degree of prompting. All seem to be equally effective (Campbell, 1971).

Other Problems in Change Programs

Trainer Variables

In terms of research data on the kinds of individuals who make the best trainers in formal organizations, the need for credibility has already been stressed. What else is desirable? There is little research available if we limit ourselves to the study of formal industrial training programs. While this is somewhat of a problem, it is, perhaps, not quite as serious as it first appears since it must be realized that training is, very often, part of the managerial and supervisory role and does, in fact, constitute one of its most important segments. We may, in a sense, equate the characteristics of a good supervisor with the characteristics of a good trainer, since the two are so intimately bound up with each other.

A good example of this is described in a paper by Griener (1967) who concluded after a review of various studies of organizational change that the best approach was what he called the shared power approach, as typified by group decision making and problem solving. This was found to be more satisfying than unilateral action and what he called a delegated authority approach. The resemblance here to our discussion of leadership behavior and organization structure is striking. Furthermore, Griener's conclusions are supported by a variety of other studies such as the following:

1. Sarason (1967) has reported that one of the major reasons change programs fail in school systems is the tendency for change proposals to emanate from high authority figures who do not take into account the feelings and opinions of those who must implement the changes.
2. Boocock (1966) concluded from a wide-ranging review of learning factors that giving students a greater degree of responsibility and autonomy vis-a-vis school authorities may produce a high level of achievement and intellectual interest in some students.
3. Gottesfeld and Dozier (1966) found in a community action program that when low-socioeconomic people assume decision-making roles, they become more ambitious.
4. There are a wide number of experimental laboratory reports which indicate that the higher the level of task difficulty imposed relatively early in the learning sequence, the greater the later learning (Barch, 1953; Barch and Lewis, 1954; Szafran and Welfand, 1950).

All in all, a consistent pattern of evidence exists that the kinds of trainer behavior which lead to effective learning and performance are highly similar to the kinds of supervisory behavior which we suggested should be related to performance in general. This is as it should be, since the change process and the techniques by which it is introduced constitute a social influence process that affects a person's self-perceived competence and his motivation to perform. The importance of the process holds whether we are talking about the day-to-day activities of the supervisor, his training activities, or any authority figure or structure.

Trainee Variables

Judging from the comments in the previous section, the reader will probably come to the conclusion that if there is a great similarity between the kinds of social influence processes that lead to effective behavior in both training and performance situations, there should also be a convergence between the kinds of worker characteristics that lead to effective learning behavior and effective work and task performance behavior.

While there are not many studies available specifically relevant to this question if we limit ourselves to industrial training programs, what studies there are seem consistent with this notion. There is, for example, evidence available that supports the notion of a favorable self-concept as being important in learning (cf. Shaw, 1968; Boocock, 1966), and when one considers this, as well as the research we spoke about earlier in this book, it is probable that when the research is done in this area support will be found for the proposition.

Design of Program Content: The Problem of Curriculum

How do we decide the content of a skill-training program? In which order do we place the content? What cues do we use in helping learning at each stage of the training process? Questions such as these are gaining an increasing amount of attention, and some meaningful guidelines are beginning to be developed.

One guideline is to ascertain the types of skills and abilities that are necessary for adequate performance at each stage of the training program. If we know what these necessary skills and abilities are at a particular stage, we can use this knowledge to dictate the cues and content that should be used to help performance on that particular skill. As an example, if we find that perceptual abilities are necessary at stage 1 and linguistic skills at stage 2, the training context can be designed to help the successful performance of these skills at each stage. Fleishman (1975) has shown, in research stretching over two decades, that such skill-ability correlations can be developed for various stages of training programs and he has proposed guidelines for training structured on these relationships.

Another way of achieving this same goal in areas of work where longitudinal changes are not too great is to analyze the basic components of the job into more skill components and more specific behavior. Such components and behaviors might then be used for the design of training for that job. In an interesting illustration of this approach, Glickman and Vallance (1958) used the method of critical incidents (see chapter fifteen) to determine the specific mistakes of Naval leaders. Lists of specific mistakes were then used to design training programs for Naval officers. While the study does not report comparative evaluations between training using this type of content and that using other types, the feedback that was received suggests that it was a well-thought-of experience by those participating.

Summary

There are many change programs in work settings which are of a pragmatic nature and which have limited goals. Yet, they constitute a significant portion of change activities, particularly since they take place in organizations that are very much interested in improving their work force but which reject the organizational development framework. These programs are important also because, being limited, they lend themselves to research and thus provide a research base for the more complex programs.

Attitude change attempts in real-world settings such as the work environment have been found to be less effective than laboratory studies with the major reason being that the laboratory study does not have to compete with other sources of influence. However, despite the lower level of aspiration that needs to be accepted, appropriate attention to certain characteristics of the attitude change message can help increase its effectiveness. Among the important factors to consider are structuring the message to meet the curiosity and intellectual level of the recipient and using credible communicators, although there is doubt as to how persisting the latter effects are. Still unclear, also, is how to effectively use fear in influencing people to change.

Skill-training programs are probably the single most common change programs in work settings. Among the various techniques used are lecture methods, group discussion techniques, simulation methods, and programmed learning. Each of these has advantages and disadvantages, although most research data support the latter as being consistently of greater value in those situations where it is appropriate. Studies of characteristics of effective trainers and successful trainees are not often found in the literature. It may be, however, that these characteristics are the same as those found in good supervisors and good learners in general.

A recent development in training research is to study the characteristics of the factors associated with different aspects of the curriculum. This provides a guideline as to which factors to emphasize in the learning process.

SUGGESTIONS FOR FURTHER READING

BASS, B. M. and VAUGHAN, J. A. *Training in industry: The management of learning*. Belmont, Calif.: Wadsworth, 1968.
Although a decade old, this book remains a useful review of some of the major practical techniques available for training purposes in work organizations.

CAMPBELL, J. P. Personnel training and development. *Annual Review of Psychology*, vol. 22. Palo Alto, Calif.: Annual Reviews, 1971, pp. 565–602.
The author of this article has little patience with trivia and fads. As a result he does an excellent job of distinguishing between what we know about training techniques and methodologies and what may safely be ignored.

McGUIRE, W. The nature of attitudes and attitude change. In G. Lindzey and E. Aronson (eds.), *The handbook of social psychology*, second ed., vol. 3. Reading, Mass.: Addison-Wesley, 1969, pp. 136–314
This is not an easy paper but will repay the serious student willing to go through it several times. The author is a contributor to attitude research who here presents a scholarly, well-reasoned, and sober assessment of the field of attitude change.

RUBINSKY, S., and SMITH, N. Safety training by accident simulation. *Journal of Applied Psychology*, 1973, *57*, 68–73.
An experimental study illustrating the use of accident simulation as a mechanism for increasing safety orientation. Wide applicability of the findings may occur as you read the techniques used and study the results.

chapter fourteen

Measuring Job Behavior and Reactions to Jobs: Conceptual Issues

Throughout this book the major work outcomes we have been trying to understand include job performance, self-estrangement, job satisfaction, changes in self-evaluation, and the other variables we have previously mentioned. This goal carries with it the assumption that these outcomes can be conceptualized in meaningful ways and subjected to empirical measurement. In this chapter we shall concern ourselves with the problems involved in developing an understanding of these variables, reserving for the next chapter a discussion of specific measurement techniques.

Job Performance: Conceptual Issues

What is Good Performance?

A dozen years ago this question would probably not have been posed in this manner. We knew what good performance was: the more goods produced, the better; the greater the number of services performed, the better; the more roads built, the better; the more stores one was able to run effectively, the better, and so on. Now, however, new ways of thinking are coming to the fore and the question of what should be considered good company and employee performance has become complex. Briefly, there no longer seems to be a generally accepted definition of "good." Consider, for example, the following:

1. The behavior of the oil companies during the oil crisis of 1973–1974. What was legitimate behavior in the name of profit? What was not?
2. The refusal of banks to consider it a good risk for them to invest in deteriorating urban areas, with such lack of investment helping to accelerate the deterioration.
3. The general responsibility of companies toward their stockholders as opposed to their responsibility for environmental quality.
4. The policies of companies that lead to greater organizational effectiveness but which may also exacerbate societal problems and tensions, e.g., the movement of some companies from the inner city to a suburb, with a consequent acceleration of urban economic social problems.
5. The stimulation of greater organizational effectiveness by company policies that also may lead to personal and interpersonal difficulties, e.g., the implicit demands of some companies that their executives take work home and, in general, subordinate their family and personal lives to organizational requirements, including frequent geographic moves.

How does one evaluate these behaviors? Are they good or bad? Before I give you my opinion, let me point out two important aspects. First, I believe that the decision as to what you define as good is a value question that is decided by one's personal code of meanings, values and ethics. From a viewpoint of research you can find out the empirical consequences of these different behaviors, but no matter what you find out, the decision as to which of these outcomes you decide is "good" is purely subjective. Thus, if you were to determine that the result of a company's move to the suburbs is a 5% increase in company performance and a 5% increase in the welfare roles of the inner city left behind, your decision as to whether this company has performed effectively would be based on values, not empirical data. The second point I want to make is that you cannot avoid value judgments in assessing the quality of performance of a given individual or organization. Any time you decide that one person has performed well and another person has not, you are implementing a value judgment about what you consider to be good and bad in that particular context.

My own position is that any assessment of performance needs to consider both long and short-term consequences as these affect the company, the employees, and society at large. It seems to me that all three of these perspectives on what is considered to be good performance are quite legitimate. I think we are long past the day when we can allow companies to operate without regard for the many consequences of their actions. However, I also do not believe that one should adopt dogmatic positions consistently favoring one perspective over another. Life is not that simple and, from a long-range perspective, it is as necessary to have healthy companies as to have healthy individuals and a healthy environment. All are necessary, and the choice of which needs to consider has to be made on a case-by-case basis. I believe, for example, that it is crucial to keep Lake Superior a viable body of water, but I also think that it is important to be concerned about the jobs of the people in that area's companies when evaluating the need for those companies to change their practices. Similarly, it is important to keep an organization healthy and profitable, but it is also important that the individuals in the organization feel that their jobs are sources of positive self-regard and satisfaction.

Operationally, what does this mean? If all of these dimensions are important, then all need to be utilized in assessing performance and all would be relevant on an a priori basis. This means that a decision on how good performance is in a specific situation would be a function of the levels of each of these dimensions and the particular philosophical framework of the judge. This leads to a tridimensional view of the "goodness of functioning" that looks something like Figure 14.1. Any given behavior can then be located in the appropriate cell of the cube, and on the basis of that location and the evaluator's value systems, both in general and for that situation, a decision as to goodness or badness of the behavior may be made. I generally like to use all three dimensions of evaluation (individual, organizational, and societal) equally in making a judgment, but I can certainly see that they could be used differently in different situations. In addition, there are questions as to whether and when they should be combined, a matter I will deal with below.

A second decision to make is which specific measurement tech-

Figure 14.1
Tridimensional View of Job Performance

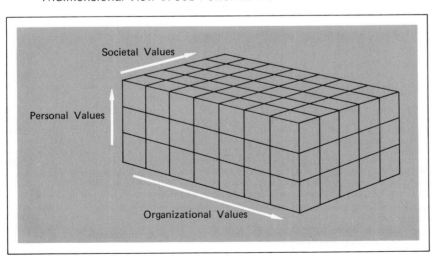

niques to use once we have decided on the dimensions we will use to evaluate performance. For example, how do we measure good performance from an organizational perspective? From a personal perspective? From a societal perspective? We will turn to some of these questions later.

The Multidimensionality of Job Performance

Once we define and conceptualize job performance, we need to consider an important principle: individual differences in performance on a given job will vary over time, using the same measure of performance (criterion), and across different criteria, with the degree of tenure held constant. More specifically, what this statement suggests is that the nature of job performance is highly complex and that the problem of deciding who is good and who is bad, using either the three dimensions I outlined above or others, is frequently going to be quite different depending on the measures used and the time of measurement. For example, the individuals who are high on job performance when using measure of performance A may not be the same individuals who are high on performance when using measure B. An example of this can be seen in Table 14.1, which summarizes a study of relationships among different measures of job performance for delivery truck drivers (Seashore, Indik, and Georgopoulos, 1960). If we look at the correlation levels between different measures in this situation (recalling that

Table 14.1

Intercorrelations among Five Job Performance Variables in 27 Operation Stations of a Delivery Service (Decimals Omitted)

Criteria	POPULATION A (STATION) N=27				POPULATION B (INDIVIDUALS) N=975				POPULATION C[a] (INDIVIDUALS WITH STATION) N=975			
	2	3	4	5	2	3	4	5	2	3	4	5
Effectiveness	74	25	-10	-46^b	28^b	-02	-08	-32^b	36^b	-05	-17^b	-42
Productivity		30	08	-39^b		-12^b	-01	-26^b		-01	02	-23
Chargeable accidents			02	-65^b			-03	-18^b			09	04
Unexpected absences				-11				15				17
Errors (nondelivery)												

Source: S. Seashore, B. Indik, and B. Georgopoulos, Relationships among criteria of job performance, *Journal of Applied Psychology,* 1960, *44,* 195–204. Copyright 1968 by the American Psychological Association, and reproduced by permission.

Note: Correlations based on delivery station mean scores (i.e., there were 975 individuals grouped into 27 stations).

[a] Correlations shown here are the weighted average station correlations, when individuals are grouped according to station membership.

[b] Significant at the .05 level.

correlations of .00 signify no relationship between the variables), we see that it is likely that differing patterns of abilities and sources of motivation are determining performance on each of these different measures. Using similar dimensions to those I suggested, a very similar pattern of low intercorrelations was found in a study of 97 firms by Pickle and Friedlander (1967). In this study, the researchers obtained measures of each firm's adequacy from the viewpoint of owner, community, government, customer, supplier, creditor, and employee perspectives, and found little similarity among company rankings on each.

In addition, the statement also suggests that a person performing effectively at one time may not be classified in the same way when using the same measure of performance at a later time. An example of this type of finding is given in Figure 14.2, which depicts the changes in the predictive validity of various tests (interest in people, mechanical principles, and distance discrimination) over time against a production criterion for a group of 56 cab drivers (Ghiselli and Haire, 1960). As can be seen, the first test generally decreased in validity, the second fluctuated, and the third increased. The sum total of these findings was that those who were high in production during the first two weeks were not those who were high in production later.

These are two examples of what is a basic principle of human work performance: performance is a multidimensional variable, people high on one measure may not be high on another, and such standings may change over time (MacKinney, 1967). This finding suggests some important questions concerning implications of this complexity. If there is more than one important dimension to job behavior (and I have postulated that there is) and people differ in their standings on them, we need to decide whether these dimensions should be combined in order to reach an overall judgment or whether the dimensions should be analyzed separately for their relationship to other variables of interest such as selection tests, training programs, and others. If they should be combined, how should we combine them? Should we add the standings of each individual (or group) on each measure? Should we weight one measure of performance greater than another? When should we do each? There is no agreement on any of these questions; we can make strong arguments both for and against each of the various alternatives.

Looking at the question of whether we should combine at all, some prominent industrial psychologists have argued very much in the negative (Dunnette, 1963; Guion, 1961; Ghiselli, 1956). To summarize their arguments, they claim that the low intercorrelations among the different performance variables indicate that these are conceptually different aspects of behavior and are not imperfect indicants of the same underlying variable, a variable that might be called overall job performance. Since these are different, the argument goes, combining these

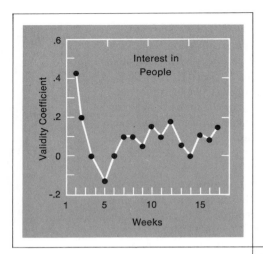

Figure 14.2
Changes in the Validity Coefficients of Three Tests During the First Weeks of Employment

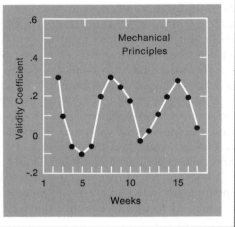

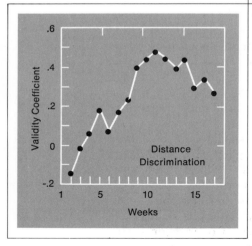

Source: E. Ghiselli and M. Haire. The validation of selection tests in the light of the dynamic character of criteria, *Personnel Psychology,* 1960, *13,* 225–231.

dimensions would be like combining apples and oranges. Furthermore, in addition to the lack of theoretical justification, such combining would be practically harmful since it would be harder to relate such composites to other variables such as selection tests than if the measures were conceptually clean and distinct. Hence, the dimensions should be studied separately for the tests that predict them. In addition, the stability of such test-criterion relationships should be monitored over time. As for which dimension to use in decision making at any particular time, this is a matter for managerial judgment anyway.

There are several arguments against this point of view and in favor of a composite criterion. For example, it could be argued that these criterion dimensions can be combined on the basis of overall worth to company, individual, or society, or on an overall basis of all these dimensions. Thus, although different measures of performance may not be related, they can all be viewed in terms of their degree of worth and therefore can be combined on that basis. A second reason some psychologists have for combining criteria is that the multiple dimensions used may differ greatly from study to study. This limits the generality of any study and leaves us lost in a myriad of specifics. A third reason for preferring the composite criterion is that it is conceptually much simpler to sell to management who must pay for the research. Finally, the argument that composite variables are less likely to relate to other variables is not necessarily so, with the prime example being the Stanford-Binet Intelligence Scales. This test, while mostly verbal, has other components and is related to a wide variety of educational criteria.

A good way of resolving this question has been suggested by Schmidt and Kaplan (1971). Conceptually, they suggest that an overall judgment is of significant administrative value and possibly even necessary for decision making. On the other hand, separate criteria are more likely to provide greater theoretical understanding in that developing predictors of separate dimensions of work behavior is more likely to insure greater understanding of the types of factors that influence different kinds of work behavior. This problem of whether to combine is, therefore, to be resolved by one's purposes at the time. If you are interested in administrative decisions, you should combine the criteria and if you are interested in theoretical understanding, you should study them separately.

Considering, now, the situation in which a combination is called for, what procedures might be used in developing a total score? Various methods have been suggested, of which the most important are the following:

1. Combine criteria by having expert judges weight them according to importance. (Obviously, this technique involves explicit recognition of the

point we have been making all along that subjective evaluations continuously influence the performance measurement process.)

2. Combine criteria by weighting more heavily those criteria that are more stable over time. The problem here is that if an aspect of behavior is stable, it does not necessarily mean that it is important.

3. Combine criteria by weighting more heavily those that are best predicted by tests. The major problem here is that the tail would now wag the dog since the test is supposed to predict significant behaviors and should be chosen on that basis, rather than the other way around. This type of approach is known as criterion contamination and should be avoided at all costs.

To sum up, there is no clear solution to the question of how one should combine criteria into an overall composite. In the last analysis the choice of procedure depends on the judgment of the people involved. Whatever they happen to like and think best, whether it is one of the methods we have suggested or a different one, it will have as many disadvantages as most of the other possible choices.

The Quality of Performance Criteria

Assume for a moment that we have resolved all or most of the questions we have been discussing and we have decided on a measure. How do we know that we have a good one or that the values we have chosen to implement are being effectively assessed by our chosen operational measure? As it turns out, there are several ways and although none of them is perfect, they do, when taken as a whole, provide us with relatively adequate guidelines.

One of the guidelines for establishing the worth of criteria when they are subjective evaluations is to establish the construct validity of the ratings by using a multitrait, multirater matrix (Lawler, 1967). The basic requirement of this procedure is that people should be rated on the same traits by more than one rater and that these ratings should show the following characteristics (Campbell and Fiske, 1959):

Convergent Validity   Correlations between the same traits as rated by different raters should be significantly different from zero.

Discriminant Validity   (a) The correlation between the same traits as rated by different raters should be higher than the correlation between different traits rated by the same rater. (b) The correlation between the same traits as rated by different raters should be higher than the correlation between different traits rated by different raters.

The logic here is that a rating of performance along dimension A of behavior is a good measure of performance along dimension A if it agrees with other ratings of performance along dimension A, but it is not a good measure of performance of dimension A; that is, it does not have good construct validity, if it agrees more with measures of dimension B and C. Before we get too confused, consider the following situation: Forty-five salesclerks are rated by two separate superiors on their interest in selling, pleasantness to customers, and acceptance of clerical nonselling duties (such as stock taking, returns, etc.). If we correlate the ratings of the two superiors over the three dimensions, we obtain the results given in Table 14.2A.

In this case, the criteria for convergent and discriminant validity have been met; that is, higher correlations are obtained for the ratings on the same dimensions than for the ratings along different dimensions, and so on. Hence, we have some basis for inferring that the ratings have construct validity and that the raters were thinking of and evaluating along the same dimensions when they were rating along dimensions A, B, and C, respectively. One might still argue, of course, that while they were thinking of the same dimension, it might not have been the one named, for example, interest in selling. Although this is so, and there is no way of knowing for sure, the presumption is that, all other things being equal, they were more likely to be thinking of the dimen-

Table 14.2
(A) Examples of Ratings Showing Both Convergent and Discriminant Validity

TRAITS		FIRST SUPERIOR			SECOND SUPERIOR		
		A	*B*	*C*	*A*	*B*	*C*
First superior	A	.83					
	B	.32	.84				
	C	.17	.25	.91			
Second superior	A	.74			.85		
	B	.42	.83		.28	.79	
	C	.08	.13	.81	.04	.17	.86

(B) Examples of Ratings Showing Neither Convergent Nor Discriminant Validity

TRAITS		FIRST SUPERIOR			SECOND SUPERIOR		
		A	*B*	*C*	*A*	*B*	*C*
First superior	A	.37					
	B	.83	.14				
	C	.38	.51	.47			
Second superior	A	.53			.32		
	B	.72	.41		.74	.67	
	C	.38	.46	.28	.73	.38	.14

sion named. Hence, as Lawler (1967) has pointed out, to the degree to which the results obtained are like the example given, we have more confidence in the rating than if the correlations obtained, using a similar form of analysis, were as in Table 14.2B. In this case, it is more likely that whatever the first superior was thinking of when he was rating along dimension A, it was not the same thing as what the second superior was thinking of, and so on.

In addition to this method, there are other ways of assessing the value of performance criteria, either when they are of a performance evaluation nature or when they are based on more objective behavioral measures such as sales or absenteeism. One of these is to make sure that the criteria are not contaminated by the predictors themselves in that the way that people rank on them does not result from a rater's attempt to make their ratings agree with differences on a predictor of that measure of performance. An example of such contamination is when a superior adjusts his ratings so that he rates a trainee from Harvard higher than one from a state university on the implicit assumption that the first trainee must be better than the second since he is from Harvard. Under this procedure, college attended cannot help but predict superior ratings!

Another way of assessing the value of a performance measure is that it must be acceptable to those using it. If it is not, it should never be used since despite whatever technical sophistication it may have, it will be sabotaged by the raters.

Third, as an offshoot of acceptability, a characteristic of a performance measure of particular relevance for objective measures of performance is the degree to which it is comprehensible. In some cases the manner in which sales and production figures are computed and the resulting attribution to individual sources is so complex that one almost needs a higher degree in mathematics to understand it. Such a situation is unsatisfactory for obvious reasons.

Finally, a criterion measure should be realistic in that it should be representative of meaningful behavior. It does not make much sense to rate a secretary by her usage of paper clips when her job contains much more meaning than this.

Ratee and Rater Characteristics as Influences on Ratings

Despite the obvious hypothesis that the characteristics of the rater and the ratee may affect what happens on a performance evaluation independently of the behavior that is being evaluated, the amount of research on this question has been relatively minimal. However, some recent work has dealt with this question and there is some evidence to support the following conclusions:

1. Rating ability is at least partially a function of the intelligence of the rater; the higher the intelligence of the rater, the better his ratings (cf. Bayroff, Haggerty, and Rundquist, 1954; Mandell, 1956).

2. The better the supervisor, the more likely he is to discriminate between good and poor employees and the less likely he is to be subject to the leniency effect (Kirchner and Reisberg, 1962).

3. The value of special training in judging other people accurately, such as that received by clinical psychologists, is doubtful. Taft (1955), among others, has found that physical scientists are as good as, if not better than, clinical psychologists in judging others.

4. The greater the propinquity between the evaluator and the evaluated, the higher the ratings (Kipnis, 1960; Rothaus, Morton, and Hanson, 1965).

5. The higher the self-esteem of the person being evaluated, the more likely he is to try to ingratiate himself with the evaluator and secure a favorable rating (Jones, 1964).

6. The higher the cognitive complexity of the rater, the more likely he is to differentiate between others (Bieri, 1961).

7. The more the rater engages in analytical thinking as opposed to global, the more likely he is to differentiate others (Gruenfeld and Arbuthnot, 1969).

8. Individuals who exhibit good behaviors are more likely to be rated accurately than those who exhibit poor behaviors (Gordon, 1970).

In addition to these findings, which concern themselves with ratee and rater characteristics as viewed separately, there are also research findings on how particular rater–ratee combinations influence ratings over and above the particular behaviors involved. These studies also pose severe conceptual problems for those trying to understand the processes influencing the measurement of performance. Most prominent of these studies has been the research on particular combinations of different racial groups and different sexes as they influence performance evaluation:

1. White supervisors use objective data in evaluating black subordinates much more than they do in evaluating white subordinates (Bass and Turner, 1973).

2. Both males and females are more likely to see male competence as being due to ability and female competence as due to luck (Deaux, 1974).

3. Males are more likely to evaluate females less favorably than equally qualified males for various personnel decisions and to discipline them more severely for identical rule infractions (Rosen and Jerdee, 1974).

4. In the peer rating situation there seems to be no race effect when blacks and whites rate one another (Schmidt and Johnson, 1973).

Obviously, we have learned much about some of the processes that influence the rating and evaluation procedure, information that has helped us to understand what makes a good rater in terms of accuracy, what makes a person get a good rating, and what influences one person to give another a good rating. It is not clear, however, how we can improve rating procedures. One answer is better rating structures and methods, a matter about which we will talk later. Another answer is to train individuals to take account of these problems. Unfortunately, for this option, there is little research concerning how valuable this type of training might be.

Reactions to Jobs: Conceptual Problems

The Measurement of Job Reactions

Emotional and attitudinal reactions to jobs can be conceptualized and measured in a variety of ways that are related to but not directly comparable to one another. A study illustrating this point in the area of job satisfaction is one reported by Wanous and Lawler (1972). In this study, nine ways of measuring job satisfaction were defined as follows:

1. Job satisfaction is a result of the sum of satisfactions with different aspects of the job.
2. Job satisfaction is a result of the sum of satisfactions with different aspects of the job, weighted by the importance of each aspect.
3. Job satisfaction is a result of the amount of need fulfillment in the job at the time.
4. Job satisfaction is a result of the amount of need fulfillment in the job at the time, weighted by the importance of each need.
5. Job satisfaction is a result of the discrepancy between the amount of need fulfillment a person thinks should be on the job and the amount there is at the time.
6. Job satisfaction is a result of the discrepancy between the amount of need fulfillment a person thinks should be on the job and the amount there is at the time, weighted by the importance of each need.
7. Job satisfaction is a result of the amount of need fulfillment a person would like to see on the job as opposed to what he has currently.
8. Job satisfaction is a result of the amount of need fulfillment a person would like to see on the job as opposed to what he has currently, weighted by the importance of each need.
9. Job satisfaction is a result of the importance of needs as opposed to what there is currently.

Wanous and Lawler found that while each of these definitions was related to one another, they were also somewhat independent as, perhaps, they should be, when we consider that these models are really based on different theories of job satisfaction. For example, numbers 3 and 4 imply an equity model, whereas 7 and 8 imply a personal need fulfillment model. In line with our earlier discussion in this book, 1, 3, 5, and 7 are additive models, whereas 2, 4, 6, and 8 are multiplicative. It seems clear, then, that the measurement of job reactions such as job satisfaction, self-estrangement, and feelings of isolation depends very much on the theory that one is using. Different theories will lead to different measurement operations.

Incidentally, the inclusion of an importance term as in numbers 2, 4, 6, and 8 does not seem to make the measurement of job reactions any better in terms of either construct validity (see below) or in predicting other variables. Wanous and Lawler, as well as others, have found this to be the case.

The Quality of Job Reaction Measures

Given, then, that there are various ways of measuring job reactions, how do we know when we have a good measure? Like job performance ratings, a good approach is the multitrait, multimethod matrix. (Rater and method are analogous variables here.) Probably the best example of this technique is the work of a group at Cornell University who attempted to determine the convergent and discriminant validity of four different methods for measuring five dimensions of job satisfaction. Figure 14.3 shows their results and considering that these are actual data, as opposed to the examples we made up previously, the results are quite good. That is, in general, the highest correlations tend to occur when the different methods are measuring the same job satisfaction dimension. Perhaps the major exception to this is the boxes instrument, which does not seem to be quite as satisfactory as the others.

In addition to the multitrait, multimethod approach for determining the quality of job reaction measures, the other general qualities of a measuring instrument should be employed. That is, it should be understandable to the respondent, and it should be acceptable. In line with the latter, there has been an increasing amount of research interest in developing nonverbal measures of attitudes, an example of which is the faces method in Figure 14.3. In this scale, drawn faces with expressions indicating happiness or unhappiness are used, with the respondent being directed to check which face approximates his job feelings. As can be seen from Figure 14.3, the faces method did have value, although, perhaps, not as great as the other measures.

Summary

Coming to a decision of what good worker and company performance is constitutes a matter of great societal controversy today. In the past, the "more is better" perspective defined what was good work behavior. Today, however, many individuals dispute this approach and argue that what may be good from one perspective may not be from another. The first part of this chapter was concerned with discussing

Figure 14.3

Correlations between Different Methods of Rating Satisfaction with Different Areas of Jobs for a Random Sample of Employees of a Farmers' Cooperative

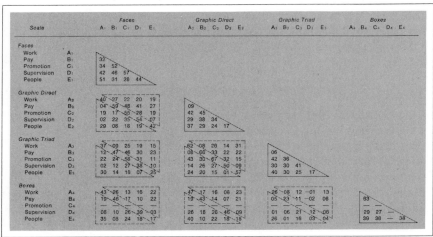

Source: E. A. Locke, P. C. Smith, L. M. Kendall, C. L. Hulin, and A. M. Miller, Convergent and discriminant validity for area and methods of rating job satisfaction, *Journal of Applied Psychology,* 1964, *48,* 313–319. Copyright 1964 by the American Psychological Association, and reproduced by permission.

Note:$-N = 41$ male and 40 female combined; decimals omitted.

this conceptual issue, with the conclusion reached that good performance needs to be looked at from the viewpoint of the individual, the organization, and the society in general and what is good for each. All need to be considered.

A second conceptual issue discussed concerns the multidimensionality of job performance. Whether one uses individual, organizational, or societal overall measures, or the different specific measures within each, those who score higher on one dimension may score either high or low on the other. This finding generates questions as to when different measures should be combined and how this should be done. One answer is to use a combined measure of performance for administrative purposes and separate measures for theoretical understanding.

A continuing question in any measure of behavior or attitudes concerns the degree to which the measure is actually measuring what it is supposed to. This constitutes a question of the construct validity of the measure and in meeting this goal a technique known as the multitrait, multimethod matrix seems useful. This involves seeing whether the measures correlate with those measures they should relate to if they are valid.

Among the other problems in measuring performance and job reactions are that subjective ratings may reflect interactive effects due to particular combinations of raters and ratees and different conceptual frameworks may generate different measurement operations.

SUGGESTIONS FOR FURTHER READING

Business and Society Review/Innovation. Boston: Warren, Gorham and Lamont.
> A journal that is concerned with evaluating the activity of work organizations for their social value. It is scholarly, nonradical, and worth reading, even if you do not agree with some of the arguments.

DEAUX, K., and EMSWILLER, T. Explanations of successful performance in sex-linked tasks: What is skill for the male is luck for the female. *Journal of Personality and Social Psychology,* 1974, *29,* 80–85.
> An experiment that aptly illustrates how our cultural stereotypes influence our evaluations in an inequitable manner, with this affecting *both* males and females. The type of study that needs to be read by anyone concerned with effective sexual integration of the work setting.

ROTHSCHILD, E. *Paradise lost: The decline of the auto-industrial age.* New York: Random House, 1973.
> An excellent case study illustrating the complexities of trying to determine what good performance is and the possible conflicts between societal, organizational, and individual perspectives. Although some of the issues raised are unique to the automobile industry, some are applicable far beyond that setting.

SCHMIDT, F. L., and KAPLAN, L. B. Composite vs. multiple criteria: A review and resolution of the controversy. *Personnel Psychology,* 1971, *24,* 419–434.
> A scholarly review of some of the basic issues involved in the multiple-criteria approach and the possible solutions. You may not agree with the recommendations, but the article remains worth reading.

chapter fifteen

The Measurement of Job Performance and Reactions: Measures and Techniques

In addition to the conceptual problems of measuring job outcomes, a second major difficulty that needs to be faced is the choosing and developing of adequate measures of the important dimensions. A wide variety of measures can be chosen and in developing my discussion I will try to relate some of these techniques to each of the three major criterion dimensions outlined previously—organizational value, personal value, and societal value. However, it will also be possible to go through the following and evaluate each of the techniques we shall be discussing on their own, without accepting this particular aspect of the discussion.

Objective Measures of Organizational Value

Often, when one talks about the nature of job performance and how to measure performance differences, somebody will offer an opinion that the ideal measure would be independent of biases, favoritism, conscious and unconscious distortion, and other problems such as the halo, leniency, and central tendency effects, all of which are felt to be endemic to the subjective ratings we shall talk about later in this chapter. Thus, the goal, it is often stated, is to find some method that eliminates these contaminating effects and measures differences in an objective, impartial manner.

While hardly anyone would argue with the desires which underlie this point of view, the fact is that, in practice, the search for a purely objective measure of performance has run into much difficulty. The reason for this is that the so-called objective measures are not objective at all, but involve a considerable number of subjective judgments. Hence, although these measures exist and are useful, the ideal of complete objectivity seems to be a somewhat unreal, difficult-to-achieve goal. Let us see why this is so by looking at some frequently suggested objective measures of performance and then examining them to see (1) the degree to which they might be expected to be free of contaminating influences and (2) how wide-ranging they might be in their usefulness, if such possibilities for contamination-free measurement are high. Our conclusion, to anticipate, will be that objective measures are neither objective nor useful in many occupations in real organizational life. For this reason, more meaningful efforts might be made toward understanding the subjective rating procedures which we shall talk about later, since these are generalizable to different occupations and some information is already available on them.

Absenteeism

A frequently suggested measure of performance adequacy has been absences since it is obvious that if a person is not at work, his performance will be zero. This is a good place to start since, at first glance, it would appear that this criterion of performance would very much meet the desired norm of objectivity. In other words, a person is either physically present or he is not, and this is not subject to misinterpretation. Or is it? Could one argue the point of view that the use of absences as a measure of performance assumes that one must be physically present in the organizational work space in order to perform and that this is not a good assumption for managers, researchers, and perhaps others? For example, suppose that a research chemist has been working on a puzzling problem that he is extremely involved with and that he must relax if he is to resolve it. Suppose, also, that his best means of relaxing is to go to a baseball game. Should he go to the baseball game or should he go to work? If he goes to the game, is he relaxing or working? This is an extreme example, perhaps, but it does indicate an important point.

Other problems arise if number of absences is used as a measure of performance. How do we decide whether to use only medically excused absences or absences in general? (Remember that some people have medical practitioners as friends and that such friendships are probably positively correlated with socioeconomic class.) Shall a person who is absent for a single 10-day stretch during the course of a year be counted in the same way as a person who has 10 single-day absences during the course of the year, with these coming particularly on Mondays or Fridays?

Chadwick-Jones, Brown, and Nicholson (1973) reviewed this whole issue and came to the conclusion that total time lost is not a good measure, since it includes unavoidable medical absences. Instead, they suggest the use of a frequency index; that is, the number of incidents of absence for each individual. This, they suggest, is more likely to reflect the attitudinal and behavioral factors that are likely to result in absenteeism.

Whether one uses the frequency index or other measures such as the percentage of Monday and Friday absences as compared to all absences, absenteeism is an important measure of performance for lower-level individuals, although it is not really applicable for those at higher levels. Organizations with a high degree of absenteeism are subject to the following (Jeswald, 1974):

1. higher fringe costs than necessary (since these costs are being paid for those not producing)
2. higher overtime costs (in order to complete the work not done during the time of absence)
3. underutilization of facilities already paid for
4. loss of overall productivity

Absenteeism, however, may not be all bad. Sometimes a company may want it (if business is bad, for example, and employees are paid by the day). Most of the time, however, it is a problem and the company normally will want to cut down on it. Yet, the fact that this not always is so supports further the contention that even using absences as a criterion measure does not meet the fully objective criterion goal.

Productivity

In common everyday stereotypical thinking it is likely that when we talk about performance the measure that comes first to mind is productivity, or the number of units produced. Such a stereotype probably has two related major bases, neither of which is valid today (if they ever were) and both of which indicate the inappropriateness of this type of objective measure of performance in today's organizational world.

The bases on which this stereotype rests are (1) the traditional belief that work consists of hard physical labor that has a tangible outcome (i.e., "man works by the sweat of his brow") and (2) the fact that most jobs were, in years gone by, physical activities. However, we are now a white-collar society and becoming increasingly more so, as various labor statistics indicate. The stereotype is the problem, though, since it seems to be so deeply ingrained in our culture that when suggestions are made that this is no longer a valid way to judge most work activities, the response is one of incredulousness. For example, how often have we either heard or made the comment ourselves to a white-collar worker at the end of the day, "Why are you so tired? You only sit behind a desk all day!" This, and similar remarks, indicate our deep-seated attitude about what we consider real work, even though this attitude is increasingly incorrect. Most people do not perform physical labor resulting in tangible outcomes that are subject to a counting operation as a measure of performance. Furthermore, even for the minority who do, it is by no means sure that such a counting operation is actually worth the trouble it takes or is as fair as its objective nature would indicate. As an example, let us take the job of a sewing-machine operator in a dress factory. At first glance, one would think that a measure of the number of garments produced would be a fair measure of performance. Consider, however, the assumptions involved. First, one must assume that each of the sewing machines has equal performance potential and that some are not older than others and more liable to break down. Second, we must also assume that the light, heat, and other physical environmental factors are equal around the work space and that some of the operators are not more favored than others along these dimensions. Third, we must also assume that each operator is treated equally in terms of supplies and other materials needed. It is obvious that unless these conditions are equal for each operator, the use of productivity in terms of units employed as a measure of performance is no more objective than any other measure.

It appears, then, that despite its cultural support, productivity as a measure of performance has very serious limitations. More important, it cannot be applied meaningfully to most jobs and attempts to do so by finding objective measures in these subjective jobs may constitute a perversion of the notion of performance measurement. An example of such a perversion is when we attempt to objectify a teacher's performance quality by using as a measure of performance the accuracy with which the teacher fills out forms relating to her students' participation in after-school recreational activities. The use of such a measure of performance, objective though it may be, is ludicrous.

We could discuss other commonly used objective measures, but the point would be the same. It is clear that these measures have their uses in certain conditions. However, these conditions are limited and there is no reason to suppose that the so-called objective criterion is necessarily the best way of measuring individual differences in performance. Rather, it seems likely that a more useful procedure in developing a satisfactory measure of job performance is to use a subjective performance evaluation (e.g., rating) since a subjective evaluation constitutes a way of measuring job performance that is applicable across all jobs and is, thus, wide-ranging in its generality. However, there are all sorts of subjective performance evaluations, both from the viewpoint of the techniques used and the person who does the evaluating. Since each of these approaches has various disadvantages and advantages, it is important to know what these are.

Subjective Measures of Organizational Value

The major psychological essence of a subjective performance rating is when a person evaluates another by saying "I think your behavior (performance) is about the following level . . ." Ideally, such an evaluation should be a measure of performance and of nothing else; that is, a measure of performance is assigned and classification is made of the individual. The problem is that such an ideal outcome is never attained since a variety of contaminating influences may affect the measure assigned, independent of the actual performance involved. The typical procedure, therefore, in research on performance evaluation has been to develop various rating techniques, determine the nature of the contaminating influences that affect each of these various rating techniques, and examine how these contaminating influences may be overcome.

Who Should Make the Evaluations?

Conceptually, there are at least four individuals who might evaluate the performance of a given individual: a superior, a peer, a subordinate (rarely used), and the individual himself. Traditionally, it is the superior who does most of the ratings and this continues to be true today. In a recent article Miner (1974) has said that about 98% of all forms are designed to be completed by immediate superiors. However, he also points out that evaluations by the others are becoming increasingly common and, though they are not the same, a judicious use of all of them may, in fact, be highly effective. For example, it is generally the case that peer and self ratings are higher than superior ratings and emphasize interpersonal skills more. However, this doesn't necessarily make one better than the other. They might all be useful. Thus, a look at all these ratings and the discrepancies between them would provide an indication of how much the person fits the need to meet the varied types of behaviors desired (i.e., the different factors covered by the superior, peer, and self-ratings). Such information, if it is in disagreement, may also provide development opportunities in that it provides graphic indication of where different perceptions of the adequacy of behavior and the potential for conflict exists.

In addition to these benefits and the consistent evidence of the ability of peer ratings to predict leadership success (Korman, 1968), there is another benefit to using self ratings and that is their developmental value. Thus, in the management-by-objectives approach (in which people set their own goals and evaluate their own achievements), there is research that has shown this technique to be of considerable value in stimulating higher levels of performance (cf. Meyer, Kay, and French, 1965). (In addition, a study by Heneman, 1974 indicates that it is not invariably true that self ratings are more lenient than superior ratings.)

Assuming, then, that different individuals will be involved in the evaluation process, a number of other factors need to be considered in planning the ratings. Among the most important of these are the following:

1. If it is possible, and if there are individuals who have had adequate opportunity for observation, more than one rater should be used from any particular source in order to overcome the effects of individual bias.
2. Evaluations should be made at a different time from salary recommendations in order to decrease the tendency (real or imagined) to let the salary recommendations influence the evaluation. (There are few situations in the real world in which salary is a function solely of performance.)
3. Feedback by a superior is crucial if appropriate development of the person being rated is to take place. Yet, it is also true that a superior evaluation is distorted upward if feedback is part of the process. One way of dealing with this is to make the feedback a continuing, everyday, behaviorally linked process, instead of an annual or semiannual activity remote from the behaviors that led to the evaluation.

Subjective Evaluation Techniques

the graphic rating scale

Probably the most common form of performance evaluation technique is known as the graphic rating scale, a typical version of which is presented in Table 15.1. It has been estimated by some that perhaps as many as 87% of U.S. companies use this type of procedure.

The typical method of using this scale is to indicate somewhere along the given rating dimension (cf. the dimensions of adaptability, etc., in Table 15.1) the appropriate place where the rater thinks the ratee belongs. The actual physical characteristics of the scale may be that a line with appropriate verbal descriptions may be used, or perhaps letter grades such as A down to F, and so on.

Despite its wide usage, we do not know very much about the graphic rating scale as a measure of performance. For a long time it was felt that it lent itself to all kinds of rating errors, in particular the

Table 15.1
Example of Graphic Rating Scale

The following factors are to be rated. The factors are listed alphabetically; therefore, their position as listed in no way reflects the respective value of individual factors. Pleace check the point on each scale which corresponds to your evaluation.

Adaptability: versatility; adjustment to job or changed conditions; ease with which new duties are learned

Is slow to learn; has trouble adjusting himself to changed conditions; needs constant instruction	Learns fairly well; is a routine worker and needs detailed instructions for a new job	Learns well with minimum amount of instruction; adjusts himself well in a short time	Meets changed conditions with little effort; has outstanding ability to pick up new jobs

Dependability: Your confidence in employee's ability to accept responsibility

Does top-grade work with minimum of supervision; outstanding ability to follow through	Willing to accept responsibility; requires very little follow-up	Usually follows instructions; needs some follow-up	Refuses to or not able to carry much responsibility; needs constant follow-up

Job knowledge: Technical knowledge of job and related work

Has excellent knowledge of his job and related work; is very well informed	Seldom needs help; has good knowledge of his job and related work; is well informed	Knows his job fairly well; has little knowledge of related work	Has limited knowledge of his job; nothing of related work

Quality: Accuracy in work; freedom from errors

Makes practically no mistakes; highest accuracy	Seldom makes errors; is accurate; does high-grade work	Makes some errors but does passable work	Makes mistakes frequently

Quantity: Output speed

Output below standard; definitely slow	Output meets standard; is satisfactory	Does more work than expected; is fast; exceeds standard	Exceptionally fast; unusual output

errors of halo, leniency, and central tendency that we spoke of in an earlier chapter. However, it has become doubtful, as also indicated earlier, that these errors are as great or pervasive as we previously thought. For example, it used to be thought that if you asked a rater to evaluate a person on all his traits before going on to the next individual, the rater would be more likely to allow one important trait to affect all his evaluations (i.e., the halo effect) than if he evaluated all of the individuals on one trait at a time, evaluating each trait separately in turn. However, research has cast doubt on whether this is really so and whether the so-called susceptibility of the graphic method to halo effects is really as important as thought. Johnson (1963) has shown, for example, that such problems may not be as great as imagined. On the other hand, Campbell et al. (1970) have found that the problems are greater here than for the critical incidents technique, a type of scale we will discuss below. Until there are more data there seems little point in recommending against the usage of the graphic scale, particularly since it is convenient, flexible, and objectively scored. Furthermore, Barrett (1966a) has formulated a list of recommendations that would even further increase its effective usage, with these suggestions appropriate for most other techniques in performance evaluation as well. His recommendations are as follows:

1. "Express one, and only one, thought in a scale." As an example, one should not have to evaluate attitude and ambition on a single scale. These are different qualities and should be rated on different scales.
2. "Use words the rater understands." One of the biggest problems in the construction of performance evaluation scales is that the psychologist, who has had approximately 20 years of education, assumes that those who will be using the scales have the same level of verbal ability that he does. This is obviously not the case and must be taken into account.
3. "Have the raters rate what they observe, not what they infer." The point here is that, sometimes, an evaluator is asked to rate an individual on some quality that can only be inferred, not observed, and that the quality to be inferred has only a tangential relationship, at best, to whatever behavior can be observed. Consider the case of the salesman who is to be evaluated by his superior. To make a more meaningful rating, both go out together into the field for perhaps a day or two. The supervisor is then asked to rate the salesman on a quality such as "persistence in the face of frustration." Can he do this fairly? It would seem doubtful because even if the supervisor had been able to observe an incident of this nature during the brief period, he still does not know of the afternoons that the salesman may have spent at a ball game or the movies after a frustrating morning.
4. "Eliminate double negatives." The use of double negatives is never justified since such usage is confusing. As Barrett points out, the phrase "gets reports in on time" is far less confusing than "never fails to get reports in on time." (However, one might use "often fails to get reports in on time.")
5. "Keep statements internally consistent." There is nothing as confusing as first asking an individual evaluator to use one standard of judgment and then switching to another standard involving different processes. Thus, if a rater is asked to evaluate a person's abilities in general after first being told he should rate him only in relation to job requirements, the result is confusion. A nuclear physicist obviously has a great deal of intelligence

compared to the average person but he might be only average as far as his job requirements are concerned.

6. "Avoid universals." The point here is that words such as *all, always,* or *never* should not be used since no one takes them literally, leading to an ambiguity of interpretation.

7. "Avoid vague concepts." The rationale here is similar to that immediately above in that words such as *honesty, reliability,* and the like are vague in terms of their actual behavioral implications and, hence, lead to ambiguous interpretations.

In addition to these recommendations Barrett suggests, on the basis of a comprehensive literature review, that the following points be considered in building a graphic rating scale:

1. The number of different steps of each dimension to be evaluated should be from five to nine.

2. There is probably little difference between having an odd or even number of steps to be rated on each dimension.

3. There is probably little value in rating more than five separate characteristics.

a weighted checklist: the critical incidents approach

A performance evaluation method that has become increasingly common in recent years is the weighted checklist method. This is a procedure whereby a list of descriptive statements of specific behaviors is presented to the performance evaluator who is requested to check or indicate in some way those that are most applicable to the person being rated. Crucial to this method is that each of the statements has previously been weighted according to the degree it is indicative of effective (or ineffective) performance. The person is then given a performance score derived from the weights of the behaviors that have been rated as being most descriptive of him.

How does one derive the specific behaviors that are indicative of good performance? Probably the best way is to use the method of critical incidents. The basic logic of this technique is that the major overall differences in performance between people lie in the unusual behaviors in which they engage, whether good or bad, as opposed to the everyday, almost automatic activities that almost all individuals perform adequately. Hence, it is argued, the best way to get an adequate measure of an individual's performance is to keep a record of these unusual or critical behaviors, both good and bad, so that a periodic recording of them on a person's record can provide a ready-made evaluation of performance.

As another example of how this technique might be used, let us look at how a well-known scale of this type was developed by Smith and Kendall (1966) in conjunction with the people who would be using it. Dunnette (1966) has summarized their procedure as follows:

1. Several groups of head nurses participated in conferences devoted to discussing the use of personnel evaluations for improving nursing performance. Information was gathered by mail from additional groups.
2. Each group listed the major qualities in successful nursing and critical incidents were gathered and classified to illustrate examples of behavior related to each quality. Throughout, the nurses' own terminology was retained.
3. The groups also formulated statements defining high, low, and acceptable performance for each quality and additional examples of actual performance incidents were suggested for each quality.
4. The head nurses then indicated independently the quality illustrated by each incident. Incidents were eliminated if there was not clear agreement concerning the quality to which it belonged. Qualities were eliminated if the incidents were not consistently reassigned to the quality for which they were originally chosen as illustrative.

Smith and Kendall made certain that the meaning of both the job qualities and the behavioral incidents chosen to illustrate them would be tightly specific and unambiguous. This step, the crucial innovation in their approach, is basically similar to procedures used in cross-cultural research that are designed to ensure that translations from one language to another adhere to the connotations as well as the denotations of the original. Material is translated into a foreign language and then translated back into the original by an independent translator.

5. The incidents were then judged by another group of head nurses on a scale ranging from 0.0 to 2.0 according to the proper behavior for nursing. Incidents were eliminated if the judgments showed a large dispersion or if they fell into more than one distinct group. This procedure provided another safeguard assuring agreement and lack of ambiguity.

The outcome of this painstaking work was a job behavior evaluation form including scales for judging six major qualities—knowledge and judgment, conscientiousness, skill in human relationships, organizational ability, objectivity, and observational ability—each firmly defined behaviorally and anchored at various points by incidents stated in the nurses' own language and rigidly fixed according to the scale location. Table 15.2 shows the scale for judging skill in human relationships. Even a cursory examination indicates the degree of precision in its development and the probable ease with which it can be completed for any given nurse. Finally, in order to check the consistency of scale judgments, Smith and Kendall correlated the judgments made by the several different groups of judges. The lowest value obtained was .972, suggesting an extremely high degree of agreement.

Since the development of the Smith and Kendall "retranslation of expectations" approach to the utilization of critical incidents in performance evaluation, a wide number of studies have appeared concerning its value in reducing rater biases like halo, leniency, and so on. For the most part these have been favorable, although not completely so.

If we assume, however, that overall there is some value to the Smith and Kendall approach, we may reasonably ask "why"? There are several possible answers and none is antithetical to the others. First, there is the participation by the individuals involved, an impor-

Table 15.2

Example of Job Behavior Scale for Describing Nurses' Skill in Human Relationships

Even when there is considerable emotional self-involvement, behavior with others is so skillful and insightful that it not only smooths but often prevents difficult emotional and social situations; this implies the ability to recognize the subtle as well as the more obvious components of basic emotional reactions in self and others (e.g., anxiety, fear, frustration, anger, etc.).	2.00	
	1.75	This nurse could be expected, whenever possible, to sit down and talk with a terminal-cancer patient who is considered to be "demanding."
	1.50	If two aides asked this nurse, acting as team leader, if they could exchange assignments because of rapport problems with the patients assigned, would expect this nurse to discuss the problem with the aides and make certain changes which would be satisfying to them.
		If this nurse were admitting a patient who talks rapidly and continuously of her symptoms and past medical history, could be expected to look interested and listen.
	1.25	If this nurse were assigned for the first time to a patient who insists upon having her treatment done in a certain order, could be expected to do as the patient wishes without making an issue about it.
If emotional self-involvement is minimal, behavior with others is such that it does not complicate difficult emotional and social situations; this implies the ability to recognize the more obvious components of basic emotional reactions in self and others.	1.00	
		If the husband of a woman who is post-operative and in good condition asks about his wife, this nurse could be expected to reply as follows: "Her condition is good."

Table 15.2 (*cont.*)

	0.75	If a convalescent patient complained about the service in the hospital, this nurse would be likely to tell the patient that the hospital is short of nurses and the needs of the sickest patients have to be met first.
	0.50	If this nurse were assigned to care for a terminal-cancer patient in a two-bed room who is depressed and uncommunicative, could be expected to carry on a conversation with the other patient while giving care to the terminal-cancer patient.
		In the presence of a woman who is crying because her husband is dangerously ill, this nurse would be expected to tell the woman not to cry.
	.025	If this nurse were told by an ambulatory patient that a patient in the ward was having difficulty breathing, could be expected to tell the ambulatory patient that his help in caring for the patients was not needed.
Behavior with others is such that it tends to complicate or create difficult emotional or social situations; this implies an inability to recognize even the obvious basic emotional reactions of self and others.	0.00	

Source: National League for Nursing, Research and Studies Service; *A Method for Rating the Proficiency of the Hospital General Staff Nurse; Manual of DIrections* (New York, 1964).

tant matter in gaining psychological acceptance in using the scales properly. Second, the participation leads to the use of a language structure that makes the scales easier to use in a cognitive sense. (The significance of these two factors in influencing the effectiveness of the scale has been supported in a recent study by Borman and Vallon, 1974). Finally, there is the critical incidents themselves. One reason these have value is that they lead to greater agreements between raters on evaluations because the basis for the evaluation is based on critical or extreme cases about which it is much easier to get agreement. For example, it is easier to agree that a person who has hit three home runs in baseball has done better than a person who has hit one, all other things being equal.

Another advantage of this method is that it does not force differences where there are none, an accusation that has occasionally been made with regard to other performance evaluation techniques. Thus, if all the workers in a group do pretty much the same thing and none of them does anything unusually good or bad, there is no basis for differentiating any of them. This conclusion would be only just and equitable.

Finally, there is good evidence that the general concept of evaluation (e.g., rating someone from poor to excellent), in an overall sense, seems to be based on a psychological process fairly akin to the notion of critical incidents in that apparently these overall judgments are a function of the number of critical incidents observed, with such a relationship apparently being the same for raters differing on the basis of such variables as jobs, experience, background, and work competence (Whitlock, 1963, 1974).

the forced-choice performance scale

A revised version of the checklist type of rating scale that grew out of World War II experiences is a procedure that is expressly designed to overcome the tendency to fake ratings high or low. Known as the forced-choice rating method, its basic underlying logic is as follows:

Assumption One   There exists a variety of behaviors on any job that one may engage in; some are good and some are bad.

Assumption Two   Some of the good behaviors are highly relevant and critical for job performance, whereas some of the other good behaviors are nice but not really important for job performance effectiveness.

Assumption Three   Some of the poor behaviors are highly relevant and critical for job performance, whereas the other poor behaviors are not particularly desirable but they do not really affect performance effectiveness one way or another.

Given these assumptions, one might set up rating scales in the following manner:

Type A   A rater might be asked to choose one of a pair of behavior description items, each of which says something favorable about a person, with the degree of favorability being equal for the two alternatives; however, only one of the behaviors involved is considered to be critical or relevant for effective job performance.[1]

Type B   A rater might be asked to choose one of a pair of behavior description items, each of which says something unfavorable about a person, with the degree of unfavorability being equal for the two alternatives; however, only one of the behaviors involved is considered to be critical or relevant for effective job performance.

Given these pairs, the logic of the forced-choice method is that a person is more likely to tell the truth about another individual on his

---

[1] It may not be crucial that these statements be highly specific. Obrodovic (1970) has shown that general statements applicable to a variety of jobs work just as well.

evaluation since (1) in the first case he must say something favorable, no matter what he says, and (2) the converse is true in the second case; that is, he must say something unfavorable, no matter what he says. Hence there is no reason to fake in either case. An example of this type of scale is given in Table 15.3.

The idea behind the forced-choice scale is intriguing and there has been a considerable amount of work on these scales, with the results sometimes, but not always, favorable. These results lead, first, to the conclusion that it is still doubtful that the original reason for the development of the forced-choice scale is as much of a problem as claimed. That is, the basis for the development was the belief that graphic rating scales were highly susceptible to faking, something that we have seen may not be as much of a problem as we think.

Second, even if one were to grant the necessity for the development of scales to overcome this problem, it is not at all certain that this is the way to do it. As Travers (1951), among others, has pointed out, one can fake forced-choice scores in a favorable direction not by evaluating the given ratee but by thinking of the best person for that job and then filling out the scales on that basis. In addition, the manner in

Table 15.3
Example of Forced-Choice Rating Forms

In each group place a check mark in front of the statement that you believe best characterizes the employee under consideration. Be sure to put only one check mark in each group of statements.

_____ Is very patient
_____ Arrives at conclusions logically
_____ Assumes responsibility for his own mistakes

_____ Delegates work very wisely
_____ Is exceptionally fair
_____ Inspires his associates

In each group place a check mark in front of the statement that you believe best characterizes the employee under consideration, and another check mark in front of the statement that you believe least characterizes him. Be sure to put two and only two check marks in each group of statements.

_____ Has a well-rounded personality
_____ Lacks force and drive
_____ Tends to be overbearing
_____ Shows foresight

_____ Displays disloyalty
_____ Is almost indispensable
_____ Makes many mistakes
_____ Has a very promising future

---

which the alternatives are equated for equal favorability (and/or unfavorability) leaves considerable room for doubt as to whether these goals are actually accomplished. Typically, the procedure has been to pair statements on the basis of their mean rated desirability, as these ratings are derived from some groups. There are two major problems with this. First, although the means of the two behaviors in terms of favorability may be equal when taking the group scores as a whole, some individuals may disagree with this and for them one behavior may be more desirable than the other, with all the implications that this may have for faking. Second, behaviors that appear similar when viewed singly may present differences when viewed as pairs. Consider, for example, the favorability of (1) finding a new method for teaching disadvantaged students and (2) raising funds for the construction of new schools. Each of these might be considered to be equally desirable when viewed singly, but if they were presented as a pair, significant differences might be seen between them by most people.

In addition, there is a third technical problem with these scales, and in a sense it is a paradoxical one that results only from a good forced-choice scale, as opposed to a poor one. This is the point that if alternatives are well equated for favorability and a person must choose one or the other, he has lost some of the basis for choosing consistently between one or the other if neither is particularly meaningful to him. Hence, he will be more likely to make random choices between one or the other and the reliability (or consistency) of measurement will be low.

Probably the most serious problem with the forced-choice technique is that the users of it rarely like it and its "have you stopped beating your wife?" format. Many people feel in responding to scales of this nature that their usage implies mistrust in the evaluator's competence to give a good rating, a type of social evaluation that we have run into previously and which the research with the Smith and Kendall scales shows has a negative influence on later performance. With all these problems, though, the forced-choice method remains in usage and probably will continue so because it does provide objective scores, it attempts to correct errors, and some of its problems may be resolved by better scale construction.

the ranking method

Perhaps the simplest way of evaluating performance and a method preferred by many is the ranking procedure, the goal of which is simply to order people in comparison to one another. There are two basic types of ranking procedures. The first is the simplest one in that the entire group is taken at one time and placed in relative order on some evaluation continuum. One common way of doing this is known as the alternation-ranking technique, whereby first one chooses the best, then the worst, then the second best, then the second worst, and so on until all individuals are placed in rank order. The advantage of this procedure is that it is easier to choose the extremes first and then attempt to distinguish between those not so different from each other, rather than the other way around.

A more technically sophisticated but extremely laborious ranking method is known as pair comparisons. Each rankee is compared individually with every other rankee, with each individual's rank dependent on the number of times he is preferred compared to those he is being compared with. The problem with this procedure is that the number of comparisons to be made becomes very great when there are more than just a few rankees involved. This can be seen by the following:

$$\text{Number of comparisons to be made when each individual is paired with every other individual} = \frac{N(N-1)}{2}$$

where N = size of group to be evaluated.

Thus: when $N = 4$,

$$\text{the number of comparisons} = \frac{4\,(3)}{2} = 6;$$

when $N = 8$,

$$\text{the number of comparisons} = \frac{8\,(7)}{2} = 28;$$

and when $N = 16$,

$$\text{the number of comparisons} = \frac{16\,(15)}{2} = 120.$$

The most important disadvantage of the ranking method is that it orders people along a continuum but does not give any consideration to the degree between ranks. For example, the fourth-ranked person may be twice as good as the fifth-ranked individual, but the latter may be only a little bit better than the one ranked sixth. This can be an important disadvantage if one is going to give a different treatment to the person ranked fifth as opposed to the one ranked sixth, a common enough situation.[2]

Two other disadvantages to the ranking method also deserve mention. The first is that it has a "have you stopped beating your wife?"

[2] Technically, a similar disadvantage can be stated for the rating methods, since they, too, despite their appearances, have the same flaw. Even though a rating method may assign a value of 10 to person A, 6 to person B, and 2 to person C, it is extremely doubtful that the differences between A and B are equal to the differences between B and C. This may happen sometimes, but not very often.

character (i.e., someone must be ranked low even though all may be high, etc.), and the second is that it is difficult to compare the scores of people who were ranked in different groups.

simulation as a performance criterion

Because of the problems of the rating and objective performance measures that we have discussed, increasing attention is being paid by some psychologists to the use of simulations of the work environment as mechanisms by which one can measure individual differences in performance. There are many types of simulations for this purpose, but they generally consist of some version of the following two major types:

1. The types of management games that are used as training exercises in management seminars. An increasingly popular game of this nature is the in-basket technique, in which the trainee is presented with a basket of problems typical of the kinds of activities that an administrator in his area may actually face in a typical day. He is then asked to solve these problems by writing the appropriate memos, making the called-for decisions, and so on. The technique is general and has been adopted for such diverse jobs as school administrator and military officer. It has been suggested by some that performance on this simulation be utilized as a performance criterion measure.
2. Trade tests, consisting of a person's knowledge of the called-for activities and behaviors in a given job position. In these tests, commonly used in the skilled trades, a person is called upon to show that he actually knows the skills and behaviors needed for a specific job.

The advantages and disadvantages of simulations as performance criteria are obvious. On the plus side, they allow a considerable amount of control over the conditions under which the performance is measured, and they allow the development of more precise measures than would be available in the real organizational environment. On the other hand, they are unreal, and even if a person does know what should be done and actually does it in a simulation, there is little justification for concluding that the person will engage in the desired behaviors in the real world on a day-to-day basis. The lack of generalizability is particularly true since we have little knowledge of what constitutes an effective simulation, the characteristics it must have, how long a person must be in it, and so on.

Measures of Job Reactions

Just as in the measurement of job performance, the techniques for measuring personal reactions to jobs are varied, with each having its particular strengths and weaknesses. Similarly, there seems to be no real way to resolve these, and the choice of which one to use will frequently depend on the attitudes of the particular investigator.

However, there are at least two important differences between measuring reactions to jobs and measuring job performance that have implications for technique development. The first is that the concept of objective measures of personal reactions seems to be even less significant than it is for objective measures of job performance. Consider, for example, the question of grievances or absences. Can we consider these to be purely objective measures? Some might believe so, but I would argue that logically this does not make much sense, since it is quite simple to conceive of a variety of organizational situations where the better the personal reaction to the job, the higher the grievances. Suppose that a person felt totally secure in a situation and knew he would not be fired. This might lead him to (1) like his job and (2) submit grievances without fear of retribution. On the other hand, consider the case where the job is totally insecure, the risk of discharge is high, and few other jobs are available. This might lead him to (1) dislike his job and (2) be afraid to submit grievances. Other examples can be cited, but it does seem obvious that there are certain logical problems to using such variables as absences and grievances as objective measures of personal reactions to a job.

The second difference is that in the measurement of job performance it has been typically the case that ratees have not evaluated themselves, but rather have been evaluated by someone else either directly through a rating procedure or indirectly through the choice of which objective criterion of performance to use. It seems to be true, though, in measuring reactions to jobs that self-evaluation is much more the norm and it is less common, although often desirable, to utilize judgments or ratings made by others. This difference between the two kinds of measures has meant that, to some extent, the problems concerned with the development of techniques of measuring job reactions have been somewhat different from those in the area of job performance but there have been some similarities also, as we shall see.

Given these conceptual differences between the nature of performance and job reaction measurement, what kinds of measures have been and are being used in the latter area? In this section we shall discuss a group of measurement techniques that have as a base of commonality the fact that they all consist of measuring job reactions by direct question procedures; that is, they ask the person in some direct way what his (or somebody else's) job reactions are. Most typically, they inquire about job satisfaction, but they are equally applicable to the measurement of other job reactions. Following, we shall discuss those kinds of measures that attempt to get at this information indirectly.

Direct Measures of Job Reactions

the questionnaire method

The simplest and easiest way to ask a person what his job reactions are is to ask him questions and provide him with alternatives for answering. "Do you like your job?" (yes, no, not sure). "How satisfied are you with your pay?" (highly satisfied, moderately satisfied, not satisfied). "Are you getting the satisfactions you think your should get?" These are the types of questions used in measures of this sort and psychologists frequently find them to be highly satisfactory, citing the data that indicate that these simply developed methods give results highly comparable to those of the more sophisticated techniques that we shall cite below. Why, then, are the more sophisticated techniques that take longer to develop utilized?

Except for one reason, which we shall see is of somewhat doubtful importance, I am not really sure myself. Certainly, it cannot be that the major weakness of the questionnaire procedure, its susceptibility to faking, is overcome by these other direct procedures. This is definitely not the case. Even if it were, it is still a moot point as to how important an advantage this would be anyway, since the problem of faking does not seem to be as relevant in measuring job satisfaction as it is in measuring personality variables. Although it is certainly true that some people might fake their level of job satisfaction for some specific reasons, the rationale for doing so is not very clear in most cases. Perhaps one case in which it might be understandable is when the person has made a high ego commitment to his job and feels forced to protect his ego by saying it is a good job even when it is not. There are little data, though, on how frequently this occurs or how important faking is on job satisfaction assessments in general.

the Thurstone scale

The oldest type of attitude scale in psychology is one developed in the 1920s by a psychologist we have previously discussed in connection with intelligence measurement, Leon Thurstone. The basic logic underlying a Thurstone scale is as follows:

1. For any type of social object that can have attitudes directed toward it, e.g., a person's job, there exists a continuum ranging from favorability of evaluation to unfavorability of evaluation.

2. For any specific point along that continuum, there exist various descriptive statements concerning the job that correspond to the favorability of the evaluation. For example, "This job is one of the worst I've ever seen" would correspond to a very negative evaluation. "This has some problems, but I'd like to stay with it" is a moderately favorable one, and

so on. Hence, if one were to have a pool of descriptive statements toward the job, each of these could be scaled in terms of their degree of favorability toward the job in question.

3. Each individual's attitude toward the job can then be assessed by looking at the statements that he says correspond to his own attitude. If he agrees with the moderately favorable one but not with the extremely favorable or the unfavorable ones, he can be classified differently from those who agree with the unfavorable but not with the moderately favorable or extremely favorable ones.

As an example, let us look at the collection of job attitude statements listed in Table 15.4. If these statements are used in a specific job situation, we could safely assume that the individuals who agree with statements that have a median scale value of 3.7 have a different job attitude than those who agree with statements that have a median scale value of 6.4 or 1.7.

There are numerous problems with the Thurstone scale. One of these revolves around the scale construction process itself and the logic

Table 15.4

Statements Used in Uhrbrock's Scale for Measuring Attitude of Employees toward Their Company

SCALE VALUE	STATEMENT
10.4	I think this company treats its employees better than any other company.
9.5	If I had to do it over again, I'd still work for this company.
9.3	They don't play favorites in this company.
8.9	A man can get ahead in this company if he tries.
8.7	I have as much confidence in the company physician as I do in my own doctor.
8.5	The company is sincere in wanting to know what its employees think about it.
7.9	A wage incentive plan offers a just reward for the faster worker.
7.4	On the whole, the company treats us about as well as we deserve.
6.3	I think a man should go to the hospital for even a scratch, as it may stop blood poisoning.
5.4	I believe accidents will happen, no matter what you do about them.
5.1	The workers put as much over on the company as the company puts over on them.
4.4	The company does too much welfare work.
4.1	Soldiering on the job is increasing.
3.6	I do not think applicants for employment are treated courteously.
3.2	I believe many good suggestions are killed by the bosses.
2.9	My boss gives all the breaks to his lodge and church friends.
2.5	I think the company goes outside to fill good jobs instead of promoting men who are here.
2.1	You've got to have "pull" with certain people around here to get ahead.
1.5	In the long run this company will "put it over" on you.
1.0	The pay in the company is terrible.
0.8	An honest man fails in this company.

Source: R.S. Uhrbrock, Attitudes of 4430 employees, *Journal of Social Psychology,* 1934, *5,* 365–377.

on which it rests. This is the basic assumption that the rated scale value of a statement is independent of the rater's own attitude toward the social object in question. Consider the statement, "This company has generally progressive personnel policies." Would a person who has an overall favorable attitude toward the company rate this the same as a person with negative attitudes? The requirements of the Thurstone scale are such that the answer to this must be yes. If it is not, the answers of the two groups are not comparable since they are not responding to the same stimuli. For a time it was thought that this assumption was being met in Thurstone scales fairly well, but more recent evidence suggests that this may not be so (Sherif and Hovland, 1961). Although these studies have not concerned themselves with job attitudes particularly, there seems to be little reason to doubt that their conclusions would be generally applicable to this area as well. A good example of this applicability might be if one were to ask the black employees of a company to rate the degree of favorability of the statement, "This company has generally progressive personnel policies" at a time when they are successfully attaining desegregated facilities. It would not be particularly profound to note that such ratings of the degree to which this is a favorable aspect of the company might be considerably lower if submitted to a group of prejudiced white employees.

A second problem with the Thurstone scales that has been responsible for its relatively low degree of usage is that the ratings of the statements must be relatively agreed upon and invariant; in other words, there should be great agreement as to what each statement means. While this is not impossible to achieve, the fact that ratings are subject to a number of rater influences that increase the variability of the judgments has meant that often many more statements of attitudes must be constructed and analyzed than will eventually be used. Hence, the economy of effort is not high.

For both of these reasons, we may conclude that although the Thurstone scale is sophisticated, at least in theory, its applicability has posed many problems that have limited its usage.

the Guttman scale

A goal for attitude scales that has always intrigued those trained in the logic of psychological measurement is whether it is possible to develop attitude scales that are unidimensional rather than being a complex mixture of various dimensions. The reason for this is that the same score for different individuals would always mean the same thing. If a scale is multi-dimensional, a particular statement could mean different things for different individuals. A good example of the latter type is that a positive answer to the statement, "This company has progressive personnel policies," may reflect attitudes toward anyone or a combination of such diverse areas as selection, training, and pension systems. It would not necessarily refer to only one type of practice. Multidimensionality tends to be quite common to both questionnaires and Thurstone scales and many psychologists feel that it would be better for interpretative purposes to develop unidimensional scales (e.g., attitudes toward desegregation in the company and attitudes toward training policies). How does one do this? There have traditionally been two answers, the Guttman scale and the Likert scale. The former is the theoretically more sophisticated, but the latter has been by far the most commonly used attitude scale in industry today. Let us see why, looking at the Guttman scale first.

The logic of the Guttman scale is relatively simple and can be illustrated by looking at height as a variable. In Table 15.5 I have listed in the left column the height of a group of people in inches, and along the top I have listed each of a group of questions to which each of the persons at the left must respond. The entry value in the table consists of their answers to each question, Y for yes and N for no.

Looking at this table, we see that there is a certain pattern of entries when we are measuring a unidimensional variable such as height. The essence of this pattern, which defines unidimensionality, is that from a person's total score on the variable under question we can predict his score on each of the questions making up the scale. Thus, for this scale we know that a person who is 76 inches tall will answer yes to any query as to whether he is taller than 75 inches, or any number less than that, whereas he will answer no to any query as to whether he is taller than 77 inches, or any number more than that.

The question for us is whether we can develop attitude scales with the same properties. If we do, we have what is called a Guttman

Table 15.5
Illustration (Height) of a Guttman Scale with High Reproducability

HEIGHT IN INCHES		ARE YOU MORE THAN?								
		83	81	79	77	75	73	71	69	67	65
Individual A	= 84	Y	Y	Y	Y	Y	Y	Y	Y	Y	Y
Individual B	= 82	N	Y	Y	Y	Y	Y	Y	Y	Y	Y
Individual C	= 80	N	N	Y	Y	Y	Y	Y	Y	Y	Y
Individual D	= 78	N	N	N	Y	Y	Y	Y	Y	Y	Y
Individual E	= 76	N	N	N	N	Y	Y	Y	Y	Y	Y
Individual F	= 74	N	N	N	N	N	Y	Y	Y	Y	Y
Individual G	= 72	N	N	N	N	N	N	Y	Y	Y	Y
Individual H	= 70	N	N	N	N	N	N	N	Y	Y	Y
Individual I	= 68	N	N	N	N	N	N	N	N	Y	Y
Individual J	= 66	N	N	N	N	N	N	N	N	N	Y

scale, named for its originator (Guttman, 1950). If we can find a set of attitude items that will exhibit this pattern, or not have more than 10% inversions, we have a set of items that are unidimensional and that are "scalable," to use Guttman's term. Unfortunately, the answer to this question has almost always been negative. Guttman scales are rarely found in applied research, and when they are, they are almost invariably found to be a series of rewordings of the same statement. When care is taken that statements relating to different phenomena are included, scalability in the sense we have described it above is rarely achieved. Hence, although the Guttman scale is theoretically desirable and would be desirable if achieved, this is so rarely the case that the method is not common for the measurement of job reactions.

the Likert scales

By far the most common type of attitude scale in use today is a measurement method known as the Likert scale. The reasons for this are that it does not have the disadvantages of the Thurstone scale in that there is no necessity for the items to be scaled for favorability by a judging group. It also approximates some of the advantages of the Guttman scale in that it can be used in developing relatively unidimensional scales.

The Likert scale consists of a collection of positive and negative statements about some social object, such as a job, with which a person is asked to indicate his or her degree of agreement. Most typically this is done on a five-point scale with the alternatives being strongly disagree, disagree, neither agree nor disagree, agree, and strongly agree. From the patterns of agreement and disagreement toward the statements about the job, a total score for each individual is determined, and this total score is correlated with the scores on each item. The higher the correlation, the more the item is measuring whatever the total number of items in general are measuring, whereas the lower the correlation, the more likely the item is measuring some extraneous factor. By eliminating the extraneous factors, an attitude scale can be developed that is relatively unidimensional and that has the additional advantage that such unidimensionality is based on empirical data rather than on the judgments of investigators. Table 15.6 depicts an overall job attitude questionnaire developed by Brayfield and Rothe (1951) using this procedure.

These are the major types of direct job attitude measures, with the most popular by far being the questionnaire and the Likert scale. Is this popularity deserved? Would it not pay to put more effort into the theoretically sophisticated methods? Perhaps, but the data do not justify such an inference. The fact is that most studies show extremely high degrees of correlation among all of these measures; that is, rs in

Table 15.6
Revised Job Satisfaction Blank

JOB QUESTIONNAIRE

Some jobs are more interesting and satisfying than others. We want to know how people feel about different jobs. This blank contains 18 statements about jobs. You are to cross out the phrase below each statement which best describes how you feel about your present job. There are no right or wrong answers. We would like your honest opinion on each one of the statements. Work out the sample item numbered (0).

0. There are some conditions concerning my job that could be improved.
   Strongly agree   Agree   Undecided   Disagree   Strongly disagree

1. My job is like a hobby to me.
   Strongly agree   Agree   Undecided   Disagree   Strongly disagree

2. My job is usually interesting enough to keep me from getting bored.
   Strongly agree   Agree   Undecided   Disagree   Strongly disagree

3. It seems that my friends are more interested in their jobs.
   Strongly agree   Agree   Undecided   Disagree   Strongly disagree

4. I consider my job rather unpleasant.
   Strongly agree   Agree   Undecided   Disagree   Strongly disagree

4. I consider my job rather unpleasant.
   Strongly agree   Agree   Undecided   Disagree   Strongly disagree

5. I enjoy my work more than my leisure time.
   Stronglya gree   Agree   Undecided   Disagree   Strongly disagree

6. I am often bored with my job.
   Strongly agree   Agree   Undecided   Disagree   Strongly disagree

7. I feel fairly well satisfied with my present job.
   Strongly agree   Agree   Undecided   Disagree   Strongly disagree

8. Most of the time I have to force myself to go to work.
   Strongly agree   Agree   Undecided   Disagree   Strongly disagree

9. I am satisfied with my job for the time being.
   Strongly agree   Agree   Undecided   Disagree   Strongly disagree

10. I feel that my job is no more interesting than others I could get.
    Strongly agree   Agree   Undecided   Disagree   Strongly disagree

11. I definitely dislike my work.
    Strongly agree   Agree   Undecided   Disagree   Strongly disagree

12. I feel that I am happier in my work than most other people.
    Strongly agree   Agree   Undecided   Disagree   Strongly disagree

13. Most days I am enthusiasticc about my work.
    Strongly agree   Agree   Undecided   Disagree   Strongly disagree

14. Each day of work seems like it will never end.
    Strongly agree   Agree   Undecided   Disagree   Strongly disagree

15. I like my job better than the average worker does.
    Strongly agree   Agree   Undecided   Disagree   Strongly disagree

16. My job is pretty uninteresting.
    Strongly agree   Agree   Undecided   Disagree   Strongly disagree

17. I find real enjoyment in my work.
    Strongly agree   Agree   Undecided   Disagree   Strongly disagree

18. I am disappointed that I ever took this job.
    Strongly agree   Agree   Undecided   Disagree   Strongly disagree

Source: A. Brayfield andd H. Rothe, An index of job satisfaction, *Journal of Applied Psychology,* 1951, *35,* 307–311.

the .70s and .80s. This finding suggests that it would be stupid to use a complex procedure when a simple one would do just as well.

Indirect Measures of Job Reactions

In addition to measuring job reactions by direct questionnaire or scaling methods, it is possible to use indirect methods. Such procedures are particularly useful when we have some reason to think that the respondents may not answer honestly or when an attitude survey might have some deleterious performance effects.

One way of measuring job satisfaction indirectly is through the use of projective tests. These may range from sentence completion tests to ambiguous pictures of a TAT type (cf. Stagner, 1956).

One interesting example of this approach that had some vogue a number of years ago but which has not really been worked on since is known as the error-choice technique. This consists of presenting the person with a so-called knowledge test of a multiple-choice nature. In actuality, all of the alternative answers given are wrong, but they are keyed so as to reflect a person's basic attitudes. For example, one question might concern the salaries of labor union officials. A person who is antiunion might be likely to overestimate such salaries, whereas someone who is prounion might be likely to underestimate them.

Probably the most extensive indirect attitude survey ever run was that by General Motors in 1946 when about 150,000 employees submitted essays entitled "Why I Like My Job." This contest provided the company with a gold mine of information about the various aspects of the organization that were sources of satisfaction to the employees. Indirectly, the same essays told the company which of the company's characteristics were not sources of satisfaction because they were not mentioned (Evans and Lauseau, 1950). For example, the fact that a given division's employees mentioned such aspects as the cafeteria, the steady work, and the opportunities for advancement much more than the average worker for the company did, and such things as the working hours and the medical benefits much less, told the management a great deal about what the sources of job satisfaction were for that division.

With the exception of these approaches to indirect job reaction measurement, the literature in this area is sparse. Perhaps this reflects the fact that one of the major motives for indirect measurement, the problem of faking, seems to be largely absent, although there are some cases in which it could occur. Another reason might be that most industrial psychologists and behavioral scientists have been trained in a research tradition that stresses direct measurement as opposed to indirect measures such as projective techniques. Whatever the reason, research interest in indirect job attitude measurement can hardly be considered flourishing.

New Trends in the Measurement of Work Outcomes

Human Resource Accounting

A new way of thinking in measuring job outcomes that combines a concern with the measurement both of job performance and reactions to jobs has come to be known as human resource accounting. Basically, this approach, much of which got its impetus from a paper by Likert and Bowers (1969), reflects the argument that we need to assess the effectiveness of organizational policies and of different types of leadership along several dimensions. First, there is the dimension of how well the organization is achieving its profit (or in the case of governmental agencies, its efficiency) goals. Just as important as profit in the financial sense is the need for the leadership to stimulate and develop a motivated, committed work force for the future. The more the company has high levels of motivated employees, the better. According to this way of thinking, measuring affectual reactions to jobs is as important as measuring profitability, since affectual reactions come before and predict profitability, according to Likert and Bower. Hence, in trying to assess the current conditions of an organization and the effects of a particular type of management (and/or manager), one would want to know the levels of profit the manager has stimulated, the levels of performance he has influenced, and the levels of motivation and job-related attitudes of his employees. All of these are crucial, with an important factor being that the last type of measure predicts the first two at a later point in time. In other words, it is these types of variables, Likert and Bower argue, that directly influence the future performance of the system.

Human resource accounting comes from this perspective. Basically, it is a way of thinking that brings into the accounting system and measures, in financial terms for the purposes of evaluation, the extent to which the organization (or its subunits) has the following:

1. a skilled, interested, capable work force committed to employment with the organization
2. a work force that provides benefits (work outcomes) relative to its costs that are greater than the benefits that would be obtained relative to the costs that would be involved in recruiting, attracting, and retaining a new work force
3. characteristics that generate the motivation and commitment to work, among which are characteristics scoring high on the following dimensions:

Figure 15.1
Revised Model of the Determinants of an Individual's Value
to a Formal Organization

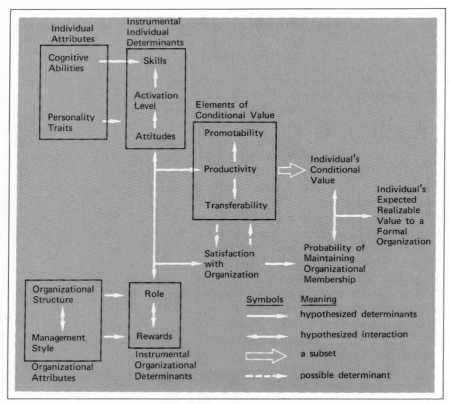

Source: Dunnette, Milkovich, and Motowidlo, 1973

a. the extent to which standards have been established in ways that are perceived as legitimate
b. the extent to which the individual has had a role in the establishment of his performance goals
c. the extent to which feedback is available
d. the extent to which standards have been established in ways that allow the freedom to fail

The idea is that these dimensions should be part of the accounting system in addition to the profit and loss statement, since these human characteristics constitute organizational resources in addition to the money and profits that the organization has accumulated.

How can human resource accounting be performed? A number of ways. One way is to utilize directly some of the measures of the personal values of a job I described earlier. Measures of job satisfaction, job commitment, tension, and so forth are all certainly involved. The problem, though, is that these are psychological data, whereas the term we are using here is human resource accounting. Ideally, the measurement procedure we use should be acceptable to accountants. A number of such models are now being developed by Flamholtz, an accountant with behavioral science training. Figure 15.1 outlines his basic approach as it has been revised by Dunnette, Milkovich, and Motowidlo (1973). According to them, the individual's expected realizable value (IERV) is the actual measure of the current value of the human resource in the organization. (This is a measure analogous to the financial resources available to the organization.) The IERV, as can be seen, is a function of two things: the individual's conditional value and his likelihood of remaining a member of the organization. The latter, is, in turn, a function of such variables as job satisfaction, organizational commitment, and work motivation, while conditional value is a function of abilities and activation level; for example, the willingness to use skills as these affect the person's current productivity, promotability, and transferability.

For these reasons such variables as job satisfaction, commitment, motivation, and the like are legitimate dependent variables with which organizations can be concerned. However, we are just starting to learn how to measure different levels of these variables in an accounting sense. Therefore, human resource accounting, though exciting and full of interesting implications, is really a promissory note for the future.

Measuring the Social Value of the Performance of Organizations and Individuals

How do we know which organizations and individuals are doing well along the social-value criterion we have talked about earlier? Our problem here is not so much choosing the types of measures available as it is choosing the dimensions of evaluation; in other words, what do we mean by social value anyway? Obviously, this is inherently a subjective judgment, one that would vary to some extent with the particular individuals, groups, and organizations involved. If you remember the questions with which we started our discussion on the measurement of organizational outcomes, there are no easy answers as to what social value is. Traditionally, many have argued that the greatest social value of a corporation is its profitability.

Despite these problems, I, and others, think that although profit is crucial, it is not enough. Furthermore, there has been some agreement as to what is meant by social value using this type of thinking and work has been done on conceptualizing appropriate variables for measuring this outcome. Below I have listed the dimensions that have typically been suggested for helping in this evaluation. It is the assumption of this way of thinking that these goals are highly meaningful and that companies and individuals may eventually be assessed on the degree to which they contribute to achieving them. Among the goals that are seen as particularly relevant to evaluating the performance of organizations and individuals along a social-value criterion are:

1. the enhancement of personal dignity and individual growth
2. the elimination of racial discrimination
3. the development of an informed citizenry
4. the improvement of the standard of living
5. the alleviation of general poverty and urban decay

I doubt that all would agree on the applicability of these dimensions for evaluating the social value of a particular behavior, or that all would agree that this should even be done. That's the point! Evaluation is a subjective judgment that defines what is good and what is bad, and there really is no other way to view it. For some people (including myself), this type of social evaluation is increasingly important today and is taking its place as one of the basic criteria by which we evaluate organizational performance on both an individual and organizational level.

Summary

Measuring job performance and reactions to job experience constitutes one of those bread-and-butter activities that has little glamour but is, nevertheless, crucial if we are to progress in our understanding of work behavior. The purpose of this chapter has been to review some of the techniques available for this process.

One major goal of performance measurement has traditionally been that of objectivity. To this end, there has always been interest in such ostensibly objective measures as absenteeism and productivity. Yet, an examination of these shows that while they can be and are useful under some conditions, they are not as objective as assumed and are lacking in applicability to many jobs. For these reasons, it may be more useful to try to improve subjective evaluation methods. A review of the various techniques available shows (1) the graphic rating scale as having the greatest popularity and not being as subject to distortions as assumed, (2) the critical-incidents technique having considerable usefulness because of its focus on extreme behaviors about which it is easy to agree, (3) the forced-choice scale as having some value but some serious disadvantages also, and (4) the ranking method as having some usefulness under some conditions.

While there are a variety of sophisticated measures of job reactions such as the Thurstone, Guttman, and Likert scales, examination shows that simple questionnaire techniques of a relatively nonsophisticated nature give results of approximately equal value. This recommendation is strengthened even further by the fact that indirect and projective measures are still relatively undeveloped and of doubtful value.

Promising newer developments include human resource accounting and measurement of the social value of organizations. Both of these are based on the assumption that organizational life needs to contribute to the quality of both work life and social life. However, disagreement still exists as to the value of this type of thinking.

SUGGESTIONS FOR FURTHER READING

CAMPBELL, J. P., DUNNETTE, M. D., ARVEY, R. D., and HELLEWIK, C. V. The development and evaluation of behaviorally based rating scales. *Journal of Applied Psychology,* 1973, *57,* 15–22.
An excellent illustration of how to develop a rating scale based on carefully planned, research-based procedures. Some of the arguments have been disputed in later research, but the major arguments remain essentially valid.

FLANAGAN, J. C. The critical-incident technique. *Psychological Bulletin,* 1954, *51,* 327–358.
The original statement on this technique by the individual most responsible for its development. Although more than two decades old, few of the arguments made need to be changed and the technique enjoys greater vogue than ever today.

RHODE, J. G., and LAWLER, E. E., III. Auditing change: Human resource accounting. In M. D. Dunnette (ed.), *Work and nonwork in the year 2001.* Monterey, Calif.: Brooks-Cole Publishing Co., 1973, 153–177.
A review of the logic and theory of human-resource accounting and a discussion of how it has been applied in several work settings. Not easy reading, but worth going through several times.

SMITH, P. C., KENDALL, L. M., and HULIN, C. L. *The measurement of satisfaction in work and retirement.* Chicago: Rand-McNally, 1969.

This monograph details the development of the job description inventory (JDI), the most widely used measure of job satisfaction today. While I would argue with some of the theory (or lack of it), the research reported stands as a model of how to establish the construct validity of a set of job attitude measures.

chapter sixteen

Concluding Remarks

We have come to the end of our discussion of behavior in work organizations. Starting from an examination of the history of the field we have, in succession, examined the research methodology used in examining work behavior, motivational and cognitive processes, organizational and environmental effects on behavior, the attitudinal and cognitive effects of organizational and work experience, procedures for regulating the conditions of organized entry, training and development techniques and theory, and the theoretical and practical questions involved in measuring work performance and work reactions.

Looking over these diverse topics and the different theory and methodologies employed in the examination of each, can we cite any common themes? Are there some general conclusions or ideas on which discussion of all (or most) of these topics tends to converge? I think there are and I have tried to point out these common threads throughout this book. However, since much of this discussion has been dispersed and since there is some value in weaving these threads into a thematic pattern, this concluding chapter is devoted to a summary of what I believe about behavior in work organizations today.

1. *The meaning of work as a form of human experience is changing today for men, women, and society in general.*

Throughout this book you can find such phrases as "women's liberation," "men's liberation," "loss of work ethic," and "alienation". These terms were virtually unheard of a few years ago when we were in a cultural epoch in which men went to work with the belief that this was good, proper, and valuable. At the same time, women worked outside the home only when they were unmarried and/or only when it was financially necessary. This, also, was proper and good, according to the ethic of the time. Now, of course, this is all over for a great number of people, and for these individuals there have been (and continues to be) an examination of the advantages and disadvantages of the traditional male and female roles and an interest in how these may be changed.

These developments have tremendous implications for those who manage our work organizations. On the one hand, like it or not, they can no longer count on an almost automatic saliency of work motivation for males. Interest in work for some males is far less than it has been *regardless of what management does*. Furthermore, these males can be found at any level of the work organization from top management on down. On the other hand, the saliency of work may be increasing among those groups that have been traditionally ignored as sources of high-level talent; for example, women, minority group members, and others. Somehow, the people who are responsible for the functioning of organizations are going to have to deal with these changing norms, even though they may not like it and even though these changes violate some of their strongly held beliefs. I have discussed some of the possible responses that might be made by management to this situation. Others will, I believe, be developed and evaluated as acceptance of this situation becomes internalized and mechanisms for reaction are developed.

2. *There is no longer any basis (if there ever was) for viewing the social institution of work separately from other social institutions such as government, education, and the family. The fates of all of these are intimately interrelated with one another in today's world.*

If there is one fact that has been learned by the administrators of work organizations in the last decade, it is that they cannot isolate themselves from the movements and changes of the world around them. While it is historically the case and perhaps still ideologically valued that management can "hire whom they want," they no longer have the right today. As we have seen, the civil rights movements have effectively limited such a right. Similarly, the implications of work experience for self-value, for family life, and for mental and physical health in general are now commonly accepted legitimate areas of inquiry and practical recommendation. Furthermore, work is not only being reexamined, but it is also being changed if it is not benefical to these other forms of social life. In other words, it is no longer the dominant institution to many, but only one of an interlocking set of dimensions of social life.

3. *Theoretical analysis is of significant value in understanding work behavior. Yet, we must never forget that work is important to everyday life. For this reason, the theories developed cannot be allowed to stray too far from the concerns of practically oriented organizational life.*

In a very real sense I think that this is one of the most important aspects of the study of work behavior. All academic disciplines have some application eventually, but some have it quicker than others. This is, I believe, an area in which application is of relatively quick importance. It is fun and often challenging to develop an interesting theoretical model on utilizing mathematical techniques for evaluating an organizational development program. However, if it is a model that assumes a freedom on the part of the researcher to set up adequate control groups and a stability of the groups studied, it may be a pedantic exercise and nothing else. The model may be fun to develop, but the realities of everyday life need to be recognized.

4. *Despite the cultural changes, the personal reevaluations and the criticisms, real or legitimate, work behavior and organizational life still remain among the most critical dimensions of human behavior. For this reason it is crucial that we continue to study work, the organizations in which it takes place, and how to make them both more effective and ego-enhancing to the individuals and groups involved.*

This remains the justification for this book and others like it. The dimensions of work and organizations may change but their significance for providing human satisfactions will remain with us for a long, long time.

References

ADAMS, J. S. Inequality in social exchange. In L. Berkowitz (ed.), *Advances in experimental social psychology*, vol. 2. New York: Academic Press, 1965, pp. 267–299.

ADAMS, J. S., and JACOBSEN, P. R. Effects of wage inequities on work quality. *Journal of Abnormal and Social Psychology*, 1964, *69*, 19–25.

ADAMS, J. S., and ROSENBAUM, W. E. The relationship of worker productivity to cognitive dissonance about inequities. *Journal of Applied Psychology*, 1962, *46*, 161–164.

ADAMS, S. Status congruency as a variable in small-group performance. *Social Forces*, 1953, *32*, 16–22.

ADORNO, T. W., FRENKEL-BRUNSWICK, E., LEVINSON, D. J., and SANFORD, R. N. *The authoritarian personality*. New York: Harper and Row, 1950.

ALPER, T. G. Achievement motivation in college women: A "now-you-see-it, now-you-don't" phenomenon. *American Psychologist*, 1974, *29*, 194–203.

ANDERSSON, B., and NILSSON, S. Studies in the reliability and validity of the critical incident technique. *Journal of Applied Psychology*, 1964, *48*, 398–403.

ANDREWS, I. R. Wage inequity and job performance: An experimental study. *Journal of Applied Psychology*, 1967, *51*, 39–49.

ARGYRIS, C. *Interpersonal competence and organizational effectiveness*. Homewood, Ill.: Irwin, 1962.

ARGYRIS, C. *Integrating the individual and the organization*. New York: John Wiley, 1964.

ARGYRIS, C. *Organization and innovation*. Homewood, Ill.: Irwin, 1965.

ARGYRIS, C. Today's problems with tomorrow's organizations. *Journal of Management Studies*, 1967, *4*, 31–55. (a)

ARGYRIS, C. On the future of laboratory education. *Journal of Applied Behavioral Science*, 1967, *3*, 153–183. (b)

ARGYRIS, C. Some unintended consequences of rigorous research. *Psychological Bulletin*, 1968, *70*, 153–197.

ARGYRIS, C. Dangers in applying results from experimental social psychology. *American Psychologist*, 1975, *30*, 469–485.

ARONSON, E., and CARLSMITH, J. M. Performance expectancy as a determinant of actual performance. *Journal of Abnormal and Social Psychology*, 1962, *65*, 178–182.

ARONSON, E., and GERARD, E. Beyond Parkinson's law: The effect of excess time on subsequent performance. *Journal of Applied Psychology*, 1966, *3*, 336–339.

ARONSON, E., CARLSMITH, J. M., and DARLEY, J. M. The effects of expectancy on volunteering for an unpleasant experience. *Journal of Abnormal and Social Psychology*, 1963, *66*, 220–224.

APPLEY, M. H. Derived motives. *Annual Review of Psychology*, 1970, *21*, 485–518.

ARVEY, R. D. Task performance as a function of perceived effort-performance and performance-reward contingencies. *Organizational Behavior and Human Performance*, 1972, *8*, 423–433.

ARVEY, R. D., and MUSSIO, S. J. A test of expectancy theory in a field setting using female clerical employees. *Journal of Vocational Behavior*, 1973, *3*, 421–432.

ASCH, S. Studies of independence and conformity: I. A minority of one against a unanimous majority. *Psychological Monographs*, 1956, *70*, Whole No. 9, 1–70.

ASH, P. Presidential message. *Industrial Psychologist*, 1968, *5*, 1–2.

ATKINSON, J., and LITWIN, G. Achievement motive and test anxiety conceived as motive to approach success and motive to avoid failure. *Journal of Abnormal and Social Psychology*, 1960, *60*, 52–63.

ATKINSON, J. W. *Motives in fantasy, action and society*. Princeton, N.J.: Van Nostrand, 1958.

ATKINSON, J. W., and FEATHER, N. T. (eds.), *A theory of achievement motivation*. New York: John Wiley, 1966.

BABARIK, P. Automobile accidents and driver reaction pattern. *Journal of Applied Psychology*, 1968, *52*, 49–54.

BACHMAN, J., SMITH, C., and SLESINGER, J. Control, performance and satisfaction: An analysis of structural and individual effects. *Journal of Personality and Social Psychology*, 1966, *4*, 127–136.

BADIN, I. J. Some moderator influences on relationships between consideration, initiating structure and organizational criteria. *Journal of Applied Psychology*, 1974, *59*, 380–382.

BALDAMUS, W. Type of work and motivation. *British Journal of Sociology*, 1951, *2*, 44–58.

BANAS, P. "An investigation of transsituational moderators." Ph.D. dissertation, University of Minnesota, 1964.

BANDURA, A., and WALTERS, R. H. *Social learning and personality development.* New York: Holt, Rinehart and Winston, 1963.

BANDURA, A., Ross, D., and Ross, S. A. Imitation of film-mediated aggressive models. *Journal of Abnormal and Social Psychology,* 1963, *66,* 3–11.

BARCH, A. M. The effect of difficulty of task on proactive facilitation and interference. *Journal of Experimental Psychology,* 1953, *46,* 37–42.

BARCH, A. M., and LEWIS, D. The effect of difficulty and amount of practice on transfer. *Journal of Experimental Psychology,* 1954, *48,* 134–141.

BARITZ, L. *The servants of power.* Middletown, Conn.: Wesleyan University Press, 1960.

BARON, R. Social reinforcement effects as a function of social reinforcement history. *Psychological Review,* 1966, *73,* 527–539.

BARON, R. A. Aggression as a function of ambient temperature and prior anger arousal. *Journal of Personality and Social Psychology,* 1972, *21,* 183–189.

BARRETT, R. Performance suitability and role agreement, two factors related to attitudes. *Personnel Psychology,* 1963, *16,* 345–357.

BARRETT, R. *Performance rating.* Chicago: Science Research Associates, 1966. (a)

BARRETT, R. The influence of the supervisor's requirements on ratings. *Personnel Psychology,* 1966, *19,* 375–387. (b)

BARRETT, R. Gray areas in black and white testing. *Harvard Business Review,* 1968, *46,* 118–126.

BARRON, F. The psychology of creativity. In *New Directions in Psychology,* vol. 2. New York: Holt, Rinehart and Winston, 1965, pp. 1–134.

BARSALOUX, J., BOUCHARD, T. J., JR., and BUSH, S. Object manipulation and creative behavior. *Proceedings, 80th Annual Convention, of the American Psychology Association,* 1972, pp. 447–448.

BARTLETT, A. C. Changing behavior as a means to increased efficiency. *Journal of Applied Behavioral Science,* 1967, *3,* 381–403.

BARTLETT, C., and GREEN, C. G. Clinical prediction: Does one sometimes know too much? *Journal of Counseling Psychology,* 1966, *13,* 267–270.

BARTOLOMÉ, F. Executives as human beings. *Harvard Business Review,* 1972, *50,* 62–69.

BASS, A. R., and TURNER, J. N. Ethnic-group differences in relationships among criteria of job performance. *Journal of Applied Psychology,* 1973, *57,* 101–109.

BASS, B. Further evidence on the dynamic character of criteria. *Personnel Psychology,* 1962, *15,* 13–24.

BASS, B. Experimenting with simulated manufacturing organizations. In S. B. Sells (ed.), *Stimulus determinants of behavior.* New York: Ronald Press, 1963, pp. 117–196.

BASS, B., and VAUGHAN, J. *Training in industry: The management of learning.* Belmont, Calif: Wadsworth Publishing Co., 1967.

BASS, B. M., and FRANKE, R. H. Societal influences on student perceptions of how to succeed in organizations: A cross-national analysis. *Journal of Applied Psychology,* 1972, *56,* 312–318.

BASSETT, G. A., and MEYER, H. H. Performance appraisal based on self-review. *Personnel Psychology,* 1968, *21,* 421–443.

BAUMGARTEL, H., and SOBOL, R. Background and organizational factors in absenteeism. *Personnel Psychology,* 1959, *12,* 431–433.

BAYROFF, A. G., HAGGERTY, H. G., and RUNDQUIST, E. A. Validity ratings as related to rating techniques and conditions. *Personnel Psychology,* 1954, *7,* 93–112.

BELL, D. *The coming of post-industrial society.* New York: Basic Books, 1973.

BEM, D. J. *Beliefs, values and human affairs.* Wadsworth, Calif.: Brooks-Cole, 1970.

BENNIS, W. *Changing organizations.* New York: McGraw-Hill, 1966.

BERGER, A. "The relationship of self-perception and job component perception to overall job satisfaction: A 'self-appropriateness' model of job satisfaction." Ph.D. dissertation, New York University, 1968.

BERKOWITZ, L. Group standards, cohesiveness, and productivity. *Human Relations,* 1954, *7,* 509–519.

BERKOWITZ, L. *Aggression: A social psychological analysis.* New York: McGraw-Hill, 1962.

BERKOWITZ, L., and RAWLINGS, E. Effects of film violence on inhibition against subsequent aggression. *Journal of Abnormal and Social Psychology,* 1963, *66,* 405–412.

BERLEW, D. "Early challenge, performance and success." Paper presented at the meeting of the Eastern Psychological Association, Atlantic City, April, 1965.

BERLEW, D. E., and HALL, D. T. The socialization of managers: Effects of expectations on performance. *Administrative Science Quarterly,* 1966, *11,* 207–223.

BERLYNE, D. Arousal and reinforcement. In D. Levine (ed.), *Nebraska symposium on motivation,* vol. 15. Lincoln, Neb.: University of Nebraska Press, 1967, pp. 1–110.

BERNBERG, R. E. Socio-psychological factors in industrial morale: I. The prediction of specific indicators. *Journal of Social Psychology,* 1952, *36,* 73–82.

BERRY, P. C. Effect of colored illumination upon perceived temperature. *Journal of Applied Psychology,* 1961, *45,* 248–250.

BEXTON, W., HERON W., and SCOTT, T. Effects of decreased variation in the sensory environment. *Canadian Journal of Psychology,* 1954, *8,* 70–76.

BIERI, J. Complexity–simplicity as a personality variable in cognitive and preferential behavior. In D. Fiske and S. Maddi (eds.), *Functions of varied experience.* Homewood, Ill.: Dorsey Press, 1961, 355–379.

BIGELOW, D. A., and DISEROLL, R. H. Effect of minimizing coercion on the rehabilitation of prisoners. *Journal of Applied Psychology,* 1973, *57,* 10–14.

BIRNEY, R. C., BURDICK, H., and TEEVAN, R. C. *Fear of failure.* Princeton, N.J.: Van Nostrand-Reinhold, 1969.

BLAKE, R., and MOUTON, J. *The managerial grid.* Houston, Texas: Gulf Publishing Co., 1964.

BLAKE, R., MOUTON, J. S., BARNES, L. B., and GREINER, L. E. Breakthrough in organization development. *Harvard Business Review,* 1964, *42,* 133–155.

BLAUNER, R. *Alienation and freedom*. Chicago: University of Chicago Press, 1964.

BLOCK, J. R. A test that tells who is accident-prone. *Psychology Today*, 1975, *9*, 84–85.

BLOOD, M., and HULIN, C. Alienation, environmental characteristics, and worker responses. *Journal of Applied Psychology*, 1967, *51*, 284–290.

BLOOD, M. R. The validity of importance. *Journal of Applied Psychology*, 1971, *55*, 487–488.

BLOOM, R., and BARRY, J. R. Determinants of work attitudes among Negroes. *Journal of Applied Psychology*, 1967, *51*, 291–294.

BLUM, A. A. The prospects for office employee unionism. In G. E. Somers (ed.), *Proceedings of the 16th Annual Meeting, Industrial Relations Research Association*, 1963, pp. 182–193.

BLUM, M., and NAYLOR, J. *Industrial psychology: Its theoretical and social foundations*, third edition. New York: Harper and Row, 1968.

BLUMENFIELD, W. S. Perceived importance and obtainability of certain values associated with naval service. *Psychological Reports*, 1965, *17*, 603–606.

BOEHM, V. R. Negro-white differences in validity of employment and training selection procedures: Summary of research evidence. *Journal of Applied Psychology*, 1972, *56*, 33–39.

BOOCOCK, L. Toward a sociology of learning: A selective review of existing research. *Sociology of Education*, 1966, *39*, 1–45.

BORMAN, W. C., and VALLON, W. R. A view of what can happen when behavioral expectation scales are developed in one setting and used in another. *Journal of Applied Psychology*, 1974, *59*, 307–312.

BOUCHARD, T. J., JR., DRAUDEN, G., and BARSALOUX, J. A comparison of individual, subgroup, and total group methods of problem-solving. *Journal of Applied Psychology*, 1974, *59*, 226–229.

BOWERS, D. G. Organization control in an insurance company. *Sociometry*, 1964, *27*, 230–244.

BRAY, D. W., and GRANT, D. L. The assessment center in the measurement of potential for business management. *Psychological Monographs*, 1966, *80*, Whole No. 625.

Brayfield, A., and CROCKETT, W. Employee attitudes and employee performance. *Psychological Bulletin*, 1955, *52*, 396–424.

BRAYFIELD, A., and ROTHE, H. An index of job satisfaction. *Journal of Applied Psychology*, 1951, *35*, 307–311.

BREER, P., and LOCKE, E. A. *Task experience as a source of attitudes*. Homewood, Ill.: Dorsey, 1965.

BROADBENT, D. Effects of noise on behavior. In C. M. Harris (ed.), *Handbook of noise control*. New York: McGraw-Hill, 1957.

BROADBENT, D., and LITTLE, E. A. J. Effects of noise reduction in a work situation. *Occupational Psychology*, 1960, *34*, 133–140.

BROCK, T. Relative efficacy of volition and justification in arousing dissonance. *Journal of Personality*, 1968, *36*, 49–66.

BROCK, T. C. Communicator-recipient similarity and decision change. *Journal of Personality and Social Psychology*, 1968, *7*, 650–654.

BRODY, M. "The relationship between efficiency and job satisfaction." Master's thesis, New York University, 1945.

BROOKOVER, W. B., and THOMAS, S. Self-concept of ability and school achievement. *Sociology of Education*, 1963-1964, *37*, 27-28.

BROVERMAN, I. K., VOGEL, S. R., BROVERMAN, D. M., CLARKSON, F. E., and ROSENKRANTZ, P. S. Sex-role stereotypes: A current appraisal. *Journal of Social Issues*, 1972, *28*, 59-78.

BROWN, E. Influence of training, method and relationship on the halo effect. *Journal of Applied Psychology*, 1968, *52*, 195-199.

BRYAN, J., and LOCKE, E. Parkinson's law as a goal-setting phenomena. *Organizational Behavior and Human Performance*, 1967, *2*, 258-275.

BUCKLEY, J. W. Programmed instruction in industrial training. *California Management Review*, 1967, *10*, 71-79.

BUCKLOW, M. A new role for the work group. *Administrative Science Quarterly*, 1966, *11*, 59-78.

BURNASKA, R. F., and HOLLOMAN, T. D. An empirical comparison of the relative effects of rater response biases on three rating scale formats. *Journal of Applied Psychology*, 1974, *59*, 307-312.

Business Week, April 19, 1969, pp. 88-89.

BYRNE, D., and McGRAW, C. Interpersonal attraction toward Negroes. *Human Relations*, 1964, *17*, 201-214.

BYRNE, D., and NELSON, D. Attraction as a linear function of proportion of positive reinforcements. *Journal of Personality and Social Psychology*, 1965, *1*, 659-663.

CAHOON, D., PETERSON, D., and WATSON, C. Relative effectiveness of programmed text and teaching machine as a function of measured interests. *Journal of Applied Psychology*, 1968, *52*, 454-456.

CAMMAN, C., and LAWLER, E. E., III. Employee reactions to a pay incentive plan. *Journal of Applied Psychology*, 1973, *58*, 163-172.

CAMPBELL, D. Reforms as experiments. *American Psychologist*, 1969, *24*, 409-429.

CAMPBELL, D., and FISKE, D. Convergent and discriminant validation by the multitrait-multimethod matrix. *Psychological Bulletin*, 1959, *56*, 81-105.

CAMPBELL, D., and LeVINE, R. A. Ethnocentrism and intergroup relations. In Abelson, R. P., Aronson, E., McGuire, W. J., Newcomb, T. M., Rosenberg, M. J. and Tannenbaum, P. H. (eds.) *Theories of cognitive consistency: A sourcebook*. Chicago: Rand McNally, 1968, pp. 551-564.

CAMPBELL, J. P. Personnel training and development. *Annual Review of Psychology*. Palo Alto, Calif.: Annual Reviews, 1971, pp. 525-612.

CAMPBELL, J. P., and DUNNETTE, M. D. Effectiveness of T-group experiences in managerial training and development. *Psychological Bulletin*, 1968, *70*, 73-104.

CAMPBELL, J. P., DUNNETTE, M. D., ARVEY, R. D., and HELLERVIK, L. V. The development and evaluation of behaviorally based rating scales. *Journal of Applied Psychology*, 1973, *57*, 15-22.

CAMPBELL, J. P., DUNNETTE, M. D., LAWLER, E. E., and WEICK, K. E. *Managerial behavior, performance and effectiveness*. New York: McGraw-Hill, 1970.

CANTRIL, H. Identification with social and economic class. *Journal of Abnormal and Social Psychology*, 1943, *38*, 74-80.

CARLSON, R. E. Selection interview decisions: The relative influence of appearance and factual information on an interviewer's final rating. *Journal of Applied Psychology,* 1967, *51,* 461–468. (a)

CARLSON, R. E. Selection interview decisions: The effect of interviewer experience, relative quota situation and applicant sample on interviewer decisions. *Personnel Psychology,* 1967, *20,* 259–280. (b)

CARLSON, R. E. Effect of applicant sample on ratings of valid information in an employment setting. *Journal of Applied Psychology,* 1970, *54,* 217–222.

CAREY, A. The Hawthorne studies: A radical criticism. *American Sociological Review,* 1967, *32,* 403–416.

CARROLL, S. J., and TOSI, H. L. *Management by objectives.* New York: Macmillan, 1973.

CARTWRIGHT, D. Determinants of scientific progress: The case of research on the risky shift. *American Psychologist,* 1973, *28,* 222–231.

CASE, H. "Reactions to auditory stress as a function of self-esteem." Senior honors paper, New York University, 1969.

CENTERS, R. J., and BUGENTAL, D. E. Intrinsic and extrinsic job motivations among different segments of the working population. *Journal of Applied Psychology,* 1966, *50,* 193–197.

CENTERS, R. J., and CANTRIL, H. Income satisfaction and income aspiration. *Journal of Abnormal and Social Psychology,* 1946, *41,* 64–69.

CHADWICK-JONES, J. K., BROWN, C. A., and NICHOLSON, N. Absence from work: Its meaning, measurement, and control. *International Review of Applied Psychology,* 1973, *22,* 137–156.

CHAPANIS, A. Knowledge of performance as an incentive in repetitive, monotonous tasks. *Journal of Applied Psychology,* 1964, *48,* 263–267.

CLARK, J. V. Motivation in work groups: A tentative view. *Human Organization,* 1960, *19,* 199–208.

CLELAND, S, *Influence of plant size on industrial relations.* Princeton, N.J.: Princeton University Press, 1955.

COCH, L., and FRENCH, J. R. P. Overcoming resistance to change. *Human Relations,* 1948, *1,* 512–532.

COHEN, A. *Attitude change and social influence.* New York: Basic Books, 1964.

COLE, S., and LEJEUNE, R. Illness and the legitimization of failure. *American Sociological Review,* 1972, *37,* 347–356.

COLEMAN, J. S., ET AL. *Equality of educational opportunity.* Washington, D.C.: U.S. Government Printing Office, 1966.

COOPERSMITH, S. *The antecedents of self-esteem.* San Francisco: Calif.: Freeman, 1967.

COSTELLO, T., and ZALKIND, S. *Psychology in administration.* Englewood Cliffs, N.J.: Prentice-Hall, 1963.

COWEN, E., BOBROVE, P., ROCKWAY, A., and STEVENSON, J. Development and evaluation of an attitude to deafness to scale. *Journal of Personality and Social Psychology,* 1967, *6,* 183–191.

COWEN, E., UNDERBERG, R. P., and VERRILO, R. T. The development and testing of an attitude to blindness scale. *Journal of Social Psychology,* 1958, *48,* 297–304.

COX, O., and BAUER, R. Self-confidence and persuasibility in women. *Public Opinion Quarterly,* 1964, *28,* 453–456.

CRAWFORD, M. Dimensions of simulation. *American Psychologist,* 1966, *21,* 788–796.

CRONBACH, L. J. Beyond the two disciplines of scientific psychology. *American Psychologist,* 1975, *30,* 116–127.

CUMMIN, P. TAT correlates of executive performance. *Journal of Applied Psychology,* 1967, *51,* 78–81.

DAHL, R. A. *Modern political analysis,* second edition. Englewood Cliffs, N.J.: Prentice-Hall, 1970.

DATTA, L. E. Remote associates test as a predictor of creativity in engineers. *Journal of Applied Psychology,* 1964, *48,* 183. (a)

DATTA, L. E. A note on the remote associates test, United States culture, and creativity. *Journal of Applied Psychology,* 1964, *48,* 184–185. (b)

DAVIES, E. This is the way Crete went. *Psychology Today,* 1969, *3,* 42–47.

DAVIES, J. Toward a theory of revolution. *American Sociological Review,* 1967, *27,* 5–19.

DAVIS, L. E., and VALPER, E. S. Studies in supervisory job designs. *Human Relations,* 1968, *19,* 339–347.

DAWSON, J. A., MESSE, L. A. and PHILLIPS, J. L. Effects of instructor-leader behavior on student performance. *Journal of Applied Psychology,* 1972, *56,* 369–376.

DAY, R. C., and HAMBLIN, R. L. Some effects of close and punitive supervision. *American Journal of Sociology,* 1964, *69,* 499–510.

DEARBORN, D. C., and SIMON, H. A. Selective perception: A note on the departmental identification of executives. *Sociometry,* 1958, *21,* 140–144.

DEAUX, K. "Women in management: Casual explanations of performance." Paper presented at the annual convention of the American Psychological Association, New Orleans, La., Sept. 1974.

DECHARMS, R., and DAVE, R. Hope of success, fear of failure, subjective probability, and risk-taking behavior. *Journal of Personality and Social Psychology,* 1965, *1,* 558–568.

DECI, E. L. The effects of contingent and noncontingent rewards and controls on intrinsic motivation. *Organizational Behavior and Human Performance,* 1972, *8,* 217–229.

DECI, E. L., BENWARE, C., and LANDY, D. The attribution of motivation as a function of output and rewards. *Journal of Personality,* 1974, *42,* 652–667.

DEESE, J., and ORMOND, E. *Studies of detectability during continuous visual search.* United States Air Force-Wright Air Development Center Technical Report, 53–8, 1953.

DENMARK, F., and GUTTENTAG, M. Dissonance in the self-concepts and educational concepts of college and non-college oriented women. *Journal of Counseling Psychology,* 1967, *14,* 113–115.

DERIVERA, J. H., and ROSENAU, J. M. *Psychological dimensions of foreign policy.* Columbus, Ohio: C. E. Merrill Publishing Co., 1968.

DEUTSCH, M., and GERARD, H. A study of normative and informational social influences upon individuals' judgment. *Journal of Abnormal and Social Psychology,* 1955, *51,* 629–636.

DOLLARD, J., DOOB, L., MILLER, N., MOWER, O. H., and SEARS, R. *Frustration and aggression.* New Haven, Conn: Yale University Press, 1939.

DONLEY, R. E., and WINTER, D. G. Measuring the motives of public officials at a distance: An exploratory study of American presidents. *Behavioral Science,* 1970, *15,* 227–236.

DRAKE, C. Accident proneness: A hypothesis. *Character and Personality,* 1940, *8,* 335–341.

DUNNETTE, M. A note on the criterion. *Journal of Applied Psychology,* 1963, *47,* 251–254.

DUNNETTE, M. Predictors of executive success. In F. R. Wickert and D. E. McFarland (eds.), *Measuring executive effectiveness.* New York: Appleton-Century-Crofts, 1967, pp. 7–48.

DUNNETTE, M., and CAMPBELL, J. Laboratory education: Impact on people and organizations. *Industrial Relations,* 1968, *8,* 1–27.

DUNNETTE, M., and KIRCHNER, W. *Psychology applied to business and industry.* New York: Appleton-Century-Crofts, 1965.

DUNNETTE, M. D. *Personnel selection and placement.* Belmont, Cal.: Wadsworth Publishing Co., 1966.

DUNNETTE, M. D. "Mishmash, mush and milestones in organizational psychology: 1974." Paper presented at the convention of the American Psychological Association, New Orleans, La., Sept. 1974.

DUNNETTE, M. D., and CAMPBELL, J. P. *A research center for the study of organizational performance and human effectiveness.* Annual Progress Report, University of Minnesota Center for the Study of Human Performance, Technical Report No. 4007, 1970–1971.

DUNNETTE, M. D., and TOWNSEND, J. *"Sensitivity and openness: Why, when and toward whom?"* Unpublished paper, University of Minnesota, 1970.

EARLE, H. Ph.D. dissertation, University of Southern California, Not seen; reported in Shaw, David. Sheriff's Aide Retracts Theory, *Washington Post,* September 3, 1972, p. K4.

EHRLICH, H., and LEE, D. Dogmatism, learning and resistance to change: A review and a new paradigm. *Psychological Bulletin,* 1969, *71,* 249–260.

ELLIS, A. *Executive leadership: A rational approach.* Secaucus, N.J.: Citadel Press, 1972.

ELLIS, A. The no cop-out therapy. *Psychology Today,* 1973, *7,* 56–62.

ELLIS, A., and BLUM, M. L. Rational training: A new method of facilitating management and labor relations. *Psychological Reports,* 1967, *20,* 1267–1284.

ELLUL, J. *The technological society.* New York: Alfred A. Knopf, 1965.

ELTON, C. F., and SHEVEL, L. R. *Who is talented? An analysis of achievement.* American College Testing Program, Research Report No. 31, Iowa City, Iowa, 1969.

ENGLAND, G. W., and STEIN, C. The occupational reference group—a neglected concept in employee attitude studies. *Personnel Psychology,* 1961, *14,* 299–304.

ETZIONI, A. *Modern organizations.* Englewood Cliffs, N.J.: Prentice-Hall, 1964.

EVANS, C. E., and LAUSEAU, L. N. My job contest. *Personnel Psychology,* Monograph No. 1. Washington, D. C., 1950.

EWEN, R. B., SMITH, P. C., HULIN, C. L., and LOCKE, E. A. An empirical test of the Herzberg two-factor theory. *Journal of Applied Psychology,* 1966, *50,* 544–550.

FARRIS, G. Organizational factors and individual performance: A longitudinal study. *Journal of Applied Psychology, 1969, 53,* 87–91.

FAUNCE, W. *Social problems of an industrial civilization.* New York: McGraw-Hill, 1968.

FAYOL, H. *General and industrial management,* C. Stons (trans). London: Sir Issac Pitman, 1949.

FEATHER, N. The relationship of expectation of success to need achievement and test anxiety. *Journal of Personality and Social Psychology, 1965, 1,* 118–126.

FEATHER, N. T., and RAPHELSON, A. C. Fear of success in Australian and American student groups: Motive or sex-role stereotype? *Journal of Personality, 1974, 42,* 190–201.

FESHBACH, S., and SINGER, R. A. *Television and aggression.* San Francisco: Jossey-Bass, 1971.

FESTINGER, L. Informal social communication. *Psychological Review, 1950, 57,* 271–292.

FESTINGER, L. Theory of social comparison processes. *Human Relations, 1954, 7,* 117–140.

FESTINGER, L. *A theory of cognitive dissonance.* Evanston, Ill.: Row, Peterson and Co., 1957.

FIEDLER, F., and MEUWESE, W. Leaders' contribution to task performance in cohesive and noncohesive groups. *Journal of Abnormal and Social Psychology, 1963, 67,* 83–87.

FIEDLER, F. E. The effect of leadership and cultural heterogeneity on group performance: A test of the contingency model. *Journal of Experimental Social Psychology, 1966, 2,* 237–264.

FILLENBAUM, S., and JACKMAN, A. Dogmatism and anxiety in relation to problem solving: An extension of Rokeach's results. *Journal of Abnormal and Social Psychology, 1961, 63,* 212-214.

FINKELMAN, J. Unpublished paper, New York University, 1969.

FINKELMAN, J. M., and GLASS, D. C. Reappraisal of the relationship between noise and human performance by means of a subsidiary task measure. *Journal of Applied Psychology, 1970, 54,* 211–213.

FINKELMAN, J. M., ZEITLIN, L. R., ROMOFF, R. A., and BROWN, L. *The effect of physical stress and noise on information processing performance and cardiac response.* Baruch College of The City University of New York, Human Factors Simulation Laboratory, Research Report No. 103, February 1976.

FISKE, D., and MADDI, S. *Functions of varied experience.* Homewood, Ill.: Dorsey Press, 1961.

FLAMHOLTZ, E. "Human resource accounting: A review of theory and research." Paper presented at the annual convention of the Academy of Management, Minneapolis, Minn., August 1972.

FLANAGAN, J., and BURNS, R. K. The employee performance record: A new appraisal and development tool. *Harvard Business Review, 1955, 33,* 95–102.

FLANAGAN, J. C. The critical incident technique. *Psychological Bulletin, 1954, 51,* 327–358.

FLEISHMAN, E. The description and prediction of perceptual-motor skill learning. In R. Glaser (ed.), *Training research and education.* Pittsburgh, Pa.: University of Pittsburgh Press, 1962.

FLEISHMAN, E., HARRIS, E., and BURTT, H. *Leadership and supervision in industry: An evaluation of a supervisory training program.* Columbus, Ohio: Ohio State University, Bureau of Educational Research, 1955.

FLEISHMAN, E. A. Twenty years of consideration and structure. In E. A. Fleishman and J. G. Hunt (eds.), *Current developments in the study of leadership.* Carbondale, Ill.: Southern Illinois University Press, 1973.

FLEISHMAN, E. A. Toward a taxonomy of human performance. *American Psychologist,* 1975, *30,* 1127–1149.

FLEISHMAN, E. A., and HEMPEL, W. E. Changes in factor structure of a complex psycho-motor test as a function of practice. *Psychometrika,* 1954, *12,* 239–252.

FLEISHMAN, E. A., and PETERS, D. A. Interpersonal values, leadership attitudes, and managerial success. *Personnel Psychology,* 1962, *15,* 127–143.

FORD, R. N. *Motivation through the work itself.* New York: American Management Association, 1969.

FORM, W. H. Auto workers and their machines: A study of work, factory and job satisfaction in four countries. *Social Forces,* 1973, *52,* 1–15.

FORM, W. H. and GESHWENDER, J. A. Social reference basis of job satisfaction: The case of manual workers. *American Sociological Review,* 1962, *27,* 228–236.

FRANKMAN, J. P., and ADAMS, J. A. Theories of vigilance. *Psychological Bulletin,* 1962, *59,* 257–272.

FRASER, D. C. The relation of an environmental variable to performance in a prolonged visual task. *Quarterly Journal of Experimental Psychology,* 1953, *5,* 31–32.

FRASER, D. C. Recent experiment work in the study of fatigue. *Occupational Psychology,* 1958, *32,* 258–263.

FREEDMAN, J., KLEVANSKY, S., and EHRLICH, P. R. The effects of crowding on human task performance. *Journal of Applied Social Psychology,* 1971, *1,* 7–25.

FREEDMAN, J. C., LEVY, A. S., BUCHANAN, E. W., and PRICE, J. Crowding and human aggressiveness. *Journal of Experimental Social Psychology,* 1972, *8,* 528–548.

FRENCH, J. R. P., JR., and CAPLAN, R. D. Organizational stress and individual strain. In A. Marrow (ed.), *The failure of success.* New York: American Management Association, 1973, pp. 30–65.

FRENCH, J. R. P., JR., and RAVEN, B. The bases of social power. In D. Cartwright and A. Zander (eds.), *Group dynamics: Research and theory.* Evanston, Ill.: Row, Peterson and Co., 1960, pp. 607–623.

FREY, R., GOODSTADT, B., ROMANCZUK, A. R., GLICKMAN, A. S., and KORMAN, A. K. *More is not better.* Paper presented at the annual convention of the Eastern Psychological Association, Philadelphia, Pa., April 1974.

GAILBREATH, J., and CUMMINGS, L. An empirical investigation of the motivational determinants of task performance: Interactive effects between instrumentality-valence and motivation-ability. *Organizational Behavior and Human Performance,* 1967, *2,* 237–257.

GAVIN, J. F. Ability, effort and role perception as antecedents of job performance. *Experimental Publication System,* 1970, *5,* Manuscript No. 190A.

GEORGOPOULOS, B. S., MAHONEY, G. M., and JONES, N. W. A path-goal approach to productivity. *Journal of Applied Psychology,* 1957, *41,* 345–353.

GERGEN, K. J. Social psychology as history. *Journal of Personality and Social Psychology,* 1973, *26,* 309–320.

GETZELS, J. W., and JACKSON, P. W. *Creativity and intelligence.* New York: John Wiley, 1962.

GHISELLI, E. *The self-description inventory manual.* Available from author, University of California, Berkeley, n.d.

GHISELLI, E. Differentiation of individuals in terms of their predictability. *Journal of Applied Psychology,* 1956, *40,* 374–377.

GHISELLI, E. Traits differentiating management personnel. *Personnel Psychology,* 1959, *12,* 535–544.

GHISELLI, E. The validity of management traits related to occupational level. *Personnel Psychology,* 1963, *16,* 109–113.

GHISELLI, E. *The validity of occupational aptitude tests.* New York: John Wiley, 1966.

GHISELLI, E. *Explorations in management talent.* Pacific Palisades, Calif.: Goodyear Publishing Co., 1971.

GHISELLI, E. Some perspectives for industrial psychology. *American Psychologist,* 1974, *29,* 80–87.

GHISELLI, E., and BROWN, C. *Personnel and industrial psychology,* second edition. New York: McGraw-Hill, 1955.

GHISELLI, E., and HAIRE, M. The validation of selection tests in the light of the dynamic character of criteria. *Personnel Psychology,* 1960, *13,* 225–231.

GIBB, C. A. Leadership. In G. Lindzey, and E. Aronson (eds.), *Handbook of Social Psychology,* second edition, vol. 4. Reading, Mass.: Addison-Wesley, 1969, pp. 205–282.

GIBSON, J. Organizational theory and the nature of man. *Academy of Management Journal,* 1966, *9,* 233–245.

GIESE, W. J., and RUTER, H. W. An objective analysis of morale. *Journal of Applied Psychology,* 1949, *33,* 421–427.

GILES, B. A., and BARRETT, G. V. Utility of merit increases. *Journal of Applied Psychology,* 1971, *55,* 103–109.

GLASS, D., and SINGER, J. *Urban stress.* New York: Academic Press, 1972.

GLICKMAN, A. S. Effects of negatively skewed ratings on motivations of the rated. *Personnel Psychology,* 1955, *8,* 39–47.

GLICKMAN, A. S., and BROWN, Z. H. *Changing schedules of work: Patterns and implications.* Washington, D. C.: American Institutes for Research, February 1973.

GLICKMAN, A. S., GOODSTADT, B. E., FREY, R. L., JR., KORMAN, A. K., and ROMANCZUK, A. P. *Navy career motivation programs in an all-volunteer condition.* American Institutes for Research, Final Report, Washington D.C., June 1974.

GLICKMAN, A. S. and VALLANCE, T. R. Curriculum assessment with critical incidents. *Journal of Applied Psychology,* 1958, *42,* 329–335.

GOLDSTEIN, L. Human variables in traffic accidents. National Academy of Science, National Research Council. Highway Research Board Bibliography No. 31, Washington, D.C., 1962.

GOLDSTEIN, O., FINK, D., and METTEE, D. Cognition of arousal and actual arousal as determinants of emotion. *Journal of Personality and Social Psychology,* 1972, *21,* 41–51.

GOLDTHORPE, J. H. Stratification in industrial society. *Sociological Review Monographs,* 1964, *8,* 97–110.

GOLEMBIEWSKI, R. *Men, management and morality.* New York: McGraw-Hill, 1965.

GOODALE, J. G., and AAGAARD, A. K. "Varying Reactions to the Four-Day Workweek." Paper presented at the annual convention of the American Psychological Association, New Orleans, La., Sept. 1974.

GOODMAN, M. Expressed self-acceptance and interpersonal needs: A basis for mate selection. *Journal of Counseling Psychology,* 1964, *11,* 129–135.

GOODMAN, P., and BALOFF, N. Task experience and attitudes toward decision-making. *Organizational Behavior and Human Performance,* 1968, *3,* 202–216.

GOODMAN, P., and FRIEDMAN, A. An examination of Adam's theory of inequity. *Administrative Science Quarterly,* 1971, *16,* 271–286.

GOODMAN, P., and THEODORE, E. D. Task experience and attitude toward delaying reward. *Social Forces,* 1973, *51,* 434–439.

GOODMAN, P., FURCON, J., and ROSE, J. Examination of some measures of creative ability by the multitrait-multimethod matrix. *Journal of Applied Psychology,* 1969, *53,* 240–243.

GOODMAN, P. S., ROSE, J. H., and FURCON, J. E. Comparison of motivational antecedents of the work performance of scientists and engineers. *Journal of Applied Psychology,* 1970, *54,* 491–495.

GOODSTADT, B. E. and HJELLE, L. A. Power to the powerless: Laws of control and the use of power. *Journal of Personality and Social Psychology,* 1973, *27,* 190–196.

GORDON, M. E. Examination of the relationship between the tendency to be lenient and the accuracy of ratings. *Proceedings, 78th Annual Convention of the American Psychological Association,* 1970, pp. 571–572.

GORDON, W. J. J. *Synectics.* New York: Harper, 1961.

GOTTESFELD, H., and DOZIER, G. Changes in feelings of powerlessness in a community action program. *Psychological Reports,* 1966, *19,* 978.

GOTTMAN, J. When in Milwaukee, do as Bostonians do. Well, then, what do Bostonians do? What Atlantans do. What do Atlantans do? See their city change. *The New York Times,* June 2, 1975.

GRAEN, G. B. Instrumentality theory of work motivation: Some experimental results and suggested modifications. *Journal of Applied Psychology Monographs,* 1969, *53,* part 2.

GRAYSON, R. R. Air-controller syndrome: Peptic ulcer in air traffic controllers. *Human Behavior,* 1973, *11,* 33–34.

GREEN, R. F. Transfer of skill in a following tracking task as a function of difficulty. *Journal of Psychology,* 1955, *39,* 355–370.

GREENE, C. N. The reciprocal nature of influence between leader and subordinate. *Journal of Applied Psychology,* 1975, *60,* 187–193.

GREENHAUS, J. H. Self-esteem as an influence on occupational choice and occupational satisfaction. *Journal of Vocational Behavior,* 1971, *1,* 75–84.

GREENHAUS, J. H., and BADIN, I. J. Self-esteem, performance and satisfaction: Some tests of a theory. *Journal of Applied Psychology,* 1974, *59,* 722–726.

GREENSHIELDS, B. D., and PLATT, F. N. Development of a method of predicting high-accident and high-violation drivers. *Journal of Applied Psychology,* 1967, *51,* 205–209.

GRIENER, L. Patterns of organization change. *Harvard Business Review,* 1967, *45,* 119–122.

GRIFFITT, W., and VEITCH, R. Hot and crowded: Influence of population density and temperature on interpersonal affective behavior. *Journal of Personality and Social Psychology,* 1971, *19,* 92–98.

GRUENFELD, L., and ARBUTHNOT, J. Field independence as a conceptual framework for prediction of variability in ratings of others. *Perceptual and Motor Skills,* 1969, *28,* 31–44.

GRUENFELD, L. N. Personality needs and expected benefits from a management development program. *Occupational Psychology,* 1966, *40,* 75–81.

GUETZKOW, H. The creative person in organizations. In G. Steiner (ed.), *The creative organization.* Chicago: University of Chicago Press, 1965, pp. 35–45.

GUION, R. Criterion measurement and personnel judgments. *Personnel Psychology,* 1961, *14,* 141–149.

GUION, R., and GOTTIER, R. F. Validity of personnel measures in personnel selection. *Personnel Psychology,* 1965, *18,* 135–164.

GUION, R. M. *Personnel testing.* New York: McGraw-Hill, 1965.

GUION, R. M. A note on organizational climate. *Organizational Behavior and Human Performance,* 1973, *9,* 120–125.

GUTTMAN, L. The basis for scalogram analysis. In S. Stouffer (ed.), *Measurement and prediction.* Princeton, N.J.: Princeton University Press, 1950.

HACKMAN, J. R., and LAWLER, E. E., III. Employee reactions to job characteristics. *Journal of Applied Psychology Monographs,* 1971, *55,* 259–286.

HACKMAN, J. R., and PORTER, L. Expectancy theory predictions of work effectiveness. *Organizational Behavior and Human Performance,* 1968, *3,* 417–426.

HACKMAN, J. R., OLDHAM, G. R., JANSON, R., and PURDY, K. *A new strategy for job enrichment.* Yale University, Department of Administrative Sciences, Technical Report No. 3, New Haven, Conn., May 1974.

HAGGERTY, H. *Personnel research for the U.S. Military Academy, 1942–1953.* U.S. Army Personnel Research Board, Technical Research Report 1077, Washington, D.C., October 1953.

HAGGERTY, H. *Status report on research for the U.S. Military Academy.* Cadet Leaders Task, U.S. Army Personnel Research Office, October 1963.

HAIRE, M., and GRUNES, W. F. Perceptual defenses: Processes protecting an organized perception of another personality. *Human Relations,* 1958 *3,* 403–412.

HAKEL, M. D. Similarity of post-interview trait rating intercorrelations as a contributor to interrater agreement in a structured employment interview. *Journal of Applied Phycology,* 1971, *55,* 443–448.

HAKEL, M. D., OHNESORGE, J. P., and DUNNETTE, M. D. Interviewer evaluation of job applicants' resumes as a function of the qualifications of the immediately preceding applicants: An examination of the contrast effects. *Journal of Applied Psychology,* 1970, *54,* 27–30.

HALL, D. T., and GORDON, F. Career choices of married women: Effects on conflict, role behavior and satisfaction. *Journal of Applied Psychology,* 1973, *58,* 42–48.

HANER, C. F. Use of psychological inventory in writing insurance for youthful male drivers. *Traffic Safety,* 1963, *7,* 5–14.

HARRELL, T. W., and HARRELL, M. S. Army general classification test scores for civilian occupations. *Educational and Psychological Measurement,* 1945, *5,* 229–239.

HEIDER, F. *The psychology of interpersonal relations.* New York: John Wiley, 1958.

HELLER, F., and YUKL, G. Participation, managerial decision-making and situational variables. *Organizational Behavior and Human Performance,* 1969, *4,* 227–239.

HELSON, H. *Adaptation-level theory: An experimental and systematic approach to behavior.* New York: Harper and Row, 1964.

HENEMAN, H. G., III. Comparisons of self-and-superior ratings of managerial performance. *Journal of Applied Psychology,* 1974, *59,* 638–642.

HERMAN, J. B. Are situational contingencies limiting job attitude-job performance relationships? *Organizational Behavior and Human Performance,* 1973, *10,* 208–224.

HERZBERG, F., MAUSNER, B., PETERSON, R. O. and CAPWELL, D. F. *Job attitudes: Review of research and opinion.* Pittsburgh, Pa.: Psychological Service of Pittsburgh, 1957.

HERZBERG, F., MAUSNER, B., and SNYDERMAN, B. *The motivation to work,* second edition. New York: John Wiley, 1959.

HICKSON, D. J., PUGH, D. S., and PHEYSEY, D. C. Operations technology and organization structure. *Administrative Science Quarterly,* 1969, *17,* 378–397.

HINRICHS, J. R. Value adaptation of new Ph.D.'s to academic and industrial environments—A comparative longitudinal approach. *Personnel Psychology,* 1972, *25,* 545–566.

HOFFMAN, L. R. Conditions for creative problem-solving. *Journal of Psychology,* 1961, *52,* 429–444.

HOFFMAN, L. R., HARBURG, E., and MAIER, N. R. F. Differences and disagreement in creative group problem-solving. *Journal of Abnormal and Social Psychology,* 1962, *64,* 206–214.

HOFFMAN, L. W. Fear of success in males and females: 1965 and 1971. *Journal of Consulting and Clinical Psychology,* 1974, *42,* 353–358.

HOFFMAN, L. W., and NYE, F. I. *Working mothers.* San Francisco: Jossey-Bass, 1974.

HOLLAND, J. Human vigilance. *Science,* 1958, *128,* 161–167.

HOLLAND, J. L., and RICHARDS, J. M., JR. *Academic and non-academic accomplishments: Correlated or uncorrelated?* American College Testing Program, Research Report No. 2, Iowa City, Iowa, 1965.

HOLLANDER, E. P. Conformity, status and idiosyncracy credit. *Psychological Review,* 1958, *65,* 117–127.

HOLLANDER, E. P. Validity of peer nominations in predicting a distant performance criterion. *Journal of Applied Psychology,* 1965, *49,* 434–438.

HOMANS, G. *The human group.* New York: Harcourt, 1950.

HORNER, M. S. "Sex differences in achievement motivation and performance in competitive and noncompetitive situations." Ph.D. dissertation, University of Michigan, 1968.

HORNER, M. S. Toward an understanding of achievement-related conflicts in women. *Journal of Social Issues,* 1972, *28,* 157–174.

HOUSE, J. S. Occupational stress and coronary heart disease: A review and theoretical integration. *Journal of Health and Social Behavior,* 1974, *15,* 12–27.

HOUSE, R. J. T-group education and leadership effectiveness: A review of the empirical literature and a critical evaluation. *Personnel Psychology,* 1967, *20,* 1–32.

HOUSE, R. J. A path-goal theory of leader effectiveness. *Administrative Science Quarterly, 16,* 3, 1971, 321–338.

HOUSE, R. J., and DESSLER, G. The path-goal theory of leadership: some post hoc and a priori tests. In J. G. Hunt (ed.), *Contingency approaches to leadership.* Carbondale, Ill.: Southern Illinois University Press, 1974, 29–55.

HOUSE, R. J., SHAPIRO, H. J., and WAHBA, M. A. Expectancy theory as a predictor of work behavior and attitude: A reevaluation of empirical evidence. *Decision Sciences,* 1974, *5,* 481–506.

HOUSTON, J. P., and MEDNICK, S. A. Creativity and the need for novelty. *Journal of Abnormal and Social Psychology,* 1963, *66,* 137–141.

HOVLAND, C. Reconciling conflicting results derived from experimental and survey studies of attitude change. *American Psychologist,* 1959, *14,* 8–17.

HOVLAND, C. I., JANIS, I. L., and KELLEY, H. H. *Communication and persuasion: Psychological studies of opinion change.* New Haven, Conn.: Yale University Press, 1953.

HOWARD, A. An assessment of assessment centers. *Academy of Management Journal,* 1974, *17,* 115–134.

HOWARD, J. *Please touch.* New York: McGraw-Hill, 1972.

HULIN, C. L. Effects of community characteristics on measures of job satisfaction. *Journal of Applied Psychology,* 1966, *50,* 185–192.

HULIN, C. L., and WATERS, L. K. Regression analysis of three variations of the 2-factor theory of job satisfaction. *Journal of Applied Psychology,* 1971, *55,* 211–217.

HUNDAL, R. S. A study of entrepreneurial motivation: Comparison of fast-and-slow progressing small-scale industrial entrepreneurs in Punjab, India. *Journal of Applied Psychology,* 1971, *55,* 317–323.

HUSE, E. F., and TAYLOR, E. K. Reliability of absence measures. *Journal of Applied Psychology,* 1962, *46,* 159–160.

INDIK, B. P., and SEASHORE, S. E. *Effects of organization size on member attitudes and behavior.* Ann Arbor, Mich.: University of Michigan, 1961.

INSKO, C. *Theories of attitude change.* New York: Appleton-Century-Crofts, 1967.

IVANCEVICH, J. M. Effects of the shorter workweek on selected satisfaction and performance measures. *Journal of Applied Psychology,* 1974, *59,* 717–721.

IZARD, C. E. Personality characteristics of sociometric status. *Journal of Applied Psychology,* 1959, *43,* 89–93.

JACQUES, E. *Work, creativity and social justice.* New York: International Universities Press, 1970.

JANIS, I. L. *Victims of groupthink.* New York: Harcourt Brace Jovanovich, 1973.

JENKINS, D. *Job power.* Garden City, N.Y.: Doubleday, 1973.

JENKINS, H. M. The effect of signal rate on performance in visual monitoring. *American Journal of Psychology, 1958, 71,* 647–661.

JESWALD, T. A. The cost of absenteeism and turnover in a large organization. In W. C. Hamner and F. L. Schmidt (eds.), *Contemporary problems in personnel.* Chicago: St. Clair Press, 1974, pp. 352–357.

JOHANNESON, R. E. Some problems in the measurement of organizational climate. *Organizational Behavior and Human Performance, 1973, 10,* 118–144.

JOHNSON, D. H. Reanalysis of experimental halo effects. *Journal of Applied Psychology, 1963, 47,* 46–47.

JONES, E. E. *Ingratiation.* New York: Appleton-Century-Crofts, 1964.

JONES, J. *Prejudice and racism.* Reading, Mass.: Addison-Wesley, 1972.

JORGENSON, D. O., DUNNETTE, M. D., and PRITCHARD, R. D. Effects of the manipulation of a performance-reward contingency on behavior in a simulated work setting. *Journal of Applied Psychology, 1973, 57,* 271–280.

JULIAN, J. W., HOLLANDER, E. P., and REQULA, C. R. Endorsement of the group spokesman as a function of his source of authority, competence and success. *Journal of Personality and Social Psychology, 1969, 11,* 115–120.

KARABENICK, S. A. Effect of sex of competitor on the performance of females following success. *Proceedings, 80th Annual Convention of the American Psychological Association,* 1972, pp. 275–276.

KATZELL, R., BARRETT, R., and PARKER, T. Job satisfaction, job performance and situational characteristics. *Journal of Applied Psychology, 1961, 45,* 65–72.

KATZELL, R. A., EWEN, R., and KORMAN, A. K. Job attitudes of black and white workers: Male blue-collar workers in six companies. *Journal of Vocational Behavior, 1974, 4,* 365–376.

KAUFMAN, H. Task performance and response to failure as functions of imbalance in the self-concept. *Psychological Monographs, 1963, 77,* Whole No. 569.

KAUFMAN, H. *Aggression and altruism: A social psychological analysis.* New York: Holt, Rinehart and Winston, 1970.

KAVANAGH, M. J. "The correlation between life and job satisfaction for men and women." Paper presented at the convention of the American Psychological Association, New Orleans, La., Sept. 1974.

KAY, E., MEYER, H., and FRENCH, J. R. P., JR. Effects of threat in a performance appraisal interview. *Journal of Applied Psychology, 1965, 49,* 311–317.

KEEHN, J. D. Factor analysis of reported minor personal mishaps. *Journal of Applied Psychology, 1959, 43,* 311–314.

KEENAN, V., KERR, W., and SHERMAN, W. Psychological climate and accidents in an automotive plant. *Journal of Applied Psychology, 1951, 35,* 108–111.

KELLEY, H. H. Attribution theory in social psychology. In D. Levine (ed.), *Nebraska symposium on motivation,* vol. 15. Lincoln, Neb.: University of Nebraska Press, 1967, pp. 192–237.

KELMAN, H. C. Violence without moral restraint: Reflections on the dehumanization of victims and victimizers. *Journal of Social Issues,* 1973, *29,* 25–62.

KENT, D. A., and EISENBERG, T. The selection and promotion of police officers. *Police Chief,* February 1972, pp. 20–29.

KERR, C., DUNLOP, J. T., HARBISON, F. H., and MYERS, C. A. *Industrialization and Industrial Man.* Cambridge: Harvard University Press, 1960.

KERR, S. A., SCHREISHEM, C. A., MURPHY, C. J., and STOGDILL, R. M. Toward a contingency theory of leadership based upon the consideration and initiating structure literature. *Organizational Behavior and Human Performance,* 1974, *12,* 62–82.

KERR, W. A. Experiments on the effects of music on factor production. *Applied Psychological Monographs,* 1945, *1,* Whole No. 5.

KERR, W. A. Accident proneness of factory departments. *Journal of Applied Psychology,* 1950, *34,* 167–170.

KERR, W. A. Complimentary theories of safety psychology. *Journal of Social Psychology,* 1957, *45,* 3–9.

KERR, W. A., KOPPLEMAIER, G. J., and SULLIVAN, J. J. Absenteeism, turnover and morale in a metals fabrication factory. *Occupational Psychology,* 1951, *25,* 50–55.

KING, G. F., and CLARKE, J. A. Perceptual-motor speed discrepancy and deviant driving. *Journal of Applied Psychology,* 1962, *46,* 115–119.

KIPNIS, D. Some determinants of supervisory esteem. *Personnel Psychology,* 1960, *13,* 377–392.

KIPNIS, D. A noncognitive correlate of performance among lower aptitude men. *Journal of Applied Psychology,* 1962, *46,* 76–80.

KIPNIS, D. Does power corrupt? *Journal of Personality and Social Psychology,* 1972, *24,* 33–41.

KIRCHNER, W., and DUNNETTE, M. D. Identifying the critical factors in successful salesmanship. *Personnel,* 1957, *34,* 54–59.

KIRCHNER, W., and REISBERG, D. J. Differences between better and less effective supervisors in appraisal of subordinates. *Personnel Psychology,* 1962, *15,* 295–302.

KIRKPATRICK, J. J., EWEN, R. W., BARRETT, R. S., and KATZELL, R. A. *Testing and fair employment: Fairness and validity of personnel tests for different ethnic groups.* New York: New York University Press, 1968.

KIRSCH, B. A., and LENGERMANN, J. J. An empirical test of Robert Blauner's ideas on alienation in work as applied to different type jobs in a white-collar setting. *Sociology and Social Research,* 1972, *56,* 180–194.

KISH, G. B., and BUSSE, W. Correlates of stimulus-seeking: Age, education, intelligence and aptitudes. *Journal of Consulting and Clinical Psychology,* 1968, *32,* 633–637.

KLEIN, S. M., and MAHER, J. R. Education level and satisfaction with pay. *Personnel Psychology,* 1966, *19,* 195–208.

KLINGER, E. Fantasy need achievement as a motivational construct. *Psychological Bulletin,* 1966, *66,* 291–308.

KLINGER, E., and McNELLY, F. W., JR. Fantasy need achievement and performance: A role analysis. *Psychological Review,* 1969, *76,* 574–591.

KOGAN, N., and WALLACH, M. Risky-shift phenomenon in small decision-making groups: A test of the information exchange hypothesis. *Journal of Experimental Social Psychology,* 1967, *3,* 75–84.

KOLB, D. A. Achievement motivation training for underachieving high school boys. *Journal of Personality and Social Psychology,* 1965, *2,* 783–792.

KOONTZ, H., and O'DONNELL, C. *Principles of management,* third edition. New York: McGraw-Hill, 1964.

KOPPELMAN, R. E. "Factors complicating expectancy theory prediction of work motivation and performance." Paper presented at the convention of the American Psychological Association, New Orleans, La., Sept. 1974.

KORMAN, A. Selective perceptions among first-line supervisors. *Personnel Administration,* 1963, *26,* 31–36.

KORMAN, A. "Some interrelationships between measures of managerial motivation." Paper, New York University, 1965.

KORMAN, A. Self-esteem variable in vocational choice. *Journal of Applied Psychology,* 1966, *50,* 479–486. (a)

KORMAN, A. "Consideration," "initiating structure," and organizational criteria—A review. *Personnel Psychology,* 1966, *19,* 349–362. (b)

KORMAN, A. Self-esteem as a moderator of the relationship between self-perceived abilities and vocational choice. *Journal of Applied Psychology,* 1967, *51,* 65–67. (a)

KORMAN, A. Ethical judgments, self-perceptions and vocational choice. *Proceedings, 75th Annual Convention, American Psychological Association,* 1967, 349–350. (b)

KORMAN, A. "Some correlates of satisfaction as moderated by self-esteem." Paper presented at the meeting of the Eastern Psychological Association, Boston, Mass., April, 1967. (c)

KORMAN, A. Relevance of personal need satisfaction for overall satisfaction as a function of self-esteem. *Journal of Applied Psychology,* 1967, *51,* 533–538. (d)

KORMAN, A. "Self-esteem, social influence and task performance: Some tests of a theory." Paper presented at the meeting of the American Psychological Association, San Francisco, Ca., Sept. 1968. (a)

KORMAN, A. The prediction of managerial performance: A review. *Personnel Psychology,* 1968, *21,* 259–322. (b)

KORMAN, A. Task success, task popularity and self-esteem as influences on task liking. *Journal of Applied Psychology,* 1968, *52,* 484–490. (c)

KORMAN, A. Self-esteem as a moderator in vocational choice: Replications and extensions. *Journal of Applied Psychology,* 1969, *53,* 188–192.

KORMAN, A. Toward a hypothesis of work behavior. *Journal of Applied Psychology,* 1970, *54,* 31–41.

KORMAN, A. K. Organizational achievement, aggression and creativity: Some suggestions toward an integrated theory. *Organizational Behavior and Human Performance,* 1971, *6,* 539–613. (a)

KORMAN, A. K. Environmental ambiguity and locus of control as interactive influences on satisfaction. *Journal of Applied Psychology,* 1971, *55,* 339–342. (b)

KORMAN, A. K. On the development of contingency theories of leadership: Some methodological considerations and a possible alternative. *Journal of Applied Psychology,* 1973, *58,* 384–387. (a)

KORMAN, A. K. "A theoretical model." Paper presented at Symposium on Occupational Research and the Navy—Prospectus 1980. San Diego, Cal., June, 1973. (b)

KORMAN, A. K. *The psychology of motivation.* Englewood Cliffs, N.J.: Prentice-Hall, 1974.

KORMAN, A. K. A hypothesis of work behavior revisited and an extension. *Academy of Management Review,* 1976, *1,* 50–63.

KORMAN, A. and FINKELMAN, J. "Urban experience and achievement." Paper presented at the annual convention of the American Psychological Association, New Orleans, La., Sept. 1974.

KORMAN, A., NOON, J., and RYAN, S. "Career development programs for management." Paper presented at the convention of the New York State Psychological Association, Kiamesha Lake, New York, May 1975.

KORMAN, A. K., and TANOFSKY, R. Statistical problems of contingency models in organizational behavior. *Academy of Management Journal,* 1975, *18,* 393–397.

KORNHAUSER, A. *Mental health of the automobile worker.* New York: John Wiley, 1965.

KORNHAUSER, A., and SHARP, A. Employee attitudes: Suggestions from a study in a factory. *Personnel Journal,* 1932, *10,* 393–404.

KRAUT, A. I. Prediction of managerial success by peer and training staff ratings. *Journal of Applied Psychology,* 1975, *60,* 14–19.

KUHLEN, R. Needs, perceived need satisfaction opportunities and satisfaction with occupation. *Journal of Applied Psychology,* 1963, *47,* 56–64.

KUHN, J. W. Success and failure in organizing professional engineers. G. E. Somers (ed.), *Proceedings of the 16th Annual Meeting of the Industrial Relations Research Association.* Boston, Mass., Dec. 1963, pp. 194–208.

KUNCE, J. T. Vocational interests and accident proneness. *Journal of Applied Psychology,* 1967, *51,* 223–225.

LACEY, J. L. Individual differences in somatic response patterns. *Journal of Comparative and Physiological Psychology,* 1950, *43,* 338–350.

LANA, R. Pretest-treatment interaction effects in attitudinal studies. *Psychological Bulletin,* 1959, *56,* 293–300.

LANDSBERGER, H. A. *Hawthorne revisited: Management and the worker, its critics and developments in human relations in industry.* Ithaca, N.Y.: New York State School of Industrial and Labor Relations, 1958.

LANE, I. M., and MESSÉ, L. A. Distribution of insufficient, sufficient and over-sufficient rewards: A clarification of equity theory. *Journal of Personality and Social Psychology,* 1972, *21,* 228–233.

LARSON, L. L., and ROWLAND, K. A. Leadership style and cognitive complexity. *Academy of Management Journal,* 1974, *17,* 37–45.

LATANE, B., and ARROWOOD, J. Emotional arousal and task performance. *Journal of Applied Psychology,* 1963, *47,* 324–327.

LAWLER, E. The multitrait-multirater approach to measuring managerial job performance. *Journal of Applied Psychology,* 1967, *51,* 403–410.

LAWLER, E. Equity theory as a predictor of productivity and work quality. *Psychological Bulletin,* 1968, *70,* 596–610.

LAWLER, E., and PORTER, L. Antecedent attitudes of effective managerial performance. *Organizational Behavior and Human Performance,* 1967, *2,* 122–142.

LAWLER, E. E., III. *Pay and organizational effectiveness: A psychological view*. New York: McGraw-Hill, 1971.

LAWLER, E. E., III., HALL, D. T., and OLDHAM, G. R. Organizational climate: Relationship to organizational structure, process and performance. *Organizational Behavior and Human Performance*, 1974, *11*, 139–155.

LEMASTERS, E. E. *Blue-collar aristocrats: Life styles at a working class tavern*. Madison, Wis.: University of Wisconsin Press, 1975.

LEONARD, R. C. "Self-concept as a factor in the similarity-attraction paradigm." Paper presented at the American Psychological Association, Montreal, Canada, Sept. 1973.

LEONARD, S. C., and WEITZ, J. Task enjoyment and task perseverance in relation to task success and self-esteem. *Journal of Applied Psychology*, 1971, *55*, 414–421.

LEVINE, E. L. Patterns of organizational control in microcosm: Group performance and group member satisfaction as a function of differences in control structure. *Journal of Applied Psychology*, 1973, *58*, 186–196.

LEVISON, A. *The working-class majority*. New York: Coward, McCann and Geoghegan, 1974.

LEWIN, K., LIPPITT, R., and WHITE, R. K. Patterns of aggressive behavior in experimentally created climates. *Journal of Social Psychology*, 1939, *10*, 271–299.

LEWIN, K., DEMBO, T., FESTINGER, L., and SEARS, P. Level of aspiration. In J. M. V. Hunt (ed.), *Personality and the behavior disorders*. New York: Ronald Press, 1944, pp. 333–378.

LIKERT, R. *New patterns of management*. New York: McGraw-Hill, 1961.

LIKERT, R., and BOWERS, D. G. Organizational theory and human resource accounting. *American Psychologist*, 1969, *24*, 585–592.

LINDGREN, H. C. *An introduction to social psychology*. New York: John Wiley, 1969.

LOCKE, E. A. Relationship of goal level to performance level. *Psychological Reports*, 1967, *20*, 1068.

LOCKE, E. A. Toward a theory of task motivation and incentives, *Organizational Behavior and Human Performance*, 1968, *3*, 157–189.

LOCKE, E. A. Personnel attitudes and motivation. *Annual Review of Psychology*, 1975, *26*, 457–488.

LOCKE, E. A., SMITH, P. C., KENDALL, L. M., HULIN, C. L., and MILLER, A. M. Convergent and discriminant validity for areas and methods of rating job satisfaction. *Journal of Applied Psychology*, 1964, *48*, 313–319.

LOWIN, A., and CRAIG, J. The influence of level of performance on managerial style: An experimental object-lesson in the ambiguity of correlational data. *Organizational Behavior and Human Performance*, 1968, *3*, 440–458.

MACKINNEY, A. The assessment of performance change: An inductive example. *Organizational Behavior and Human Performance*, 1967, *2*, 56–72.

MACKWORTH, N. H. *Researches on the measurement of human performance*. Medical Research Council, Special Reports Series, Her Majesty's Office, No. 268, London, 1950.

MAIER, N. R. F. *Frustration*. New York: McGraw-Hill, 1949.

MAIER, N. R. F. *Psychology in industry*, second edition. Boston: Houghton-Mifflin, 1955.

MAIER, N. R. F., and HOFFMAN, L. R. Organization and creative problem solving. *Journal of Applied Psychology,* 1961, *45,* 277–280.

MANDELL, M. M. Supervisory characteristics and ratings: A summary of recent research. *Personnel,* 1956, *32,* 435–440.

MANN, F. C., and HOFFMAN, L. R. *Automation and the worker.* New York: Holt, Rinehart and Winston, 1960.

MANN, L., and JANIS, I. A follow-up study on the long-term effects of emotional role playing. *Journal of Personality and Social Psychology,* 1968, *8,* 339–342.

MARACEK, J., and METTEE, D. P. Avoidance of continued success as a function of self-esteem, level of esteem certainty and responsibility for success. *Journal of Personality and Social Psychology,* 1972, *22,* 98–107.

MARCH, J. G., and SIMON, H. A. *Organizations.* New York: John Wiley, 1958.

MARROW, A., BOWERS, D. G., and SEASHORE, S. E. *Management by participation.* New York: Harper and Row, 1967.

MASLOW, A. H. *Motivation and personality.* New York: Harper and Row, 1954.

MAYFIELD, E. C. The selection interview—a reevaluation of published research. *Personnel Psychology,* 1964, *17,* 239–260.

MAYFIELD, E. C., and CARLSON, R. E. Selection interview decisions: First results from a long-term research project. *Personnel Psychology,* 1966, *18,* 41–55.

MCBAIN, W. Noise, the arousal hypothesis and monotonous work. *Journal of Applied Psychology,* 1961, *45,* 309–317.

MCBAIN, W. Arousal, monotony and accidents in line driving. *Journal of Applied Psychology,* 1970, *54,* 509–519.

MCCLELLAND, D. *Assessing human motivation.* New York: General Learning Press, 1971.

MCCLELLAND, D., ATKINSON, J., CLARK, R., and LOWELL, E. L. *The achievement motive.* New York: Appleton, 1953.

MCCLELLAND, D. C. *The achieving society.* Princeton, N.J.: Van Nostrand, 1961.

MCCLELLAND, D. C. Toward a theory of motive acquisition. *American Psychologist,* 1965, *20,* 321–333.

MCCLELLAND, D. C. Testing for competence rather than "intelligence." *American Psychologist,* 1973, *28,* 1–14.

MCCLELLAND, D. C., and WINTER, D. G. *Motivating economic achievement.* New York: Free Press, 1969.

MCCORMICK, E. J., CUNNINGHAM, J. W., and GORDON, C. G. Job dimensions based on factorial analyses of worker-oriented variables. *Personnel Psychology,* 1967, *20,* 417–430.

MCDAVID, J. W., and HARARRI, H. *Social psychology: Individuals, groups, and societies.* New York: Harper and Row, 1969.

MCFARLAND, R. A., and MOSELY, A. L. *Human factors in highway transport safety.* Boston: Harvard University, School of Public Health, 1954.

MCGREGOR, D. *The human side of enterprise.* New York: McGraw-Hill, 1960.

McGuire, W. Personality and susceptibility to social influence. In E. F. Borgatta and W. W. Lambert (eds.), *Handbook of personality theory and research*. Chicago: Rand McNally, 1969.

McGuire, W. J. Some impending reorientations in social psychology: Some thoughts provoked by Kenneth Ring. *Journal of Experimental Social Psychology*, 1967, *3*, 124–139.

McKenny, J. L., and Keen, P. G. W. How manager's minds work. *Harvard Business Review*, May–June 1974, *52*, 79–90.

McKinnon, D. The nature and nurture of creative talent. *American Psychologist*, 1962, *17*, 484–495.

Mednick, S. The associative basis of the creative process. *Psychological Review*, 1962, *69*, 220–232.

Meehl, P. *Clinical vs. statistical prediction*. Minneapolis: University of Minnesota Press, 1954.

Megargee, E. I. Influence of sex roles on the manifestations of leadership. *Journal of Applied Psychology*, 1969, *53*, 377–382.

Mercer, J. R. Latent functions of intelligence testing in the public schools. In L. P. Miller (ed.), *The testing of Black students: A symposium*. Englewood Cliffs, N.J.: Prentice-Hall, 1974.

Meyer, H. H., Kay, E., and French, J. R. P. Split role in performance appraisal. *Harvard Business Review*, 1965, *43*, 123–129.

Milgram, S. Some conditions of obedience and disobedience to authority. In G. Steiner and M. Fishbein (eds.), *Current studies in social psychology*. New York: Holt, Rinehart and Winston, 1965, pp. 243–261.

Milgram, S. *Obedience to authority*. New York: Harper and Row, 1973.

Miller, N. E. The frustration-aggression hypothesis. *Psychological Review*, 1941, *48*, 337–342.

Milner, E. *The failure of success*, second edition. St. Louis: W. H. Green, 1968.

Miner, J. B. *The management of ineffective performance*. New York: McGraw-Hill, 1963.

Miner, J. B. *Studies in management education*. New York: Springer, 1965.

Miner, J. B. Management appraisal: A review of procedures and practice. In W. C. Hammer and F. L. Schmidt (eds.), *Contemporary problems in personnel*. Chicago: St. Clair Press, 1974, pp. 246–257.

Miner, J. B., and Dachler, P. Personnel attitudes and motivation. *Annual Review of Psychology*, *24*, 1973, 379–402.

Miner, J. B., Harlow, D. N., Rizzo, J. R., and Hill, J. W. Role motivation theory of managerial effectiveness in simulated organizations of varying degrees of structure. *Journal of Applied Psychology*, 1974, *59*, 31–37.

Mintz, A., and Blum, M. A. A re-examination of the accident-proneness concept. *Journal of Applied Psychology*, 1949, *33*, 195–211.

Mintzberg, H. *The nature of managerial work*. New York: Harper and Row, 1973.

Mischel, W. *Personality and assessment*. New York: John Wiley, 1968.

Mischel, W. Toward a cognitive social learning reconceptualization of personality. *Psychological Review*, 1973, *80*, 252–283.

Mitchell, T. R. Expectancy model of job satisfaction, occupational preference and effort: A theoretical, methodological and empirical appraisal. *Psychological Bulletin,* 1974, *81,* 1053–1077.

MITCHELL, T. R., and ALBRIGHT, D. W. Expectancy-theory predictions of the satisfaction, effort, performance and retention of Naval aviation officers. *Organizational Behavior and Human Performance,* 1972, *8,* 1–20.

MITCHELL, T. R., BIGLAN, A., ONCKEN, G. R., and FIEDLER, F. E. The contingency model: Criticisms and suggestions. *Academy of Management Journal,* 1970, *13,* 253–267.

MITCHELL, T. R., and POLLARD, W. E. *Effort, ability and role perceptions as predictors of job performance.* Office of Naval Research, University of Washington, Contract # N00014-67-A-0103-0032, May 1973.

MOHR, L. B. Organizational technology and organizational structure. *Administrative Science Quarterly,* 1971, *16,* 444–459.

MOORE, M. H., and CHAMPION, J. E. "The influence of ethnic-group membership on job attitudes and performance." Paper presented at the Convention of the American Psychological Association, New Orleans, La., Sept. 1974.

MORSE, N., and REIMER, E. The experimental change of a major organizational variable. *Journal of Abnormal and Social Psychology,* 1956, *52,* 120–129.

MOULTON, R. W. Effects of success and failure on level of aspiration as related to achievement motives. *Journal of Personality and Social Psychology,* 1965, *1,* 399–406.

MYERS, M. S. Conditions for manager motivation. *Harvard Business Review,* 1966, *44,* 58–71.

NASH, A. Vocational interests of effective managers: A review of the literature. *Personnel Psychology,* 1965, *18,* 21–38.

NEEL, R. G., and DUNN, R. Predicting success in supervisory training programs by the use of psychological tests. *Journal of Applied Psychology,* 1960, *44,* 358–360.

NEELEY, J. D., JR. A test of the need gratification theory of job satisfaction. *Journal of Applied Psychology,* 1973, *57,* 86–91.

NEWMAN, R. I., JR., HUNT, D. L., and RHODES, F. Effects of music on employees' attitude and productivity in a skateboard factory. *Journal of Applied Psychology,* 1966, *50,* 493–496.

NORD, W. R., and COSTIGAN, R. Worker adjustment to the four-day week: A longitudinal study. *Journal of Applied Psychology,* 1973, *58,* 60–66.

OBRADOVIC, J. Modification of the forced-choice method as a criterion of job proficiency. *Journal of Applied Psychology,* 1970, *54,* 228–233.

OGILVIE, B. C., and PORTER, A. Business careers as treadmills to oblivion: The allure of cardiovascular death. *Human Resource Management,* Fall 1974, pp. 14–18.

OPPENHEIMER, E. The relationship between certain self-constructs and occupational preferences. *Journal of Counseling Psychology,* 1966, *13,* 191–197.

ORNE, M. T. On the social psychology of the psychology experiment: With particular reference to demand characteristics and their implications. *American Psychologist,* 1963, *17,* 776–783.

OSGOOD, C. E. *An alternative to war or surrender.* Urbana, Ill.: University of Illinois Press, 1962.

O'TOOLE, J. Work in America and the great job satisfaction controversy. *Journal of Occupational Medicine*, 1974, *16*, 710–715.

PALLAK, M. S., BROCK, T. C., and KIESLER, C. A. Dissonance arousal and task performance in an incidental verbal learning paradigm. *Journal of Personality and Social Psychology*, 1967, *7*, 11–20.

PARNES, S. J. *Creativity: Unlocking human potential.* Buffalo, N.Y.: D.O.K. Publishers, 1972.

PATCHEN, M. *The choice of wage comparisons.* Englewood Cliffs, N.J.: Prentice-Hall, 1961.

PEPITONE, A., FAUCHEAUX, C., MOSCOVICI, S., CESA-BIANCHI, M., MAGISTIETH, G., and IACONO, G. "The role of self-esteem in competitive behavior." Paper, University of Pennsylvania, 1969. (Not seen, cited in Maracek and Mettee, 1972.)

PERLMUTTER, H. V. Relations between the self-image, the image of the foreigner, and the desire to live abroad. *Journal of Psychology*, 1954, *38*, 131–137.

PETTIGREW, T. F. Social evaluation theory: Convergence and applications. In D. Levine (ed.), *Nebraska symposium on motivation.* Lincoln, Neb.: University of Nebraska Press, 1967, pp. 241–311.

PHARES, E. J. *Locus of control.* New York: General Learning Press, 1973.

PICKLE, H., and FRIEDLANDER, F. Seven societal criteria of organizational success. *Personnel Psychology*, 1967, *20*, 165–178.

PORTER, L. W. A study of perceived need satisfactions in bottom and middle management jobs. *Journal of Applied Psychology*, 1961, *45*, 1–10.

PORTER, L. W. Job attitudes in management: I. Perceived deficiencies in need fulfillment as a function of job level. *Journal of Applied Psychology*, 1962, *46*, 375–384.

PORTER, L. W. Job attitudes in management: II. Perceived importance of needs as a function of job level. *Journal of Applied Psychology*, 1963, *47*, 141–148.

PORTER, L. W., and HENRY, M. Job attitudes in management: Perception of the importance of certain personality traits as a function of job level. *Journal of Applied Psychology*, 1964, *48*, 31–36.

PORTER, L. W., and LAWLER, E. Properties of organization structure in relation to job attitudes and job behavior. *Psychological Bulletin*, 1965, *64*, 23–51.

PORTER, L. W., and LAWLER, E. Managerial attitudes and performance. Homewood, Ill.: Irwin, 1968.

PORTER, L. W., and STEERS, R. M. Organizational, work and personal factors in employee turnover and absenteeism. *Psychological Bulletin*, 1973, *80*, 151–176.

PRESSEY, S. C. Two basic neglected psychoeducational problems. *American Psychologist*, 1965, *20*, 391–395.

PRITCHARD, R. D. Equity theory: A review and critique. *Organizational Behavior and Human Performance*, 1969, *4*, 176–211.

PRITCHARD, R. D., and DeLEO, P.J. Experimental test of the valence-instrumentality relationship in job performance. *Journal of Applied Psychology*, 1973, *57*, 264–270.

PRITCHARD, R. D., and KARASICK, B. W. The effects of organizational climate on managerial job performance and job satisfaction. *Organizational Behavior and Human Performance,* 1973, *9,* 126–146.

PRITCHARD, R. D., and SANDERS, M. S. The influence of valence, instrumentality, and expectancy on effort and performance. *Journal of Applied Psychology,* 1973, *57,* 55–60.

PRITCHARD, R. O., DUNNETTE, M. D., and JORGENSON, D. O. Effects of perceptions of equity and inequity on worker performance and satisfaction. *Journal of Applied Psychology Monographs,* 1972, *56,* 75–94.

PRUDEN, H. O. The interorganizational link. *California Management Review,* 1971, *14,* 39–45.

PUCKETT, E. S. Productivity achievement: A measure of success. In F. G. Lesieur (ed.), *The Scanlon Plan.* New York: Published jointly by the M.I.T. Press and John Wiley, 1958, p. 113.

PUGH, D. S., HICKSON, D. J., HININGS, C. R., and TURNER, C. The context of organization structures. *Administrative Science Quarterly,* 1969, *14,* 91–114.

QUINN, R. P., and MANGIONE, T. W. Evaluating weighted models of measuring job satisfaction: A Cinderella story. *Organizational Behavior and Human Performance,* 1973, *10,* 1–23.

QUINN, R. P., KAHN, R. L., TABOR, J. M., and GORDON, L. K. *The chosen few.* Ann Arbor, Mich.: University of Michigan Institute for Social Research, 1968.

RAMEY, J. W. Communes, group marriages and the upper middle-class. *Journal of Marriage and the Family,* 1972, *34,* 647–655.

REILLY, C. A., III., and ROBERTS, K. H. Job satisfaction among whites and nonwhites: A cross-cultural approach. *Journal of Applied Psychology,* 1973, *57,* 295–299.

REISSMAN, F. The culturally deprived child: A new view. In E. P. Torrance and R. D. Strom (eds.), *Mental health and achievement.* New York: John Wiley, 1965, pp. 312–319.

RICCIUTI, H. Ratings of leadership potential at the U.S. Naval Academy and subsequent officer performance. *Journal of Applied Psychology,* 1955, *34,* 194–199.

RICE, A. K. Productivity and social organization in an Indian weaving shed. *Human Relations,* 1953, *6,* 297–329.

RICE, A. K. *The enterprise and its environment.* London: Tavistock Publications, 1963.

ROADMAN, H. An industrial use of peer ratings. *Journal of Applied Psychology,* 1964, *48,* 211–214.

ROBARDS, T. Britain's 3-day week. *New York Times,* April 24, 1974, pp. 55, 57.

ROETHLISBERGER, F. J., and DICKSON, W. J. *Management and the worker.* Cambridge: Harvard University Press, 1939.

ROGERS, C. R. Interpersonal relationships: U.S.A. 2000. *Journal of Applied Behavioral Science,* 1968, *4,* 265–280.

ROKEACH, M., MILLER, M. G., and SNYDER, J. A. The value gap between police and policed. *Journal of Social Issues,* 1971, *27,* 155–169.

ROSEKRAUS, F. M. Choosing to suffer as a consequence of expecting to suffer: A replication. *Journal of Personality and Social Psychology,* 1967, *7,* 419–423.

ROSEN, B., and JERDEE, T. H. The influence of sex-role stereotypes on evaluation of male and female supervisory behavior. *Journal of Applied Psychology,* 1973, *57,* 44–48.

ROSEN, B., and JERDEE, T. H. "Experimental effects of the effects of sex stereotypes on administrative decisions." Paper presented at the annual convention of the American Psychological Association, New Orleans, La., Sept. 1974.

ROSENTHAL, R. Covert communication in the psychological experiment. *Psychological Bulletin,* 1967, *67,* 356–367.

ROSENTHAL, R., and JACOBSON, L. Teacher expectancies: Determinants of pupils' IQ gains. *Psychological Reports,* 1966, *19,* 115–118.

ROSENTHAL, R., FRIEDMAN, N., and KURLAND, D. Instruction-reading behavior of the experimenter as an unintended determinant of experimental results. *Journal of Experimental Research in Personality,* 1966, *1,* 221–226.

ROTHAUS, R., MORTON, R. B., and HANSON, P. G. Performance appraisal and psychological distance. *Journal of Applied Psychology,* 1965, *49,* 48–54.

ROTTER, J. B. Generalized expectancies for internal vs. external control of reinforcement. *Psychological Monographs,* 1966, *80,* 1–28.

ROWE, P. Individual differences in selection decisions. *Journal of Applied Psychology,* 1963, *47,* 304–307.

ROWE, P. M. Order effects in assessment decisions. *Journal of Applied Psychology,* 1967, *51,* 170–173.

RUBINSKY, S., and SMITH, N. Safety training by accident simulation. *Journal of Applied Psychology,* 1973, *57,* 68–73.

RUNYON, K. E. Some interactions between personality variables and management styles. *Journal of Applied Psychology,* 1973, *57,* 288–294.

SALEH, S. D. A study of attitude change in the preretirement period. *Journal of Applied Phycology,* 1964, *48,* 310–312.

SALEH, S. D., and OTIS, J. L. Age and level of job satisfaction. *Personnel Psychology,* 1964, *17,* 425–430.

SALES, S. M. Economic threat as a factor in authoritarianism: The case of the great depression. *Proceedings, 80th Annual Convention of the American Psychological Association,* 1972, pp. 249–250.

SAMUEL, W. *Contemporary social psychology: An introduction.* Englewood Cliffs, N.J.: Prentice-Hall, 1975.

SANFORD, N. The approach of the authoritarian personality. In J. L. McCrary (ed.), *Psychology of personality.* New York: Grove Press, 1956, pp. 253–319.

SARASON, S. Toward a psychology of change and innovation. *American Psychologist,* 1967, *22,* 227–233.

SCHACTER, S. *The psychology of affiliation.* Stanford, Calif.: Stanford University Press, 1959.

SCHACTER, S., and SINGER, J. E. Cognitive, social and physiological determinants of emotional states. *Psychological Review,* 1962, *69,* 379–399.

SCHACTER, S., and WHEELER, L. Epinephrine, chlorpromazine and amusement. *Journal of Abnormal and Social Psychology,* 1962, *65,* 121–128.

SCHACTER, S., ELLERTSON, N., McBRIDE, D., and GREGORY, D. An experimental study of cohesiveness and productivity. *Human Relations,* 1951, *4,* 229–238.

SCHACTER, S., FESTINGER, L., WILLERMAN, B., and HYMAN, R. Emotional disruption and industrial productivity. *Journal of Applied Psychology,* 1961, *45,* 201–213.

SCHAFFER, R. H. Job satisfaction as related to need satisfaction in work. *Psychological Monographs,* 1953, *67,* 14, Whole No. 364.

SCHEIN, E. H. *Organizational psychology.* Englewood Cliffs, N.J.: Prentice-Hall, 1965.

SCHEIN, E. H. The individual, the organization and the career: A conceptual scheme. In D. A. Kolb, I. M. Rubin, and J. M. McIntyre (eds.), *Organizational psychology.* Englewood Cliffs, N.J.: Prentice-Hall, 1971, pp. 301–317.

SCHLENKER, B. R. Social psychology and science. *Journal of Personality and Social Psychology,* 1975, *29,* 1–15.

SCHLETZER, V. SBIV as a predictor of job satisfaction. *Journal of Applied Psychology,* 1966, *50,* 5–8.

SCHMIDT, F. L., and JOHNSON, R. The effect of race on peer ratings in an industrial situation. *Human Behavior,* 1973, *1,* 49.

SCHMIDT, F. L., and JOHNSON, R. H. Effect of race on peer ratings in an industrial situation. *Journal of Applied Psychology,* 1973, *57,* 237–241.

SCHMIDT, F. L., and KAPLAN, L. B. Composite vs. multiple criteria: A review and resolution of the controversy. *Personnel Psychology,* 1971, *24,* 419–434.

SCHNEIDER, B., and SNYDER, R. A. Some relationships between job satisfaction and organizational climate. *Journal of Applied Psychology,* 1975, *60,* 318–328.

SCHWAB, D. P., and DYER, L. D. The motivational impact of a compensation system on employee performance. *Organazational Behavior and Human Performance,* 1973, *9,* 215–225.

SCHWAB, D. P., and WALLACE, M. J. J. Correlates of employee satisfaction with pay. *Industrial Relations,* 1973, *12,* 408–430.

SCOTT, W. E., JR. Activation theory and task design. *Organizational Behavior and Human Performance,* 1966, *1,* 3–30.

SEASHORE, S., INDIK, B., and GEORGOPOULOS, B. Relationships among criteria of job performance. *Journal of Applied Psychology,* 1960, *44,* 195–204.

SEASHORE, S. E. *Group cohesiveness in the industrial work group.* Ann Arbor, Mich.: University of Michigan, Institute for Social Research, 1954.

SEEMAN, M. Antidote for alienation. *Trans-Action,* 1966, *3,* 35–39.

SENNETT, R., and COBB, J. *The hidden injuries of class.* New York: Alfred A. Knopf, 1972.

SHAW, M. C. Underachievement: Useful construct or misleading illusion. *Psychology in the Schools,* 1968, *5,* 41–46.

SHEPARD, J. *Automation and alienation.* Cambridge, Mass.: MIT Press, 1971.

SHEPARD, J. M. Alienation as a process: Work as a case in point. *Sociological Quarterly,* 1972, *13,* 161–173.

SHERMAN, P., KERR, W., and KOSINAR, W. A study of accidents in 147 factories. *Personnel Psychology,* 1957, *10,* 43–51.

SHURKIN, J. Policemen, stress and the John Wayne syndrome. *Washington Star-News,* August 30, 1973, p. A-3. (Report of a symposium at the 1973 American Psychological Association Convention.)

SIEGEL, J., and BOWEN, D. Satisfaction and performance: Casual relationships and moderating effects.*Journal of Vocational Behavior,* 1971, *1,* 263–269.

SIMMONS, D. Self-concept, occupational stereotype, and engineering career plans. *Psychological Reports,* 1967, *20,* 514.

SIMON, H. *Administrative behavior,* second edition. New York: Macmillan, 1957.

SIMPSON, R. L. Beyond rational bureaucracy: Changing values and social integration in post-industrial society. *Social Forces,* 1972, *51,* 1–6.

SINHA, D., and SARMA, K. C. Union attitude and job satisfaction in Indian workers. *Journal of Applied Psychology,* 1962, *46,* 247–251.

SLAKE, S., and BROZEK, J. Effects of intermittent illumination of perceptual motor performance. *Journal of Applied Psychology,* 1965, *49,* 345–347.

SLATER, P. *Earthwalk.* Garden City, N.Y.: Doubleday, 1974.

SLATER, P. *The pursuit of loneliness.* Boston: Beacon Press, 1970.

SMITH, C. G., and BROWN, M. E. Communication structure and control structure in a voluntary association. *Sociometry,* 1964, *27,* 449–468.

SMITH, P. C. The curve of output as a criterion of boredom. *Journal of Applied Psychology,* 1953, *37,* 69–74.

SMITH, P. C., and CURNOW, R. Arousal hypothesis and the effects of music on purchasing behavior. *Journal of Applied Psychology,* 1966, *50,* 255–256.

SMITH, P. C., and KENDALL, L. M. Retranslation of expectations: An approach to the construction of unambiguous anchors for rating scales. *Journal of Applied Psychology,* 1963, *47,* 149–155.

SOBEL, R. S. Tests of preperformance and postperformance models of satisfaction with outcomes. *Journal of Personality and Social Psychology,* 1971, *19,* 213–221.

SOLEM, A. An evaluation of two attitudinal approaches to delegation. *Journal of Applied Psychology,* 1958, *42,* 36–39.

SOLOMON, R. An extension of control-group design. *Psychological Bulletin,* 1949, *46,* 137–150.

STAGNER, R. *The psychology of industrial conflict.* New York: John Wiley, 1956.

STAGNER, R. *Psychological aspects of international conflict.* Belmont, Calif.: Wadsworth Publishing Co., 1967.

STAGNER, R., and ROSEN, H. *Psychology of union-management relations.* Belmont, Calif.: Wadsworth Publishing Co., 1965.

STARK, S. Research criteria of executive success. *Journal of Business,* 1959, *32,* 1–14.

STAW, B. M. Attitudinal and behavioral consequences of changing a major organizational reward: A natural field experiment. *Journal of Personality and Social Psychology,* 1974, *29,* 742–751.

STEDRY, A. C., and KAY, E. The effects of goal difficulty on performance. *Behavioral Science,* 1966, *11,* 459–470.

STEINER, G. Introduction. In G. Steiner (ed.), *The creative organization.* Chicago: University of Chicago Press, 1965, pp. 1–24.

STELTZER, N. E., and KOCK, G. V. Influence of emotional role playing on smoking habits. *Psychological Reports,* 1968, *22,* 817–820.

STRODTBECK, F. L. Family interaction, values and achievement. In D. C. McClelland (ed.), *Talent and society.* Princeton, N.J.: Van Nostrand, 1958, pp. 135–194.

SUSMAN, G. I. Job enlargement: Effects of culture on worker responses. *Industrial Relations,* 1973, *12,* 1–15.

SZAFRAN, A., and WELFAND, B. On the relation between transfer and difficulty of initial task. *Quarterly Journal of Experimental Psychology,* 1950, *2,* 88–99.

SZALAGYI, A. D., and SIMS, H. P. An exploration of the path-goal theory of leadership in a health care environment. *Academy of Management Journal,* in press.

TAFT, R. The ability to judge people. *Psychological Bulletin,* 1955, *52,* 1–23.

TANNENBAUM, A. S. Control in organizations: Individual adjustment and organizational performance. *Administrative Science Quarterly,* 1962, *7,* 236–257.

TANNENBAUM, A. S. *Social psychology of the work organization.* Belmont, Calif.: Wadsworth Publishing Co., 1966.

TANNENBAUM, A. S., and KAHN, R. L. *Participation in union locals.* Evanston, Ill.: Row, Peterson and Co., 1958.

TANNENBAUM, R., and SCHMIDT, W. H. How to choose a leadership pattern. *Harvard Business Review,* 1958, *36,* 95–101.

TANNENBAUM, R., WECHSLER, I., and MASSARIK, F. *Leadership and organization: A behavioral science approach.* New York: McGraw-Hill, 1961.

TARNOWIESKI, D. *The changing success ethic.* New York: American Management Association, 1973.

TEFFT, S. K. Task experience and intertribal value differences on the Wind River Reservation. *Social Forces,* 1971, *49,* 604–614.

TEICH, H. P. "Validity of a business game." Master's thesis, University of Oregon, 1964.

TERKEL, S. *Working: People talk about what they do all day and how they feel about what they do.* New York: Pantheon Press, 1974.

THOMPSON, J. D. *Organizations in action.* New York: McGraw-Hill, 1967.

THOMPSON, V. A. Bureaucracy and innovation. *Administrative Science Quarterly,* 1965, *10,* 1–20.

THORNDIKE, R. L., and HAGEN, E. *10,000 careers.* New York: John Wiley, 1959.

THURSTON, L. L. Primary mental abilities. *Psychometric Monographs,* 1938, No. 1.

TIFFANY, D. W. and TIFFANY, P. G. Powerlessness and/or self-direction? *American Psychologist,* 1973, *28,* 151–161.

TIFFIN, J., and McCORMICK, E. *Industrial psychology,* fifth edition. Englewood Cliffs, N.J.: Prentice-Hall, 1965.

TIMMONS, J. A. Black is beautiful—is it bountiful? *Havard Business Review,* 1971, *49,* 81–94.

TORNOW, W. W. The development and application of an input-outcome moderator test on the perception and reduction of inequity. *Organizational Behavior and Human Performance,* 1971, *6,* 614–638.

TOSI, H. A re-examination of personality as a determinant of the effects of participation. *Personnel Psychology,* 1970, *23,* 91–99.

TRAVERS, R. M. W. A critical review of the validity and rationale of the forced-choice technique. *Psychological Bulletin,* 1951, *48,* 62–70.

TRESEMER, D. Fear of success: popular, but unproven. *Psychology Today,* 1974, *8,* 82–85.

TRIANDIS, H. C. Cognitive similarity and interpersonal communication. *Journal of Applied Psychology,* 1959, *43,* 321–326.

TRIANDIS, H. C., BASS, A. R., EWEN, R. B., and MIKESELL, E. H. Team creativity as a function of the creativity of the members. *Journal of Applied Psychology,* 1963, *47,* 104–110.

TRIST, E. L., HIGGIN, G. W., MURRAY, H., and POLLACK, A. B. *Organizational choice.* London: Tavistock Publications, 1963.

TSCHEULIN, D. Leader behavior measurement in German industry. *Journal of Applied Psychology,* 1973, *57,* 28–31.

TUDDENHAM, R. D., BLUMENKRANTZ, J., and WILKIN, W. R. Age changes on AGCT: A longitudinal study of average adults. *Journal of Consulting and Clinical Psychology,* 1968, *32,* 659–663.

TURNER, A. N., and LAWRENCE, P. R. *Industrial jobs and the worker.* Boston: Harvard University, Graduate School of Business Administration, 1965.

TURNEY, J. R. Activity outcome expectancies and intrinsic activity values as predictors of several motivation indexes for technical professionals. *Organizational Behavior and Human Performance, 11,* 1974, 65–82.

UHRBROCK, R. S. Attitudes of 4430 employees. *Journal of Social Psychology,* 1934, *5,* 365–377.

UHRBROCK, R. S. Music on the job: Its influence on worker morale and production. *Personnel Psychology,* 1961, *14,* 9–38.

URWICK, L. *The elements of administration.* New York: Harper and Row, 1943.

VALECHA, G. K. Construct-validation of inter-external locus of reinforcement related to work-related variables. *Proceedings, 80th Annual Convention of the American Psychological Association,* 1972, pp. 455–456.

VANCE, S.C., and GRAY, C. F. Use of performance evaluation model for research in business gaming. *Academy of Management Journal,* 1967, *10,* 27–38.

VAN ZELST, R. H. Sociometrically selected work teams increase productivity. *Personnel Psychology,* 1952, *5,* 175–185.

VAN ZELST, R. H. The effect of age and experience upon accident rate. *Journal of Applied Psychology,* 1954, *38,* 313–317.

VAN ZELST, R. H., and KERR, W. A. Workers' attitudes toward merit rating. *Personnel Psychology,* 1953, *6,* 159–172.

VERNON, P. Ability factors and environmental influences. *American Psychologist,* 1965, *20,* 723–733.

VILAR, E. *The manipulated man.* New York: Farrar, Straus and Giroux, 1972.

VROOM, V. Some personality determinants of the effects of participation. *Journal of Abnormal and Social Psychology,* 1959, *59,* 322–327.

VROOM, V. *Some personality determinants of the effects of participation.* Englewood Cliffs, N.J.: Prentice-Hall, 1960.

VROOM, V. Ego-involvement, job satisfaction, and job performance. *Personnel Psychology,* 1962, *15,* 159–177.

VROOM, V. *Work and motivation.* New York: John Wiley, 1964.

VROOM, V. H., and PAHL, B. Relationship between age and risk-taking among managers. *Journal of Applied Psychology,* 1971, *55,* 399–405.

VROOM, V. H., and YETTON, P. W. *Leadership and decision-making.* Pittsburgh, Pa.: University of Pittsburgh Press, 1973.

WAHBA, M. A., and BRIDWELL, L. G. Maslow reconsidered: A review of research on the need hierarchy theory. *Organizational Behavior and Human Performance,* in press.

WALKER, C., and GUEST, R. *Man on the assembly line.* Cambridge: Harvard University Press, 1952.

WALKER, E., and HEYNS, R. *An anatomy for creativity.* Englewood Cliffs, N.J.: Prentice-Hall, 1962.

WALKER, E. L. Psychological complexity as a basis for a theory of motivation and choice. In D. Levine (ed.), *Nebraska symposium on motivation,* vol. 12. Lincoln, Neb.: University of Nebraska Press, 1964, pp. 47–97.

Wall Street Journal, August 17, 1974.

WALLACE, J. *Psychology: A social science.* Philadelphia: W. B. Saunders Co., 1971.

WALLACH, M., and KOGAN, N. The roles of information, discussion and consensus in group risk taking. *Journal of Experimental Social Psychology,* 1965, *1,* 1–19.

WALLACH, M., KOGAN, N., and BEM, D. J. Group influence on individual risk-taking. *Journal of Abnormal and Social Psychology,* 1962, *65,* 78–86.

WALLACH, M., KOGAN, N., and BEM, D. J. Diffusion of responsibility and level of risk-taking in groups. *Journal of Abnormal and Social Psychology,* 1964, *68,* 263–274.

WALSTER, E., ARONSON, E., and BROWN, Z. Choosing to suffer as a consequence of expecting to suffer: An unexpected finding. *Journal of Experimental Social Psychology,* 1966, *2,* 400–406.

WALSTER, E. E., BERSCHEID, E., and WALSTER, G. W. New directions in equity research. *Journal of Personality and Social Psychology,* 1973, *25,* 151–176.

WATSON, G. Work satisfaction. In G. Hartmann and T. Newcomb (eds.), *Industrial conflict.* New York: Cordon Co., 1939.

WANOUS, J. P. "The role of individual differences in human reactions to job characteristics." Paper presented at the convention of the American Psychological Association, Montreal, Can., Sept. 1973.

WANOUS, J. P. Tell it like it is at realistic job previews. *Personnel,* July–August 1975, pp. 50–60.

WANOUS, J. P., and LAWLER, E. E., III. Measurement and meaning of job satisfaction. *Journal of Applied Psychology,* 1972, *56,* 95–105.

WATERS, L. K., and WATERS, C. W. An empirical test of five versions of the two-factor theory of job satisfaction. *Organizational Behavior and Human Performance,* 1972, *7,* 18–24.

WEBB, E. J., CAMPBELL, D. T., SCHWARTZ, R. D., and SECHREST, L. *Unobtrusive measures: Nonreactive research in the social sciences.* Chicago: Rand McNally, 1966.

WEBB, W. B., and HOLLANDER, E. P. Comparison of three morale measures: A survey, pooled group judgments, and self-evaluations. *Journal of Applied Psychology,* 1956, *40,* 17–20.

WEBER, M. *The theory of social and economic organization,* trans. and ed. T. Parsons and A. M. Henderson. New York: Oxford University Press, 1947.

WEBSTER, E. C. *Decision making in the employement interview.* Montreal: Industrial Relations Center, McGill University, 1964.

WECHSLER, I., and REISEL, J. Inside a sensitivity training group. *Industrial Relations Monograph,* 1959, No. 4.

WEICK, K. Amendments to organizational theorizing. *Academy of Management Journal,* 1974, *3,* 487–502.

WEICK, K. E., and NESSET, B. Preference among forms of equity. *Organizational Behavior and Human Performance,* 1968, *3,* 400–416.

WEINER, B. *Theories of motivation: From mechanism to cognition.* Chicago: Markham Publishing Co., 1972.

WEINER, B. Achievement motivation as conceptualized by an attribution theorist. In B. Weiner (ed.), *Achievement motivation and attribution theory.* New York: General Learning Press, 1974, pp. 3–48.

WEINSTEIN, M. S. Achievement motivation and risk preference. *Journal of Personality and Social Psychology,* 1969, *13,* 153–172.

WEISS, H., and SHERMAN, J. Internal-external control as a predictor of task effort and satisfaction subsequent to failure. *Journal of Applied Psychology,* 1973, *57,* 132–136.

WEIST, W., PORTER, L. W., and GHISELLI, E. Relationships between individual proficiency and team performance and efficiency. *Journal of Applied Psychology,* 1961, *45,* 435–440.

WEITZ, J. Selecting supervisors with peer ratings. *Personnel Psychology,* 1958, *11,* 25–35.

WEITZ, J., and ADLER, S. The optimal use of simulation. *Journal of Applied Psychology,* 1973, *58,* 219–224.

WEITZ, J., and NUCKOLS, R. C. The validity of direct and indirect questions in measuring job satisfaction. *Personnel Psychology,* 1953, *6,* 487–494.

WEITZ, J., and NUCKOLS, R. C. Job satisfaction and job survival. *Journal of Applied Psychology,* 1955, *39,* 294–300.

WESCHLER, I. R. An investigation of attitudes toward labor and management by means of the error-choice method. In M. L. Blum (ed.), *Readings in experimental industrial psychology.* Englewood Cliffs, N.J.: Prentice-Hall, 1952, pp. 140–147.

WHEELER, K. E., GURMAN, R., and TARNOWIESKI, D. *The four-day week.* New York: American Management Association, 1972.

WHITE, R. K. Three not-so-obvious contributions of psychology to peace. *Journal of Social Issues,* 1969, *25,* 23–40.

WHITLOCK, G. H. Application of the psychophysical laws to performance evaluation. *Journal of Applied Psychology,* 1963, *47,* 15–23.

WHITLOCK, G. H. "Sensitivity of raters to variations on performance stimuli." Paper presented at the annual convention of the American Psychological Association, New Orleans, La., Sept. 1974.

WHITLOCK, G. H., CLOUSE, R. J., and SPENCER, W. F. Predicting accident proneness. *Personnel Psychology,* 1963, *16,* 35–44.

WILD, R. Job needs, job satisfaction and job behavior of women manual workers. *Journal of Applied Psychology,* 1970, *54,* 157–162.

WILD, R., and KEMPNER, T. Influence of community and plant characteristics on job attitudes of manual workers. *Journal of Applied Psychology,* 1972, *56,* 106–113.

WILLIAMS, F. J., and HARRELL, T. W. Predicting success in business. *Journal of Applied Psychology,* 1964, *48,* 164–167.

WILLIAMS, S. B., and LEAVITT, H. J. Group opinion as a predictor of military leadership. *Journal of Consulting Psychology,* 1947, *11,* 283–291.

WILSON, D. Ability evaluation, post-decision dissonance and co-worker attractiveness. *Journal of Personality and Social Psychology,* 1965, *1,* 486–489.

WILSON, J. O. *Quality of life in the U.S.—an excursion into the new frontier of socio-economic indicators.* Midwest Research Institute, 1970. (Not seen; quoted in Dunnette, Milkovich and Motwilde, 1973.)

WINTER, D. G. *The power motive.* Homewood, Ill.: Free Press, 1973.

WINTERBOTTOM, M. R. The relation of need for achievement to learning experiences in independence mastery. In J. W. Atkinson (ed.), *Motives in fantasy, action and society.* Princeton, N.J.: Van Nostrand, 1958, pp. 453–478.

WISSLER, C. The correlation of mental and physical traits. *Psychological Monographs,* 1901, *3,* Whole No. 6.

WOFFORD, J. C. The motivational bases of job satisfaction and job performance. *Personnel Psychology,* 1971, *24,* 501–518.

WOLLACK, L., and GUTTMAN, I. *Prediction of OCS academic grades and post-OCS performance of junior officers with a battery of speeded tests.* Washington, D.C.: U.S. Naval Personnel Research Field Activity, 1960.

WOOD, I., and LAWLER, E. E., III. Effects of piece-rate overpayment on productivity. *Journal of Applied Psychology,* 1970, *54,* 234–238.

WOODWARD, J. *Industrial organization: Theory and practice.* London: Oxford University Press, 1965.

WREGE, C. D., and PERRONI, A. G. Taylor's pig-tale: A historical analysis of F. W. Taylor's pig-iron experiments. *Academy of Management Journal,* 1974, *17,* 6–27.

WRIGHTSMAN, L. *Social psychology in the seventies.* Belmont, Calif.: Brooks-Cole Publishing Co., 1972.

WYATT, S., FRASER, J. A. and STOCK, F. G. *The comparative effects of variety and uniformity in work.* Industrial Fatigue Research Board, Report No. 52, London, 1929.

WYATT, S., FRASER, J. A., and STOCK, F. G. *The effects of monotony in work.* Industrial Fatigue Research Board, Report No. 56, London, 1929.

YANKELOVICH, D. Turbulence in the working world: Angry workers, happy grads. *Psychology Today,* 1974, *8,* 80–89.

Youth's attitude toward work. *Business and Society Review,* 1974, *11,* 46–48.

YUKL, G. A. Toward a behavioral theory of leadership. *Organizational Behavior and Human Performance,* 1971, *6,* 414–440.

ZAJONC, R. B. Social facilitation. *Science,* 1965, *149,* 269–274.

ZALEZNIK, A., CHRISTENSEN, C. R., and ROETHLISBERGER, F. J. *The motiva-*

tion, productivity and satisfaction of workers: A prediction study. Boston: Harvard University Graduate School of Business Administration, 1958.

ZAND, D. Trust and managerial affectiveness. In R. T. Golembrewski and A. Blumberg (eds.), *Sensitivity training and the laboratory approach,* second edition. Itasca, Ill.: F. A. Peacock Publishing Co., 1973, pp. 553–572.

ZANDER, A., and NEWCOMB, T., JR. Group levels of aspiration in United Fund campaigns. *Journal of Personality and Social Psychology,* 1967, *6,* 157–162.

ZANDER, A., FORWARD, J., and ALBERT, R. Adaptation of board members to repeated failure or success by their organization. *Organizational Behavior and Human Performance,* 1969, *4,* 56–76.

ZILLER, R. C. Communications restraints, group flexibility and group confidence. *Journal of Applied Psychology,* 1958, *42,* 346–352.

ZILLER, R. C., BEHRINGER, R., and GOODCHILDS, J. Group creativity under conditions of success or failure and variations in group stability. *Journal of Applied Psychology,* 1962, *46,* 43–49.

ZIMBARDO, P. G. The human choice: Individuation, reason, and order versus deindividuation, impulse, and chaos. In D. Levine (ed.), *Nebraska symposium on motivation,* vol. 17. Lincoln, Neb.: University of Nebraska Press, 1969, pp. 231–307.

ZIMBARDO, P. G. Pathology of imprisonment. *Transaction,* 1972, *9,* 4–8.

ZLUTNICK, S., and ALTMAN, I. Crowding and human behavior. In J. F. Wohlwill and D. H. Carson (eds.), *Environment and the social sciences: Perspectives and applications.* Washington, D.C.: American Psychological Association, 1972, pp. 44–60.

ZUCKERMAN, M., KOLIN, E. A., PRICE, L., and ZOOB, I. Development of a sensation-seeking scale. *Journal of Consulting Psychology,* 1964, *28,* 477–482.

ZUCKERMAN, M., NEARY, R. S., and BUSTMAN, B. A. Sensation-seeking scale correlates in experience (smoking, drugs, alcohol, hallucinations and sex) and preference for complexity (designs). *Proceedings of the 78th Annual Convention of the American Psychological Association,* 1970, pp. 317–318.

NAME INDEX

SUBJECT INDEX

DATE DUE

JUN 26 '84			
OCT 01 1986			
OCT 15 1986			
NOV 28 1987			
NOV 30 1988			
OCT 1 8 1990			
DEC 1 1 2000			
30 505 JOSTEN'S			